Interdiction

Kevin L. Kingsbury

Dinglemay Publishing
Elkhart, Indiana

This book is a work of fiction. The characters, other than recognized historical figures, and the events depicted herein are fictitious. Any resemblance to actual persons, living or dead, is purely coincidental. The names, circumstances, dialogues and opinions expressed are the product of the author's imagination and should not be considered real. No part of this book is intended to represent or should be interpreted as expressing the views of the U.S. Navy or of any other department or agency of any governmental body.

INTERDICTION

published by Dinglemay Publishing

Edited by Ardis A. Kingsbury and Julie J. Anglemyer

Cover design by Sean Seal

For information:

Dinglemay Publishing
Post Office Box 2956
Elkhart, IN 46515-2956

Printed in the United States of America

International Standard Book Number: 0-9709852-0-7

Library of Congress Control Number: 2001089083

Acknowledgments

I would like to thank my editors, Ardis Kingsbury and Julie Anglemyer, for their time and efforts in bringing my manuscript to its finished form.

Thanks also to my friends and family, who have been nothing but supportive of my venture.

And finally, thanks to my wonderful wife, Lori "Mayvis" Kingsbury, for her undying love and support. Without her, my journey would be a lonely one.

Dedication

This book is dedicated to my boys, Zeke and Nico.

"Let love and faithfulness never leave you; bind them around your neck, write them on the tablet of your heart.

Then you will win favor and a good name in the sight of God and man.

Trust in the Lord with all your heart and lean not on your own understanding; in all your ways acknowledge him, and he will make your paths straight.

Do not be wise in your own eyes; fear the Lord and shun evil. This will bring health to your body and nourishment to your bones."

Proverbs 3:3-7

Boys, don't let anything turn you from the ways of God. He may not do things the way you want, and He may not do them in your timing, but keep your eyes on Jesus and He will take care of you. He will give you the desires of your heart, just like He promised.

Dedication

[illegible]

~1~

There is nothing quite as black as midnight on the Caribbean. When the light of the moon and stars cannot penetrate the cloud cover, the darkness seems to stretch on into eternity. The gentle breeze created by the ship's slow movement through the water is the only evidence that one has not been sucked through a hole in the universe and deposited into an endless void where there exists nothing except the realization of one's presence there and the memory of having once been someplace better. The blackness is so deep, a person could begin to doubt that his hand really was in front of his face, despite messages received by the brain from the arm and hand confirming a location of two inches away from and slightly to the left of the nose. Sometimes one would actually reach up and touch his elevated hand with the other, just to make sure that it was in fact where he believed he had placed it. Such were the conditions on this warm, cloudy night, as the ominous form of the USS *Mississippi* moved quietly across the dark blue water of the Caribbean Sea, cruising due east at eight knots.

It was 0000 local time aboard the USS *Mississippi* CGN-40, a six-hundred-foot nuclear-powered Guided Missile Cruiser flying the flag of the United States Navy. She was part of the aging fleet of Virginia Class surface warships, most of which had been in service for over twenty years. Their primary function was that of aircraft carrier escort ships, traveling with, and in support of, an Aircraft Carrier Battle Group. Like a bodyguard, their task would be to detect and neutralize any external threat to the carrier including, if worse came to worst, taking incoming fire to preserve the integrity of the carrier and to keep it operational. In addition to their duties as aircraft carrier escort ships, the versatility of the cruisers also made them capable of carrying out solo missions while awaiting the next obligation to a six-month carrier battle group deployment. Being stationed on the east coast meant that the USS *Mississippi* would be assigned to accompany a carrier group to the Mediterranean Sea about once every two years.

While awaiting such a deployment, the '*Mighty Mississippi*' had been dispatched to assist the Coast Guard with its 'War on Drugs' in the Caribbean Sea. The *Mississippi* and the USS *Ticonderoga* CG-47, a conventional Guided Missile Cruiser, would alternate six-week tours-of-duty in the Caribbean until a few months prior to the time when the USS *Theodore Roosevelt* CVN-74 was due to proceed to the Mediterranean Sea with a complete battle group for its tour-of-duty rotation. Both cruisers would then go to the Portsmouth Naval Shipyard in Portsmouth, Virginia for routine maintenance and systems upgrades in preparation for their Mediterranean deployment.

At present, the *Mississippi* and her men were underway for their second six-week stint in the Counter-Drug Operations (CD Ops) rotation. After being at sea for three weeks, the excitement, when there had been any, had worn off and the crew had settled in to the dull, daily routine of life aboard a naval vessel patrolling the high seas. There was very little activity at this hour of the night. Those unfortunate men who had the night watch were at their posts, while most of the others were sleeping in their pits (racks/beds). A few were still awake, either watching television, writing letters, playing cards, or reading. For the most part, however, the interior of the *Mississippi* looked like a ghost ship. The illumination in the passageways and living complexes had been switched from the bright white lights to the much dimmer red lights, giving the vessel a doleful, other-worldly appearance. Occasionally someone would stroll along the passageway, usually in shorts and flip-flops, sometimes in uniform, taking care of some type of personal business or fulfilling the duties of a roving watch.

Outside the skin of the ship, condition 'Darken Ship' had been set, during which all sources of external light must be extinguished, covered, or re-directed. This ensures that the vessel is completely bathed in blackness. During this time, the use of clear lenses in personal flashlights as well as regular white bulbs in compartments whose doors opened outside the skin of the ship was strictly prohibited. Although one could feel the ocean breeze and hear the hull of the great warship cutting through the water, the sense of sight was rendered completely useless by the near total absence of light and the incalculable depth of the darkness of the night. Only one tiny ray of blue light prevented the night from completely swallowing all visual evidence of the *Mississippi*'s presence. That was the result of Signalman Second Class (SM2) Jonathan (Jack) Douglass making his way across the Signal bridge using a small pocket flashlight with a piece of blue plastic covering the lens. Though far above average in performance, Jack was about as average as a guy could be in appearance. Average height, medium build, nondescript hazel eyes, short brown hair. He was the kind of guy who would never be chosen from a police line-up because there was nothing peculiar about him that would cause someone to take any special notice of him. He was a good looking fellow, but not one who would stand out in a crowd.

Jack had exited the skin of the ship through a watertight door on the aft part of the forward superstructure, four levels above the main deck on the port/starboard centerline. From there, he chose to proceed around to the port side, where he had to step over a series of three ten-inch deep elliptical doorways made of steel and painted dark gray. Each was two-and-a-half feet wide by five-and-a-half feet tall and positioned twelve inches above the deck, where it was welded to the bulkhead (wall). As he emerged from the third doorway, he entered the open area on the port side of the signal bridge. This would take him to the forward part of the forward superstructure, where the signal shack was located. He lifted his face to the sky to look at the moon and stars, only to be quickly reminded that none were visible tonight. Still, the cool ocean breeze whisked across his face and through his hair, threatening to ruin his sour mood and make this night bearable after all.

Even in the pitch black of the night, Jack could easily navigate the signal bridge without the use of a flashlight, and without causing any major damage to his shins or other extremities. But tonight he was conducting a pre-watch tour of the space before he relieved the current Signalman of the Watch, so he used his small flashlight to check for equipment deficiencies and all-around space readiness before he assumed responsibility for it. He was not looking forward to standing his rotation of Signalman of the Watch tonight, as was evidenced by his quiet grumbling to himself as he looked over the equipment. He stood up after verifying that the gear locker padlock had been properly secured, drew in a deep breath, then forcefully blew it out through clenched teeth. He raked his fingers through his hair and continued on his way, carefully assessing the condition of the area where he would spend the next twelve hours.

The signal bridge, one level above the Captain's bridge and four levels above the main deck, consisted of a central signal shack surrounded by a weather deck (a deck which remains exposed to the weather) on the forward, port, and starboard sides. Inside the shack area, an inclined draftsman-style desktop lined the forward bulkhead, measuring about twenty-eight feet from port to starboard. It was supported by drawers and cabinets containing various technical manuals, log books, an assortment of signal flags in differing states of disrepair, and, most importantly, a #10 can of coffee grounds with a healthy supply of filters and condiments. There was just enough room for two men to pass side by side between the desk and the aft bulkhead, which was covered mainly with communications equipment. In the center was the J-dial telephone, which works just like a regular rotary-dial telephone for communication throughout the ship. Immediately to the starboard side of the J-dial was the sound-powered telephone, which was activated by the sound of the speaker's voice and used for communication with several specifically designated places, such as the Captain's Bridge and the Combat Information Center, or CIC. Right next to the starboard bulkhead was the Squawk Box; an intercom system allowing communication between several designated boxes pertinent to the watch and duties of the

Signalman. Next to the J-dial telephone on the port side was the sound tube, which is a big brass tube going directly from the signal shack to the Captain's Bridge, used in the event of a loss of all other communication circuits. On either side of the signal shack, there was a two-and-a-half by five-and-a-half foot oval doorway cut in the bulkhead twelve inches above the deck, with a knife-edge seating surface extending outboard of the shack along the entire length of the oval. The rubber gasket of the equally shaped and slightly larger steel doors which hung on the bulkheads outside the shack would be pressed against this knife-edge to form a watertight seal. The access to any space on the ship which passed through a structural bulkhead was equipped with one of these watertight doors. Across the forward bulkhead of the shack was a row of windows stretching from door to door just above desk level. Tonight, one window on each side of the shack was open, allowing the cool Caribbean breeze to filter through the dim blue light emanating from the small desk lamp the Signalmen used to fill out their log book.

SM2 Douglass continued his pre-watch inspection tour of the signal bridge. Since he was the on-coming watch supervisor tonight, the condition of the signal bridge was his responsibility. Anything that was discovered to be out of regulation specs in the morning would have to be made right by either Douglass himself or by his junior Signalman before they could be relieved, just as he would require of the off-going watchstanders tonight. Advancing forward along the port side, Douglass inspected the 'big eyes,' basically a huge pair of binoculars mounted on a steel stand which is welded to the deck. This apparatus allows the Signalmen to see and classify other vessels, or 'contacts,' several miles away on the horizon. Satisfied that they were in acceptable working order, he continued forward. On the forward port corner of the weather deck, he stopped to check that the night vision scope was on, and that the proper startup maintenance had been performed on it. Rounding the front of the signal shack, he visually inspected the various antennae jutting out forward from the signal bridge like the feelers on a cockroach. All seemed to be in order. "So far, so good," he muttered to himself. After duplicating his inspection on the starboard side, SM2 Douglass announced to the current Signalman of the Watch that he was ready to assume the watch.

"Nothing to report, SM2 *Dufus*," responded Petty Officer Patterson. Jack would have preferred 'Union Jack' or just 'Douglass,' but he expected as much from Patterson. SM3 Kip Patterson had been a continuous source of irritation to Jack since his first day aboard the *Mississippi*. He didn't really do anything wrong, but he didn't really do anything right, either. He was one of those sailors with no motivation to excel and no pride in himself or in the Navy. He constantly looked like he had ironed his uniform shirt with a rock, shaved with the wrong side of his razor, and polished his shoes with a spade shovel and potting soil. The leading Signalman chief, Chief Petty Officer Johnson, had given Jack the task of 'squaring away' SM3 Patterson. "I want that boy to earn a minimum of 3.4 on his next evaluation. If he does not, it will reflect significantly on the 'leadership' portion of YOUR next evaluation." Such was the curse laid upon him by SMC Johnson. Since Jack was the senior blue shirt* in the division, he was the Leading Petty Officer (LPO), and was responsible to the leading chief for the performance of all the blue shirts in the division. True, there were only four including Jack, but Patterson messed up enough for any two regular sailors. On the 4.0 scale used by the Navy for evaluating its enlisted men, SM3 Patterson had only achieved a score of 2.8 for the last two quarters in a row, and the chief would have no more of it. To Jack's dismay, however, Patterson's disheveled appearance was a 3.8 compared to his attitude and work ethics. In many cases, pre-watch tours are disregarded, because both parties trust the other not to bag them with things to fix. However, everybody did a pre-watch tour when relieving Patterson.

"I'll figure it out," Jack retorted. "You are relieved."

"But, we have contacts," said Patterson. "Three off the starboard bow, and--"

---

*ranks of 1st class petty officer and below (E-1 to E-6) wear the blue dungarees as their working uniform, while the chief petty officers and above (E-7 to E-9) wear the khaki uniform as their working uniform.

"I said I'd figure it out, SM3 Patterson, now just go away!" Jack growled.

"Touchy, touchy, *Dufus*!! Somebody whiz in your coffee this morning?" Patterson teased as he walked out of the shack. "I stand relieved!" he called over his shoulder.

Jack took a deep breath and walked over to sign the Signalman of the Watch Log Book, officially assuming the watch. He hated the idea of putting Patterson in charge of anything, but since SM1 Wheeler had taken early retirement the previous month, his options had dwindled to next to zero. Wheeler had been replaced with Thomas Wilson, a seaman fresh out of Deck Division who had only been awarded his designation of Signalman (SMSN) two weeks earlier, and another third class who had just transferred on board from a slack shore duty job while he recovered from knee surgery. Having no intention of letting a screw-up like Patterson train a new kid, Jack was forced to assign Patterson as Signalman of the Watch with SM3 McCoy, so that he could see to the new kid's training personally. So far, a miracle in itself, there had been no major mishaps as a result of Patterson's position. The log book seemed to be in order—all contacts had been properly logged and classified. "Probably SM3 McCoy did it," Jack said aloud to no one in particular. Having familiarized himself with all contacts and business affecting his watch, Jack told Seaman Wilson to monitor the horizon with the 'big eyes' and notify him of any new contacts. Then he walked out to the port weather deck to enjoy the greatest privilege of the Signalmen. He climbed up onto the ledge of the forward bulkhead, and sat looking up at the empty sky. He would have preferred to be able to watch the stars and the moon, for they are never so beautiful as when they are viewed from the side of his signal bridge. Unfortunately, tonight they were hidden from view by thick cloud cover. So he tried to relax, now that his confrontation with Patterson was over, and talk himself into a little bit better mood. He felt the cool tropical breeze across his face and listened to the water splash as the hull cut through it. His tension slowly eased and melted away as his mind filled with thoughts of Megan.

*　　　*　　　*

Jack Douglass had attended church nearly every Sunday when he wasn't out to sea for a very good reason: he couldn't lie to his mother. Connie Douglass kept in very close contact with the only one of her sons to have left his hometown after high school. She always kept informed of his sea schedule by talking to Jack himself or by calling the USS *Mississippi* ombudsman line—the telephone number which connected the caller to an informational recording about the ship's activities. She called Jack nearly every Sunday just to chat. Jack didn't mind; he had a close relationship with his mother, and since he had no family in the Norfolk area, he rather enjoyed hearing about home and how things were going back at his old stomping ground. But after hearing the disappointment in her voice the first three times he had said, "No, Mom, I haven't found a church yet," he decided to find one he could tolerate and attend just to make her happy. Connie knew he was only attending to appease her, but she was content with that. At least he was attending. And the mother's prayer was that if she could get her son to promise to attend church, God would find a way to reach his heart while he was there. Then one Sunday, Jack discovered his own reason for being a regular attendee of the First Church of the Nazarene in Hampton Roads, Virginia.

Since Jack was single, he didn't receive Basic Allowance for Quarters (BAQ) like the married servicemen did. He wasn't willing to part with his base pay just to be able to live off the ship, so the USS *Mississippi* CGN-40, Pier 10, Naval Station Norfolk was his home. All his mail was delivered directly to the ship, and the personal belongings he couldn't keep with him on the ship were in a storage unit near the base. The Yellow Pages of the local phone book were the medium he used to determine which church was right for him. He wanted one as close as possible to the base, but it had to be a denomination his mother would recognize rather than a generic one whose doctrinal teachings he would be obligated to explain to her when she called. He had no intention of getting that involved; just being there at all would be enough to keep his mother happy. There were many churches much nearer to the base than the one he chose, but Jack concluded that making a longer drive to this church would be easier than the explanation of an 'interdenominational church' to his mother.

First Church of the Nazarene, Hampton Roads, Virginia, was a big church by Jack's standards; one in which he would have little difficulty remaining anonymous. The foyer was a wide hallway that ran along the perimeter of the audience section of the hexagonal sanctuary, branching off into rest rooms, offices, classrooms and more hallways, with a set of glass double-doors at each end. There were four pairs of wooden double-doors, each with tall narrow windows along large brass handles, which led from the foyer to the back of the sanctuary. Inside the sanctuary, there were three sections of pews from which to choose, separated by wide aisles that led from the rear doors to the dark wooden altar. Behind the altar, two steps led to the elevated platform which was home to the large wooden pulpit, the piano, the organ, the choir loft, and several high-backed chairs where the pastor, the minister of music, and any guests would await their turn to perform their various Sunday morning duties. Jack would arrive just before the worship service began, slip into a seat near the back, then make a hasty exit as soon as the service was over. He didn't fill out any visitor cards, and he didn't attend Sunday school where he might be placed on the class roster. He remained a nameless face in the crowd, exactly as he preferred to be. He didn't stop to chat with the friendly ushers on his way in, nor did he join the line of parishioners shaking the pastor's hand and congratulating him on yet another award-winning sermon on his way out. He had no ties with anyone in the church, and he didn't want any. There were enough people in his mother's church praying for him already; he wasn't about to bring upon himself a whole new group of well-wishers spouting off encouraging phrases to him every time they saw him. He was quite content with things just as they were. With one possible exception ...

She came in during the first hymn and eased behind a family of four into an open seat in the third row from the back, middle section left of center. One row in front of Jack and about three seats over to the right. He noticed her long blonde hair as it fell across her shoulders and came to a point in the middle of her back. As she looked down at her hymnal, Jack could see her long black eyelashes and the beginnings of what was certain to be a fantastically attractive face. "Now when God created woman," Jack grinned to himself, "that was what he had in mind." The breeze her approach had created was filled with her perfume, which Jack inhaled heartily, as though filling his lungs with the scent of her would enable him to keep a part of her with him when he left.

He lingered after church that day for the first time, busying himself with his jacket or his bulletin, trying to edge closer to her so that he could overhear while several church members introduced themselves and welcomed her to their church home.

Unfortunately, there was little to be learned at this time. No wedding band on the left hand, and no tell-tale tan line to indicate that one did in fact reside there but had been lost down the shower drain or something. Very pretty, apparently single and available, and apparently new to the church. She had expressed some interest in the Young Adults Sunday school class, and Jack thought to himself that perhaps it was time for him to strengthen his ties with the church just a little. Suddenly this field looked ripe for the harvest. "Megan Gallagher," Jack said, quietly nodding his head as he unlocked his Honda Accord and climbed in behind the wheel. "Miss Megan Gallagher, you are the next contestant..."

* * *

Jack jumped with a start when he saw the steaming cup of coffee floating ten inches from his face. "Sorry, Jack, I thought you heard me coming. You were looking right at me!"

"S'okay, Phil. I was just thinking about something," Jack replied as he patted his startled heart with one hand and took the cup of coffee with the other. "Strong and black?"

"Navy coffee, all the way, bud. If you can't chew it, it ain't strong enough," Phil laughed.

"What? How do you Coasties drink it? Girlie style, with

two creams and a handful of sugar?"

"Hardly, Stud. You Navy boys think this strong junk makes you tough. In the Coast Guard, we just let the package speak for itself," Phil said as he brushed the back of his hand down his body, then fanned it out like Vanna White pointing out a purchased vowel. "We drink it this way *because* we're tough."

"I think I'm going to be sick. Did you bring me a barf bag with this coffee?" Jack teased.

They both chuckled as they sipped their coffee in the still black night. This had become nearly a nightly ritual on the signal bridge of the USS *Mississippi*. There was a full complement of fourteen Coast Guard men on board the *Mississippi* for their joint task of Drug Interdiction Operations off the coast of South America in the Caribbean Sea. The Coasties would use the sophisticated radar of the *Mississippi* to track all sea and air traffic in the area, since the powerful radar allowed them to track many targets at the same time. They could watch all the airports, commercial ones as well as those little unknown runways between the fields of coca trees, and all the seaports. They could track the activities of all boats, ships, and planes in the area, and monitor their positions and courses. Any suspicious activity by air traffic would be reported to the authorities at the most probable destination of the aircraft. Any suspicious behavior in a seagoing vessel, however, came under the jurisdiction of the US Coast Guard. On the fantail (aft main deck) of the USS *Mississippi*, the Coasties had rigged a RIB (Rigid Inflatable Boat) which would allow a boarding team of armed Coast Guard men to approach and board any vessel exhibiting peculiar behavior. The *Mississippi* would steam quietly nearby, providing a subtle recommendation of submission to the civilian vessels by posting *Mississippi* sailors in battle dress at each of the fifty caliber machine guns mounted on the weather decks. If the appearance of an armed U. S. Coast Guard Assault Team alongside a suspect vessel didn't sufficiently intimidate its crew, the presence of a fully functional United States warship steaming nearby would usually do the trick.

"So, what's her name?" asked Phil, not looking at Jack in the glow of the blue light coming from the signal shack.

"Who's name?" replied a confused Jack Douglass.

"The girl you were thinking about when I came up. Come on, Jack, I have spent five years floating around the oceans on these silly boats. We have been out here for three weeks. After a while, you get to know the looks that come onto the guys' faces. There's one that just says, 'I miss my own bed on land.' There's one that says, 'I'd give my left arm for a six-pack of Bud Light.' There's one that says, 'I wonder who my wife's cheating on me with tonight.' And there's a very distinct one, 'Union Jack' Douglass, that says '**SIGH**.........Ahhhhhh, ____________,' where the 'blank' is filled with the name of that girl back home that completely owns your heart, whether you have had the guts to tell her yet or not. So, partner, I asked you what her name is."

"Sometimes you bug me, Phil. I don't like being so transparent. Is it really that obvious?" Jack asked. He had only met Phil three weeks ago, when they had first deployed from Norfolk, Virginia, the home port of the USS *Mississippi*, to spend six weeks in the Caribbean doing their rotation of CD Ops. But Phil knew things. Relationships build rather quickly out to sea, since people tend to spend all of their time with the same group of men. That can be great if you and your co-workers share common interests. It can also make for a very long six-week cruise if you work with a bunch of—well—gentlemen with whom you would not elect to spend your leisure time, given the opportunity to do otherwise. But Phil was different. Very tall and very slim, with a kindly demeanor that put people at ease when they were with him. His hair was thick and black as coal, and his pale blue eyes looked completely non-threatening, though they seemed to be able to penetrate right into a person's soul. He was christened Emerson Phillip Anthony Prescott by his father, a high school history teacher, and his mother, head librarian at the public library in his home town. The unlikely combination of names was the blending of his parents' most beloved authors and literary figures, and was intended to be an honor to him. He didn't have the heart to tell them that he would have preferred Jim, or Tom, or something a little less... well, just a little less. He didn't see himself as an Emery, or a Tony, so he settled on the part of his name that meant something special to him: his grandfather's name of Phillip. Thus, he became E. Phillip Anthony Prescott, or Phil.

After graduation from high school, Phil had been uncertain about what he wanted to do with his life. His parents strongly encouraged him to choose a college, but he didn't feel ready for that yet. He wanted to see some things and experience some things before he did a four-year college stint and landed a career that would take him to retirement. That sounded too plain. Phil wanted more excitement. Something to tell his grandkids about in front of the fireplace at night. He chose the Coast Guard. That way, he reasoned with his distraught parents, he could use the GI Bill to help pay his own way through college, thereby relieving them of some of the burden. Plus, he would get the chance to see some of the world and do some things before he settled into an educational path that would almost certainly make his doubts prophetic and lead to a great career from which he would most likely never depart. They reluctantly supported his decision by offering to help in any way they could.

Phil Prescott had joined the Coast Guard as a seaman, a basic recruit holding the lowest rank of E-1. His diligence, hard work and positive attitude had helped him to advance on the first try whenever his time in service allowed him the opportunity. Therefore, in exactly five years he had attained the rank of E-5, or a second class petty officer. Since he enjoyed the hard work of the Boatswain's Mates in deck division, he didn't 'strike' for any other rate, but concentrated his efforts at being the best 'Boats' that he could be. Thus, he was now BM2 E. Phillip Prescott; and right now he was seeing through Jack Douglass as if he were holding up a sign with Megan's name on it.

"Well, it is obvious to me, Jack. Tell me about her. Your secret will be safe with me."

"I know, Phil. I just don't like talking about personal stuff much, you know. There aren't very many people I trust, especially on this boat."

Phil grunted in agreement as he blew on his coffee and took a sip. He and Jack had spent a lot of time chatting in this very spot since their departure three weeks ago. Phil was the kind of guy a person felt comfortable opening up to, and Jack was a guy who had not been open with anyone in a very long time.

"Hey, it's your business, Jack. I'm not trying to be nosy.

You just look like you are going to explode if you don't tell somebody about her. You have been alluding to her for over a week now, but I haven't asked because I don't want to pry. But I, for one, really enjoy our talks and I hope you know that anything you tell me stays right here between us. Who knows, I might even be able to offer you a tiny morsel of helpful advice!"

"Thanks, Phil. I like our talks, too, but, you know, I just don't have that many friends, and it takes me a while to feel comfortable talking to anyone about personal stuff."

"So don't talk then. Maybe it's none of my business. Sorry."

"No, that's not it. You're not out of line or anything. You see, man, I don't know how to feel about her. Megan. Her name is Megan. I met her at church a few weeks ago..."

* * *

Jack Douglass had had a strong and unusual urge to subject himself to Sunday school at First Church of the Nazarene that next Sunday morning, just on the off chance that Megan would be there. "How pathetic!" he thought to himself. "What am I, twelve? Maybe I should just pull her hair and chase her around the sanctuary after church!" After minimal deliberation, he concluded that seeing her in Sunday school might be more effective than the chasing and hair-pulling. He arrived promptly at 9:45 a.m. and was joyfully directed by an egg-shaped usher upstairs to a long room with an elliptical arrangement of chairs, most of which were filled with people his age talking about the weekend's activities and the impending drudgery of the coming week. This seemed to be what they all looked forward to. The week, to them, was merely a necessary evil which had to be endured before they could come back here and talk about it amongst themselves. Jack wondered to himself if the prospect of seeing and possibly meeting Megan was going to be worth spending the morning with these people; that is, until he saw her long blonde hair falling across the shoulders of her lime green mini dress, of the sort Marcia Brady would have worn to her senior prom. Jack could no longer hear the mind-numbing chatter of the rest of the class members. The world melted away as her face burned its image forever onto his mind. "This," he thought, "is a picture that will be displayed for all time in the Louvre of my mind. The Hall of Beauty, within which are preserved for eternity the frozen images of a hundred such breathtaking visions, will forever be adorned with this miracle in lime green, this sacred work of art will grace the forbidden depths of my inner world, and...and..." and he smiled rather stupidly and most uncomfortably as she caught him staring at her and offered a polite if uneasy "Hello." He could only imagine the various shades of red his face must have been turning as he sheepishly selected an empty chair a few steps away from where he had been standing, smiled, and returned the greeting. "Smooth, Jack…real smooth," he silently muttered as he lowered himself into the chair, hoping that somehow the wood grains would conceal him for the rest of the class time. This was not to be, Jack assured himself, as the class leader announced that they would go around the room and introduce themselves, since there were several new class members today. Each person was expected to give his name, where he was from, and tell one thing about himself that he didn't think anybody else there would already know. "Well, at least that part will be easy," Jack said to himself.

The remainder of the class was concluded without any additional embarrassment to Jack, despite his pre-occupation with Megan. For the church service that followed, he had returned to his seat at the back of the middle-left section and, to his pleasure, so did Megan. But this time she greeted him with a handshake and a comment about the morning's class.

"Yeah," Jack replied, "it was a little different than what I'm used to, too." His attempt to continue the conversation was rudely interrupted by the song leader, who authoritatively instructed them to stand together, acquire their hymnals, and locate page number 223. Jack wanted to shout "Sir, yes, Sir!!" while offering a snappy salute, but he thought better of it and obediently reached for the hymnal.

After the service was over, Jack's usual hasty retreat was

foiled by the pastor. He approached the end of the pew just as Jack was exiting his row and Megan was reaching the end of hers. With a smile that belonged on a television commercial for dental floss, Pastor John Mackey held out his hand and greeted Jack by name. "So much for my stealthy anonymity," Jack thought to himself with a wry grin that he tried unsuccessfully to hide. Pastor Mackey, who was much larger close up than he appeared to be when behind the pulpit, looked like a lumberjack and had a voice that Jack suspected could easily be heard from one treetop to another. He stood at the end of Megan's row, effectively blocking her exit, and invited them both to join him for lunch. A handful of members commonly meet at the Country Kitchen after church, and he would be delighted if both of them would join the group today. Jack hesitated as he tried to come up with a good enough excuse for why he couldn't possibly join them today, when he heard himself say, "Thank you, Pastor Mackey, I would love to. What do you say, Megan?"

With Pastor Mackey in the lead in his light blue station wagon, what looked like a funeral procession leaving the church slowly made its way across town to the Country Kitchen restaurant and their infamous lunch buffet. The pastor smiled and waved at Shirley, the hostess, who seemed quite familiar with the weekly gathering as she grabbed a handful of menus and led the way to a large and largely unoccupied room in the corner of the building. Several tables had been pushed together to form one long table in the center of the room, where Shirley plopped down a handful of menus, directed everyone to find a seat, and announced that the waitress would be Susan and that she would be over shortly. Of course, if anyone was having the buffet, he was welcome to proceed to the U-shaped food bar and begin filling his plate. Everyone present went directly to the food bar, dragging Jack and Megan along.

Once back at their seats, they each prayed individually for their respective meals and began eating. The conversation continued non-stop all through the meal. Jack wondered how the group had managed to fill and empty all the plates that littered the table from one end to the other while simultaneously maintaining a continuous conversation with several different people at different places around the table. "Must be one of the gifts of the Spirit," Jack chuckled to himself.

Even so, Jack was amazed at how comfortable he felt with these people. He told them about his home in Sandusky, Michigan, and a few of his more interesting sea stories about life on board the USS *Mississippi.* He had been seated next to Megan since, as a result of Jack encouraging her to join them, the pastor thought they were already acquainted. This suited Jack just fine. She was becoming more attractive by the minute. Besides the obvious physical attraction, which was intensified by the close proximity in which he happily found himself, he learned that she was also intelligent, clever, easy to talk to, and had a great sense of humor. She was even a bit bold and mischievous, as was exemplified when she related the story of Jack's unfortunate trip into his own mind at the beginning of Sunday school. Megan also enlightened him, as well as the rest of the group, to the fact that she had actually said "Hello" to him two times prior to the one which had succeeded in jerking him back to reality. When questioned as to what had so captured his thoughts that he would not hear such a lovely girl greeting him, he had casually commented on the juicy tastiness of the fried chicken that he had picked up from the buffet. As one would expect, this not terribly clever and not in the least bit successful change of subject was greeted with raucous laughter from everyone at the table. As the blood rose in Jack's cheeks until he thought his face would ignite, he noted the satisfied smile on Megan's face as she reveled in the laughter at his expense. Surrendering to the obvious humor of the situation, Jack joined in the laughter, too. This was one impressive woman, he concluded.

* * *

Machinist's Mate Third Class Jimmy Davis hooked the bucket on the fire plug next to Number Two Turbine Generator and forcefully tapped on the handle that would charge the fire plug with one hundred-fifty pounds of sea water pressure from the

Firemain System. He did this once a quarter to each of the fire plugs located within the spaces maintained by Machinery Division, because he had the added responsibility of being the Damage Control Petty Officer of the division. Once the ball valve inside the fire plug was opened enough to charge the plug, Davis would observe it to ensure that there was no leakage past the rubber gasket that served as a barrier between the firemain system and the machinery spaces. Next, he would isolate the plug from the rest of the system by shutting the globe valve immediately upstream of the plug, then crack open the ball valve in the other direction, allowing the sea water to drain into the bucket. When all the sea water had drained from the plug, he would disassemble, clean, and lubricate the fire plug. Finally, he would reassemble the fire plug, attach the fire hose, and leave it in a condition of peak readiness, should any unfortunate situation arise where its services would be needed. As Davis was finishing up his mundane task of fire plug preventative maintenance, he heard his name being called from the upper level of the engine room. He glanced up through the deck grating and saw a shipmate lighting a cigarette for himself and motioning with another one for Davis to join him. Davis pocketed his wrenches and other paraphernalia, picked up the bucket and climbed the ladder to the upper level. He usually dumped his bucket of sea water into the bilge on the lower level, but this time he figured he could find a drain funnel on the upper level that would work just as well. He placed the bucket on the bulky lagging that encased the steam piping and retrieved the lit cigarette from his friend.

Having reached an agreement on which football team was destined for the Super Bowl this year, they crushed out their cigarette butts in the ashtray and each returned to whatever it was that he had been doing prior to their unscheduled break. Davis reached for his bucket with his right hand while he picked up his tools with the other. Glancing at it out of the corner of his eye, he misjudged the height of the bucket, thus making contact with it two inches below the handle and sending it tumbling down to the deck. The sea water spilled onto the lagging, finding its way into cracks in the paint, and seeping in at the joint where two pieces of lagging were connected. Davis scraped the water from the deck with the side of his boot, brushed off the pipe lagging with the back of his hand, and left the engine room.

That night, Davis sat on the floor by his rack and began a letter to his mother. He dated it July 7, 1977.

"Dear Mom," he wrote. "Greetings from the USS *Ticonderoga* CG- 47, somewhere off the coast of Virginia . . ."

*　　　*　　　*

Pablo Linares looked out over his family's fields from the home-made rocking chair that was a permanent fixture on the front porch of the main house. His grandfather had made it during the rainy season some fifty years earlier while waiting for harvest time to come. Always the most comfortable of the outdoor furniture that lined the porch, it had become the throne upon which sat the patriarch of the Linares family. He stirred his custom blended tea with a sterling silver spoon, then placed it on the imported china saucer, while the family crest engraved in the spoon's handle watched him like the souls of a hundred dead kings scrutinizing his leadership of the family. He drew in a deep breath, filling his lungs to capacity, then blew it out forcefully, as if by the act of exhaling he could rid himself of his guilt just as his body was ridding itself of carbon dioxide. He wondered if his father had felt so small when he had sat in this chair.

Pablo was a rather small man, slightly less than average height, with thick black hair and a bushy black mustache. His deep set black eyes held the power to intimidate men much larger than himself, while they shielded his family from his inner turmoil like a frosted glass window prevents passersby from seeing into a bathroom. He mentally surveyed the estate, which now belonged solely to him, the eldest of four sons. The main house, with its twenty-seven rooms, the four-bedroom guest house with the three acre lawn in between, the garage, the barns, the stables, the fields. –Ah, yes, the fields. What had begun as five fields, each almost as large as the three remaining, had dwindled through the years due to various family hardships. For six generations, the Linares

Plantation had produced sufficient revenues from the sale of its sugarcane crops to permit a rather lavish lifestyle, as well as to make the Linares name a symbol of the social elite. Nothing was more important to a Linares than family honor and heritage. Blood was the membership card to an elite social club, heritage was the gold bullion upon which the club's status was based, and tradition served both as evidence of current membership and as the honored remembrance of those since retired. A back injury, suffered by Pablo's father while his sons were still too young to pick up the workload, had caused the most recent sale of a portion of the beloved Linares Plantation several years ago. Pablo, the head of the family since his father's passing two years previous, had vowed that the Linares estate would never again suffer the dismemberment it had endured in the past. It was now up to him to continue the family traditions and the family business.

It was for this reason that Pablo now sat silently on the porch of his magnificent home, pondering the wisdom of his recent business ventures. He had known who the men were before they had even introduced themselves. The suits, the shoes, the car, even the manner with which they had presented their request to him had told him who they were—or at least who they worked for—Don Miguel Ramirez. Once upon a time, the only rival to the Linares Plantation was that of Luis Ramirez, patriarch of the Ramirez family. Both derived their livelihood from the land, both had vast influence in the business world. Ramirez, however, had the desire to diversify his holdings, while the Linares' were content to preserve their family heritage and depend upon the land in the same manner generation after generation. Each understood the deep roots of family and lineage, and therefore spoke the other's name with a respect born of common beginnings and many similar trials and successes.

Pablo watched the events unfold in his memory. Two years earlier, an infestation of beetles had wiped out nearly eighty percent of the Linares harvest. Most of the following year had been spent exterminating the beetles, and the land had only healed itself to a degree which would yield a fifty percent crop for the current year. His father's stubborn refusal to hire accountants and upgrade to modern agricultural techniques in the years leading up to the beetle infestation had cost the estate dearly, to the point of nearly wiping out any liquid assets and the majority of the cash on deposit with the Bank of Puerto Cristobol. Two back-to-back years of diminished earnings was almost more than the estate could handle. Pablo had spent many a frustrating evening walking along the edge of the fields, probing his mind for a solution to his financial difficulties. On one such evening, he had seen a car pull off the dirt road and onto the path beside the field. Two men had approached him with an invitation to the Ramirez mansion for coffee late the following morning. Pablo had hesitantly, but respectfully, accepted.

Miguel Ramirez was an average looking man of medium build and of medium height. His expensive suit and bejeweled fingers portrayed an image of success far exceeding that of one who draws his living from tilling the land and dabbling in various business interests. No one seemed able to prove anything, but it was well known that Don Miguel Ramirez, although he did own and operate several legitimate businesses, had made and maintained his own personal fortune primarily with the exportation of marijuana and cocaine to America. Miguel had avoided the authorities for years by being completely ruthless in all dealings of a questionable nature. No one dared cross him or inform the authorities about him. His reputation was very well known: you would only cross Don Miguel Ramirez once. He extended his hand to Pablo, who took it and shook it courteously. The two men had never been friends, as their parents and grandparents had, but they honored the relationships cultivated by their fathers. Miguel got right to the point.

"Pablo, I want to help you. I am aware of your financial situation, and I am aware of the unforeseen events that led to your current financial situation. I am also aware of your late father's reluctance to bring the working side of the plantation up to speed with modern agricultural technology, and how that resistance to change has contributed to your current financial situation. As you well know, I am a very successful businessman. I did not get this way by giving my money away. However, I do wish to help your family through this difficult time. If I may be so bold, what would it take to secure your business and sustain your estate until the next harvest?"

Pablo sat stunned. For a long while, he didn't respond. His mind was racing, trying to discern the motive behind Miguel's implied offer. Would he attempt to foreclose on the land? The house? Pablo's thoughts were bouncing off one another and not really making sense. He decided to just let Miguel have his say. He made a few mental calculations then volunteered a sum to Miguel.

"Ah," Miguel said as he shook his head up and down, "very close to what I had calculated. Now then, Pablo, here is what I propose."

Miguel outlined his plan. The Linares Plantation would be given one-hundred fifteen percent of the sum Pablo had quoted up front to seal the deal. The deal was this: for the next five growing seasons, Pablo would lease one-third of each of his fields to Miguel. Miguel could use them however he wished, so long as they remained the property of the Linares Plantation, and their fertility was in no way harmed or compromised. In return, Pablo would receive a cash payment at harvest time equal to two hundred percent of the total projected earnings of the leased land, based upon the profits generated by the remaining land still used by the Linares Plantation for production.

* * *

"Sigs, Bridge! Identify contact at bearing 024."

"Sigs, Aye!" SN Wilson answered.

"Who is this?" the voice from the bridge asked.

"Seaman Wilson, Bridge."

"This is Ensign Barker, the OOD (Officer of the Deck, the senior duty officer of the bridge). Where is Petty Officer Douglass, SN Wilson?"

"On the weather deck, Sir, monitoring for contacts."

"And why are you answering the phone, Wilson?"

"I'm on watch, Sir. SM2 Douglass is the supervisor."

"Bridge, Aye. Seaman Wilson, notify SM2 Douglass of

our request and report to the bridge immediately."

"Yes, Sir. Right away, Sir," Wilson snapped as he replaced the handset. He quickly walked out of the signal shack to inform Jack of his orders.

"Did he say what he wanted, Wilson?" Jack asked.

"Nope, he just said to tell you he wants you to identify the contact at bearing 024 and he wants me to report to the bridge immediately."

"All right, take off then. Hey, one thing Wilson—don't let them get to you."

"Sure, Jack," he said as he walked aft along the weather deck, pointing his blue-lensed flashlight a couple of yards in front of his feet.

"Poor sap," Phil commented. "I have seen Barker grill some of the new kids before. It's not pretty. He just keeps asking them questions about their rate or their watch until he gets them totally confused and totally irate, then he laughs and dismisses them."

"Yep, he is a pig," Jack agreed. "But it's part of the game, you know. Gotta have something fun to do out here in the middle of the sea at two o'clock in the morning. Now, about that contact..."

An hour later, Jack was back on his perch at the forward port corner of the signal bridge, and Wilson was making his way back to the shack from his grilling on the bridge by Ensign Barker.

"Did you school him, Wilson? Teach old 'Bob' Barker which price was really right?" Jack asked with a chuckle.

"What a jerk!" Wilson exclaimed. "I would just like to see him out of his uniform one time..."

"Easy there, Killer, he is just messing with you. He is bored and he has no life and he is power-tripping. Here," Jack said as he fished some quarters out of his pocket, "go get us a couple of Cokes, and one for Phil, too."

"Sure, Jack. Thanks," Wilson replied as he once again made his way aft to the ladder.

"All right, Jack, so you have made contact," Phil prompted as Wilson rounded the corner and walked out of sight. "What happens after lunch with the clergy?"

"Huh?" Jack said. "Oh, yeah, back to Megan. Storybook, Phil. Just like something you would see in a little girl's bedtime story collection..."

* * *

The next Sunday, Jack walked into the classroom and took the seat right beside Megan. At least now they each knew somebody. They followed the lead of the others and chatted about how their week went. Apparently, none of these people ever saw one another outside of the church. Jack was determined not to let that be the case with him and Megan. In fact, just to ensure it did not happen with them, Jack told Megan he had a couple of stories to share with her that would only be sufficiently amusing if told over a seafood platter at Captain Charlie's, a greasy little seafood joint not too far from the base. She cheerfully accepted, and Jack didn't hear a word of the sermon that day. Sitting beside Megan in the pew, his mind was everywhere but on the service. He wasn't nervous, for she was so comfortable to be with, but he was very concerned that everything would be just right for his afternoon plans. Maybe she would want a tour of his ship after lunch. Maybe she would have a rotten time and not want to see him again. Maybe she would change her mind even before the service was over. Maybe she would just pick up her purse and walk toward the door without saying a word to him. "Maybe I am being an idiot," Jack suggested to himself.

As it turned out, he was completely correct. He was being an idiot. Lunch went wonderfully, and yes, she would love to see his ship after the meal. They parked their cars in the lot closest to Pier 10 and began walking in that direction. As they reached the pier, Megan looked in awe at the rows of warships on either side, moored end to end along both sides of the pier. The huge gray monsters looked ominous with all of their cables, antennae, and equipment covering the decks from the main deck all the way up the superstructure to where the sails would be, had they been sailing vessels of that sort. Each of their radar was idle, though each would be rotating continuously while out to sea. The various missile launchers and gun mounts sat motionless on the decks, waiting for some conflict to call on them to discharge their respective weaponry for the cause of preserving freedom and democracy. Megan carefully climbed the aluminum ladder to the brow which led them to the aft starboard quarterdeck of the USS *Mississippi*. Jack flashed his military identification to gain access for himself and his guest, who would be required to remain under his observation at all times. That would definitely not be a problem. He tucked his wallet back into the pocket of his pants and led Megan across the main deck to the aft port quarterdeck, where they would be permitted to enter the skin of the ship. As they crossed the main deck, Jack pointed out the aft missile launcher, LS-2, located in the exact center of the fantail, and the aft five-inch gun mount, located at the forward end of the fantail, immediately aft of where the interior spaces of the ship extended above the main deck. Each of the aft corners of the main deck sported the latest in Tomahawk Missile Automated Box Launcher (ABL) technology. The pair of ABLs were twelve feet high, twelve feet wide, forty feet long, and mounted lengthwise on either side of the main deck as an afterthought where the *Mighty Miss*' had originally been designed to carry an Apache attack helicopter. They had boarded the ship in the late afternoon when most of the crew was ashore on liberty. Jack opened the watertight door and led Megan into a vestibule. In the bulkhead in front of her was a regular door leading somewhere deeper into the interior of the ship. In the deck at her feet, there was a large hole and an odd-looking contraption that resembled something out of an Edgar Allen Poe poem. In reality, it was merely a watertight hatch containing a watertight scuttle, the normal means of gaining access to the second deck from the main deck. The hatch was similar in construction to the watertight door, except that it was designed for preserving vertical watertight integrity as opposed to horizontal. It consisted of a three by four-and-a-half foot square hole in the deck, with a knife edge seating surface extending six inches up into the space above it. The heavy steel hatch was raised up and held in place by two solid steel one-and-a-half inch diameter removable stanchions, in turn held fast at each end by quarter-inch pins with rotating ends like cotter keys. The hatch would be fastened in the shut position during General Quarters by flipping up the ten swing-bolts secured to the deck into ten hooks welded to the hatch and tightening their respective nuts. In the center of the hatch was the scuttle, which served as a quick access to the space during periods when General Quarters was set. An iron handwheel on the top, measuring about nine inches in diameter, rotated a mechanism of bars and another handwheel on the underside of the scuttle to allow it to be tightened against the twenty-two inch diameter round hole with a one-and-a-half inch raised knife edge seating surface. Immediately inside the hatch was an aluminum ladder extending down into the passageway below. Again Jack led the way, cautioning Megan to use the handrails and watch her head as she descended. Even though aluminum is a relatively soft metal, it is still quite unforgiving when in conflict with the soft tissue of a human body. At the bottom of the ladder, they proceeded aft along the passageway which, even though it was one of only two passageways running fore and aft through the ship, was still too narrow for them to walk side by side. The steel walls, or bulkheads, had been painted white, the floor covered with some shiny royal blue surface with light blue specs randomly interspersed over its entire length. There were valves and pipes jutting out from the overhead and the bulkheads in all directions, little stenciled identification tags labeling their contents and direction of flow for the crew. Every fifty feet or so, they would have to step up over a twelve inch 'knee knocker' to pass through a watertight door held open by a steel hook at the top. They took a hard right through a watertight door, went down through another hatch and descended one more ladder to the next deck, then stepped up through one more watertight door to get into Jack's berthing compartment.

"And here it is, my home away from home—Crew Living Complex Sixteen," Jack said as he bowed and stretched out his hand like the hero of a melodrama taking an extra curtain call. "This is where it all happens, Megan. Men and their fortunes are made and lost within the confines of these steel walls. This is the proverbial hub around which the spokes of the universe turn, each extending to a...okay, you're not buying it. So, uh, this is where

26 guys play cards and watch TV."

"Now that, I'll buy," Megan said, shaking her head and chuckling. "You are a nut, Jack Douglass."

Jack grabbed her hand and continued the tour, which consisted of pulling aside a deck-to-overhead curtain to reveal a twenty-four-foot-long room with three columns of three pits on the right side, and two columns of three pits on the left side. Lockers stretched from deck to overhead where the third column of pits would be. That was the tall end of the L-shaped room. Jack's pit was on the bottom of the L, around the corner from the crew lounge. The lounge was a ten by fourteen foot area in the crotch of the L, less than half the size of the classroom at the church. On the outboard side of the lounge area, on the other side of what seemed to be a rather thin steel wall, was the Chesapeake Bay. On the inboard side was a small bathroom, called a 'head' in Navy lingo, where one could find a small stainless steel shower, one sink surrounded by a small Formica countertop, a porcelain stool inside a stainless steel stall, and a porcelain urinal hanging on the bulkhead by the door. Jack led the way around the corner to where his pit was located. There was a crude curtain hanging across the front of a space barely bigger than Jack himself. The curtain stretched almost from one end of his pit to the other, the closest he could come to having any privacy while he slept or read a book or listened to his compact disc player through his headphones. Each pit had a light and a vent fan at one end with a small towel rack and a vent fan suction opening at the other. Jack unlocked the padlock on the front of his pit and lifted it up to reveal a six-inch deep horizontal storage locker where he kept the majority of his belongings. He was also provided with a tiny steaming locker, also six inches wide, but tall and deep enough to hang his clean uniforms in without wrinkling them. Megan smiled and shook her head in amazement. She couldn't believe that he could keep everything he needed for a six-week or six-month deployment in just those two small lockers the ship provided him with. Jack let his pit slam shut, replaced the lock, and ushered Megan back to the door. They exited his living complex, climbed up one deck, walked forward to the center of the ship, cut across to the starboard passageway, then climbed up three more ladders until they reached the 04 (pronounced "oh-four") level, where the signal bridge was located. She was fascinated with all the equipment spread out over the various decks of the big cruiser. Jack told her what most of it was used for, trying to relay what part each played in the ship's operation. As they strolled across the signal bridge, he told her how he would come out during the mid-watch and sit on the ledge on the forward bulkhead, watching the stars and listening to the water splash against the hull. Sometimes he would feel so large and powerful sitting up here, like a lookout on a pirate ship, watching the world go by below him. He felt like a king presiding over a jousting match, where he held the lives of his pawns in his hands, choosing who would fight whom, and letting fate have its way. Other times, he felt so small. Floating out on the vast ocean, merely a tiny speck that could so easily be swallowed up by the great sea, Jack knew insignificance. There would be mourning, to be sure; there would be sadness, of course; but if their ship were to suffer some disastrous fate out there and end up sinking to the ocean depths, he knew that the world would continue on without them. Highland Appliance would still be having a sale, the NFL would still watch its members struggle for the privilege of playing at the Super Bowl, and Dick Clark would still ring in the new year from Time Square in New York.

"Did anybody ever tell you that you think too much?" Megan asked as Jack voiced his philosophical pondering.

"Well, I guess there is a lot more time out there than there are things to do when we go underway," Jack replied. "Sorry if I was rambling. It's your fault, anyway—you are too easy to talk to."

"That's okay," she said sweetly. "I don't mind listening, it's just that I don't think, even with all that time on my hands, I could come up with some of that stuff you just did. It must get awfully lonely out there."

"Yeah, it does," Jack agreed with a sigh.

A comfortable silence ensued as Jack's mind flashed back to evenings underway, memories usurping his thoughts like oil climbing up the dry wick of an oil lamp. Megan tried to imagine what it must be like out there on the lonely sea for weeks at a time in this giant steel box. Breaking the silence and jolting Jack back to the present, Megan asked about the mail service on board while the ship was underway.

"We have a postal service on board the ship," Jack replied. "Usually we get mail delivered by helicopter two or three times a week, depending on where we are. I mostly get letters from my mom every couple of weeks. We talk on the phone when I'm in port, but she knows how lonely it is out to sea, so she writes to me about all the hometown news. Sometimes she includes newspaper clippings about people I know back home."

"I could write to you if you would like," Megan offered. I really don't have any friends here anyway, so it would give me someone to talk to, even if there is a two week delay in getting a response."

"That would be wonderful, Megan. I would really appreciate that. I'll try not to ramble on too much or think too much about my responses." They laughed together as they began descending ladders to leave the ship.

They said good-bye at her car after making plans to meet at the ship on Friday to catch a movie together.

* * *

"Sure sounds like a storybook to me, pal," Phil agreed. "How long ago did all this happen?"

"Well," Jack thought, "the Friday we went to the movie was the Friday before we deployed. She came to the pier to see us off when we left that next Thursday."

"That's kind of like getting a great toy for Christmas the night before you leave on a vacation. Now here you are with all this time on your hands and nothing much to do except think about your new toy back at home. Gee, no wonder you were spacing out."

"Yeah, and if you could see the toy, you would understand even more. Except there really isn't anything to miss yet. I mean, we haven't even kissed or anything. We have only had one date. The next time I saw her, outside of church, I was standing right here waving good-bye to her on the pier."

"But, Jack, she was on the pier for you. That has to mean something. So, you two haven't talked about the relationship or where it might be headed at all?" Phil asked.

"Nope," Jack replied. "We're still in that 'getting-to-know-you' phase, when you talk about past and present, who you are, what you like, what you don't, and all that garbage before you decide if the other person is worth talking with about the future."

"You do think too much, Jack!" Phil chided as he finished his coffee and stretched. "As for me, I think it's time to hit the rack for the night. Take it easy, Jack. Kiss her once for me."

Jack smiled as he regained his seat, looked up at the endless black sky, and thought about the letter he had received from Megan that afternoon. It was a very safe letter. At times like this, Jack hated safe letters. Not suggestive, not particularly inviting, and at the same time, exciting and enticing. She really had had nothing of consequence to say; no mention of missing him, no talk of emotions or feelings at all. She had merely rambled about her job, a couple of movies she had watched, and what the Sunday school lesson was about the previous week. A handful of people from the church sent greetings, but none sent cookies. The only blurb of particular interest to Jack was that last sentence before she signed off. Jack pretended to struggle to remember, as though he hadn't memorized it after the very first time he had read it:

"Are you still getting back on Monday, the 10th? Maybe I'll see you on

the pier. Thanks for the letters, it is nice to hear from you."

"Gotta go, Jack. You know, carrying on a one-way conversation like this

is a bit more difficult than I had expected..." -blah, blah, blah........whatever.

Jack let a grin spread across his face. "Hmm," he thought to himself. "Maybe she will see me on the pier. Now, wouldn't that be lovely. After all, it *is* nice to hear from me..."

*   *   *

Miguel Ramirez slammed the pearl handled receiver down onto the gold plated telephone cradle. Then he threw it against the far wall of his home office and furiously verbalized a rather long and distinguished list of expletives, assigning new and not terribly pleasant nicknames to several of his employees and a few diligent law enforcement officers. The catalyst to this outburst was the interrupted travel plans of a special package which was being shipped from a small fruit packaging company, to which Don Miguel Ramirez could never be linked, to a distributing warehouse in Miami, to which Don Miguel Ramirez could also never be linked. The package had just been intercepted by the port authority of Puerto Cristobol. As a result, a quantity of fine grade Venezuelan marijuana, street-valued at just over fifty thousand American dollars, would not fulfill its destiny of converting itself into a five-digit number appearing in the deposit column of one of Miguel Ramirez's bank statements. Such an unfortunate turn of events was not acceptable. Miguel had not built his dynasty by tolerating failure. Someone would be punished for this. Miguel could easily dismiss the loss of fifty thousand dollars, but the attack on his business could not be overlooked. He would find out who was responsible for this bust, and they would receive a fifty-thousand-dollar lesson in why it is not prudent to cross Don Miguel Ramirez.

When he had once again regained his composure, he called Victor, his most trusted assistant, into his office. Victor, having listened to Miguel's side of the telephone call and the subsequent tantrum, cautiously entered the office. He quickly surveyed the room; the mahogany bookshelves, the expensive Persian rug on the tile floor, the large mahogany desk and chair which acted as a throne for Miguel. His eyes swept across the wet bar to the right of the desk, and the locked gun cabinet to the left. He bent down to retrieve the remnants of the telephone when Miguel stopped him.

"Victor," he began, "I want to know how this happened.

Somebody talked. Somebody told the Puerto Cristobol Port Authority that there was a shipment going out today. Somebody betrayed Don Miguel Ramirez, and I want to know who it was. I don't want to see your face again until you can tell me the name of the person responsible for this treachery, Victor. Do I make myself clear?"

"Yes, Don Miguel," Victor obediently nodded. "I will take care of it. May I take Raul to assist me?"

"You can do whatever is required to get this done. I want a name, and I want it NOW."

"It will be done, Don Miguel," Victor pledged as he backed out of the office.

Later that night, as the Venezuelan sun had disappeared beneath the crest of the majestic Andes mountain peaks, Miguel Ramirez typed his password into the box provided, positioned his mouse arrow over the 'log on' box, and pressed the left button. His computer beeped and chirped, connecting him to the information superhighway. He navigated his way into the pre-selected chat room, logged in under the proper user name, and waited. Once a week, Tuesday night at midnight, Miguel was contacted by Belinda. Their secret Internet meetings had been organized and planned out months earlier. The first through the tenth of each month, they would log in to the 'entrepreneurs' chat room; he was machoman22, she was stella24. The eleventh through the twentieth, it was the 'motorcycle racers' chat room; he was whoopte_doo, she was bighill2jump. The twenty-first through the end of the month, it was the 'love line' chat room; he was wanting_ubad, and she was nothinghere_4u. At six minutes after midnight, 'stella24' blinked onto the screen.

A bit impatient after his disappointing day, 'machoman22' began to type.

machoman22: you're late, stella. I've been waiting.
stella24: greetings to you too, machoman.
machoman22: how was your day? any rude customers?
stella24: no more than expected
machoman22: are you using the new menus yet?

stella24: they're not back from the printer yet but
they promised them by the tenth. we should
be able to start using them then.
machoman22: will the food choices still be the same?
stella24: definitely.
machoman22: have sales dropped on any items?
stella24: not at all. Sales are in no danger of dropping
machoman22: let me know how the new menus work
out.
stella24: sure will. How's your business going?
machoman22: not bad. One of our drivers lost 50
dollars today. Police took statements, but
the money is lost.
stella24: that's too bad. your drivers should never
carry more than 20 dollars:)
machoman22: very funny.
stella24: well, better luck the rest of the week. talk
to ya later.
machoman22: sure. take care.

Miguel logged off and shut down his computer. He refilled his brandy snifter from the bar in his office and walked out onto the balcony. Belinda would come through for him. Then things would be different.

~2~

"Blossom Ship! Blossom Ship! All hands, man the rails!" the loudspeaker squawked, summoning every sailor not actually on watch to muster on the weather decks in his service dress white uniform. The men would then be lined up along the rails on every weather deck, creating a very impressive spectacle for those waiting on the pier for the *Mighty Mississippi* to moor, bringing their loved ones home. There were 600 men in the ship's company, so the pier was usually quite full of wives, children and friends when the ship pulled into port. The men had found that, no matter how well you knew the face of your wife, it was very difficult to spot her in the sea of people lining the pier. Jack had one distinct advantage—well, actually two. He grinned to himself as he walked over to the 'big eyes' on the port side of the ship and began to search the crowd for the beautiful face of Miss Megan Gallagher. He was a confused bundle of nerves as he scanned the crowd for her. Half of him expected to see her, half of him expected not to, and all of him hoped and prayed that she would be there. He had paced and fidgeted all night long on his watch, wondering if the clock had deliberately slowed itself just to torment him. He had tried to get some rack time after lunch, but he was too uptight and excited to sleep. Instead, he had spent the time perfecting his uniform and polishing his shoes to a glassy mirror finish. If Megan did happen to be on the pier, he wanted her to be proud of him. He continued surveying the pier with the 'big eyes', slowly panning the crowd from left to right.

All manner of people were present—tall and short, big and small, from newborn infants to white-haired grandparents. There were brothers, sons, sisters, mothers, fathers, wives and daughters. The crowd sported more hairdos than a year's subscription to Hairstyles Magazine could offer and represented every variation of fashion from late sixties polyester for the grandparents to whatever the current fad for the young kids happened to be. Finally, after several minutes of searching, Jack's eyes locked onto a familiar face. A beautiful face. A face he had seen every night in his dreams; smiling at him, talking to him, taking the edge off the loneliness of the nights. A face that even now caused his heart to beat faster, his breath to come quicker. His chest tightened, and a lump that he was certain would choke him to death in a matter of seconds lodged itself in his throat. She was even more beautiful than he had remembered, looked more stunning than he had anticipated. After six weeks of thinking about her and missing her every day, she was finally here. Here, but still thirty yards away and inaccessible. He could see her long blonde hair being gently tousled by the ocean breeze, but it would be yet another thirty minutes before he could reach out and touch her. Another thirty minutes before he could smell her perfume and hold her in his arms. He felt like a puppy who, when teased with a hunk of beef or a doggie treat, gets so excited that he just can't contain himself so he dances around yapping at the top of his lungs and wets himself all over the carpet. Fortunately, Jack was able to control his excitement, thus avoiding the puppy pitfall and the resulting social faux pas of wetting himself all over the carpet.

Even still, he became overwhelmed with emotion. His face paled and he steadied himself on the rail.

"Whatsamatter, Jack, did she get ugly over the last six weeks?" Phil teased. "Or did she show up with a couple of kids?"

"Ha, ha. You should be in show business, Phil," Jack retorted, feeling more than a little self-conscious about his own over-emotional state.

He returned to the 'big eyes' and found Megan again. She was looking straight at him and waving, with a big smile on her face. "Life is good," Jack smiled.

"Moored. Shift colors!" the loudspeaker announced. That was the order for the duty Signalman to shift the location of the American flag from the forward superstructure to the flagpole on the fantail. Jack could also see the duty electricians in their blue coveralls preparing to hook up the shore power cables, and the duty Deck Division sailors were busy setting up the ladder and the brow that would allow the men freedom in a matter of minutes. Jack made his way down to the main deck where he could see Megan only a few yards away on the pier. He motioned that she should get in the line to come aboard the ship. She nodded and began making her way toward the brow.

The sweetest words a sailor can hear finally came across the loudspeaker: "Liberty Call, Liberty Call. Liberty Call for duty sections one, three, and four. Liberty to expire in accordance with the Plan of the Day." There were two lines on the brow; one going off the boat, and one coming on the boat. Megan finally got through the crowd and walked up to Jack with her arms outstretched. They embraced, and Jack held her for as long as he dared before they pulled themselves apart, giggling about absolutely nothing. They embraced again, then Jack took her hand and led her across the main deck to where Phil was standing by the rail.

"Phil, this is Megan Gallagher. Megan, Phil Prescott."

"It is indeed a pleasure to meet the girl who has messed up Jack's head so much," Phil said with a mischievous grin.

Jack punched him in the arm and told him to shut up. Megan lifted an eyebrow to Jack, who once again felt his cheeks flush with embarrassment.

"Really, Jack?" she asked. "Just what have you boys been talking about out there, anyway?"

"Phil is just being a pain," Jack said. The eyebrow again. Jack hesitated. "Well, I may have mentioned you to him a couple of times."

"Just a couple of times?" she teased. "That's all the press I get? Just a couple of times?"

"Can we go now?" Jack pleaded. They all laughed as they said their good-byes and parted ways. Jack and Megan went down to his berthing to collect his bags, then off the ship on liberty until 0700 the next morning.

"I thought we could go out and have a nice dinner together," Megan suggested as they walked past the McDonald's and into the parking lot.

"Sounds great," Jack agreed. "Any place but the galley on the ship, I am all for it. And it won't be half bad having you there, either."

"Wow, Jack, you really are a sweet talker. You make me feel so special," Megan teased, returning his grin.

They located Jack's Honda, tossed his bags in the back, then climbed into the front seats. Jack pumped the accelerator pedal a few times then turned the key in the ignition. After the slightest hesitation, the little car sputtered to life and purred softly, like a faithful cat welcoming its master back from a vacation.

Jack gave the car a few minutes to warm up, then joined the line of vehicles filled with anxious sailors attempting to exit the base and reclaim their land-based lives. As they neared the gate at the exit of the base, Jack asked Megan where she wanted to go for dinner.

"It's up to you, Jack," Megan replied. "You are the one who has been away, so you can choose the restaurant tonight. We can go wherever you want to."

"Okay, that works for me. How about Luciano's? Does Italian sound good?" Jack asked.

"Sounds wonderful," Megan agreed. "Drive on."

Since it was still over an hour before the dinner rush, Jack and Megan were immediately ushered to a small booth in the back corner of a deserted section of the dining area. Megan's comment about this being Jack's first day back after six weeks out to sea had elicited a knowing smile from the hostess, who had giddily led them to their secluded dining place with a twinkle in her eye.

While they waited for their waitress to bring them their beverages, Jack and Megan chatted continuously about the previous six weeks. Megan told Jack all about her job, the Sunday School class, how everybody was doing, and how she had been doing. They discussed which movies she had seen and whether they were any good or not, and some significant happenings in the local and world news department. Megan asked Jack about his latest experience underway, the liberty ports he had visited, and how things had gone during the deployment.

The waitress appeared to deliver their beverages and take their dinner order, then she disappeared to pass their order on to the kitchen.

"Jack, what is it like coming back home?" Megan asked. "I mean, I will never be able to understand what it is like to be out there, but what is it like when you get back in? What things do you miss the most?"

"You mean, besides you?" Jack asked.

Megan's face acquired the slightest pinkish hue. She looked down at the table. "Yes, silly, besides me." She raised her eyes to look back up at him, her head still lowered, a warm grin on her face.

"Glass doors," Jack replied.

The grin faded, the head came up with a quizzical look.

"Glass doors?" Megan asked, not certain she had heard him correctly. "You mean, glass doors—like, *glass* doors? Like *doors* that are made of *glass*?" she asked, confused, surprised at his immediate transition from a suggestive and flattering comment like "Besides you?" to something completely unrelated and impertinent like "glass doors." What in the world was that supposed to mean? Sure, she had dismissed his flirting flattery like women were supposed to do, but that didn't mean that she didn't want him to do it any more!! Why could men never seem to understand that?

"Yeah," Jack said. "Glass doors. All the doors on the ship are steel. You can't see through them, and they're all painted and ugly with big, stupid numbers on them. I miss glass doors."

"Okay, then," Megan said, still taken aback by Jack's response, for which she had been totally unprepared and from which she had no idea where to take the conversation. "Glass doors."

"Glass doors," Jack repeated, grinning and thoroughly enjoying himself. He took a swig of his Coke, then glanced up at Megan. "Not exactly what you were expecting, eh?" he asked.

"No, uh, no, not really," Megan replied. "Really wasn't looking for glass doors, Jack. You got me on that one."

Jack smiled. Oh, but this was fun, he thought.

"And wood. On the ship, everything is made of metal. I miss wood. And trees and grass and dirt. I mean, dirt that is supposed to be there and doesn't have to be swept up."

"Interesting," Megan said. "All right, then, what do you miss the *most*?"

"Freedom," Jack replied.

"Explain..." Megan prompted, waving her hand in a circular motion.

"Freedom," Jack repeated. "The freedom to come and go as I please. The freedom to not be bothered by the Navy after the workday is over. The freedom to wear what I want, do what I want, say what I want, and to hang out with whomever I want." A pause. "And space. On the ship, even after working hours, I still can't go anywhere farther than 600 feet from wherever I am standing. And 'the man' can always get to me. On land, I can at least avoid him during the evening by not answering my pager or by not going back to the ship at night. Underway, there is no escape."

"You are one abstract, ideal-oriented individual, Jack Douglass."

"Hey, you asked!" Jack said.

The waitress returned with their meals, grated cheese onto everything, and placed the hot plates of Italian cuisine on the table. Jack attacked his plate with a determination bred from six weeks of eating in the galley aboard the ship.

The evening progressed as well as Jack could have hoped. Megan seemed really to have missed him, though she hadn't let on in her letters. The food was great, and the conversation was light and fun. They savored each other's company, drinking in the intense emotion that only an extended separation can create. After dinner, they went to the Military Circle Mall. They bought drinks at the food court, then found an empty bench by the fountain where they sat and talked until the mall closed and they were asked to leave. The rent-a-cop locked the door behind them as they began making their way toward the parking lot. They found Jack's Honda right where they had left it. Jack fished the keys out of his pocket, opened the door for Megan, then walked around to his own. They sat in comfortable silence as Jack drove back to Megan's car on the base. It had been a very intense day. They both looked forward to a good night's sleep. At Megan's car they embraced again. When they pulled apart, Jack kept his hands on her waist, fingers locked behind her. He looked deep into her eyes.

"Thanks, Megan," he said.

"For what?" she asked.

"Just for being you," Jack said. "And for coming to meet me today."

"I wouldn't have missed it, Jack," she said.

They hugged each other again, then Megan got into her car. Jack waved, watched her drive away, then started toward the ship with a big ole' goofy smile covering his whole face.

* * *

Pablo Linares was not a fool. He knew exactly what Miguel was asking him for. He knew that Miguel was going to plant marijuana in the sacred soil of the Linares Plantation, which for so many years had been a symbol of honor and nobility in the community. Miguel had given Pablo a week to consider his offer, during which Pablo had become very irritable, seldom eating a decent meal and sleeping only fitfully during the night. He had gone over the family's financial standings again and again, hoping that somewhere he had missed something, that they really were not in such sad shape as to have to resort to dealings of any kind with Miguel Ramirez. Pablo worked at his desk for hours at a time, getting up only to crack his knees and get the blood flowing through his legs again. Finally, against his better judgment but motivated by his vow of protecting the physical integrity of the plantation, he had met with Miguel and accepted his offer.

And so, he had done it. Pablo Linares had succeeded in protecting his beloved plantation from the predatory jaws of the Bank of Puerto Cristobol. And yet, he was not at peace. He couldn't call a family meeting and tell them about his latest deal that would save the plantation from bankruptcy. He couldn't tell anyone. He could only try to convince himself that it had been his last resort; something he had to do, and not something that would come back to destroy him later.

* * *

BT3 Lonnie Duncan walked across the engine room of the USS *Ticonderoga* and stooped over the metal bin full of clean rags. He put his clipboard under his arm and selected a jagged piece of what must once have been either a very tacky pair of pajamas or a very gaudy set of curtains. He wadded up the rag and wiped the sweat from his forehead before shaking the wrinkles out of it and shoving one end of it into his back pocket.

The temperature in the engine room averaged about ninety-five degrees when the ship was underway, and this evening was no exception. In the main areas of the engine room, where the ventilation ducting supplied cooling to the space, one could enjoy a strong sixty-degree breeze; however, in the nether regions of the engineering spaces where heat-generating equipment or large steam piping was located, the temperature would often hover between ninety-five and one hundred twenty-five degrees. Ventilation ducting didn't exhaust into these areas because they were not normally inhabited by people for extended periods of time and the equipment located there did not require external cooling. But BT3 Duncan had to pass through them once an hour to take gauge readings on several pieces of equipment pertinent to his watch station. On a day as hot as this, he knew he would need a fresh rag to wipe his face off once he was finished with his log readings. He would always start on the lower level, since his particular watch had log readings on all three levels, and work his way up to the upper level, where, at the beginning of each watch, he would stash his fifty-two ounce insulted mug half full of 'bug juice', the Navy's sad excuse for a fruit drink, and half full of ice chips from the mess decks. He would finish taking his log readings, then lean up against the workbench under the ventilation duct for a small break and a big drink of ice-cold bug juice. Since this was also a popular smoking area in the engine room, he could almost always find an interesting conversation to get involved in while he rested and sipped his beverage. Duncan didn't notice that all eyes were on him as he rounded the corner and tossed his clipboard on the workbench. He pulled the rag out of his pocket, mopped his face and neck with it, then replaced it and reached inside the ventilation duct where he always stored his cold mug of bug juice. What BT3 Duncan didn't know, of course, was that one of the gentlemen who stood a short distance away, smoking an unfiltered cigarette and talking about the harmful effects of the hole in the ozone layer, had taken his mug out of the duct and replaced the ice cold bug juice with warm sea water from the re-circulation valve on a sea water circulation pump. Now, sea water at any temperature would be a rather repulsive drink, but warm sea water would have to be the worst. And what would make the prank even more effective is the fact that Duncan was *expecting* it to be ice cold bug juice.

Right on cue, Lonnie Duncan had reached up into the ventilation duct and grabbed his mug. He popped open the sliding drinking-hole cover and lifted the huge mug up to his mouth. Tipping it back like a shot glass, he filled his whole mouth with what he thought would be icy-cold liquid refreshment, gulping down three swallows in rapid succession. Then, to the sheer pleasure of those watching, his face began to turn an odd shade of green; he spit out the rest of his mouthful and hunched over, coughing and spitting on the deck. He could just barely be heard over the roaring laughter of everyone present as he verbally linked a freight-train-length of expletives and colorful, descriptive nicknames together. When he finally began to regain his composure, he looked up and noticed that one very guilty-looking sailor was enjoying the festivities significantly more than all the others. Assuming this man to be the culprit, Duncan quickly popped the lid off his mug and slung the remainder of its contents at his assailant's face. The jokester ducked, allowing the remaining 50-some ounces of sea water to land on the bulkhead, the deck, and the steam piping behind him. Still chuckling, he dodged Duncan and bolted from the engine room. One of the smokers crushed out his cigarette butt in the ashtray and offered to refill Duncan's mug for him. Duncan gladly accepted. As the men filtered out of the engine room and Lonnie walked over to the scuttlebutt to rinse the sea water taste out of his mouth, the sea water that had been thrown onto the pipe found its way into cracks in the paint, penetrating the lagging and seeping in at the joint where two pieces of lagging were connected.

BT3 Lonnie Duncan sat on the workbench and began filling out his logs for the next day, since his watch was the one that crossed the midnight hour and began the next day. He clicked his government-issue black pen, set it to his log sheet and wrote, "0000 August 16, 1987. Status is as follows..."

*　　　　*　　　　*

"Olivares, Miguel," Victor said as he came into the office. "It was Hector Olivares, one of the fork lift operators at the fruit packaging plant."

"Victor, come in, sit. Now, tell me all about Mr. Olivares. Tell me about the man who has just asked me to rid him of his pitiful life."

"It seems the noble Mr. Olivares had a problem of conscience. He became aware of the special package because of the unusual loading requirements. Once he knew what was going on, he could not live with himself if he were to be a part of it. So, he decided to go to the authorities and tell them what he knew in return for a profitable relocation to another town."

"And," Miguel prodded, "where is he now, Victor?"

"He is in the protective custody of the Puerto Cristobol Police Department. They have relocated him and his family to a safe house in the country."

"Can I assume we know the whereabouts of this safe house, Victor?"

"Miguel, I would not have returned without that information," Victor calmly asserted.

"That is why I gave you the assignment, Victor. I can always count on you to deliver," Miguel said approvingly. "Perhaps we should pay Mr. Olivares a little visit."

Victor got to his feet to leave as Miguel walked behind his desk and sat down. He finished his brandy with a gulp, giving Victor a dismissing wave of his hand.

"Okay, Mr. Hector Olivares," Miguel said to the ceiling as he leaned back in his chair, "How would you like to demonstrate to anyone else who may think of betraying me that such a course of action would be fatally unwise? Perhaps you would be so kind as to be vaporized in an explosion while nestled safely in the arms of the law? Or perhaps you would prefer to be gunned down while trying to escape from the safe house? Or perhaps your demonstration of death would be more effective if a personal touch were added, let's say, with a knife..."

*   *   *

"Why don't you come on out, then, Jack. It's going to be a lot of fun," Kirt prodded.

"Okay, sure, Kirt. What time does it start?"

"How about if I meet you at the ship at about seven?" Kirt suggested. "Then you can follow me here and save me trying to give you directions. Sound good?"

"Sure," Jack replied reluctantly. "I'm at pier ten."

"All right, Jack. See you there, Friday at seven."

"Right, see you then," Jack said. He hung up the phone, annoyed at Kirt's persistence and at his own inability to come up with a viable excuse why he couldn't make it. "Sure," he muttered to himself, "meet me at the ship, so I can't just blow you off and not show up." He threw his hands in the air, asking of no one in particular: "What do you people do, have recruiting training after church or something? That's textbook appointment scheduling procedure!"

Jack continued his conversation with himself as he strolled across the main deck of the Mississippi, looking at the lights across the Chesapeake Bay in Hampton Roads. He climbed up the ladder leading to the Harpoon missile deck, one up from the main deck and right in front of the bridge, and leaned against the railing along the edge. He tried unsuccessfully to place Kirt Radford's face in his mind as he mentally reviewed the Sunday school class members. The telephone message had come from the Petty Officer of the Watch, who stands guard at the aft quarterdeck where access to the ship is controlled. Jack had used one of the two pay phones located in the vestibule behind the quarterdeck to return Kirt's call. Apparently he is having a big bonfire/weenie roast at his parent's farm on Friday, and Jack is cordially invited to be in attendance. "Great, and Megan has to work on Friday night. What a thriller this was going to be. Well, I guess it won't be that bad of a night," he tried to convince himself. "I can always go for a good bonfire/weenie roast thing. Plus, it will be interesting to see what those people are like outside of church. I bet they won't have anything good to drink there, though. 'BYOB' to them probably means 'Bring Your Own Bible.'"

The evening turned out to be far from the drudgery Jack had anticipated. The Radford farm was located about ten miles north of Hampton, about halfway between the two tiny map dots of Tabb and Big Bethel. Kirt's parents, Tom and Milly Radford, could have been chosen for that famous picture of the tall, skinny old man with the pitchfork and the short, gray-haired 'Missus' standing side by side in front of the picket-fenced farmhouse. Jack smiled to himself as Milly gave him a big hug and welcomed him to their home. Behind the house was a huge lawn that joined a typical big red barn, a tool shed, two silos and another pair of smaller out buildings. In the middle of the yard was an enormous fire pit, blackened with the memories of many events just like the one Jack was attending tonight. There were probably eighteen or twenty people standing around the fire, staring at it as if it contained the answers to all the mysteries of life. Another handful of people were gathered at a long table stacked with all manner of finger foods and snacks. At one end of the table there were four gallons of apple cider, a coffeepot full of hot chocolate, and several stacks of Styrofoam cups.

"Be shy and you'll go home hungry!" Tom said as he threw his arm across Jack's shoulders and led him to the end of the table where the plates were stacked. "Kirt tells me you're a Navy boy. Here, try one of these brownies. The Missus is a genius behind a baker's apron."

"Thank you, Sir," Jack said. "I haven't had a homemade brownie in a very long time. At least not a fresh one."

"Ain't nobody around here 'name of "Sir", Jack. You call me 'Tom' or 'Gramps.' "Sir" makes it sound like I'm getting old!" He slapped Jack on the back and had himself a good old belly laugh.

They found themselves a piece of empty lawn and stretched out on the grass. Tom talked for a while about his days farming the Virginia earth, raising Kirt and the other kids, and his life prior to taking over the family farm from his father. Jack shared a few sea stories and told about some of the foreign ports he'd visited in the Caribbean. He was just finishing a tale about missing the last water taxi back to the ship one night when Kirt approached them with his hands in the air.

"Here you are!" he announced, as if there were some doubt in Jack's mind as to his own whereabouts. "I wondered where you'd disappeared to!"

Jack and Tom got to their feet, brushing little pieces of grass from their clothes. Tom excused himself to see if Milly needed any help, though Jack doubted that Milly ever needed any help, and Kirt motioned for Jack to follow him. Jack obliged, tossing his empty plate into the fire as they got close to it and snatching another cup of cider from the end of the table. Most of the guests Jack recognized from church, although there were a few couples that he didn't remember having seen there. He figured they must be neighbors or friends of the family. Greetings and pleasantries were exchanged, then people divided off into pairs and groups, like coins in a separator, sorted by common interests and experiences. Several stayed to chat with Kirt and Jack. Jack figured they just wanted the 'goods' on the new kid, which Kirt was sure to pry out of him. They reminded Jack of their names, and he politely answered their questions about where he was from, how many siblings he had, what he did in the Navy, etc. They smiled and nodded, uttering the occasional "Ah" and "Oh" as Jack continued his discourse. Sensing a lull in the 'getting to know you' conversation, and an opportunity to change the subject to anything besides himself, Jack drew in a breath and opened his mouth to speak again, only to be cut off before he could begin by the piercing voice of Brad Coulder, the short, rotund fellow with shaggy brown hair and a scraggly attempt at a beard dirtying his chin.

"Hey, Jack!" he shouted, "I got a question for you! I have heard a lot about hazing in the military lately on the news. What kind of stuff really happens on board a ship like yours?"

"Well, that just depends on the people you live and work with in your division, I guess," Jack began. "I suppose just common pranks like you would expect from any group of 600 guys all living together in a tin can for weeks at a time. You know, hiding your boots, or drawing hearts on your underwear when it comes back from the laundry. Just silly stuff like that."

"Did they do anything to you when you first got on board?" Brad asked.

"Well, they generally save that kind of stuff for the younger, lower ranking guys. I was already a second class when I came to the Miss', so I missed most of it," Jack explained.

"So, they never did anything to you?" Brad persisted.

"Well, yeah..." Jack nodded his head and hesitated.

"Come on, Jack, out with it!" someone yelled.

"Let's hear it, Jackie-boy!" another chimed in. "Do you have cute little hearts on your underwear tonight?"

"Very funny," Jack smiled. "No, they never got my clothes. In fact, what they did to me had precious little to do with my clothes."

The small crowd was suddenly silent as they waited for Jack to tell the tale. The fire snapped and popped, sending little ghouls of burnt orange light dancing back and forth across their faces, dueling with the black shadows of the night for the right to occupy the space.

"All right," Jack continued. "I'll tell you about it." He took a sip of his cider as his mind went back to that first cruise he had taken on the *Mighty Mississippi*.

There are a variety of sounds and signals aboard a ship that every sailor must be aware of, know the meaning of, and know the proper response to. The gong-bong sound of the 'General Quarters' alarm is a general warning of imminent danger, whether it be from flooding, fire, or enemy attack. The higher pitched beeping of the collision alarm warns all hands to brace for impact, as the ship is about to have an at-sea collision with another vessel or with some foreign object in the water. The radiation alarms warn all hands that the detectors up on the superstructure have detected airborne radiation, indicating a nuclear attack or a severe reactor plant accident. The Boatswain's Whistle, blown over the PA system in a ridiculous attempt to preserve a completely unnecessary and outdated Navy tradition, lets the crew know when chow is served, when the mail is available for pickup, or when to conduct periodic sweeping of the main passageways. But there is one warning sound that one will not find listed or described in the Bluejacket's Manual (the boot-camp-issue Navy training manual); one that will not appear on any Damage Control Team Qualification Card; and one that is not a pre-requisite to earning the coveted Surface Warfare Pin. And yet, this warning sound can elicit a response from a sailor quicker than any General Quarters bell or Collision alarm. It is generated when a loose flap of duct tape is grasped firmly in one hand, the roll is loosely but firmly held with the other, and the hands are jerked apart rapidly, thereby yanking a measure of tape free from the roll, poised for attachment to a variety of surfaces. The distinctive sound created as the adhesive is torn from the back of the tape beneath it is almost magical in its power. This one sound will turn every head in the room; it will cause the curtains to be opened slightly around the pits of 'sleeping' sailors; it will cause the door to the head to be opened, a pair of eyes peering out cautiously; and it will cause arms to be upraised and feet to be planted in a defensive posture. After 8 years in the Navy, Jack knew the danger that such a sound represented. He knew that someone was about to get taped up, but he never considered the possibility that it might be him. For several years, Jack had been one of the senior Signalman on his last boat. He was the man on the roll side of the tape, not on the sticky side. HE was the one who taped up the junior squids, not the other way around. What Jack failed to realize as he walked toward the shower in his underwear and tee shirt, was that *he* was the junior man on this boat. It wasn't until SM1 Wheeler, a moose of a man, grabbed Jack's arms from behind and wrapped them around the chill water pipe that he realized what was going on. By then it was too late to run, and any opportunity that there may have been to fend off the attack was long since passed. But fight he did, because he also knew that the less you fought, the less fun it was for them, the worse they taped you up, and the longer it would be before they released you.

And so, when the yelling and laughter died down, Jack found himself in a rather intimate position with the chill water pipe that was, as its designation would suggest, quite chilly. After the third chorus of 'Anchors Away', SM1 Wheeler approached Jack with his pocketknife and cut just enough of the tape loose so that Jack could eventually wriggle out of it, giving the participants one last source of amusement before the event was over.

There were mixed reactions from the crowd around the bonfire. The guys thought it was hilarious, while the girls generally dismissed it as some silly 'guy thing' that they couldn't understand and would be totally unable to cope with if it had happened to them. They dispersed for more food and drinks, then re-grouped for more sea stories, which Jack was happy to relate.

The evening went by quickly. Before Jack realized it, it was almost 11:30, the fire was dying, and the food had mostly been eaten or cleared away. The party had dwindled to only about 6 people besides the Radfords. Jack decided that he had better get going. Again, pleasantries were exchanged, and they all looked forward to seeing him on Sunday. Jack gave a firm handshake to Tom and big hug to Milly, who refused the handshake on the grounds that nobody as cute as Jack and so far from his mother was leaving her property without a hug. She was still giggling at herself as Jack opened his car door and waved good-bye one last time. He honked the horn as he pulled out onto the little unpaved gravel road that would take him back to the highway and then into town. "Wow," Jack thought to himself. "What a great night, and we didn't even have to sing kum-ba-yah."

* * *

Jack was up early Sunday morning and, for the first time, was actually looking forward to going to church for a reason other than to see Megan. Although he still took his time shaving, perfecting the double-Windsor knot in his tie, and ironing his shirt for Megan's benefit, the smile on his face and the urgency with which he readied himself this morning was different. He was looking forward to seeing the friends he had made Friday night.

Jack rolled in to the parking lot with just enough time to get to his class before it began. He pulled his Honda into the first parking spot he could locate and speed-walked toward the building. Entering the classroom as the door was being closed, he quickly made his way toward the empty chair beside Megan. She smiled sweetly and squeezed his hand as he sat down. Jack was instantly transported to that place where only the love of a beautiful woman can take you. That place that really isn't here, but really isn't anywhere else, either. That place that is filled with everything you like and nothing that you don't. Where liver tastes like steak, ice cream has no calories, and chocolate is one of the four basic food groups, necessary for sustaining life. In this place, every minute can be spent with the one that you love; the rest of the world just drifts away, leaving the two of you floating on a cloud, drinking in the essence of each other with every inhalation, feeling the electricity with every touch of the beloved...

"Riiiiiiiiip!!!"

"Riiiiiiiiip!!!"

"Riiiiiiiiip!!!"

"Riiiiiiiiip!!!"

"Riiiiiiiiip!!!"

Jack's blood ran cold. In a split second, he sat bolt upright in his chair, arms raised and tense, rigid as a pair of boat oars, teeth clenched and lips pursed, preventing the breathing his involuntary functions had apparently forgotten about anyway. His body was frozen in place as his eyes darted across the room. That sound...

Shouts of laughter filled the room. Jack relaxed as his eyes fell on Kirt Radford, Brad Coulder, Laura Wright, Kim Perkins and Steve Denison; all of whom had stayed to listen to Jack's recounting of his *Mississippi* hazing experience the previous Friday night. Each of them was now leaning on chairs or tables or other people to support themselves as they laughed uncontrollably and pointed their fingers at Jack. Each of them was holding a roll of duct tape with an arm's length torn loose from the roll.

"You should have seen your face!!" Kim yelled between waves of laughter.

"You looked like Chuck Norris in one of his bad action movies!!" Brad teased as he clumsily demonstrated a classic defensive karate posture.

"You... you..... HA!! Hahahaha..." Laura attempted

through her tears as she tried to catch her breath.

Jack patted his chest as if to restart his heart, inhaling deeply and blowing it out at the ceiling. "Oh, you guys are just hilarious," he said; but even he couldn't refrain from laughing.

Prompted by the class leader, Jack gave the rest of the class a brief version of the story he had relayed Friday night. Megan watched and listened intently as Jack told the tale of his welcome aboard the *Mighty Mississippi*. When he had finished, Megan leaned over and squeezed his arm.

"What else did I miss Friday night?" she asked.

*   *   *

Pablo carefully placed his empty teacup on the wicker stand next to the rocking chair. The silver spoon clinked in the glass as it rocked back and forth with the momentum created as Pablo released the saucer from his grip. As if responding to the jingling teaspoon like a battalion of soldiers to reveille, the ghosts began to fill Pablo's mind. They seemed to enjoy the waiting. The period of waiting between the planting and the harvest, where only minimal effort is required to care for the sugarcane, should have been a time of relaxation for him. It should have been the time when the plantation owners and the workers alike enjoyed their last free evenings before the rigorous schedule of the harvest keeps them in the fields from just before the sun rises until well after it has set. But for Pablo, the extra time on his hands served only to torment him. He would much rather have been busy working in the fields or in the shed doing maintenance on the farm equipment. At least then he would have something else to occupy his mind.

He yawned and stretched, then slowly began to walk across the porch. He descended the concrete steps, turned off the walk, and strolled across the lush grass of the front yard. The grass tickled his bare feet. The gentle breeze tousled his hair. And the night sky gave him hope.

As he watched the day and the night battle for possession

of the evening sky, Pablo Linares had an idea. He was the sun, Miguel Ramirez was the night. He may have lost this battle with Fate, but he would be back in the morning to fight again. Just as the sun had waged its war valiantly to the very end, so would Pablo Linares continue to fight until he regained his dignity and his plantation's integrity. Miguel Ramirez would not take it from him. Fate would not take it from him. He was Pablo Antonio Linares Monteverde, descended from a long line of distinguished agriculturists, and he would not be beaten by bad luck or poor business choices. For even as the sun had retreated into the night to regroup for the next day's battle, it had posted the moon in the sky to hold off the enemy until its return. Though the battle was over for the time being, the darkness of night had not achieved a complete victory. Most of the light had indeed been driven from the sky, but there still remained a thousand little rays of light interspersed throughout the sky, taunting the night; reminding him of his incomplete victory; and holding fast to the territory upon which he rested, from which the next day's battle would begin.

He held fast to what he still had, and fortified the territory he still occupied. Even in retreat, the light had prepared the way for the next day's campaign; and so would Pablo Linares. He had accepted assistance from the darkness, but he had not given it his loyalty. He had sacrificed a small portion of his land, but he had not totally given in. Miguel did not own him, nor did he own his land. He was only permitted to use the land, and this is where Pablo drew the line. He realized that this was so much more than just the production of an illegal crop. It was much more than just selling out to the selfish interests of another. Pablo had given evil a foothold in his life. A very small one, no doubt, but a foothold nonetheless. He had let his faith waiver, and as a result, was now in business with one of the most ruthless criminals in all of Venezuela. He knew the effects of the production of marijuana. He knew that it would find its way into the hands of innocent children, both locally and in foreign countries, particularly the United States. He knew that he was a part of it, even if all he had done was to sit idly by and let it happen. Pablo was not merely concerned that someone might find out about his meager participation in the drug trade; he was worried about his soul and about the damage that would come to countless people and families as a result of his actions. He had given in, using the noble intention of protecting his family and preserving their livelihood as his excuse. But he knew there was no excuse. Pride in the family name and in his own social standing had motivated him to take the steps he had taken, with no consideration given to the effects his actions may have on others. Throughout the day, as he busied himself with tasks that may or may not have needed completing, he could almost justify his actions to himself; but in the cool of the evening, when the days activities were over and it was time to close that chapter of his life and prepare for the next one to begin, Pablo could not escape the fact the he knew he had done wrong. The rock-solid voice of his own conscience tormented him. Having joined forces in a minute way with a bad person such as Ramirez was not the issue. Having leased out a part of his land was not the issue. Even taking a silent and passive role in furthering the drug trade was not the issue. No, Pablo was being tormented for one reason only; because he had placed his own wants and desires above what he knew to be right and good. He had violated his own integrity by ignoring his conscience and making a selfish choice on his own. Pablo had once told his children that God gave us a conscience to use when we did not have the presence of mind to pray. When circumstances call for an immediate decision, our gut instinct will follow the advice of our conscience and guide us in the right way. If we cultivate that instinct by centering our thoughts on God and by following the lead of our conscience whenever it directs us concerning day to day issues, then we can be assured that our conscience will be strong and true to lead us in times of crisis. This is the advice Pablo had given his own children, but he had failed to follow it himself.

As he walked through the grass in front of his home, Pablo made a decision. He then offered an apology and made a request. And this was the beginning of a new life for Pablo Linares. The decision he made was to do what he knew was right no matter what. The apology was offered to God, for violating his sacred laws and for acting in selfishness. And the request was for God to assume the leadership of his life. For Pablo knew that only through total commitment to God could he experience true peace and contentment. He had endured all the self-condemnation and feelings of guilt that he could handle, and it was time to change the course. He had let the pressure of being the head of the family detract from his responsibility as a servant of God. But no more. Tonight his goals had changed. Doing the right thing was now more important than the business, or the Plantation, or even the image of the family. He would trust God to take care of him; and for the first time in months, Pablo Linares breathed easily. The oppression of his guilt and frustration melted away like a sugar cube in a hot cup of tea. Tonight, Pablo would sleep. He would sleep soundly and deeply, and he would awake refreshed in the morning, ready to do whatever he felt God directing him to do.

Over breakfast the next morning, Pablo did indeed feel refreshed. He also felt direction. Today, he would go to the authorities and explain his situation. The danger to himself was great, however, from both sides. He and his plantation could be implicated, since his land was being used to grow the illegal substance with his full knowledge and consent. He could be imprisoned, and the plantation could be confiscated by the government or fined heavily. On the other side of the coin, Pablo knew full well the penalty for betraying Miguel Ramirez. He hoped that he could simply alert the authorities to Miguel's activities, allow them access to his land to confiscate and destroy the marijuana crop, and appear innocent to Miguel, so as not to bring his wrath upon the Linares family. Either way, Pablo had made up his mind. He would talk to the authorities and trust God to work out the details. He wouldn't be so bold as to ask God to shield him from the repercussions of his actions, however. Sin carries consequences; it is a cause-and-effect relationship. Just because one has been forgiven for the cause, that does not negate the resulting effect. The consequences of sin may linger on long after the sinner has been forgiven. Pablo hoped that somehow the authorities would keep his name out of the situation, but he was ready to accept their course of action, whatever it may be. He just prayed that God would take care of his family, regardless of what happened to him personally.

*   *   *

As the sea water evaporated from the upper level steam piping in the forward starboard corner of USS *Ticonderoga*'s Number Two Engine Room, it created a localized area of high chloride ion concentration on the surface of the steam piping. Over the course of many years, as this same area became wetted and re-wetted by various means, the concentration of chloride ions grew to a level sufficient to support chloride pitting corrosion. The presence of oxygen, a high temperature, a tensile stress on the piping, and a high concentration of free chloride ions together on a susceptible material such as austenitic stainless steel provided the optimal conditions for the corrosion to take place. And take place it did. To a degree not even noticeable to the human eye, the chloride ions attacked and consumed the steam piping until, eventually, the wall of the pipe had become so thin and pitted that it couldn't withstand the pressure of the steam inside it.

It was 2218 local time on board the USS *Ticonderoga.* Pre-watch tours had been completed in the engine room about an hour earlier, for the 2130 watch relief, and had revealed nothing out of the ordinary. The new watch team was settling in for another boring nighttime watch, waiting for 0130 to arrive when they would in turn be relieved to enjoy a nice warm shower and some peaceful time alone, while the majority of their shipmates would be asleep in their pits. Elsewhere aboard the vessel, most of the off-watch crewmen were making use of their free time to write letters, watch a movie, read a book, play on a musical instrument, or catch a hand of Euchre or Spades before turning in for the night. MM3 Donald Allann, standing his first 'Under Instruction' watch in the engine room, walked around the forward starboard corner of the upper level to take the rest of his hourly log readings. MM2 Simmons, the qualified Machinist's Mate responsible for the watch, motioned for Allann to continue taking the log readings while he stopped at the ashtray. He took out a cigarette and began tapping it on the heel of his hand. Placing the filter carefully in the corner of his mouth, he retrieved his lighter from his shirt pocket and prepared to light up. It was a cigarette he would never smoke. As he flicked the lighter and lifted it to meet the end of his cigarette, he was instantly unable to see. He also was unable to hear. And within seconds, the steam escaping from the ruptured pipe not three feet away had seared his lungs so that he couldn't breathe. His body was relieved of life before it even hit the deck, landing in a crumpled pile beside an electrical panel. MM3 Allann suffered a similar fate on the other side of the rupture, though his untimely death was achieved by jagged pieces of pipe which had become blazing hot projectiles. Their speed had been only slightly diminished by their intersection with the soft-tissue of a human body. Unfortunately, MM3 Allann's military burial would be preceded by a closed-casket funeral.

Throughout the engine room, men could be heard screaming and gasping for the air that had already been displaced by superheated steam. Clipboards and pens fell to the deck, followed immediately by the corpses of the men who had been holding them. Only three sailors escaped the engine room with their lives that night. They had been studying the portion of the main condensate system located in the lower level adjacent to the escape hatch when they were deafened by the rupture in the upper level. They rushed through the door and into the escape hatch vestibule, allowing the excessive steam pressure in the engine room to slam the door and hold it shut. In a state of sheer panic, they shot up the ladder to the second deck, where a scuttle in the deck allowed them access to the passageway.

The three survivors were led to Medical, while a casualty assistance team donned steam suits and prepared to enter the engine room to assess the situation. The boilers had been shut down, and the huge exhaust fans were slowly removing the steam from the space to again make it inhabitable. The casualty was found to have been as detrimental to the machinery as it had been to the personnel. One of the boilers had been boiled dry, exposing the inner tubing and accelerating the corrosion occurring on its walls. Much of the electrical equipment had been shorted out as the steam condensed inside it. The USS *Ticonderoga* would no longer be able to accomplish her mission of patrolling the Caribbean Sea. At best, the captain hoped the *Tico* would be able to make it to the nearest friendly port under her own power. The disgruntled and defeated captain of the great warship sent a message to Norfolk, Virginia and Guantanamo Bay, Cuba stating that the ship had suffered a severe casualty and would be traveling at her best possible speed to Guantanamo Bay for repairs.

*   *   *

After church, Jack and Megan continued their usual Sunday lunch ritual of dining together at a restaurant near the church. Jack was eager to tell Megan all about Friday night's activities, as they hadn't been able to spend any time together since the party. As the hostess guided them to a corner booth in the non-smoking section, rattling off the daily specials and handing them creased menus, Jack wondered what Megan would think of the fun she had missed on Friday night. When Amy, who would be their waitress today if they needed anything, had finally left them alone, Megan asked him to tell her what in the world had happened Friday night that she kept hearing references to. As Jack filled her in on the evening's events, she could see the excitement in his eyes. He seemed to be thrilled about the new friendships he had made that night. Apparently, Jack was not a loner on purpose. He just hadn't met the right people to become friends with until now. Megan smiled as Jack recounted his tale about the taping incident on the ship, which explained why those five people had found it necessary to brandish their rolls of duct tape in such a manner at the beginning of class this morning.

Amy made another appearance, delivering their beverages and taking their lunch orders on a crumpled note pad. She whisked their menus off the table and departed with a hasty ". . .just holler if you need anything!" over her shoulder.

Jack and Megan continued their conversation about their respective weekends; hers being the height of boredom at work, and his being almost completely wonderful, having such a great time Friday night, then just not being out to sea on Saturday. The only thing that kept it from being completely wonderful was the fact that he had been unable to spend it with Megan. He told her all about the events of Friday night, his near refusal to even show up, the yummy food, the roaring fire, and the stories he had both shared and listened to.

"You seem to be really taken with those people," Megan commented. "I haven't heard you talk this much about any one group of people before."

"Well," Jack explained, "I don't have an awful lot of friends, Megan. I grew up in a very small town, and when I left to join the Navy, well, I left everything I knew behind. I'm not complaining, I mean, there really wasn't much in Sandusky, Michigan to take with me, you know? And in the Navy, well, I have never been a super religious person, even though I was raised in the church, but I still don't have a lot in common with many of the guys on board the ship. They all have different priorities, which mainly include drinking a lot and prowling around for loose women. Hey, to each his own, you know, but I just don't think that way. There has to be more to life than that."

Megan nodded her head, acknowledging what she had just been told and encouraging him to continue.

"I guess I just haven't met anyone from the ship that I care to spend my off-time with. We get along great on the ship and in foreign ports, but that is kind of an unreal existence. Things look different when you get back to the good old U S of A. I have made several somewhat close friends while out to sea, but when we get back home, we just never see each other off the ship. And then, when we get back out on the ocean, we just pick up where we left off, like there was never any time between deployments. It is a very strange phenomenon, but it happens all the time."

"So, what is different about these church people?" asked Megan.

"I don't know," Jack admitted. "Maybe it's the same thing happening, only in reverse. This may sound crazy, especially since we have only been together outside of church one time, but they actually seem to care about me. When they ask how I am doing, they actually listen to the answer. They just seem like real people—like the kind of people you want to be around. I can't explain it, I just enjoy being with them."

"Well, that's great, Jack. Everybody needs friends. Maybe these folks can be yours."

"Sure, maybe," Jack agreed, as Amy appeared with two heaping plates full of food, a basket of bread, and fresh drinks. They declined fresh ground pepper, so Amy retrieved their empty glasses and executed a hasty departure, as seemed to be her way.

The conversation was kept in limbo while they munched on their food. Church has a way of making a person hungry.

Amy eventually returned to ask if they required anything else and to hand them their bill. Jack placed three ten-dollar bills on it and slid it to the edge of the table.

"That should cover it. Are you ready to go?" Jack asked Megan.

"Sure, lead the way," she offered.

Jack took her outstretched hand and led her toward the door, deftly dodging the swinging elbows of those still dining around the crowded tables. Megan suggested they stop by the video rental store and pick up a movie, which they could curl up on her couch and watch together. Just in case their mood changed, they could get a sappy drama and an action/comedy flick. Jack was not about to argue with such a good idea, so he took a left out of the parking lot and headed for the video store following the directions Megan had already given him.

They were both rather anxious for the 'curling-up-on-the-couch' thing, so they wasted no time picking out the movies and heading for Megan's apartment. Part-way through the first one, they were interrupted by the shrill wailing of Jack's beeper. Since he didn't have an apartment, he didn't have a telephone, so he had splurged for a beeper in the event someone needed to get in touch with him. The screen displayed a number he didn't recognize, but he knew that very few people had his beeper number, so it was probably in his best interest to find out who it was and what the person wanted. He untangled himself from Megan and walked to the phone at the end of the kitchen bar. Punching in the numbers on the display netted him three rings followed by a cheery voice and a lot of background noise.

"Hey, this is Jack, your number came up on my beeper."

"Oh, hi, Jack! This is Kirt Radford."

"Ah, Kirt," Jack replied. "I thought the number looked familiar, but I couldn't remember whose it was. So, what's up?"

"Oh, not much at the moment, but a few of us were thinking about getting together tonight for some pizza and conversation and stuff, and we were wondering if you and Megan could join us."

"I don't know, what time did you have in mind?" Jack asked as he covered the mouthpiece and relayed the invitation to Megan.

"Well, it's about three now, probably about five-thirty or six. How about it?"

Megan nodded assent, so Jack happily accepted the invitation. They would meet at the Pizza Hut at five-thirty. As for now, they had to see if the estranged couple from the movie would ever repair their differences and get back together. They resumed their seats on the couch and continued their movie viewing.

* * *

Jack and Megan entered the parking lot of the Pizza Hut just as Laura and Kim were getting out of their cars. Laura was the petite one with the long blonde hair and the big blue eyes; Kim was a size or two larger, though not a bit less attractive, with short black hair and little black eyes like a field mouse. They smiled and waved, waiting for Jack to park the Honda and join them. Taking the first available space, Jack parked and disembarked, walking quickly around the car to open Megan's door. With their new friends in tow, Kim and Laura led the way into the restaurant. The place was busier than they would have expected for a Sunday night. Nearly all of the thick wooden tables were piled high with plates, silverware, dirty napkins, glasses containing varying levels of liquid refreshment, and many with more than one stainless steel pizza stand proudly displaying the night's choice of sustenance.

The crowd was diverse. Some tables were surrounded by groups of teenagers, others by families, some by love-struck couples who didn't even seem to notice that anyone else was there. The waitresses hurried back and forth carrying hot pans of steaming pizzas and icy-cold pitchers of Coke and beer. Sighting their friends sitting at their usual table in the far left corner of the dining area, Kim and Laura dodged the waitresses and proceeded to weave their way through the congested dining area to where their friends were waiting.

Kirt, Brad and Steve were sitting around the table, laughing and munching on bread sticks.

"We waited for you," Brad mumbled through a mouthful of bread, 'Just like one pig does for another!" Brad chuckled at his own humor while the others greeted the newcomers and motioned to the empty chairs around the table.

Greetings were exchanged, the dilemma of how many pizzas with which toppings was settled, and drinks were ordered. The conversation was light and friendly, as Jack expected it to be. Kim talked about her job, Steve and Laura about their college schedules, and Brad about nothing of consequence. Megan shared a couple of funny stories about her job, Jack told them about some of his High School exploits in the small town of Sandusky, Michigan, and Kirt talked about his job and his parents. They had no agenda, no schedule. They were a group of friends simply hanging out together, and Jack strangely felt like he belonged in their company. He didn't feel threatened by them, scrutinized by them, or as though he needed to be in competition with any of them. He felt comfortable, and he hoped that Megan would feel the same way. He wanted her to enjoy their company as much as he did.

The pizzas arrived, and Kirt offered to lead them in a short prayer before they dived in to the food. He and the others joined hands, motioning to Jack and Megan to do likewise. Kirt's prayer was simple, quiet, and sincere. He didn't appear to do it to attract attention to himself; he seemed to do it simply because that's what you do before you eat, whether you are at home, at the church fellowship hall, or in a restaurant. Kirt was just like that. He reminded Jack of Phil, his Coast Guard buddy. They both seemed to have that easy-going, calm confidence about them.

As they began to devour the pizzas, Jack's mind began to wander. He thought of the various conversations he had participated in since meeting these people. Most, if not all, involved the church in one way or another. They were either discussing the sermon from Sunday morning, the activities coming up during the week, the next party to be planned, the topic of the Sunday school class, or something else directly related to the goings on of the church. Even if the subject started out to be a job, a college class, upcoming mid terms, a new song or movie, or anything else totally unrelated to God or the church, they would eventually bring it around so that it ended up being about exactly that—God or the church. Jack listened as Kim finished relating a story about being a good witness for Christ at her job and Kirt began talking about his ideas for the annual End of Summer Party. As if thinking that everyone else at the table had been following his thought process in his mind, Jack concluded aloud "That really is all you guys think about, isn't it?"

The conversation came to an abrupt halt as every head turned toward Jack, eyebrows raised inquisitively.

"How's that, Jack?" Kirt asked.

Jack felt a little silly, realizing now that he had interrupted Kirt in the middle of his party idea. "Sorry, Kirt," he said. "I didn't mean to interrupt you. I was just thinking that it seems like all you guys ever talk about is God and the church. Don't you ever do anything else?"

"Like what?" Kirt asked.

"I don't know," Jack replied, uncomfortably fidgeting in his chair, "Like just something that doesn't directly correspond to building the church roster or telling someone about God. Don't you guys ever just hang out and do nothing? Or do something just for yourselves, or just for the fun of it?"

Kirt's body language told the others that he would field this question. He raised one finger, signifying that he would take the floor, and indicating a short pause while he took a drink to wash down a mouthful of pizza. The group conceded.

"Sure, we do, Jack. All the time. I mean, it's not like we are under orders, here, or something. Fact is, this IS what we do for fun. Well, let me speak for myself. If I am hearing you right, you are suggesting that all I ever do is talk about God or do things for the church; like I devote every waking hour to God and the business of the church. Is that about it?"

"Well, I didn't mean it like that, Kirt, I just..."

Kirt stopped him by shaking his head and waving his upraised hand.

"No, it's all right, Jack, you didn't offend me. You see, I like doing things for God. And I love being involved in the church and in its activities. This is where I feel at home. This is where my friends are. This is where I feel a purpose in life. I've been on the other side, Jack. I spent a lot of years doing what I pleased, with no consideration for God or for his commands or for his gift of salvation. I did my own thing, followed my own creed. I didn't let anything get in my way; things like compassion for my fellow man, integrity in my job, decency in relationships. I was all for Kirt, and Kirt for—none, except Kirt. And I was unfulfilled. I can't say I was miserable, because I had a lot of fun. But that is all it was—pointless, empty fun. I didn't gain anything by my lifestyle. I didn't do any good for myself or for anybody else. I had no purpose in my life; no direction. I didn't feel like I counted for anything. Don't get me wrong, I wasn't a bad person. I was just a useless one.

"And then I had an encounter with Jesus Christ. Suddenly, my life had meaning. It wasn't all about what could I get for ME anymore; suddenly, it was all about what my life could accomplish for Christ and for my fellow man. And you know what, Jack? I feel a hundred times better now. I feel like I matter. I can go to sleep at night feeling contented, joyful, peaceful."

Kirt sat back in his chair, realizing that he had scooted forward to the edge of it during his enthusiastic explanation. He smiled somewhat self-consciously and shrugged his shoulders.

"Sorry, Jack—I didn't mean to get preachy on you, but I feel very strongly about this. For me, this is what life is all about."

"Uh—Wow, Kirt. That was quite a discourse," Jack finally replied.

"I know, Jack. But you strike me as the intellectual type, so I don't believe you will have any trouble processing what I said. You are a thinker, Jack Douglass. So let me know what you think about all of that sometime. As for now, I want another piece of that pepperoni and mushroom..."

Kirt dropped the subject just as quickly as Jack had brought it up. He had given Jack a lot to think about—a totally new perspective on life, and a whole new way of living it. But he knew that Jack was not yet ready to take the discussion further. He needed time to ponder what Kirt had said. And God needed time to reach his heart and make him understand. Kirt had planted a seed in Jack's mind and heart, and now he would leave it alone to take root by itself before he attempted to tend it again. He knew that Jack would approach him again when he was ready to take the next step, so he wisely changed the subject and allowed the work of God to run its course. Kirt was just like that.

~3~

The ride back to Megan's apartment was quiet and uneventful. Jack was deep in thought, and Megan was miles away and seemed content to let him think, undisturbed. When they reached her apartment, Jack pulled up the emergency brake on his Honda, but left the engine running. He got out and walked Megan to her door, where they shared a hug and said goodnight. Jack promised to call during the week to plan a date after Megan got her work schedule for the week. She let herself into her apartment as Jack turned back toward the parking lot and headed for the

Honda. He looked up and waved to Megan as she closed her door, waving back at him and smiling.

When Jack finally reached the base, he parked his car in the first slot he could find and began the walk to the pier. He flashed his ID to the pier sentry and continued to the brow of the *Mississippi*, where he again flashed his ID and proceeded across the main deck. As he descended the ladder to the second deck, he was surprised at all the activity he saw. Normally, on a Sunday night, the ship would be all but deserted. The only people on board would be the duty section and those few unfortunate men who lived on board. Many of them would already be asleep in their pits, but a few would still be up, either watching the TV in their living complexes or playing cards on the mess decks. But tonight, the ship was buzzing with activity. Officers in their khaki uniforms were purposefully scampering from here to there. The duty section watchstanders, who should have completed any necessary tasks hours ago, were angrily trudging about, uniforms in disarray, a day's worth of stubble on their previously clean-shaven faces. Jack walked through the door of his living complex and straight to his pit. He stripped off his jacket, tossed it on top of his blanket, kicked off his shoes and walked back out to the small table in the lounge area of the complex. Post was there, busily writing a letter to someone while listening to his CD player through a set of headphones. His real name was Paxel, but everyone just called him 'Post'. Some said it was because he was tall and skinny like a post, but most agreed that it was because he was as dumb as a post. That was typically how nicknames came about on the *Mighty Miss*'. Some came simply from the butchering of a person's given name, some came because of a stupid thing that a person had done, and some came about because they just seemed to fit that person. Such was the case with Post.

"Hey, Post!" Jack said as he tapped him on the shoulder. "What in the world is going on around here? What's all the hubbub about?"

"You haven't heard?" Post asked, a little shocked. "Where have you been, dude?"

"No, I haven't heard," Jack confirmed. "I have been off the ship all day. I just got back, and everybody is running around the ship like chickens with their heads cut off! What gives—is some admiral visiting tomorrow, or what?"

"Nothing that easy, dude. We're going back out. The *Ticonderoga* had some kind of an accident down in the Caribbean, and we have to go back down and relieve her. She's supposedly limping back to GITMO even as we speak."

"But, we just got back!" Jack exclaimed. "We've only been in for a week!"

"Tell me about it, dude."

"Well," Jack asked, "How long will we be out this time? Do we have to do *Tico*'s whole rotation of CD Ops?"

"Nobody knows. Or, at least they're not saying. Official announcement comes at Quarters tomorrow. This is just scuttlebutt, but you know it's true. Stock up on clean jockey shorts, pal, we're going back underway."

Jack slumped into the chair across from Post, stunned into silence. Post resumed his writing while Jack tried to accept what he had just heard. "Six more weeks." he muttered to himself. "Six more weeks."

"Could be more, Union Jack," Post volunteered. "If they can't find a replacement for *Tico* by the time we finish her rotation, we might have to stay out and do our own, too. Better get ready for a long one."

Jack stood up slowly and staggered to his pit. He was suddenly very tired. "I'm going to bed," he announced to no one in particular. "Maybe I'll wake up tomorrow and all this will not have happened." He wanted to go right back out and call Megan to tell her the bad news, but he didn't want her to hear the disappointment that would surely be evident in his voice. No need giving out too much information. Feeling defeated, he undressed silently and crawled into his pit, desperately hoping that tonight he would succeed in making himself dream about Megan.

Jack was rudely awakened Monday morning by reveille, which was spoken rather than actually being played, over the 1MC ship-wide announcing circuit. He rolled over and clenched his pillow, angry at being awakened and having to get out of his nice, warm pit, and already annoyed at what he knew the day would hold for him. He used the reveille announcement as a snooze alarm, since he knew that several routine and unimportant announcements would be made at short intervals over the next hour. After the second such announcement, he rolled himself out from under his blanket and stood up on the cold tile floor, stretching his arms up until his hands touched the maze of piping and electrical wiring that comprised the overhead in his complex. He fumbled through the storage compartment beneath his rack until he located some soap, shampoo, shaving cream and a razor, a towel and washcloth, and his shower shoes.

Someone was already using the shower, so Jack filled one of the sinks with hot water and began coating his face with shaving cream. He finished shaving about the same time the shower was free, so he moved on to the next step in his morning routine. Coming out of the head and into the complex lounge, Jack saw that everyone had already either gotten out of his rack or arrived back on board from ashore. The only topic on anyone's mind was the upcoming emergency underway rumors.

"Yes, I heard, and no, I don't want to talk about it!" Jack growled when someone called his name and attempted to draw him into the conversation. He tossed his toiletries into his pit locker, hung his towel on the tiny rack along the back wall of his pit, and opened up his steaming locker. He grabbed the first uniform he came to, not bothering to check its condition, and absent-mindedly dressed himself. Locking both of his lockers, he snatched his ball cap off his pillow and headed up to the galley for some breakfast. Maybe a hot ham and cheese omelet would help to lighten his mood a little bit.

He joined the throng of sailors in the made-to-order omelet line, taking a tray and some silverware from the bins beside the serving rack. At his request, some hash browns and strips of bacon were added to his tray before the mess crank (a non-rate or junior petty officer doing a tour of duty as an assistant to the Mess Specialists) handed it back to him. He made his way to the beverage mess, where he filled a glass with cold milk and a cup with hot coffee. He joined a group of men who looked like they had either driven all night to get back to the ship this morning, or had drunk all night and were lucky to have even found the ship this morning. He chose their company because they didn't look as though they felt like talking any more than he did, especially since the conversation all around him centered on Friday's rumored deployment. He finished his breakfast in silence, delivered his tray and dishes to the scullery, and headed back down to his complex to sit and wait for Quarters, the daily morning meeting "...for muster, instruction, and inspection."

Quarters began promptly at 0730 on the forecastle, port side, forward of the five-inch gun mount. SMC Johnson called the men to attention, then put them at ease and began to read from his clipboard about the day's schedule. He recapped the accomplishments of the weekend duty section, then stuck his clipboard under his arm. He confirmed the rumors about the deployment on Friday. The official word was that the *Ticonderoga* had suffered a steam line rupture in her number two engine room. Nine confirmed dead, three injured, and several more with temporary hearing loss as a result of the explosion. USS *Mississippi* would deploy on Friday morning at eight a.m. to finish the remainder of *Tico*'s rotation of Drug Interdiction Operations. They would be joined by the same Coast Guard team that had deployed with them the last time they were out. Bravo-Zulu to the *Mighty Miss*' for stepping up to assist her comrade in distress, yada, yada, yada. Most of the rest of the meeting flew right over Jack's head. He was thinking of all the tedious, petty work that the khaki's would find for him and his men to do before Friday. He knew that the officers would be running around in circles, trying to get their departments squared away and ready for the deployment, deciding which maintenance items actually needed done, which could be postponed until later, and contacting any men who were on leave to tell them they had to come back to the ship immediately. He also knew that there was nothing other than routine tasks that needed to be done on the signal bridge, although he was certain that the Division Officer and the Chief would come up with a list for him to accomplish anyway.

"Dismissed!!"

The bellow of the Chief's gravely voice snapped Jack back to the present. The Chief handed Jack the dreaded list that the division officer had comprised the previous night while he was on duty. Jack called to the Signalmen to meet him on the signal bridge at 0800 so he could divide up the work assignments he had just been given, while he himself made a bee-line for the signal bridge coffee pot and his favorite cup. He could enjoy at least twenty more minutes of peace before the official work day began and his men would begin gathering on the signal bridge and grumbling about their assignments. Jack reached the empty signal shack, took out his keys to unlock the door and let himself in. He put just a little extra coffee in the filter, added a dash of cinnamon, then picked up the carafe and walked out of the signal shack, across the weatherdeck to the watertight door at the aft end of the superstructure, and entered the skin of the ship. He had to go to the head just inside the door to fill up the coffee maker, because there were no faucets anywhere closer to the shack.

Soon, the wonderful aroma of fresh-brewed coffee filled the shack. As soon as it was almost done dripping, Jack grabbed the carafe and filled his waiting cup. The hot, tasty liquid ran down his throat and seemed to burn away a little of his anxiety for the coming day. Very little, but he would take what he could get. He filled his mind with pictures of Megan, while trying in vain not to conjure up the image of her waving good-bye to him from the pier as the ship sailed away on Friday. His reverie was interrupted by the arrival of two of his men, still three minutes early. He began passing out assignments to those who had arrived, and before he was finished, the last one had shown up and received his as well. Jack's motivational talk was brief and to the point.

"Guys, I know most of this is worthless busywork that doesn't need to be done at all, but you and I both know that the Div-O and the Chief will have a chicken if they see any of us NOT diligently working on completing this list. Bear in mind that I am not in the least bit amused by the prospect of going back out to sea this Friday, and I am not in the mood to be trifled with today. Please, just get this stuff done and stay out of sight. We will meet back here after lunch, at precisely 1330, to discuss what we have to do to make sure that we can get out of here on time today. Please do not be late for the afternoon meeting. I think we all want to get out of here, and you know how the Div-O likes to come up with sweat items at the end of the day. That is all. Go to it, guys."

Patterson and Miller disappeared. McCoy stayed around to finish his coffee and chat for a few minutes, then he, too, disappeared. Alone again, Jack began his own inspection of the spaces for which he was responsible, making his own list of things that actually did need to be done prior to getting underway on Friday.

The morning seemed to take forever to pass. Jack tried to busy himself with odd jobs to make it go quicker, but each time he looked at his watch, the hands had barely moved. He wished he could come up with a way to trick time—to make it pass faster when he wanted it to, then slower when he didn't, but he couldn't come up with anything. "If it could only be reversed somehow," he thought to himself. "The way it is now, when I really want time to pass quickly so that I can get to something you enjoy, it drags its feet and refuses to be rushed. But then, when I finally get to do the thing I have been waiting for so impatiently, time goes screaming by in a flash. That's kind of a flip-flopped, backwards way for it to be," Jack concluded to himself.

Finally, try as it might to resist, morning eventually gave way to afternoon. Jack grabbed a quick lunch in the galley, then went up to the main deck to use the pay phone on the Quarterdeck. He dialed Megan's number, knowing she wouldn't be there, and left her a message saying that he would be coming by tonight because something had come up and they needed to talk.

The rest of the day went pretty much as Jack had anticipated that it would. The Division Officer sent the Chief to him with a couple of items that apparently meant the end of civilization as they knew it if they weren't rectified before 1515, the prescribed time for the official work day to end and Liberty Call to go down for the non-duty section crew members. As he also suspected, no mention was made of the fact that eighty percent of the list they had been given at Quarters was completed. Jack took SM3 McCoy and SMSN Miller with him to take care of the life-threatening task from the Div-O.

They did get off the ship late that afternoon, which annoyed Jack even though he really didn't have anywhere to go anyway. Megan wouldn't get home from work until at least nine, which gave him five-and-a-half hours to kill. He didn't feel like eating on the ship again, since that was the only place he would be eating for quite some time beginning Friday, so he started driving in the direction of Megan's apartment and watching for restaurants along the way. He didn't want fast food, but he didn't want to have to interact with anyone either, so he opted for the steakhouse with the cheapest buffet dinner deal. He paid his money, made his series of trips to the various tables of food, then sat nursing a cup of coffee for half an hour. Finally, he dropped a tip on the table and headed for the door. Once outside, he was pleased to see that the sun was setting, dimming the external illumination to an eerie ghost-gray. He inhaled deeply and let it out slowly, looking over to where his car waited patiently for his return. Turning away, he tucked his keys back into his pocket, strolled across the parking lot and entered the mall. He still had some time to kill before going to Megan's. He browsed through the bookstore, the shoe store, the men's clothing store, and the pet store before he was satisfied that it was late enough to head for Megan's apartment. He walked back to where he had left the Honda, fired it up, and pulled out into the traffic on Military Highway.

He came to a stop in an unoccupied parking spot in front of Megan's apartment and killed his engine. As he got out and walked between the cars to the sidewalk, he could hear the tinking of Megan's car as the heat from the engine dissipated and the various metals contracted at different rates. She opened the door before he could knock and led him into the living room.

"What were you doing, Jack, hiding in the bushes and watching for me to get home?" she teased. "I haven't been here five minutes!"

"Just good timing, I guess," Jack offered.

"What's up, Jack? You sounded kind of bummed on the answering machine. Is anything wrong?"

"Well, not really. Not yet, anyway. But something will be very wrong on Friday," Jack said as he sat on the couch next to her. She raised an eyebrow, not sure where the conversation was going, but certain that Jack was already there.

"You see, Megan, I was really hoping to spend some time with you over the next few weeks. I mean, well, you know, some good time. I mean, I really want us to get closer, and I was hoping that over the next few weeks we could see a lot of each other and maybe that would happen."

"Jack, what are you saying? I expected that we would see a lot of each other over the next few weeks, too. We can—"

"Megan, I'm going back out," Jack interrupted.

Megan stopped mid sentence. "But,--" she began, but Jack answered before she could ask. He told her all about the *Ticonderoga*'s accident and about the *Mighty Miss*' having to go down and relieve her on station in the Caribbean. He explained that they would be getting underway Friday morning and that they would be out for a minimum of 4 weeks with the potential for another 6 on top of that, depending on the extent of the damage aboard the *Tico*. Finished with his explanation, Jack got up and walked into the kitchen to get them something to drink. He dropped ice cubes into glasses, filled them with spring water from a dispenser in the refrigerator, then walked back into the living room and plopped down on the couch next to Megan. She reached over and took her glass, drinking several swallows before setting it on the lamp stand next to the couch.

"Well, I guess we had better make these last four days count, then, hadn't we?" Megan concluded with a smirk. She seemed to enjoy watching him get all flustered when the conversation got too close to home. Jack grinned shyly as he felt the warmth creeping across his face. He felt silly that he had been worried about—whatever it was that he had been worried about. Megan promised to write to him often, even if she didn't get a response between letters. She even offered to send him a box of cookies and goodies while he was gone.

Jack leaned over and kissed her forehead. "Thanks, Megan," he whispered, feeling relieved and excited and peaceful all at the same time.

* * *

Tuesday night at two minutes to midnight, Miguel Ramirez logged on to the Internet and browsed through the chat room selections. He positioned his mouse arrow over the "motorcycle racers" chat room and clicked the button on the left. His computer displayed an hourglass to let him know that it was working on his request. The hourglass disappeared and Miguel was inside the chat room. He punched in his chat name, 'whoopte_doo,' typed "Hello?" then pressed his 'enter' key. His name and message appeared inside the window. He didn't type anything else. He just sat there and waited, reading all the greetings from the current chatters who responded to his 'hello'. After about a minute, bighill2jump logged on.

bighill2jump: yo, whoopte_doo. what's up?
whoopte_doo: hey, jump. same old. whassup with you?
bighill2jump: busy, busy. my big brother wrecked his new bike. trashed it good. it's on its way to castro's shop right now. he doesn't even know if he can fix it.
whoopte_doo: wow. tough break for him, eh? is he getting another new one?
bighill2jump: he doesn't know yet. depends on how hard it will be to fix his dead one. might just put the old one back on the track for a while.
whoopte_doo: how long will it take him to get his old one track-ready again? will he be able to run it immediately?
bighill2jump: not a chance. it's already in storage. it'll probably take a few days just to get it running again. then there's the matter of hauling it to the track for trials. you know how it goes.
whoopte_doo: sure do. stinks to be him.
bighill2jump: I'm supposed to meet him Friday morning at 8 to time him at the track.

whoopte_doo: 8 at the track, you say? let me know his best time. I can't let him beat me this year. Hey, how's your puppy working out? got him going outside yet or on a paper or something?

bighill2jump: yep, he's great. doesn't even make messes anymore. just give him a treat when he's good, and he'll do anything you want.

whoopte_doo: have you taught him to speak yet?

bighill2jump: sure. I just give the command word, and he snaps to it. anything for the treat...

whoopte_doo: great work. I could never get our dog to do anything. stupid mutt.

bighill2jump: you gotta have the touch. so, how's your bike coming along? purring like a kitten?

whoopte_doo: most of the time. a few minor adjustments to make, but nothing I can't handle.

bighill2jump: great. then I'll talk to ya later.

whoopte_doo: right. later.

Miguel logged off the Internet and shut down his computer. Leaning back in his desk chair, he put his hands behind his head and interlaced his fingers. He drew in an easy breath and let it out slowly. "Excellent," he whispered to himself. "Excellent. I believe I have some calls to make." He picked up the telephone and began dialing.

*   *   *

The sun was warm on Pablo's back as he walked from the house to the garage. He looked out over his land, observing the crops nearing the end of their growing season and the stately buildings dotting the landscape like memorials to his ancestry. Today Pablo would justify that ancestry. Today he would prove himself worthy to be the head of the proud line of Linares' dating back to the first settlers of the region. Today he would redeem himself in his own eyes. He saw the birds circling overhead, darting from one tree to the next, then back again, singing their songs to each other. Pablo smiled as he reached for the handle of the garage door. He felt as free as those birds today. He felt like he was above the petty worries of life, soaring through the sky without a care. He knew that the events of the day could destroy him and all the things he held dear, but he knew with even more certainty that God was in control, and that he needn't concern himself with the outcome of what he was about to do.

He lifted the heavy door and walked over to his dirty Land Rover. It simply wasn't worth the effort of trying to keep it clean. His house was several miles from the nearest town, and the drive to town was across many dusty or muddy roads, depending on season and precipitation. Besides, most of the miles the Land Rover had accumulated had been accumulated on the plantation, going to and from the fields, through the fields, or back and forth between the house and the outbuildings. He could have the workers wash it and wax it one day, and by the end of the next, there would be no evidence that cleaning had ever taken place. Pablo slapped the seat and blew the dust away, then climbed in behind the wheel and turned the key in the ignition. The monster roared to life, belching out a puff of black smoke from the tailpipe. He carefully backed it out of the garage, dropped the gearshift into drive, and set out for the city of Puerto Cristobol, proudly eager to face whatever the day might have in store for him.

As the Range Rover bounced through mud holes and ruts in the crude dirt road, Pablo hummed a chorus to himself. The tall green grass grew in patches on either side of the road, reluctantly giving way to pasture land or commercial crops. He crossed several streams and one river, each boasting a vast array of water fowl and other water creatures. The landscape was beautiful, shades of green intermingled with the yellows and blues of dead weeds and bodies of water. Wild animals could be seen from time to time, roaming the countryside in search of water or their next meal prospect. Pablo watched the hummingbirds hovering over flowering plants and the macaws sitting passively on tree branches. Butterflies and bees covered the wild flowers on either side of the road, rising up in a swarm at the noise of the approaching vehicle. Pablo could see parts of the neighboring plantations as he drove along; some tobacco, some sugar cane, some livestock. Occasionally he would pass a pedestrian walking along the road or see some workers in the fields, but the majority of his journey was made without encountering another soul.

The thirty-eight mile trip took nearly an hour, due in part to the unfavorable road conditions in the rural areas, but due mostly to the leisurely pace at which Pablo traveled. As he approached the city from the south however, the roads were paved and fairly well maintained, so progress was more rapid, whether intentionally or not. The road upon which Pablo traveled became Calle Miranda as he entered the outskirts of the city of Puerto Cristobol. He proceeded into the center of town, where he turned left on Avenida Bolívar, right on Avenida Carabobo, then left again onto Calle Sucre. He drove for two blocks, then turned right into the parking lot across the street from the police station. He parked his Land Rover in the first row, along Calle Sucre, facing the police station. He killed the engine and pocketed the keys. Taking a deep breath and sending up one last prayer, he opened the door, climbed out of the vehicle and walked across the street to the sidewalk in front of the building. The building was a tall, three-story sandstone structure with a gabled roof and large sandstone pillars along the porch on either side of the front doors. The basement level housed a crude jail, complete with barred windows on the outside. The main level served as the police station proper, and the two upper floors contained offices. Fifty feet in front of the porch, the sidewalk leading to the building merged into a great circular garden, in the center of which was a large fountain. From the middle of the fountain rose a tall bronze statue of Simón Bolívar, "El Libertador" (The Liberator), who is credited with liberating South America from Spanish rule in the early 1800's. His statues could be found at one place or another in every significant city in Venezuela. The flags of the City of Puerto

Cristobol, the State of Sucre, and the Republic of Venezuela flapped in the gentle breeze at the tops of three flagpoles which stood in a row like soldiers guarding the entrance to Camelot. At the entrance to the building, there were huge wooden double doors, each looking like it must weigh over two hundred pounds, with gaudy brass handles shaped like crescent moons mounted vertically near the center. Pablo pulled open the door on the right, exerting much more force than was necessary, so that he had to lunge after the door to keep it from slamming into the stone wall beside it. He had expected such a large door to be more difficult to open. The man at the desk seemed quite amused by Pablo's experience with the door. He sat chuckling to himself and grinning widely, as though the door had intentionally been designed to operate that way, thereby putting off guard anyone who would venture into the halls of the Puerto Cristobol Police Department.

Pablo identified himself to the duty patrolman and respectfully requested that he be directed to the office of the Chief of Police. No, he didn't have an appointment, and yes, he would be happy to wait while the chief was contacted. Pablo strolled around the room, looking at the old framed pictures of those who had previously held the office of Chief of Police, while the patrolman mumbled something into his telephone. At his behest, Pablo repeated his name and stated that no, it was not an emergency, although it was a matter of utmost importance. The patrolman gingerly placed the receiver back in its cradle and sheepishly announced that the chief would see him immediately in the large office at the end of the hall.

Halfway down the hallway, Pablo was greeted warmly with a firm handshake by Captain Emilio Escobar, the Puerto Cristobol Chief of Police. Apparently, though it hadn't meant much to the young patrolman at the duty desk, the name 'Linares' had caught the attention of Captain Escobar. Pablo was ushered into a huge office with a big window overlooking the north half of the city and the water of the Caribbean Sea beyond. The building was very old, but appeared to have been very well maintained over the years. The walls were paneled with wood, probably mahogany if he had to guess, the floor was hardwood, and the ceiling was painted an eggshell white. Bookshelves lined opposite sides of the room, and a wet bar took up most of the wall across from the big window. There were metal file cabinets on either side of the wet bar, their modern construction looking completely out of place with the rest of the decor. The Captain gestured to the two chairs in front of his desk as he continued to walk to his own chair between the desk and the big window. "Please, have a seat, Mr. Linares," he offered.

"Thank you. My, that is a most impressive view, Captain Escobar. You certainly have the best seat in the house!" Pablo said politely as he lowered himself into the nearest chair and straightened his pant legs over his shoes.

"Oh, thank you, Mr. Linares," Captain Escobar returned. "Sometimes it's good to be the boss."

"Just sometimes?" Pablo asked with a grin.

"Well, you know how it is. Rank has its privileges, but it also has its responsibilities. Would you care for a cup of coffee, Mr. Linares?"

"Well said, Captain. Well said. And yes, I would love a cup, thank you."

Captain Escobar nodded as he walked to the wet bar where an antique silver coffee service was displayed. The silver pot with matching cups and saucers sparkled in the light, giving Pablo the impression of a formal dining set. He had expected that the service was there as a decorative piece, and not one that would be in service on a daily basis. However, a closer look revealed a small ribbon of steam rising from the spout formed into the side of the pot. Captain Escobar selected a cup from the rack and carefully lifted the silver coffee pot from its matching tray.

"This coffee service belonged to my grandmother," he explained. "It was always one of her most treasured possessions."

He poured the steaming black liquid into the silver cup he had selected for Pablo, then continued his discourse as he lifted a silver saucer off the small stack next to the coffee pot and slowly walked across the room to where Pablo had seated himself.

"When she gave it to my wife and me on our wedding day, she told us a story about her own wedding day. She had come from a poor family, as had my grandfather. Shortly before they were to be married, Grandfather's brother was killed in a hunting accident. They were partners in a business venture, and Grandfather was unable to run it by himself. When the business subsequently went under, they lost all the money they had invested in it. When your grandfather heard that they were planning to announce the cancellation of the wedding, since they could no longer afford to fund it, he hired my grandfather to work on the Linares plantation. He promptly advanced them enough money to pay for the wedding, for which he accepted weekly payments until the debt was erased. Exhibiting a similar kindness, your grandmother said that every newly married couple had to have something fancy with which to entertain guests, so she gave them this silver coffee service as a wedding gift.

"The story behind her prized coffee service and the generosity of the Linares family has been passed down through the family from that day on. Grandmother told all of her children the story, and she told all of her grandchildren as well. She said that it represented a perfect model of how generous and kind people could be, and that we should all strive to be that sort of people."

He handed Pablo the cup he had filled for him, then retrieved his own from the corner of his bulky antique mahogany desk. Raising his cup in a toast, he said, "May we both live up to the example and expectations of our grandparents!"

Pablo raised his cup and drank to the Captain's toast, then looked down at his feet, sighing and praying to God for courage.

"Now, Mr. Linares, what can I do for you?" Captain Escobar coaxed.

"Captain Escobar, I've gotten myself into a bit of a situation. It's quite embarrassing, frankly, and I neither take pride in my actions nor make any excuse for what I am about to tell you. I understand that justice must be served, and that, above all, you must perform your duty; I ask only that you treat the situation with as much delicacy and discretion as ethics will allow."

"Rest assured, Mr. Linares, I will do whatever I can to preserve your family's good name. Please, continue."

Pablo took another long sip of his coffee, then stood and began to pace around the room. Beyond the big window, Pablo could see sailboats splashing through the waves on the gulf, the wind playing in the tops of the trees closer to the building. He saw the flag of Puerto Cristobol proudly flapping in the breeze, making a declaration of peace, justice, and freedom for all. He whispered a silent prayer for strength and felt a peaceful wave of calm confidence wash over him like a whitecap rolling over the beach. He cleared his throat and began telling his story.

He began with a quick history of the Linares plantation, briefly covering his father's old fashioned leadership, the infestation of beetles that had nearly destroyed the crop, and the subsequent financial weakening of the estate. Then he discussed his father's accident, followed by his untimely death, and the continued struggle to turn the business around. This all came easily enough, but Pablo hesitated when he broached the subject of his dealings with Miguel Ramirez. Determined to proceed, he purposefully set his coffee cup on the edge of Captain Escobar's desk and turned to face him. He detailed the invitation Ramirez's associates had delivered and the meeting with Ramirez that had followed. He explained the arrangement as it had been offered to him, and reluctantly confirmed that he had indeed accepted it. He told Captain Escobar the exact location of the parcels of land upon which Ramirez's men had planted the illegal crop of marijuana. Feeling relieved, Pablo returned to his chair and sank into it. He retrieved his coffee cup and took a drink, letting the hot liquid slowly run down his throat, soothing and moistening it.

Captain Escobar got out of his chair and walked from behind his desk. He rubbed his chin with his hand, deep in thought, nodding and grunting. After several minutes, he went back to his desk, pulled a miniature tape recorder from the top drawer, and began to question Pablo. He asked him for more details about the meeting with Ramirez; the financial arrangement, the actual transfer of funds, the disbursing of those funds by Pablo, the condition of the illegal plants, and so on. When he was satisfied that he knew as much as Pablo could tell him about the subject, he clicked off the tape recorder and placed it gently on the desk.

"Mr. Linares," he said, "you are correct. This is a very difficult and sensitive situation. I am glad you came to me about it. Perhaps we can find a mutually beneficial solution to your problem. Obviously, we want Miguel Ramirez behind bars. We are aware of the majority of his activities, but we can never prove anything, and we can never get a witness to testify against him."

"What do you want me to do?" Pablo asked.

"Give me some more time to think about it, Mr. Linares," Captain Escobar began. "I will need to speak with some people at the Directorate of Intelligence and Prevention Services (DISIP) and the State's Attorney's Office. Let me call you in a couple of days and we can meet again to discuss options."

"Thank you, Captain Escobar," Pablo stammered. "Thank you for your kind consideration. I will be at your service. You've only to let me know what I must do to help, and it will be done."

Pablo let himself out of the office and walked down the hallway, feeling very relieved and very tired. "Lord," he said aloud, looking up at the ceiling, "it is in your hands, now. I have done my part. Now I will trust you to take care of me and my family." He reached his Land Rover, climbed inside, cranked over the engine and headed across town. He would pick up a few things and do a little shopping before going home. He needed a little time to himself to unwind and relax before he got back to the plantation.

Meanwhile, Captain Escobar was on the telephone, already making plans to bust Miguel Ramirez and send him to prison. He set up meetings with the Director, DISIP and the State of Sucre State's Attorney. This was huge, and he wanted to make sure that everything was done right. He didn't want Ramirez getting off on a technicality, and he didn't want the Linares name involved unless it was absolutely necessary. He knew he could get Pablo immunity in exchange for his testimony against Ramirez; he just didn't know if he could get Pablo to agree to testify in a public trial, where Ramirez would have henchmen watching and waiting to silence him, regardless of the verdict of the trial.

*   *   *

Jack Douglass awoke at reveille Friday morning. He crawled out of his pit and stood up on the cold tile deck of his complex, the chilly air bringing coherence to him sooner than he would have liked. A myriad of thoughts raced through his mind. First, he thought of Megan, smiling sweetly as the wind played with her hair, waving goodbye to him from the pier as he walked across the main deck and into the inner areas of the ship; then he thought of leaving land for an unknown length of time, not knowing when he would see Megan again. He thought of the foreign ports he might visit over the next few weeks; then he thought how much more he would enjoy them if Megan could be there with him. He thought of beginning twelve hour watch rotation again, which would continue for however long they were required to cover CD Ops by themselves. Then he thought about Megan. Her smile, her hair, her mannerisms, her laugh. He thought about the dingy beige paint that covered his locker, wondering how it would look with blue swirls. From blue swirls, his mind went to the new blue crystal bowl freshener he had installed in Megan's toilet tank the day before. "Ahh, Megan," he sighed. He thought about that last evening they shared together, just the two of them, sitting on her couch, talking about everything and nothing, savoring every moment until the needs of the Navy pulled them apart again. But this time, Jack wasn't worried. He didn't wonder if she would forget about him while he was gone. He was quite certain that she would be there waiting for him when he returned. And she would also be there for him while he was gone—writing letters, sending goodies, thinking of him. Waiting for him to come back to her. *To her.* Jack shivered with excitement at the thought of Megan feeling what he was feeling. It was going to be a good day. Jack forced himself out of his daydream and began his morning routine of shaving, dressing, eating breakfast, etc. He had to be on the signal bridge early to observe SM2 McCoy performing all the duties required of the Signalmen when the ship is getting underway. Some flags had to go up, some flags had to come down, some flags just had to switch places, and the Signalmen were responsible for all of them.

The lines were removed from the cleats on the pier and drawn back aboard the ship by the deck hands. The tug boats pushed the six hundred foot cruiser away from the pier and out into the muddy waters of the Chesapeake Bay, where they left her to answer bells on her own main engines. Jack could still see Megan through the 'big eyes', smiling and waving as the big ship carried Jack out into the ocean for as long as the ship's services were needed in the Caribbean. Finally, when Jack could no longer make out anything other than her outline through the 'big eyes', he lifted his head and stepped back toward the signal shack, a forlorn look upon his face and a deep sigh escaping his lungs. He pulled open the water tight door to the signal shack and stepped over the door frame into the shack. To his surprise, he was greeted by his Coast Guard buddy, Phil Prescott. A big smile crossed his face as he thrust his hand in Phil's direction. Phil grabbed his hand and shook it warmly, handing Jack a cup of coffee with the other.

"Girlie style, just like you like it, with two creams and a bunch of sugar," Phil teased as Jack took the steaming cup of strong, black coffee.

Jack took a sip, feeling the hot liquid all the way down his throat. "Thanks, Phil. I needed that," he said. "Hey, what are you doing here? Well, getting underway with us, obviously, but, I mean, why? You were just on the last one with us."

"New program," Phil explained. "Our team has been assigned TAD (Temporary Active Duty) to the *Mississippi* for the duration of your CD Ops schedule. The *Tico* has her own team, too, though I don't imagine they'll be getting much action any more. They'll just get re-assigned again if the *Tico* stays down for long. Sad thing about the *Tico*, huh?"

"Yeah, tough break. You wouldn't catch me spending all my time down there in the hole with those engineering boys. Give me the strong winds and the open sea."

"I hear ya, Jack."

"Well, that's great, Phil," Jack said, slapping him on the back. "We just might have a lot to talk about this time. Even more than last time."

"Really?" Phil asked. "And why might that be? Could it have something to do with a young lady by the name of Megan? Hmmm?"

"As a matter of fact, Phil, it just might. A lot of it,

anyway. But we'll have to talk about it tonight. Right now, I have to take care of some Navy business. You know how it is."

"Sure, Jack. No problem. I'll just drink my coffee and watch the air go by. See you tonight."

"All right, Phil. Good to see ya, buddy. Be sure and come up tonight," Jack reiterated as he turned around and started filling in the Signal Bridge Log with all the necessary entries pertinent to the ship getting underway.

The rest of the day was uneventful. The *Mighty Miss*' steamed eastward, away from the coast of Virginia and out into the Virginia Capes. Then she adjusted to a southerly course to begin the long journey into the heart of the Caribbean Sea. Men were scurrying about, taking care of last minute items that hadn't been completed before the ship left port. Jack could watch them from the signal bridge, going about their duties while trying to accept the fact that they were not going to be home for a long but, as yet, undetermined length of time. He could see the dismay on many faces, particularly those with wives and children, as they thought about their loved ones at home. They had only spent two weeks with them after having been underway for six weeks, and now they would be separated again for a minimum of four weeks, but probably more along the line of ten weeks. That was the part about the Navy that most people hated. Once you got past the first day or two it wasn't so bad, but sometimes those first two days felt like they were dragging on forever. When you are in the act of leaving, it often feels like it is your fault that you are going away. Once you have made the break, then it becomes easier to blame it on the Navy and to feel less guilty about leaving your family behind. That first night, however, there are a lot of men who either hit their pits early or start writing letters home about all the things they wish they had done before they left, and that they intend to do when they get back home. Some make apologies, some make promises, and some do both. For Jack, the first night wasn't really any different than any other night. At least, it never had been, until the first night of this cruise. This time, he also had someone to miss. He couldn't use that safety net in his mind that says, 'Aw, Jack, be real—she doesn't feel anything for you! You're just dreaming! It was just flirting, and when you get back, she won't remember your name.' Because this time, he knew that he and Megan shared something a little deeper than flirting, and that she would definitely remember his name when he returned from sea. He could feel the bond even now, floating into the ever deeper and ever warmer water as the Atlantic Ocean became the Caribbean Sea.

After evening chow, Jack finished updating the log book, tidied up the shack, and turned the watch over to SN Wilson.

"I'll be out on my perch," Jack called to SN Wilson. "Give me a holler if anything happens."

"Aye, SM2. Will do," Wilson answered.

"2130 hours," Jack sighed to himself. "Just getting good and dark. Perfect for a little sig-bridge zoning." He stretched, yawned, shifted his weight on the steel surface he called his 'perch', then just let his mind wander. Contrary to what one might think, it didn't go straight to Megan this time. Not really. His thoughts centered on the small party his friends at the church had thrown for him Wednesday evening after the service.

He had been completely surprised by the party. After all, he had only begun hanging out with them two weeks earlier. He did expect the usual good luck and best wishes comments, but not a party. They held it in the fellowship hall of the church right after the service. There was a cake and some other baked goods, coffee and punch to drink, and a rather large box of gag gifts from many of the other members of the Sunday school class. Each person seemed to enjoy his or her particular gift more than Jack did—they would roar with laughter at their own cleverness as Jack's face contorted with shock or confusion, or blushed with embarrassment at their gifts. A few people had given him more serious gifts: a couple of novels, some crossword puzzles, and a devotional book.

Just in case anyone present at the party had not already heard it, Jack was coerced into re-telling the story of his hazing attack shortly after getting on board the *Mighty Miss*'. Whether it was the first, second or third time they had heard it, every person in the room was choked with laughter by Jack's story. They prodded and begged him until he told them a couple more sea stories, then they asked him if he would like them all to pray for his safe and quick return before the party broke up. He agreed, and several people prayed aloud while many of the others nodded and spoke in agreement with their prayers. Jack had never had a group of people pray for him like that. At first, he was a bit uncomfortable; but as it continued, he felt increasingly more at ease, then peaceful, until at the end he even found himself verbally agreeing with the prayers of the leaders. And once again, the bond was strengthened between Jack and his new church friends. He knew now that he was more than just another seat-warmer in the church. He had friends there. People who would wish him well and mean it, while they waited for his return. Some might even send him packages. Maybe even some more of those brownies, which could only be the handiwork of Milly Radford.

Jack's mind came back to the present. He felt the cool breeze rushing past him as the *Mississippi* steamed southward at 26 knots, eager to get to her destination. He was about to climb down off his perch when he saw a familiar figure in the light of the signal shack. BM2 E. Phillip Prescott was pouring himself a cup of coffee and chatting with SN Wilson. He left Wilson with a nod and headed to where he knew Jack would be sitting with his mind racing at a hundred miles per hour. He wasn't disappointed. Jack jumped down off his perch and smiled as they shook hands.

"It's great to see you, Phil," Jack said.

"Yeah, you too, Jack," Phil agreed.

"I sure didn't expect to be seeing you on the Miss' again—especially not so soon!"

"Well, I didn't expect to be here again quite so soon, either!" Phil agreed. "But I did know I would be staying with the *Mississippi* for a while. Since the Navy is supplying two ships at a time for continuous CD Ops rotation, the top brass in the Coast Guard decided that it would be prudent for us to provide Assault Teams for each of the vessels. So, here I am, aboard the *Mighty Miss'* once again, and apparently for who knows how long."

"Get used to it, buddy. They don't tell us much around here. We must be on a need-to-know basis, and apparently the zeros (slang term for officers, as their rank status is listed as O-1, O-2, etc.) don't think we ever need to know."

"Apparently not," Phil agreed. "Same song, different

dance."

Jack nodded as Phil took a sip of his coffee and looked out across the water.

"So, what has been going on, Mr. Douglass? How is everything with the young Miss Gallagher?" Phil asked.

"It's wonderful, Phil. Just wonderful. We're taking it really slow- well, heck, we've only had two weeks anyway- but things are progressing most satisfactorily."

"Then shall I assume we will be receiving letters sprinkled with perfume? Locks of hair? Sappy poems on gaudy stationary?" Phil teased.

"Hey, you never know!" Jack countered. "But I'm thinking it will be more of a ME, and not so much a WE who will be getting that stuff."

Phil laughed aloud. "Hey, seriously, that's great, man. You guys still going to that Nazarene church?"

"Yep. In fact, it's the coolest thing..." Jack proceeded to tell Phil all about his new friends at the church. He told him all about the night at the pizza joint, the bonfire at Kirt Radford's place, and the party after church on Wednesday. He chattered on for several minutes, while Phil just sat there listening, smiling, and praising God under his breath. He had been praying for Jack ever since they had first met on the Miss' several weeks earlier. He had prayed that God would give him opportunities to talk to Jack about his soul, and that God would send someone Jack's way while he was in port to carry on the work of introducing him to Jesus. It seemed that God had done just that, and Phil was elated. Jack continued his discourse, telling Phil all about Megan, how the relationship was progressing, the things they had done together, and the things they had talked about.

When Jack finally finished, Phil didn't have much to say. He told Jack that he was happy for him, and that it was great news about Megan and his friends at the church. They chatted for a few minutes longer, then Phil drained his cup and headed off to his pit. Tomorrow, he and the rest of the Coasties would start their training exercises on the main deck, and he would need to be well-rested.

*   *   *

Miguel Ramirez replaced the receiver of his telephone into the cradle and leaned back in his chair. The smile that covered his face was the smile of an evil man putting an evil plan into action. He chuckled to himself, thinking of the precious American battleship limping its way to Cuba.

His men would move immediately. By the end of the day, all the cocaine and marijuana that could be packaged and made ready for shipment would be transported to various ports along the coast of Venezuela. Then it would be secretly loaded into crude oil tankers, commercial fishing boats, chartered tour boats and private yachts for transport to any of a dozen ports along the southern coast of the United States, from North Carolina all the way to Texas. The U. S. Navy was taking an unscheduled break from patrolling the Caribbean, and Miguel would take full advantage of their misfortune. He would take a small risk and make bulk shipments to almost all of his contacts in the United States. He would send everything he had ready, since the American's radar would be out of service for a few days and thus unable to track his movements. The United States Air Force would still have the 'Guardian' eye-in-the-sky E2 Hawkeye snoop plane patrolling the skies and making reports to Coast Guard Headquarters in Washington D. C., but without its counterpart patrolling the seas, its effectiveness would be seriously hampered. It would therefore be a much less significant threat to Miguel's operation. This minor setback for the U. S. Navy could mean millions of dollars worth of extra revenue for Miguel, and it could also save him hundreds of thousands of dollars worth of shipping costs. Miguel smiled again. Sometimes, the Fates really seemed to like him.

*   *   *

"Ah, one week down," Jack remarked to Phil as they ate their dinner in the galley without trying to figure out what the entree was supposed to have been. Sometimes it was easier that way. The meals were often pretty good in the "*Mississippi Café*", as the Mess Specialists liked to call it, but other times, a guy would have to wonder just what the cooks must have been thinking during meal preparation. Sometimes the little yellow laminated cards labeling the various rectangular pans full of food were more than merely a regulation requirement. At times, they were quite necessary to assist in the identification of one's meal constituents.

"Yeah, Jack, you survived one week without her. Amazing." Phil teased. "Hey, we should be getting some mail sometime soon, shouldn't we?"

"Man, I hope so. Er, I mean, yeah, any time now. We've been on station for four days, and all our mail should have been sent to GITMO beginning the day we left Norfolk. We probably have a ton of it sitting on the beach, waiting for us to come and get it. Maybe they will send a helicopter out from GITMO with a load of it pretty soon," Jack speculated.

"You are so hooked, Jack Douglass." Phil observed. "You never once mentioned the mail the whole time we were out the last time. Now, it has only been one week, and you are all anxious about it. I hope this girl is worth all the press you are giving her."

"Me, too, Phil. Me, too."

The conversation lulled while they finished their meal. They got to their feet, dumped their trays off at the scullery, and headed up toward the signal bridge. It was still fairly early in the evening, so the sky remained illuminated with the light of the sun. Once inside the signal shack, Jack poured the old coffee down the scuttlebutt (drinking fountain) and made a fresh pot. He knew that there would be several sailors coming up to the signal bridge to have their after-dinner smoke within the next half hour or so, and they always preferred his coffee to what they could get in the galley. Jack filled his own cup and one for Phil, then headed for his perch on the port side forward. He chose the port side because smoking was not permitted on that side due to the flammable fuel stored on the weather deck immediately below the signal bridge.

Jack was not a smoker, and he really didn't like the smell of cigarette smoke, so he preferred to stay on the side where smoking was not allowed. He and Phil sipped their coffee in silence for a while, watching the sky slowly darken and feeling the salty ocean breeze ruffle through their hair.

"So," Phil finally said, breaking the silence and rousting Jack from his daydreaming, "What goals have you set for yourself for this underway period?"

Jack didn't answer right away. He knew that the usual response of rattling off a noble goal or two wouldn't satisfy Phil. He knew that Phil would continue prodding until Jack really looked inside himself and answered the question from his heart. Phil was just like that. They sipped their coffee while Jack considered the question and Phil patiently waited for the answer. Jack's thoughts went to the odd entity that is Navy life. It is a strange animal, indeed. At the beginning of an underway period of any significant length, say a minimum of three to four weeks, a person is given an unusual opportunity. It is similar to recess in elementary school, but it lasts much longer. It is an illusive opportunity which all receive, few perceive, and even fewer actually believe can make a difference in their lives. It is conceptually quite simple, though few take full advantage of it because to use it for the best possible good is not always easy, is occasionally quite humbling, and nearly always demands change. It is much like what many people do at New Year's Eve parties, albeit on a much grander scale. At the New Year's Eve party, a person's thinking is often clouded by strong drink, which may alter his perception of himself and of the reality that exists outside of himself. Also, at the New Year's Eve Party, most will not have taken a sufficient amount of time to evaluate their lives and to come up with an intelligent means of achieving the changes which would elevate their existence to a more satisfactory level. Therefore, a New Year's resolution will seldom result in any improvement still in evidence a couple of weeks or months down the road. The opportunity afforded the sailor, however, is quite different. For that individual who understands the chance he is being given and grasps the power of being able to change his own life for the better as a result of intensive and extended self-evaluation, there is no greater sense of controlling one's own destiny.

Even so, the Navy deployment is the ultimate oxy moron. This is because of the multi-faceted alteration of time that occurs while the ship is out to sea. From one perspective, while on board a deployed ship, time stands still. Anything a sailor didn't have a chance to do, to say, or to complete before getting underway will be frozen in time until he returns. In his mind, upon his return, it will be as if he had never left. He will expect things to be exactly as he left them. Things both under his control and completely out of his control will be expected to remain the same. Since he is in an isolated place where those things he considers 'his life' don't exist, it is as if he has been transported to a celestial penalty box out of the realm of reality, where he must remain, frozen in time where nothing else exists, until he has served his time and can return to the game.

From another perspective, time seems to accelerate. Upon his return from a six or eight week deployment, a sailor may very well step off the ship to find that everything on land has changed. All the popular songs on the radio may have been replaced with new songs that he has never heard. The movies showing at the theater may be different from those that were showing when he left. And, worst of all, the lives of his land-dwelling friends and family have continued on without his influence, without his assistance, and often times are very different upon his return than they were at the time of his departure. Everything can change while the ship is gone, and the sailor can occasionally come home to a completely different world than the one from which he departed a mere month or two earlier.

From the final perspective, time is not relative. This perspective is the one that allows the sailor the golden opportunity. While underway for an extended length of time, the first two perspectives on the alteration of time converge to create the third, which the wise man will take advantage of to get a clear picture of himself and of the world around him. The result of time both standing still and accelerating all at once, combined with the fact of the sailor's isolation from the rest of the world, is simply this: he has enough free time at his disposal to thoroughly evaluate his life and his character while he remains secluded from the distractions and distortions he may experience if attempting such soul searching within the range of influence of loved ones. He has time to review encounters he has had, things he has said and heard, not said or heard, and lessons he has learned. He has the time to remove himself from the scenes of his life and evaluate his performance. Without the burden of the normal pressures and cares of life, he can concentrate his efforts on becoming the kind of person he really wants to be. A man can get in touch with his true self, gain a better understanding of what he wants out of life and decide if his current course will result in achieving those directives. For this individual, the deployment will be a time of refreshment and renewal, rather than merely a useless morsel of time chipped off the edge of his life. He will return home to his family and friends a better person, more in tune with his inner self and better able to deal with the normal ups and downs indigenous to the journey of life.

With this in mind, Jack considered his response before saying it aloud to Phil.

"You know, Phil," Jack began, "I think, this time, I just want to figure out what I really want out of life."

"Hmm..." Phil smiled. "This ought to be a good one. Please, continue."

"So much has happened in the last couple of months, Phil. I think it is time for me to figure out where I am going with my life. You know, what I am trying to accomplish. What my lot in life is."

"Any possibilities thus far?" Phil asked. "Any idea of where you are headed?"

"Well, nothing conclusive," Jack admitted. "There have been a lot of changes in my life recently, and it is making me wonder how it is all supposed to fit together."

"Have there?" Phil coaxed. "What kind of changes?"

"You know, the church, my new friends, Megan..."

"Ah!" Phil chuckled. "I wondered when we would get around to her."

Jack looked out across the ocean. The sun had set and the crescent moon was shining out over the water. The sky was a blanket of sparkling stars, their light dancing off the hull of the great ship as it steamed across the ocean. The moist sea breeze ran through his hair, sending a chill down his spine that gave him goose bumps and made him shiver. At the same time, he felt a searing warmth in his chest which slowly crept up his body, forming a lump in his throat. The lump seemed to radiate a heat of its own, which continued ascending his face like water soaking into a sponge, forming tiny beads of sweat on his forehead

"And about God," he mumbled.

"What's that?" Phil asked. "What do you mean, 'about God'?"

"I don't know, just how He fits into the whole picture, I guess," Jack said, trying to figure out exactly what he wanted to say and how best to put the words together.

"I see," Phil nodded. "And how does He fit into the whole picture at the moment?"

"Well, at the moment, He doesn't," Jack admitted bluntly. He opened his mouth to continue, then paused, squinting, peering at an invisible spot above and behind his right eye, as though all the answers to all his questions had been written there only moments ago and could be accurately recalled if he stared at it hard enough. Surrendering to his lack of enlightenment, he clumsily continued.

"I guess I have never really given it much serious thought," he said. "I always thought that Mom went to church and all that just because it made her feel better to be able to say she was a part of a good and charitable organization. Or something like that. But now, I guess maybe there could be something more to it. Take the guys from the church back in Hampton Roads, for example. They actually seem to *like* being involved in church activities all the time. They go because they want to, not because they will feel guilty if they don't. They seem to leave the church happier than when they came in. Kirt Radford— that is one of my new friends from the church—says that before he got so involved in the church, he was a useless person. 'Not a bad person, just a useless one,'" Jack recited, attempting to mimic Kirt's voice. "That kind of got me thinking, you know. I mean, I have a pretty good life, and I try to be a decent guy, but I'm not getting anywhere. At least, I don't think I am, because I don't even know where it is that I am supposed to be going. It is very difficult to judge the distance from point 'A' to point 'B' when point 'B' is an unknown destination. All of his talk about doing things for people and making his life matter made me realize that my life doesn't matter all that much. Maybe I am supposed to be doing more. Or doing better. I really just don't know, Phil." Jack paused for a moment and watched the moonlight jump from wave to wave across the sea out to the west of them. A person could get completely lost in the beauty of the open ocean. He took a deep breath as the wind played with his hair and slapped the collar of his shirt against his face. Unable to think of anything else to say, he looked expectantly at Phil. "Have I thoroughly confused you yet?" he asked.

"Huh? Oh, sorry Jack, I wasn't listening. Did you say something?" Phil teased.

"Yeah, sometimes I even feel that way about the things my brain runs on about," Jack said.

"I'm teasing, Jack," Phil said as he shook his head and repositioned himself on the railing. "I was listening. And, you know, I was just wondering, have you ever considered praying about it?" he asked.

"Nope," Jack admitted. "Never crossed my mind, to tell you the truth. Is that your prescription, doctor?"

"Couldn't hurt," Phil responded. "After all, God did create us, so He would most likely be the best resource for discovering what our purpose in life is supposed to be. Sound reasonable?"

"Yeah, I guess," Jack allowed. "I just never thought of it that way. I never pictured God as someone who would answer questions if you asked Him."

"You know, Jack, I think that is what knowing God is all about. Having a relationship with Him. Lots of people get caught up in the religiosity of it all, when what God really wants from us is the relationship."

"Go on," Jack prompted. "I know there is more where that came from."

"Well, if you insist..." Phil smiled, pretending it was all Jack's idea. "Wouldn't it be great if you had a friend who could always be with you, who always had the right answers, and who always had your best interests in mind? Someone who would never judge you, never fail you, never leave you hanging?"

"Well, sure, Phil, that would be great, but…"

"You see, Jack, that is what God wants to be for us. Sure, He isn't a physical presence like I am to you, or like you are to me, but His presence and influence can be felt just as strongly as if He were sitting right beside you. He can give you a peace that you can't get anywhere else. And when you ask Him for guidance or assurance, He will give it to you. I don't know what your concept of God is, Jack, but that is how I see Him. To me, He really is a friend who sticks closer than a brother."

"You sound like one of those religious tracts that old people hand out," Jack said.

"Well, where do you think they come up with those things?" Phil asked. "That is how people feel about Him. They just print what God means to them on those tracts as a way of sharing their faith with others." Phil drained his coffee cup, setting it on the railing beside him. "Jack, is that what you think all Christians are like? Boring, stuffy old people passing out tracts on the street corner or in the dentist's office, wasting away their lives baking cakes for the next charity bake sale and never having a life of their own?"

"Pretty much, I guess, yeah," Jack admitted. "That is what most of the people in my home church in Michigan were like. I guess they did seem happy, though. Maybe they liked being that way."

"Yeah, I bet they did," Phil agreed. "You see, Jack, Christianity is not merely a list of 'do's and don'ts' that we have to follow in order to get into Heaven when we die. It's not about what happens when we die. I know that is what most of the bumper stickers refer to, but that is not the point at all. It's all about the relationship *now*. Sure, there is the sin problem that must be taken care of, but that is simply the entry pass, not the ultimate goal of salvation. Turning from your wicked ways and experiencing the forgiveness of God is a necessary step before you can have true *fellowship* with God. *That* is what it's all about. It all comes down to the relationship."

Jack remained silent, pondering what Phil had said. It was a whole new perception of Christianity for Jack to consider. Maybe there was more to it than singing songs and memorizing Bible verses. Maybe the church was something more than just a feel-good club where young and middle-aged people go to feel better about themselves and old people go to get ready to die.

* * *

Veronica Santos sat at her desk in the aging but elegant headquarters of the Puerto Cristobol Police Department. She had been in the employ of the city for many years, through several different administrations and several different police chiefs. She had witnessed the corruption of some administrations and the integrity of others. Though her official job description was merely the Office Manager and secretary to the Chief, she often served in the capacity of his advisor. Over the years, it had become the custom of the reigning Chief to take her advice under careful consideration and to treat her opinions with respect.

On this particular morning, the Chief had instructed her to usher the first three of his 8 a.m. meeting participants directly into the conference room, where he would be waiting to welcome them and offer them a comfortable chair and their choice of a small selection of beverages. A fourth guest would be arriving as well, but he should be sent into the Chief's private office, to be summoned to the conference room after the meeting had already begun.

They sat around the table in the elaborate conference room at Police Headquarters, Puerto Cristobol, Sucre, Venezuela, each consuming his hot or cold libation of preference. The thick mahogany table, with its hand-carved edging and shiny waxed surface, was surrounded by matching hand-carved chairs with thick, dark, maroon-colored cushions held onto the seat and the back by a series of bronze rivets. A hutch stood along the west wall, its surface covered with a lace tablecloth to protect it from the legs of the antique clock that adorned its center and the myriad of other items meticulously arranged on either side of the clock. Along the opposite wall, a pair of plastic trees stood in bronze pots on either side of the doorway like soldiers guarding the entrance to a fallen king's tomb. The remaining two walls were bare, except for a four foot tall bronze-framed mirror that hung in the center of each, three feet off the floor and nearly stretching the entire length of the room. The absence of windows and the placement of the mirrors encouraged those present at any given time to focus all their attention on Captain Emilio Escobar, who sat proudly in the high-backed chair at the head of the table, gathering his thoughts and preparing to call the meeting to order. As the antique clock completed its series of eight chimes, the Chief stood and addressed the small company who had gathered at his request.

"Gentlemen," he began, "I have asked you all to come here this afternoon because I need your assistance. A local citizen has presented me with a potential cure for a cancer which has taken root in Puerto Cristobol, as well as in many other areas of northern and western Venezuela. However, I do not have the resources with which to eradicate this cancer. I am speaking of the man they call 'Don' Miguel Ramirez."

The room fell silent. Those present were the Senior Operations Officer of the local branch of the Directorate of Intelligence and Prevention Services, Inspector Eduardo San Tielo, the State's Attorney, Mr. Jose Fernando, and the Mayor of Puerto Cristobol, the Honorable Mr. Marcos Garcia. Each man present was without aide or assistant. This was to be a closed-door meeting, the content of which would be discussed exclusively with those whose involvement would be absolutely necessary to achieve the goal: that of bringing Miguel Ramirez to justice. The need for secrecy was great, for even as Don Miguel Ramirez was known for his ruthlessness in dealing with those who would dare to betray him, he was also known for the generosity with which he rewarded those who proved their loyalty to him. Information was a valuable commodity, and Ramirez was always in the market for more. The purchase of information was considered a business expense. It was more important than any other single aspect of Ramirez's operation, and he didn't mind investing heavily to ensure that he received a continuous supply. As a result, his eyes and ears were everywhere. With the millions of Venezuelan bolívars he made from every deal he secured, he could afford to have a network of informants covering nearly every office building, every factory, every police precinct, every bar, and every significant street corner in all the major cities of north-central Venezuela. He had knowledge of every illegal operation in Puerto Cristobol, even those he didn't have a financial interest in. Captain Escobar knew that in order to bring Ramirez down, the utmost discretion would be necessary. As few people as possible must learn the details of what would be discussed during this meeting, and the subsequent course of action decided upon by those present. Even the members of the various Assault Teams that would be deployed would not be given the details of their operation until immediately before it was to begin. From that point on, no telephone calls or any other external communication would be allowed for any reason until the mission's completion.

Inspector San Tielo broke the silence. "That explains all the secrecy," he began. "And the omission of my—or, should I say, our—aides."

"Quite so, Inspector," Captain Escobar conceded. "Quite so. As all of you well know, Miguel Ramirez is a most formidable adversary. The tentacles of his organization are as far-reaching as they are deadly. Very little happens in Puerto Cristobol that does not find its way back in some form to the ears of Miguel Ramirez. It is for this very reason that I have asked the three of you here, and asked that you join me unaccompanied. The smaller the number of people who know of our intentions, the less the likelihood that Ramirez will get wind of them. And I want this to be the last time anyone attempts to bring down Mr. Ramirez. I want this to be the time that we lock him up for good."

Heads nodded in agreement around the big table. The Mayor was the next to speak. He was a short but rotund man, round of head and round of body, with matching round-lens glasses. His head was bald on the top, and he kept the ring of graying black hair above his ears and around the back of his rather bulbous head cropped short and neatly trimmed. His deep voice filled the conference room as he assumed the floor.

"We have been after this Ramirez fellow for a long time, Captain Escobar. We have secured a number of witnesses over the years, all of whom either mysteriously come up missing right before the trial, or, equally mysteriously, seem unable to remember what it was they witnessed Ramirez doing. Each time this happens, it costs us a great deal of money and it makes us look foolish in the eyes of other criminals, which therefore costs us a great deal of public support while contributing to Ramirez's feeling of invincibility. Are you saying that this time you have a reliable witness who will not fall victim to these recurring oddities?"

"Yes, Mr. Mayor, I believe I have," Captain Escobar answered. "My witness is a very prominent man in our community, the reigning head of a family as old as Puerto Cristobol itself. His character is above reproach, his reputation is solid, and his determination to assist us is unwavering. He has presented to me some very incriminating evidence, both physical and testimonial. He has requested to remain nameless as far as is possible, but not to a point that would preclude the successful prosecution of Mr. Ramirez."

The mayor began to speak again, but Captain Escobar held up his hand to retain the floor and thus continue his presentation.

"Mr. Mayor," he continued, "Gentlemen, if you will permit me just a few minutes more, I believe I can answer many of your questions before you find it necessary to ask them. I have asked my witness to join us today, so that you can see and hear for yourself both the evidence we have against Ramirez and the witness's determination to assist in his arrest and prosecution." Captain Escobar walked to the door at the end of the conference room and opened it. He greeted Pablo warmly, shaking his hand and leading him into the room. Each of the men sitting around the table was introduced to Pablo by name and title, after which the Captain introduced Pablo, beginning with a short explanation of the family's prominence and position. Walking back to his chair at the head of the table, Captain Escobar regained his seat as he asked Pablo to relay his story to the small gathering, starting at the beginning of his family's difficulties and continuing up to his decision to work with the authorities to stop Miguel Ramirez.

Pablo Linares breathed a heavy sigh, said a quick, silent prayer for courage and wisdom, then proceeded to detail his involvement with Mr. Miguel Ramirez. The other men listened intently as Pablo spoke, occasionally asking questions for further clarification or interjecting comments as to the suitability of a certain piece of evidence for trial. When he was finished and there were no more pertinent questions from the guests, Pablo was thanked for his time and cooperation and politely dismissed. Captain Escobar continued his presentation by detailing his building case against 'Don' Miguel Ramirez. The group of law enforcement officials again asked questions, each from his own perspective and based on his own area of concern and expertise. The representative of the DISIP was concerned with warrants and procedures for making the bust. The State's Attorney was concerned with the 'letter of the law' and with making sure that the charges would stick. The mayor was concerned with jurisdictional issues, human resources, and funding for the bust and the high-profile trial that would follow.

They discussed strategy amongst themselves for a while, then agreed to meet again in one week to continue the process. Each man had questions that needed researching, procedures that required verification, and/or issues that must be settled during the week so that he could present his findings to the rest of the group. Captain Escobar shook hands with each of the men as he departed, thanking him for his time and assistance thus far and for his individual promise of additional assistance in the near future. When at last he was left alone, Captain Escobar walked into his office and shut the door. He sat in his chair and, leaning back with his hands behind his head and his fingers interlaced, smiled a confident smile. "Finally," he said aloud to the empty room. "Finally, Miguel Ramirez, justice will be served! Justice will be served, and your head will be on the platter!"

~4~

Jack could feel the gentle sway of the ship as he lay awake in his pit. Although he was very tired, sleep escaped him. He could't even relax himself. He just lay there, his tired body unwilling to move while his mind was still racing at a hundred miles per hour. He needed sleep, but his busy mind wouldn't let it come. The previous two weeks had passed in a blur, the intensive schedule of drills and practice boardings taking its toll on the crew. Whenever the *Mighty Miss*' was underway, the engineering men in the propulsion plants ran drills every weekday immediately following the evening meal. This time out, the captain also wanted ship-wide drills run, such as small boat attack, man overboard, fire, flooding, collision, and even nuclear accident drills. Contrary to the scheduled propulsion plant drills, these ship-wide drills were run at random times throughout the day, and sometimes even at night. He wanted the crew to be at peak readiness to ensure the safety of the ship in the unlikely event that any of the aforementioned catastrophes actually did occur. Hence, at any time of the day or night the General Quarters alarm could be and had been sounded, that obnoxious BONG—BONG—BONG—BONG—BONG—BONG—BONG—BONG—BONG!! that seemed to go on forever, like an alarm clock equipped with a hot iron fist that could reach into your skull and thump the top of your brain one time per second while you fumbled blindly in the dark, willing to give up anything you had if you could just locate the snooze button. The captain had even thrown in a series of boarding drills so that the Coasties could participate in the grueling exercises. The Coast Guard Team was not typically subjected to such an intensive training regimen, but as long as they were temporarily assigned to the *Mississippi*, the captain owned them and he could drill them as much as he pleased. Aside from the sheer benefits of intensive training, the Coasties had been subjected to their strict drilling program right along with the Navy men on the *Mississippi* in the spirit of fairness. Working one group of men like dogs while allowing another group to slack off is a sure way to kill morale and generate poor attitudes and shoddy workmanship. This was something that the captain wanted very much to avoid. One more day at their present pace, then they would settle in to a more reasonable schedule of training, with only one or two drills each day, not normally to occur after taps (lights out) at 2200.

Every man on the *Mississippi* was looking forward to returning to the normal pace of operation, including Jack. For the last two weeks, he had let his paperwork slide, not to mention the cleaning and maintaining of the signal shack and the other spaces that fell under his cognizance. There was always chipping and painting to be done, flags to be repaired, decks to be swabbed, equipment maintenance to be performed, and the associated paperwork to be updated for each. So far, Chief Johnson had said nothing to Jack about the lack of work and documentation being completed, but that wouldn't last much longer. As soon as the drill schedule relaxed, he would make an inspection tour of all the spaces owned by the Signalmen, and he would come to Jack with a long list of items that needed his attention.

"One more day," Jack mused to himself. "One more day. Then I can relax a little and get some things done." He rolled over to face the steel wall of his pit, careful not to lift his head too high and smack it into the bottom of the pit above his. He had only done that one time, with almost enough force to knock himself unconscious, which was quite sufficient to convince him not to do it again. Experiment conclusion: physical testing confirms—steel pit bottom is without doubt much harder than the human forehead. Human subject nearly rendered unconscious, steel pit bottom unaffected. Additional testing not necessary.

Jack awoke the next morning feeling groggy but somewhat refreshed. The captain had graciously seen fit to allow the men a full night of sleep for the first time in twelve days. The *Mississippi* supported a normal workday from 0730 to 1630, during which no sleeping was allowed other than during the lunch period, which goes from 1130 to 1300. Despite the widespread employment of the 'nooner', that one-hour nap taken after scarfing down a lunch tray full of food, the men were getting tired. A daily nap can only do so much for a person who is prevented from getting a full night's sleep for an extended period of time. Even the Signalmen, who stood a twelve on/twelve off watch rotation from noon to midnight or midnight to noon, were not exempt from the injunction of the normal sleepless workday.

After a hot shower, a close shave and the donning of a clean uniform, Jack was feeling even more refreshed and only slightly groggy. One cup of steaming coffee and a couple of lungs full of fresh ocean air and that should be behind him as well. He decided to get a plate of eggs and hash-brown potatoes before venturing up to the signal bridge, for fear that the drills would begin again and he would thus be prevented from getting anything until lunch. He endured the ritual of waiting in line, ordering his eggs, waiting in line, getting his eggs, waiting in line, getting his hash-browns and a pair of sausage links, and finding a seat. As usual, he didn't feel like conversing before or during breakfast, so the seat he selected was in an uninhabited corner of the mess deck. He ate his breakfast quickly, the pleasant image of steam rising off the surface of his special blend gourmet coffee, contained in his personal "SM2 Union Jack Douglass" coffee mug, spurring him ever onward and encouraging haste in his food consumption. After completing the remainder of the dining ritual, which consisted of waiting in line again to deposit his tray and silverware in the scullery, Jack made his way to the ladder that would take him up to the signal bridge and his steaming cup of 'Good Morning' refreshment.

The only good thing about the rigorous schedule of the previous two weeks was that the obnoxious SM2 Patterson became quite subdued and manageable when deprived of sufficient rest. "The Lord truly works in mysterious ways," Jack commented to himself as he rounded the corner of the signal bridge weather deck and entered the shack. He sent out a general greeting to all who currently occupied the space as he walked straight to the coffee pot and lifted the carafe off its heated plate. No one wanted the little bit of coffee remaining, so Jack dumped it down the scuttlebutt and rinsed out the carafe. He opened the desk drawer marked "LPO" and retrieved the small bag of Morning Blend gourmet coffee, tossing it to SM3 McCoy and nodding toward the coffee maker and filters. He stepped over the knee-knocker and exited the shack, walking aft to fill the carafe with water from the sink in the nearby head. This time, he was glad that SM2 Patterson hadn't been thoughtful enough to make a fresh pot of coffee, because he wanted some of his super-rich special-blend gourmet grounds. He returned with the carafe of water to find BM2 Prescott waiting with a smile on his face and an empty cup in his hand.

"I heard you were busting out the good stuff, so I thought I'd pop in for a cup," Phil said.

"Figures," Jack retorted. "Don't see hide nor hair of you when there's work to be done, but bust out with some expensive coffee, and you drop out of the sky with your hands held out. Hmpf—must be a Coastie thing." Jack smiled as he poured the water into the top of the coffee maker and slapped the lid shut. He hadn't seen Phil for several days as a result of all the training going on, so he was very glad to see him this morning. In fact, they had't had a chance to talk since Phil's dissertation on the real meaning of the Christian life. With drills ending the next day, perhaps they would get a chance to continue their discussion in the near future. Jack knew Phil was always ready to 'get deep and philosophical', and he thought maybe he could use some in-depth brain exercise, too. They chatted about the past few days while waiting, what seemed like an eternity, for the coffee to finish dripping into the pot. Jack filled Phil's cup, then his own, then motioned for Phil to join him out on the weather deck.

Jack jumped up on his perch, snatched his coffee cup off the bulkhead, and took a long sip, savoring the flavor and the aroma. "You gotta take pleasure in the little things, Phil," he said. "If a good cup of coffee is the only thing you have to look forward to, then you should enjoy that cup to the fullest."

"Here, here!" Phil chimed, raising his cup in a mock toast. "May all our days be filled with this much joy and satisfaction." They sipped their coffee and looked out over the horizon. Water. Nothing but water as far as the eye could see. Phil was about to make a comment that was sure to be completely profound when their moment was rudely interrupted by the ship-wide 1MC announcing circuit.

"Boarding Team, Boarding Team! Now assemble the Boarding Team in the wardroom! This is not a drill!" The announcement was repeated verbatim, thus signifying that it had in fact been properly delivered.

Phil poured a large slug of coffee into his mouth, hastily placed his cup on the bulkhead next to Jack, and raced from the signal bridge.

The Boarding Team meeting in the wardroom was called to order. These were the Coast Guard members who worked with the *Mississippi*'s radar, sonar, radio, and weapons specialists to track contacts both in the air and on the ocean. The radiomen had received a signal from Washington D.C. to be on the lookout for a fifty-foot private yacht, the *Rosa de la Mañana*, as it was exhibiting suspicious behavior after departing from a small fishing village in the eastern part of Colombia. The Captain had ordered the OOD to plot an intercept course with the vessel and to let him know as soon as they were approaching range for visual contact, which would be in about 5 miles. Once the identification of the vessel was confirmed, the Coast Guard Drug Interdiction Assault Team would be placed on alert. The radiomen would contact the captain of the yacht, identify themselves as members of the U. S. Coast Guard, and request permission to board and search the vessel. If the captain consented to a boarding, the RIB on the main deck aft would be lowered into the water to take the Assault Team to the suspect vessel while the *Mississippi* steamed nearby, its spotlights and fifty caliber machine guns manned and trained on the hull of the suspect vessel.

The men in the wardroom fell silent as the captain entered and stood behind his chair at the head of the table.

"Gentlemen," he began. "We have reason to believe that the motor yacht '*Rosa de la Mañana*', or '*Morning Rose*', a private fifty-foot pleasure cruiser out of Cartegena, Colombia, is transporting illegal narcotics and is en route to an unspecified port in the southern region of the United States. In accordance with our mission of the interruption and prevention of the trafficking of illegal narcotics from South America to the United States, and in our capacity of Naval Support Representative to the Joint Navy/Coast Guard Drug Interdiction Task Force, it is our duty to detain, board and inspect any maritime vessel exhibiting suspicious behavior while on a direct course to any port in the United States of America.

"At 0438 yesterday morning, we received intelligence from Washington D.C. advising us of the departure of a private yacht from the port of Puerto Lopez in Colombia at 0406 that same morning. We began tracking the vessel, which arrived at the port of Puerto Cristobol in Venezuela later that afternoon. At 2337 last night, we received confirmation that the vessel had been loaded with sufficient supplies and provisions for several days at sea and had departed Puerto Cristobol, Venezuela at 2313. We continued our tracking of the vessel, which is now 17 miles away and dead ahead of us. We will be in visual contact range within the next ten minutes, and we anticipate intercepting the vessel within the hour.

"Men, you have been well trained, and you all know your duties. The mission of the Drug Interdiction Task Force is to keep illegal drugs out of the hands of our children and siblings back in the USA, and it all starts right here with us and with what we will do in the next couple of hours. Stay sharp, keep your minds on your work, and perform your duties as the highly trained professionals that I know you all are. God-speed, gentlemen, and good luck." The captain nodded to Lieutenant Junior Grade Malcolm Hensley, the commander of the Coast Guard unit, turning the meeting over to him. He removed his ball cap and lowered himself into his chair.

Ltjg Hensley stood and walked to the front of the wardroom. He towered over the seated Coast Guard men, since he was a head taller than most of them when they were standing. His commanding presence belied his mild manner and his all-American boy-next-door appearance. He didn't sport the 'tough guy' crewcut like many on specialized teams did, but his close-cropped black hair was well within regulation length requirements. He kept his thick, black mustache trimmed regulation style as well, off the lip and not extending past the corners of his mouth. He was fit and trim, always finishing near the top during physical readiness testing.

Taking charge of the meeting with as much confidence as the captain, he outlined the procedures to be utilized during the boarding, confirmed the position assignments of each of the men who would be participating in the boarding, and briefed the men on Coast Guard Maritime Protocol. It was a speech they had all heard countless times already, but which was required by the Coast Guard prior to deploying the Assault Team much like the reading of the Miranda Rights would be required if an arrest resulted from their boarding. Ltjg Hensley then wished them luck and dismissed them to collect their gear and muster on the fantail by the RIB.

The hull of the USS *Mississippi* cut through the three foot swells, throwing sea spray up over the main deck as the great ship steamed north-northeast at 28 knots on an intercept course with the *Rosa de la Mañana*, which now appeared as a dark dot on the distant horizon. BM2 Prescott and the other members of the Coast Guard Drug Interdiction Assault Team began to assemble on the fantail in full battle dress. They gathered in pairs by the RIB, each checking that the other had donned his protective gear properly and was ready for action. They checked that their weapons had been loaded and were in proper working order, with the safeties on, and that the extra clips and magazines were fully loaded and properly stowed for immediate use, should the situation call for it.

In the radio room, Ltjg Hensley was attempting to contact the captain of the *Rosa de la Mañana*. After two attempts in English and one in Spanish, a scraggly voice finally came over the radio identifying himself as captain of the *Rosa de la Mañana*. Ltjg Hensley continued his conversation in Spanish.

"This is Lieutenant Malcolm J. Hensley with the United States Coast Guard. I am serving aboard the United States Navy

Guided Missile Cruiser USS *Mississippi*, which is now located approximately eight miles off your starboard bow. We will be intercepting your vessel on its current course in approximately ten minutes, at which time we request permission to board your vessel and conduct a search of the vessel as well as an interrogation of yourself and any other crew members we deem necessary. Any attempt to change your vessel's course or speed will be considered an act of hostile intention and will be dealt with accordingly. Refusal to surrender your vessel to boarding and search will result in an armed Naval escort to whichever port you decide to enter, as well as notification of your impending arrival and a thorough briefing of your activities and actions to the cognizant Port Authority. I repeat, this is Lieutenant Malcolm J. Hensley with the United States Coast Guard requesting permission to board and search your vessel. Please respond."

Hensley replaced the microphone on the radio while the *Mississippi*'s Radiomen cheered and held up signs with "9.8" printed on them in black marker. Hensley shushed them, hiding a grin, and listened for the captain of the *Rosa de la Mañana* to respond. After a brief period of silence, the scraggly voice came over the airwaves again, reluctantly granting permission for the boarding.

"That's it!" Hensley said, slapping the knee of the Radioman next to him. "It's GO TIME!!" Hensley jumped out of his chair and exited the radio room. He would first go and make his report to the captain, then rush down to the fantail and take charge of the Boarding Team.

Ltjg Hensley arrived on the fantail to find his men already standing in formation next to the RIB. As the commander of the team, it was Hensley's responsibility to ensure proper readiness of his men. Before each boarding, he would perform a cursory inspection of them in full battle dress. Each of the eight men wore a Kevlar vest under his inflatable life preserver, his regular Coast Guard uniform with the pants legs tucked into the combat boots, and a navy blue ball cap with the words 'Coast Guard' embroidered in silver in a half-circle above and 'Drug Interdiction Task Force' in a half-circle below the silver Coast Guard emblem. On the back of each man's cap, his position on the team was embroidered in silver above the plastic size adjustment strip. Each man was armed with a military issue .45 caliber handgun in a black leather holster, which hung from a black nylon utility belt along with three extra clips for the handgun, a pair of handcuffs, a riot baton, and a police style black steel halogen bulb flashlight. Four of the men were also armed with a specialty weapon, either an M-16 assault rifle or a short barrel 12 gauge riot shotgun. Once satisfied that the men were properly dressed, extra magazines were loaded, weapons were loaded and safeties were on, and all necessary equipment was available and in acceptable working order, Ltjg Hensley reported to the captain of the *Mississippi* that his team was ready to go and awaiting his order to lower the RIB and disembark the ship.

The *Rosa de la Mañana* was now in full view of the Boarding Team. She was a fifty-foot pleasure yacht, stark white except for the dark blue pinstripe just above the normally submerged part of the hull, also dark blue, running from bow to stern along each side. The upper level was walled all the way around with dark brown tinted glass, completely obscuring any occupants inside from the view of passing vessels. Three men could be seen on her bow, awaiting the arrival of the Coast Guard.

The *Mississippi* came about to match the *Rosa de la Mañana*'s course and speed, running parallel to her at a distance of a thousand yards. The fifty-caliber machine guns on either side of the Miss' were manned, the one on the Boarding Team's side trained on the hull of the *Rosa de la Mañana.* On the captain's order, the RIB was lowered into the choppy Caribbean water with her full complement of armed sailors. As soon as the lines were let loose, the boat engineer revved up the motor and the coxswain made for the yacht at the RIB's best possible speed.

Inside the uncomfortable hull of the RIB, nine men silently contemplated the next couple of hours. Only six of them had ever participated in a boarding before, although each had completed the two-week training course at the Maritime Law Enforcement School in Norfolk, Virginia. As a result, tension was high in the little boat. Each man knew his part in the procedure. Each knew what to do in a small variety of situations, and what the proper response was to a handful of potential variants that may occur during a boarding. Each man had been well trained to know how he should present himself in almost any situation a boarding could throw at him, but no amount of training could take the place of experience. Knowing the right answers and the right immediate responses does not necessarily mean that a person will react in accordance with that knowledge in the heat of the moment when there is no time to think about what he should do. And, as a general rule, the crews of suspect vessels seldom followed their scripts correctly. They didn't act the same way the actors did during the training school. Every boarding called for gut instinct and common sense, something which not all the sailors possessed in noteworthy abundance.

BM2 Phil Prescott looked over the rubber side of the RIB into the deep blue water of the Caribbean Sea. His reflection was but a shadow due to the speed of the boat and the choppy swells in the sea. The other men in the RIB prepared themselves in a variety of ways. Some nervously tapped their fingers on their weapons, some silently reprimanded the suspects they would soon be meeting, and some talked incessantly about the mission to alleviate their fear. Others simply sat still and watched the yacht grow larger in their view as the RIB closed the distance between the two vessels. Phil also sat quietly, but, at the same time, he was offering a prayer to God for the safety of himself and of his team. He asked God to protect them from harm and danger while carrying out their mission, and he asked that their mission would be successful. He thanked God for the opportunity to participate in the war on drugs, and he placed the events of the next couple of hours confidently into the capable hands of God.

Four minutes later, the RIB pulled up to the aft end of the *Rosa de la Mañana*. She was a Carver 530 Voyager Pilothouse, a fifty-three-foot luxury motor yacht proudly crafted by the Carver Boat Corporation in Pulaski, Wisconsin. The bow and stern lines of the RIB were tossed onto the transom, where each was retrieved by a crew member of the yacht and securely wrapped in a figure eight around a cleat in the aft corner of the cockpit, securely fastening the RIB perpendicular to the yacht. On the RIB, the coxswain kept his M-16 assault rifle trained on the two men in the cockpit, while the boat engineer used his riot shotgun to cover the two men on the bridge. As soon as the RIB was moored to the transom of the *Rosa de la Mañana*, Ltjg Hensley stepped up onto the forward edge of the RIB and asked to speak to the captain. A burly man with a big round belly descended the stainless steel ladder from the bridge to the cockpit, stepping forward to identify himself as Captain of the vessel. He was a rugged man, his long face weathered from many years on the sea, his salt and pepper beard neatly trimmed around his face. Ltjg Hensley formally greeted him and again requested permission to board the yacht. With the captain's formal permission, Hensley climbed onto the yacht, followed by two men carrying riot shotguns who posted themselves on either side of the transom. After confirming that all of the yacht's inhabitants were present on the deck, Ltjg Hensley addressed them and explained the boarding procedure to them. All the men would be required to remain on the deck while the Boarding Team conducted its search and the Lieutenant interrogated those whom he decided may have something of consequence to say. When the sailors had confirmed that they understood the procedure, Hensley motioned to his two pairs of 'sniff dogs', the men whose job it was to conduct the actual search of a suspect vessel in lieu of real drug-sniffing dogs. Under the armed protection of the rest of the Boarding Team, they were to begin searching the yacht while he and the captain confined themselves to a more isolated area where they could discuss the purpose for the boarding without interruption.

Immediately the 'sniff dogs' split, BM2 Phillip Prescott and BM3 Bob Henderson taking the stainless steel ladder through the hatch and up to the bridge, while QM3 (Quartermaster Third Class) John Jenkins and EN3 (Engineman Third Class) Hank Steadmore headed down to the engine compartments, thoroughly searching every conceivable place where illegal drugs could have been hidden. Without the aid of real 'sniff dogs', the Coast Guard men had to rely on their own instincts and creativity to find any drugs that may have been stashed aboard the vessel.

On the bridge, BM2 Prescott and BM3 Henderson set to work with an intensity of purpose and a strong sense of duty. The most significant driving force in locating the drugs was to keep them off the streets of America and out of the hands of the young people who were often so easily enticed to give them a try. Also, in the same way that a fighter pilot wants to get the next enemy kill to earn that small figure of a bomb painted on the side of his plane, each of the 'sniff dogs' wanted to be the one to find the next stash of contraband so that he could get a silver hash mark embroidered on his ball cap directly above his right ear. BM2 Prescott, who already had three such hash marks adorning the side of his cap, proceeded forward to the instrument panel, while BM3 Henderson, as yet without any hash marks but hoping to change that on this mission, began at the aft end. The bright Caribbean sun glared off the glossy white fiberglass finish of the bridge as BM2 Prescott removed his sunglasses and took his Gerber multi-purpose tool out of the small pouch hanging from his gun belt. He opened it up to reveal a Philip's head screwdriver and began removing the access covers below the instrument panels. After removing each one, he took the small mirror attached to a telescoping handle out of his shirt pocket and used it to look up inside the dashboard behind the electronic controls. Once satisfied that nothing was out of place, he carefully replaced the access covers and went to work on the instruments themselves. He gently tugged at each one in case a false face had been installed in place of an actual instrument, and turned on any that weren't in use to make sure that they hadn't been gutted and their boxes filled with drugs instead of navigational electronics. From there he moved past the pilothouse access hatch to the starboard side where he found a fully stocked wet bar, complete with a sink and a refrigerator. He opened the bottle storage area, lifting out bottles of bourbon, vodka, rum, tequila, several varieties of schnapps, and some two-liter bottles of ginger ale. He checked to see that each bottle contained its intended liquid, then examined the storage area for false walls or removable panels. He replaced all the bottles, then went through the same ritual with the small refrigerator, finding nothing but a full complement of a local Colombian beer and a single stick of butter.

While BM2 Prescott was searching the forward half, BM3 Henderson was busily searching the aft section, with no more success than his partner. Bob Henderson was short, stocky and muscular, looking rather like a miniature professional wrestler. He had looked over the seats in the u-shaped lounge area and squeezed the cushions in case some of the stuffing had been removed and replaced with a stash of drugs. On the starboard side, he had lifted the seat on the double lounge chair and removed two life jackets, three towels and a pair of flip-flops. After checking the walls of the storage area for hidden storage compartments, he replaced the contents of the lounge seat and continued moving forward. He finished in time to help BM2 Prescott put all the cans of beer back in the refrigerator and pronounce the bridge free of contraband. They opened the hatch to the pilothouse and started down the stairs.

In the engine compartment two levels below, QM3 Jenkins and EN3 Steadmore were putting the same intensive effort into their search. They began in the engine compartment, deep within the hull of the yacht. Crawling over the pair of Cummins QSM11-635 hp diesel engines, they visually surveyed every inch of the engines and all the supporting equipment, hoses, lines, cables and pipes connected to them. Using the backs of their hands, they carefully felt the various hoses, pipes and engine parts to check that they were at their designed operating temperatures. A cold hose or pipe that should be hot during operation could indicate a piece of equipment that had been hollowed out and filled with illegal narcotics sealed in plastic bags. After finding all temperatures to be as expected and all engine parts and support equipment to be in order, they shifted their search to the compartment itself and to the storage areas within it. They went through each toolbox, every cubby hole and every storage locker, checking all the aerosol cans, grease cans, tool handles and boxes of replacement parts. They checked the batteries and their cases, the rag bin, the trash can. Anything capable of having a false bottom or top or middle was inspected scrupulously for any indication that something had been hidden inside. The hatches to the bilge were lifted, and QM3 Jenkins used his mirror and flashlight to verify the absence of contraband there while EN3 Steadmore did the same in the installed fuel, water, and waste tanks. The spare fuel and freshwater cans were also inspected, revealing nothing out of the ordinary.

Proclaiming the engine compartment free of drugs, Jenkins and Steadmore proceeded up into the aft end of the cockpit and the transom area. QM3 Jenkins began searching the two lockers on the aft bulkhead of the cockpit and the two fender storage compartments on the platform of the transom. The locker on the starboard side revealed only freshwater shower equipment, the one on the port side a coil of nylon line and a pair of connection boxes, one for cable television and one for telephone. EN3 Steadmore tackled the cockpit itself, removing covers for stereo speakers and lighting fixtures on the aft bridge extension.

Entering the pilothouse, BM2 Prescott and BM3 Henderson again split up, each beginning at the same place they had on the bridge. BM2 Prescott again removed his Gerber from its leather pouch on his belt and began removing instrument panel covers on the dash of the helm station. He inspected them as he had those on the bridge, with the same disappointing results as he had experienced on the bridge.

BM3 Henderson continued his search at the L-shaped six-person couch in the aft end of the pilothouse, examining the entire leather surface for evidence of damage or recent repair. He prodded and squeezed all the cushions to ensure that all were filled with stuffing and not with illegal drugs. He surveyed the rest of the small room, checking the decks and bulkheads, especially the seams, for evidence of tampering.

From there, BM2 Prescott and BM3 Henderson proceeded aft to the salon, beginning at the galley. This is where the search became very tedious and actually quite a bit more difficult. Where the command and control areas had very few interior compartments to search through, the living areas seemed to have little else. There was plenty of room to move around, but everywhere one looked were shelves, cupboards, cubby holes and drawers where contraband could be hidden. And, if that weren't enough, inside almost all of those shelves, cupboards, cubby holes and drawers were a myriad of smaller items within which one could have hidden various quantities of controlled substances and paraphernalia. Beginning at opposite ends of the U-shaped galley, the 'sniff dogs' emptied cupboards and drawers onto counters, examining each item as they removed it. Cans and jars that had already been opened, such as sugar and coffee, were either dumped into bowls or dug through and searched thoroughly with a spoon or other suitable utensil. The refrigerator was searched just like the one on the bridge, as was the microwave oven and the coffee maker.

When they finished with the cockpit and the transom, QM3 Jenkins and EN3 Steadmore entered the salon from the cockpit. Since BM2 Prescott and BM3 Henderson were still in the pilothouse at that time, BM2 Prescott directed them to take the companionway from the pilothouse down to the suites located below. As they entered the master stateroom, QM3 Jenkins slapped his forehead and let out a sigh.

"Man, how much cupboard space do they need on this silly thing?" he asked, rhetorically. "This is nuts!"

EN3 Steadmore silently agreed and began the task of searching through all the storage lockers, cupboards and drawers. He rifled through a couple of suitcases that hadn't been unpacked, and searched through a closet full of clothes that had. He checked each compartment for false panels, behind which he hoped to find a stash of drugs, then replaced the items he had removed and continued on to the next one.

QM3 Jenkins began at the queen size bed, lifting the mattress and examining it for hidden pouches or stitching that could have been sewn up after drugs were hidden inside. He removed the diffusers and inspected the vent ducting, then checked the rest of the stateroom for evidence of tampering. In the master head, he searched the cupboards and their contents, the toilet tank, and the medicines in the medicine cabinet. As in all other rooms, all electrical outlet covers had been removed and inspected.

QM3 Jenkins and EN3 Steadmore painstakingly searched each of the other two staterooms in the same manner, while BM2 Prescott and BM3 Henderson did the same in the salon aft of the galley. After an hour and forty minutes of extensive inspection, the two search teams met in the salon to compare notes. The conclusion was simple: their search had yielded absolutely nothing illegal. Disappointed and frustrated, they reluctantly decided to report their findings, or the lack thereof, to the Lieutenant and let him take it from there. The aft search team turned and headed toward the ladder leading down to the cockpit while BM2 Prescott, leader of the forward search team, paused to take one last look around the galley. The freak accident that followed was the only thing that made their boarding successful, resulting in the arrest of the yacht's captain and crew, and the confiscation of just over four kilos of cocaine by the US Coast Guard.

Since the Coast Guard had completed their search, the crew members of the *Rosa de la Mañana* were permitted to use the head at the base of the companionway to the forward stateroom. As the search teams were preparing to proceed down the ladder to the cockpit, one of the crew members of the *Rosa de la Mañana* exited the head, climbed the steps back up to the pilothouse and entered the salon. He stopped in the galley, pausing to strike a match and light a cigarette. He shook the match to extinguish the flame then tossed it into the wastebasket next to the wine storage rack at the end of the counter in the galley. Pausing long enough to draw in a chest full of smoke and blow it out at the Coast Guard men, he turned and started down the ladder to the cockpit with all the cocky arrogance of a teenager who has just gotten away with sneaking back in his window after going to a party against his parents' orders.

"That dirt bag really ticks me off!" remarked one of the aft team 'sniff dogs', stepping back and relinquishing use of the ladder to the crew member. "I know there's something on this boat. We just can't seem to find it. I hate the idea that these thugs will get away with transporting a stash of drugs right under our noses--even after we searched their boat ourselves!"

"I know what you mean," Phil agreed. "I feel like it's right here, staring us in the face, but we can't see it." Phil walked across the room, angry and frustrated. "But if we were to continue the search, I don't know where else we could look," he added, defeated.

As the search teams once again turned and headed for the ladder to the cockpit and Lieutenant Hensley, they saw the flames licking the top of the wastebasket where the crewman had deposited his match. They all froze for a split second, then BM2 Prescott remembered having seen a portable CO2 fire extinguisher hanging on the bulkhead inside the cupboard beneath the sink in the galley. He rushed over to the sink, grabbed the CO2 bottle, ripped off the protective tape, pointed the cone at the wastebasket and squeezed the trigger. Nothing happened.

Expertly, BM2 Prescott quickly inspected the valve mechanism of the extinguisher for damage or blockage. Realizing that Phil's extinguisher was inoperative, EN3 Steadmore ran down the companionway into the master stateroom and retrieved a different CO2 bottle. He quickly returned to the salon and put out the small fire with a couple of short blasts from his extinguisher.

"I don't understand this," BM2 Prescott said. "There's nothing wrong with this unit. The valve is new, the cone and hose are free of blockage, it weighs way too much not to be charged, and yet it won't discharge. It doesn't make any sense."

He continued to inspect the CO2 bottle from one end to the other. He unsnapped the steel band with the clip that holds the cone in place and removed it from the center of the bottle. Then he noticed something very odd. He asked for the expended bottle that had been used on the fire. As he began unsnapping the band, he asked that any other bottles that could be found on board be brought to him.

Close inspection revealed that all the bottles were single-construction units except for the one that didn't work. BM2 Prescott instructed BM3 Henderson to hold one end of the bottle and twist while he did the same to the other end, but in the opposite direction. The seal was cracked, and the CO2 bottle began to unscrew. BM2 Prescott took the bottle and, placing the bottom between his knees, slowly unscrewed the top half and lifted it off. A smile covered his face as he lifted two thick plastic bags of fine white powder out of each end of the fire extinguisher and held them up for his cohorts to see.

"Go and get the Lieutenant," he ordered, finally satisfied

with the outcome of the boarding.

"So," Phil continued, "The Captain and all his crew members were taken into custody and are being held under armed guard on the *Mighty Miss*' until we can pull into Guantanamo Bay and turn them over to the DEA."

It was just after 1900 hours on the evening of the drug bust. The ship was buzzing from bow to stern with talk of the boarding, the drugs and the prisoners. Everywhere the men customarily gathered, talk was centered around some aspect of the day's events, and the signal bridge was no exception. SM2 Douglass and SMSN Wilson had the watch, though they shared their area with more than the usual amount of sailors drinking pop or coffee and chatting like a bunch of old women at a church social. Jack was on his perch, surrounded by Phil, Tom Wilson, and a few others. Phil smiled as he overheard various accounts of the boarding, the tales growing taller with each telling.

"Yeah, then one of the druggies pulled a knife on the Lieutenant…"

"They found a stash of guns and ammo in a false compartment in a closet…"

"One of the guys is wanted for killing a cop in Colombia…"

Phil chuckled and shook his head, rolling his eyes at their embellishments. "I thought it was interesting enough the way it really happened," he said quietly.

"What about the yacht and the drugs?" Tom Wilson asked with all the eagerness of a young boy listening to his grandpa tell a ghost story around the campfire. "What will happen to them?"

"A couple of our boys are piloting the yacht to Guantanamo right behind us, and the drugs have been locked up very securely on the *Mississippi* until we can turn them over to the DEA in Cuba as well," Phil explained.

Satisfied that he now knew the real deal about the boarding, SN Wilson finished off the last warm, flat slug in the can of Classic Coke he was holding and walked around the signal shack to deposit it in the recycle bin just inside the watertight door.

"What a day, eh, Phil?" Jack asked, rhetorically.

"Boy, that's for sure," Phil answered. "It sure snapped us out of the boring rut of all those stupid drills, though."

"Well, that is true enough," Jack allowed. "By the way, pretty slick how you found that stash of coke, Phil," he smiled, nodding his head in approval. "Very smooth."

"Yeah, well, I am just glad we found it," Phil said. "I hate it when I know that something is there, but no matter how hard I look, I just can't find it. That makes the job very frustrating."

Phil sipped his coffee and looked out over the ocean across the fantail of the ship. The Caribbean sun was beginning to set over the western horizon, golden rays of light sprinting across the water like Olympic runners racing for the ship to get the gold medal. The sky was getting darker as dusk approached, the few sparse clouds electrified by the receding sun which was not willing to go away without leaving its mark on everything in its path. A smile crept across Phil's face as his mind drifted back to the yacht they had just searched. His imagination lifted him off the signal bridge of the USS *Mississippi* and transported him to the bridge of his own Carver 530 Voyager Pilothouse motor yacht. His navy blue Coast Guard uniform was replaced with a pair of white cotton tennis shorts and a matching polo shirt, his black combat boots with brown leather deck shoes. Across the transom of his yacht, Phil watched the sun set on an exciting day of cruising, fishing and swimming in the warm waters of the Gulf of Mexico while he slowly made his way west toward the South Padre Islands near the southern tip of Texas. He would remain in port there for a few days before he picked up his next charter for a three-day deep sea fishing jaunt…

"Phil!" Jack repeated, punching him in the shoulder.

"Huh? Oh, sorry, Jack," Phil mumbled.

"Hey, welcome back, buddy. Where were ya, man?" Jack asked. "Nice to know I'm not the only one who dwafts out to la-la land in the middle of a conversation."

"Yeah, sorry man. I was just thinking about that boat. That thing is awesome, Jack. Some day, I've gotta get me one of those."

"Yeah, me too," Jack agreed. "Me too."

*   *   *

Captain Emilio Escobar warmly greeted the small group of men assembled in the conference room of the Police Headquarters Building in the heart of downtown Puerto Cristobol. As at their previous meeting, those present were the mayor of Puerto Cristobol, the State's Attorney, the head of the local DISIP office, and the Chief of Police, Captain Escobar. He called the meeting to order, thanking them for their attendance and directing their attention to the small pile of documents on the table in front of each of them, which consisted of copies of the reports each had brought to distribute to the others. Captain Escobar began to deliver the first oral report to the group.

"Gentlemen, since our last meeting, I have spent countless hours reviewing innumerable cases which have been dismissed, declared mistrials, or otherwise lost due to faulty police work. I have meticulously reviewed entire manuals of police procedures and have held extensive training sessions on the same with my men. We have reviewed arrest procedures, treatment of perpetrators, definitions of necessary use of force, search and seizure warrant requirements, control of evidence at the scene and at the evidence locker here at the station, as well as procedures for maintaining the integrity of a crime scene. I have stepped up departmental training requirements for the Physical Fitness Confidence Course, and the Live-fire Situational Simulator, and I have doubled the required practice time on the Firing Range for general marksmanship with handguns, shotguns, and assault rifles. I believe my men will be prepared to assist in whatever capacity we as a group deem necessary."

Heads nodded in approval around the table. Escobar's resolve was clear. The next man to speak was the mayor.

"Sounds like you are doing an exemplary job of preparing your department, Captain. Keep up the good work. From my end, I have reviewed several special sting operation estimated cost figures drafted by a variety of city employees over the last eight to ten years. I could find no record of ever having funded such an undertaking, so I can only assume that these were drafted behind closed doors for the sole purpose of having a plan available should the need ever arise, and should any of my predecessors ever be put on the spot and required to comment on the feasibility of such an operation without the proper time allotted for sufficient research. At any rate, using the average cost of the four sting operation plans I discovered, and taking into consideration the inflated cost of materials, manpower and equipment, and also with respect to the availability of said materials, manpower and equipment, I have concluded that the City of Puerto Cristobol could reasonably provide financial and actual support for an average-cost operation similar to those I have reviewed in the amounts as follows: eighty-three percent of the necessary materials, thirty-seven percent of the manpower, and thirty-two percent of the equipment necessary to execute such an operation. I trust that our DISIP friends at the capitol are willing to provide financial and actual assistance in the event that this operation proceeds as we all hope it will," the Honorable Marcos Garcia said, directing the last statement across the table to Inspector Eduardo San Tielo.

"Of course, Mr. Mayor," San Tielo began. "It is most certainly in the best interests of the State of Sucre that Mr. Ramirez be arrested, prosecuted, and confined for the rest of his natural life. We will be happy to do anything in our power to achieve a satisfactory end to this proposed operation. In fact, I have also done extensive research, informal and covert, of course, using hypothetical situations whenever the opinions of others were needed, and have come up with figures that quite compliment those of the City of Puerto Cristobol. It seems that our strengths are your weaknesses, Mr. Mayor, as we have access to an abundance of state-of-the-art equipment and top-notch manpower, though our expendable materials budget is suffering somewhat. I also have been reviewing past operational plans, some that have never been executed, but many which have proven quite successful in the capture of criminals and the confiscation of contraband. I am confident that together we can mobilize a formidable force against Mr. Miguel Ramirez, provided Mr.

Fernando and Captain Escobar can confirm that sufficient grounds exist to ensure a successful campaign, and that this will indeed be the last campaign against the infamous 'Don' Miguel Ramirez." Inspector San Tielo, clearly finished with his report, reached for his coffee cup and swirled its contents to mix up any sugar that may have settled to the bottom during the conversation. He took a drink, then motioned to Captain Escobar that he would like to refill his cup from the pot across the room. Escobar nodded his consent, then directed his gaze to Mr. Fernando.

"Mr. Fernando," he said, "it appears as though the operation is provisionally approved, contingent upon your favorable analysis of the anticipated success in prosecuting Mr. Ramirez. Please, share your opinions with the group," he invited.

"Thank you, Captain. Yes, I believe you are correct, it seems that the field aspect of the operation is in capable hands. The legal side, however, is never so cut and dried. There are a number of misdemeanor charges that could reasonably be expected to apply to Mr. Ramirez, but none of which would carry a penalty significant enough to justify launching such an extravagant contrivance for his capture. Neither would the resulting sentence be sufficient to hold him in prison for an extended period of time. Therefore, we must be able to guarantee that he can be charged successfully with a more serious crime, such as viable, provable, undeniable trafficking of illegal drugs, manufacture of controlled substances, smuggling a controlled substance, and the like. On a related note, he could conceivably suffer the same fate as the American mobster Al Capone who, although he was a known organized crime boss, was eventually put in prison for tax evasion. Ramirez is also known to be connected to several suspicious deaths, so there is always the possibility of an arrest for murder, or even conspiracy to commit murder if it can be proven that he ordered the hit. The possibility of a racketeering charge also exists, provided sufficient evidence can be collected to support such a charge. So you see, gentlemen, it is very possible to arrest him and put him away for a long time, as long as the supporting evidence can be found and tied to him personally. He will have a very expensive and very corrupt lawyer on his side, who will no doubt use every trick in his dirty little book to get his client off on some technicality, or to get crucial evidence thrown out or something equally contemptible. There is also the very real prospect of great personal bodily harm being threatened to any witnesses we may be able to come up with. In short, gentlemen, I can guarantee nothing. It all depends upon the proper collection of iron-clad proof that Miguel Ramirez is guilty of whatever crimes we try him for, coupled with our irrefutable ability to provide absolute security to any witnesses we can convince to testify against him. Any loophole, no matter how small, will allow his fancy crooked lawyer the opportunity to squeeze him through the cracks in the justice system and, once again, put him back out onto the streets a free man."

The atmosphere in the conference room took on a deep air of solemnity. The four men around the ornate hand carved table sat in silence, each wondering the same thing: Could they really make this work? Captain Escobar was the first to speak.

"Gentlemen, as true as Mr. Fernando's statement is, I do not believe it should deter us from our objective. Yes, it will be very difficult, and no, there are no guarantees, but I, for one, am willing to take that risk. If we run this operation according to a well thought out plan, checked and double-checked by each of us, I believe we can stop Miguel Ramirez's reign once and for all. I am not deterred in my resolve to press on, and I hope that the rest of you are still in agreement."

"Let's do it," Inspector San Tielo said. "It is time for this scum to go down."

"This is my city," Mayor Garcia said, "not his. I agree with the Inspector. It is time for him to go. The operation has my full support."

"Rest assured, gentlemen, I will do my very best to get a conviction using whatever evidence you can bring to me," Fernando added. "Let's take him down."

* * *

The surface of the Caribbean Sea was a shiny mirror of

glass. The only disturbance in evidence for miles in any direction was that created by the steel hull of the USS *Mississippi* and the fiberglass hull of the confiscated motor yacht *Rosa de la Mañana* as they cut through the warm, salty water on their way to the United States Naval base on the south side of the eastern tip of the island of Cuba. It was mid morning, the sun was already high in the sky and the hot, muggy breeze coming across the weather decks of the *Mississippi* already felt thick, like the inside of a dryer full of fluffy towels that still needed another half hour to rid themselves of their excess moisture. Far across the horizon, not yet visible to the naked eye but plain enough through the magnification of the 'big eyes' on the signal bridge, a tiny dot could be seen in the middle of the vast ocean. It was actually an island closely mimicking the shape of the human spleen, measuring some seven hundred seventy miles long and occupying a total land area of 104,945 square miles. It was home to approximately eleven million people and forty-six species of lizards.

In another time, a sailor standing watch in the crow's nest of a wooden galleon might have peered through his spyglass, calling out "Land Ho!" as the lens of his glass filled with the faint form of the tropical island slowly taking shape on the distant horizon. The crewmen would tuck their daggers into their belts and ready their swords and muskets, arming themselves in preparation for whatever adventures and treasures the approaching piece of land might have for them.

Jack Douglass sometimes wished for those days, wondering what it would have been like to sail the seven seas on a pirate's schooner, making or taking his fortune wherever he could find it, creating a name for himself that would fill the pages of children's storybooks for years to come. He would be the dashing hero who makes a grand entrance at precisely the right moment to subdue the bad guy, save the damsel in distress, and add yet another thrilling victory to his long and distinguished accumulation of tales and escapades, securing for all time his place in the annals of the legends of days gone by…

But instead, he walked back into the signal shack, with no sword or dagger on his belt and no parrot perched on his shoulder, armed only with the small black government-issue Skillcraft ball-point pen. He dutifully made the appropriate notations in the Signal Bridge Log book of, not his own pirate's schooner, but the American Navy warship USS *Mississippi.* stating that they had come within sight of the island of Cuba. He diligently logged all pertinent information, noting the current time and weather conditions aboard the *Mississippi,* as well as the distance and relative bearing to the island.

Jack felt the gentle thud under his feet as the tug boat made contact with the hull of the *Mississippi*, guiding her into her berth along the pier at the US Naval Station, Guantanamo Bay, Cuba. On the way through the bay, Jack was once again amazed at the beautiful green water, so clear that he could see the rocks on the bottom, even though he knew it was well over thirty feet deep. The Petty Officer of the Watch blew his boatswain's whistle and announced that the ship was moored, the Officer of the Deck was shifting his watch to the aft port quarterdeck, and the colors should be shifted to reflect that the ship was no longer underway. Soon, the men who weren't on duty would be cut loose on liberty, even though there was very little to do on the small base in Cuba. Still, every man who could, would make a beeline for the shore, many lining up ten or twenty at a time to use the pay phones to call and talk with loved ones back in the States, many stocking up on food, snacks, clothing, CD's and other paraphernalia from the Navy Exchange (NEX) store, and still more proceeding directly to the Package Store (the base liquor store) to acquire the main constituent of their anticipated nighttime activities.

When the ship is in port, the Signalmen lock up the signal shack and secure the watch, thereafter becoming part of the Topside Duty Section rotation. Since there were more men than there were watches that required manning, not every man would have a watch to stand on every duty day. Sometimes they would even go three or four duty days without ever standing a watch. This would be one such day for Jack Douglass.

The Executive Officer (XO) held a meeting in the wardroom with the Principle Assistants (PA's- the officers assigned to head a specific department) and the rest of the officers, explaining that this was a working port, not a liberty port, and that they should use this time to complete any maintenance that needed to be done while the ship was moored and much of the underway equipment was not in use. Both reactors would remain online, but either of the engine rooms could be shutdown as necessary to support steam plant maintenance that needed to be done after four weeks of continuous steaming. After answering a couple of unimportant questions, he informed them of the captain's intentions to get underway again at 0900 the next morning and dismissed them to pass the instructions on to their enlisted men.

The PA's then met with the leading chiefs, the senior enlisted men responsible for their respective divisions, who would in turn meet with the blue-shirts under their cognizance, passing on schedule information and making the necessary work assignments for the in-port period. The last of those meetings was sure to include a lot of grumbling from the junior sailors, because they typically had a liberty port visit after three weeks out, and this time they had been out for four weeks already and had not visited a liberty port. Even if it was just GITMO, they still wanted to get off the ship and blow off some steam.

However, much to their dismay, the blue-shirts were informed that Liberty Call would go down after the normal working day was over according to in-port working hours, and that liberty would expire on board at 0000 for all hands. "Watchstander's Liberty" would be in effect, which granted duty personnel permission to leave the ship when not actually on watch, even though they were part of the duty section. The engineering men, or 'nukes', would be on a 6 and 12 watch rotation (6 hours on, 12 hours off) in the engine rooms, while the topsiders manned their watches according to their normal in-port duty schedule. They were informed of the underway time of 0900 the next morning, and given lists of items that needed their attention prior to Liberty Call that afternoon.

The day went much as Jack had expected, peculiarly similar to the last couple of days in Norfolk before getting underway for this cruise. The captain thought that the ship needed maintenance and cleaning, so the junior officers rushed to perform inspections, during which they would generate lists of hits for the enlisted men to fix. The enlisted men would in turn rush to correct the lists of hits so that their small allocation of shore liberty would not be delayed or withheld.

Finally, at just after 1530, Liberty Call was announced, and a stream of sailors in civilian clothes flowed across the brow onto the American-occupied Cuban soil. Many sailors had taken advantage of Watchstander's Liberty during the workday and had already made their way from the pier to the conglomeration of buildings that made up the naval base to take care of whatever personal business or shopping they wanted to do. The provision that anyone on such liberty must be in uniform ironically made it possible for many who were not on liberty to leave the ship anyway. If they could get someone to cover for them with their chief or LPO, or if they just had a strong enough desire to leave and were willing to brave the consequences, they would simply walk off the brow in uniform and take care of their personal business.

Even if he had wanted to, Jack could not have succeeded in such a venture, due to his position as LPO of the division. People would be looking for him at various times throughout the day, and he had to make himself available to them if he ever wanted to be able to take advantage of Liberty Call when it actually did go down. So, at 1533, Jack joined the throng of people disembarking the ship to enjoy a few hours of freedom which, for many of them, would consist mainly of a telephone call and a lot of alcohol.

Since his buddy, Phil Prescott, had been granted liberty shortly after arrival, Jack made his trek into the main area of the base unaccompanied, which suited him just fine. He was a people person, but there were times when he just wanted to be alone. Being a Signalman provided him with many such opportunities, which was one reason he had chosen that particular rate for his naval career. He looked around as he made the long walk from the pier to the shopping center, taking note of the odd shrubbery and the general lack of vegetation on the island. Far off to the north, he could see the rolling hills on the Cuban side of the fence line. "Funny," he thought to himself, "it didn't look any different than any other tropical island. The fact that it was a Communist country, ruled by a man of questionable integrity and character, and itself a nation on other than friendly diplomatic terms with the United States, couldn't be ascertained by simply gazing at the beautiful countryside, watching the birds dip and swoop near the water, and listening to the peaceful sounds of the lazy hot afternoon."

There was nothing inherently thrilling about the place of Guantanamo Bay, Cuba, other than the fact of his actually *being there*, Jack concluded. That was the oddity of travel. When sitting at home in the States, looking through a magazine or a Fodor's Travel Guide to 'wherever', the places look exotic, enticing, even magical. One would think that, upon arrival to such a wondrous place, one would be immediately swept away into a fairyland of euphoria and delight, floating around blissfully on a cloud of one's own imagination, drinking in the ambiance of the place like a thirsty flower soaking up life-giving minerals from the recently rain-moistened earth. In reality, however, there is nothing so distinctly different about being in a foreign place. Jack was still Jack, the *Mighty Miss*' was still looming in the background, pain still hurt, and he still needed air to survive. If he woke up in the morning and didn't remember where he was, he would probably not be able to tell that he was in Cuba until his head cleared and he remembered his arrival the previous day. Not that he didn't enjoy traveling, it just didn't turn out to be as magical as he had anticipated before he began a career in the Navy which afforded him such travel opportunities.

As he neared the NEX shopping center, Jack involuntarily noticed the bank of pay phones off to his left. "Boy, it would be nice to talk to Megan," Jack said to himself. "I wonder what she is doing right now..." They had agreed before his deployment that they would confine their communication to letters and packages, rather than spending a large amount of money on expensive phone calls from foreign ports. As it turned out, each phone booth had a line of at least six people impatiently waiting behind the current caller anyway, so Jack figured that he was pretty safe from an impulse call on that front. He proceeded into the NEX shopping complex and browsed through the stores. It was set up sort of like a mall, though not enclosed by walls. The central court area was filled with cheap plastic tables at which patrons of the surrounding food vendors could sit and eat their purchases in the shade of a handful of palm trees which grew up out of the floor, encased by circular iron grates. The court area was shaped like a plus sign, with restaurants and stores extending along the bottom on either side. On the upper half of the plus, the left side housed a bank of Automated Teller Machines and a couple of pay phones, while the right side was an inaccessible part of the Navy Exchange itself. At the top of the plus were two sets of automatic double doors providing access to the main Navy Exchange shopping area.

The NEX attempted to carry everything a sailor this far away from home would ever need during the extent of his tour of duty here, plus a large variety of amenities that might make his stay a little more comfortable. From groceries, linens, and crystal knick-knacks, to hip-waders, boom boxes, and bottles of toilet cleaner, the selection seemed endless. Jack wandered aimlessly around the store, listened to a few CDs on the test player in the audio department, picked up a handful of snacks from the food section, passed up a once-in-a-lifetime deal on baby formula, then strolled out into the humid Cuban air with his purchases.

As he was sitting on a bench finishing a Coke that he had procured from the friendly Cuban snack shop proprietor, a small group of his friends walked by, inviting him to join them on a short trip to a nearby beach. He agreed, collecting his bags and blending in with the group. They chatted about whatever topic came up while they made their way along the gravel road to the small beach, happy to be on land again, even if it was in Cuba.

The small gravel road stretched out before them, winding up a hill and disappearing from sight as it reached the top and continued down the other side toward the beach. Small, scraggly bushes dotted the rocky and nearly barren landscape. Sparse clumps of knee-high green grass stuck out of the earth like pale green candles on a chocolate-frosted birthday cake. Far off in the distance, a tall chain-link fence, which seemed completely out of place in such a lifeless and desolate place as this, ran along the entire perimeter of the base. It separated the friendly soil of the United States Naval Station, Guantanamo Bay, Cuba, from the tainted and oppressive soil of the Communist Republic of Cuba.

As they crested the hill, Jack was completely taken back by the sight before him. It was like something right out of one of those travel books. Down the hill and to the right stood an old wooden pavilion, with its built-in grills and its rows of picnic tables bolted to the concrete floor slab. Fifty-five-gallon barrels which had been turned into trash cans were strategically placed around the area, providing visitors with a simple means of keeping the place clean and free of litter. A crude sand-pit volleyball court separated the pavilion from the rest of the beach, its sandy surface not quite contained between the two poles which held the sagging and weathered volleyball net between them. Beyond the volleyball court, the beach, which consisted of gravel and pebbles instead of fine sand and ground seashells, extended only about twenty feet before it gave way to the incoming waves of the Caribbean Sea. The beach was only about five hundred yards long, bordered on each side by jagged rocky cliffs that jutted nearly a hundred feet into the air. This created an elevated plateau on either side of the beach, from whence legend says the ghosts of dead mariners stand guard over the small inlet like gargoyles on the roof of a castle. The small band of men jogged down the hill, eager to shed some of their clothing and jump into the warm, crystal-clear water. Jack was still in awe of the scene when he placed his bags on a picnic table and removed shoes and socks. He tucked his wallet inside one of his shoes and walked down toward the water.

Straight ahead, holding a cloudless royal blue sky in place, he could see the Caribbean Sea. Water fowl dipped into the translucent greenish-blue water and swooped back into the air. Jagged, coral-covered rocks peeked out above the surface then quickly submerged again when the waves gently rolled over them on their way in to the shore. Wading into the water, Jack could see huge boulders not thirty feet in front of him, which seemed to separate the less than knee-deep water of the beach from the significantly deeper water beyond. The men realized that the beach really was not conducive to swimming, so they returned to the pavilion to don their footwear and explore the surrounding area. A short hike to the top of the cliffs afforded them a breathtaking view of the rocky coastline, the crystal-clear water splashing against the rocks a hundred feet beneath their feet. A completely ugly iguana lurked nearby, watching from beneath a shrub and a patch of grass as the strange, colorful creatures which had invaded his world laughed and talked and jumped around. Some of them approached the iguana, talking to it and trying to get it to move. The rest seemed to ignore it altogether.

From behind him, Jack heard a scream followed by quick, thudding footsteps. Thinking the iguana had finally had enough and had decided to attack, he quickly spun around to investigate, just in time to see one of his shipmates let out a yell and hurl himself over the cliff, plunging into the surf below. Jack's initial reaction was one of shock and wonder at the foolishness of his friend's actions—not even finding out the depth of the water that separated him from the sharp, jagged rocks beneath the surface before flinging himself off the cliff anyway and hoping for the best. Even so, once convinced that the sacrificial test-idiot had survived the plunge, one by one the rest of Jack's buddies raced along the plateau and hurled themselves over the cliff.

"Well, what the heck," Jack said to the silent iguana who hadn't budged an inch, "a chance to risk your life in a foreign communist country for a cheap, momentary thrill doesn't come along every day, now does it?" And with that, he backed up several paces, let out a yell of his own, and took a nervous running leap off the edge of the cliff.

The men in the water quickly discovered that the jumping had definitely been the easy part of the adventure. Besides the obvious difficulty of swimming in their combat boots, or even in their sneakers, they also faced the force of the uncooperative waves dragging them away from the shore. The waves would come in from the open sea and splash against the huge rocks between the men and the beach, then they would pull the men away from the shore as they receded to make way for the next incoming wave. And to make matters worse, once the men finally overcame the waves, there was the very real danger of getting smashed into the rocks by the next wave with enough force to cause severe cuts and abrasions from the razor-sharp barnacles and coral covering the entire surface of the rocks.

Everyone made it back to shore eventually, sporting only a few minor cuts and scrapes. Exhausted, they sat or lay down on the picnic tables to recover from what had turned out to be a much more physically demanding exercise than any of them had anticipated.

"And this we do for fun," Jack commented to himself, shaking his head and wiping away a small stream of blood oozing from a cut on his forearm.

After a rather short rest, hunger and thirst convinced them to gather their belongings and begin the hike back to the NEX complex, where a variety of foods and beverages would be available to them for a reasonable portion of their Navy wages.

Dinner for Jack consisted of a huge burger and a basket of greasy fries at the NEX restaurant. They all passed through the line, selected their desired sustenance, and chose a pair of tables along the edge of the central court to relax and consume their meals. Conversation during the meal was minimal as they attacked their food with passion, as is common to young men with an intense appetite and no young ladies around to slap them and demand that they use proper table manners.

The small group sat at their tables, suppressing belches and letting the food and the tropical breeze rejuvenate them in preparation for the night's activities. It was already getting dark, just after 2030 hours, and the dance club across the base was already hopping.

Jack declined their invitation to accompany them to the club, opting instead to stroll back to the ship and get a shower and some fresh clothes. Clubbing didn't hold much interest for him, especially since Megan wasn't there to go with him. "Yeah, and I sure wish she were here," Jack muttered to himself as he gathered his bags and turned to leave the NEX. He crossed the parking lot, hopped up onto the sidewalk, and began his trek back to the ship. He looked to his right as he again passed the bank of phone booths. All of them were still occupied by lonely sailors sending their love to someone at home on the other end of the line and sending their money to someone at the phone company at the end of the month. Jack sighed deeply and plodded on up the sidewalk.

As he came abreast of the last phone booth, he heard someone say, "I love you, too. Goodbye." The lonely sailor dropped the receiver back into its cradle and exited the booth.

Somehow, against the laws of science and physics, a phenomenon occurred then which scientists have yet to explain. An unseen and unknown force reached out from the telephone booth, grasping Jack's head like a farmer plucking a melon off the vine, and pulled it toward the booth. Jack could no more have resisted the force than he could have resisted gravity and refused to fall into the water when he had jumped off the cliff earlier that afternoon. Once the vacuum of the telephone booth had placed him directly in front of the telephone, Jack feared that his only means of escape would be to actually place a call, thereby feeding the fiber-optic monster the money it craved and possibly breaking its hold on him to gain his freedom. But who to call? Mom? No, she would just worry, possibly even have nightmares about the fiber-optic monster and fire up the church prayer chain to counter her son's psychotic episodes. "Well, I guess that only leaves Megan," he said. "She'll understand." He picked up the receiver and began punching numbers on the keypad. He shrugged his shoulders while the phone started to ring in Norfolk, Virginia. "What else could I do?" he said, resignedly. "When you're beat, you're beat." Two more rings, then his eyes closed, a smile lighting up his face. The tension drained from his body, relaxing him as the mere sound of her voice sent the blood coursing through his veins with renewed vigor, swelling his heart so that he could feel every single twinge of the muscle inside his chest. His mind emptied of all thoughts that didn't begin or end with Megan Gallagher, his surroundings fading away as though stagehands were clearing the stage after the final curtain call of an opera. Every sense came alive with the memory of Megan, sparked to life by the sound of her voice. He could smell her favorite perfume, feel her soft, blonde hair tickling his neck, feel her crushing embrace as she hugged him with all her might. "And all this just from hearing her voice," Jack thought to himself with a shake of the head and a sigh. "Man, I might actually explode when I see her again in person!"

"Hello…?" Megan repeated. "Is anyone there?"

"Hi, Megan," he said, finally getting a grip on himself. "It's Jack."

The call only lasted 23 minutes, but it was the best 23 minutes Jack had experienced since leaving the pier in Norfolk 27 days earlier.

~5~

Once again, as though they had never been near land at all, the *Mighty Miss'* sailed out across the open ocean, with nothing but water to be seen in any direction, even through the 'big eyes' on the signal bridge. The water was as smooth as it had been during their trip to Cuba the previous day, the air just as warm and humid. The blazing Caribbean sun had given in to the approaching darkness, leaving behind a residual heat that would slowly drift away as the night pressed on, only to be revitalized again as soon as morning returned. The hint of a virtually non-existent breeze was the only palpable result of the ship's lazy movement through the stillness of the night.

As usual, SM2 Jack Douglass could be found in his favorite place on the signal bridge, perched up on the forward bulkhead, only this time without a cup of coffee in his hand. All had been extremely quiet aboard the Miss' since their departure from Cuba that morning, though an elevated level of activity would hardly have made a difference to Jack. His thoughts had taken him to a world of his own, and Megan Gallagher was the sun around which that world rotated. He could no more have banished her from his mind than Mars or Pluto could banish the sun from their world simply by willing it to be so. The phone call he had made to Megan a few hours earlier kept replaying in his mind. He could hear it in his head as clearly as if he had recorded it and was replaying it through a set of headphones. The joyful contentment in her voice resounded in the auditorium of his mind like the passionate intonations of the Philharmonic Orchestra performing for the President at Carnegie Hall in New York City. If he closed his eyes, he could almost smell her intoxicating perfume…could almost hear her playful, impish giggling…could almost reach out and touch her beautiful face…

"'Union Jack' Douglass!"

"Hey, Phil!" Jack replied. "I have been waiting for you to come up. How's it going?"

"You called her, didn't you?" Phil asked, smiling like a street cop watching a perfectly healthy person exit his vehicle after parking in the "Handicapped Only" space at the supermarket.

"What?"

"You called her. While we were in GITMO, you called her."

"What are you talking about, Phil? I told you we were just going to write letters this time—"

"Yes, Jack, you did tell me that. But you called her, didn't you?"

"Aw, Phil, she has the sweetest voice," Jack admitted, only a little starry-eyed. "And we only talked for twenty minutes."

"You are pathetic, Jack. I knew you would cave," Phil chided, flashing a knowing grin.

"Hey, I didn't even go near the phones until I was on my way back to the ship tonight—just strolling along, minding my own business—then some nuke walked out of one of the phone booths right in front of me. What was I supposed to do? It sucked me right in, man. *Totally* not my fault," Jack explained.

"Uh-huh. Hey, it happens. What's a guy to do?" Phil agreed. "So, how is she doing? Everything going all right back in Norfolk?"

"Yeah, she is fine. Getting a little restless, I guess. Bored, maybe. Seems like she was looking forward to spending a lot of time with me, too, before we found out that I had to come back out here again. It's exciting and frustrating all at the same time. I finally meet a nice girl who I would really like to get to know better, and I can't seem to get enough time to do it. Letters are fine, sometimes very fine, but there is no comparison to being together. I can't see her eyes when I read her letters. Letters are just words. In conversation, I can learn just as much about her by listening to how she says what she says, and by looking at what her eyes are saying, as I can by hearing the words she is saying."

Phil nodded, expressing agreement and encouraging him to continue.

Jack paused. He was feeling many things inside, but he didn't quite know how to get them all out. He didn't really want to talk about Megan right then, but he wasn't sure which conversation he wanted to pursue. As if talking to Megan had not been emotional enough, they had talked a lot about the church—how the services had been going, what some of the messages had been about, how the Sunday school class was going. All of his new friends missed him, asked her to say "Hi" in her letters, and asked about him all the time. Jack felt an unexplainable tugging at his heart that he had never felt before. He thought it was just that he was missing Megan, but it was more than that. He thought it might be missing the fellowship he had found with his new friends, but it was more than that, too. There was something about that whole religion/church thing that was eating away at him. He had always reasoned that it was fine for his mother, if that was what she needed to feel important and to be happy, but he was doing just fine without it. He had lived a pretty fulfilling life up to now. He had been fairly popular in school, was doing well in his naval career, and had always had plenty of friends around him. He had had several girlfriends over the years, some 'serious', some not. Looking back over the years, he couldn't place his finger on any one thing that he had lacked. But now, suddenly, something seemed to be missing. He had never given much thought to his death, or what would happen after it, either to himself or in the world in general that would have to find a way to cope and exist without his presence in it. What legacy he would leave behind had never concerned him. When the time came, he would try to leave his children a little something, and enough for his wife to carry on, if she outlived him, but that was as far as he had taken it.

"I wasn't a bad person, just a useless one," Kirt Radford had said. He had also said that now he could go to bed feeling "...contented, joyful, and peaceful." Kirt's words kept gnawing at him. Jack didn't feel that way when he hit his pit at night. Even when everything was going well, he was restless inside. How could focusing all your energy on God make a person feel more content? Or joyful? Or peaceful? It didn't make any sense. What about Jack? If all his energy was focused somewhere else, who would take care of Jack? Not to sound like a selfish pig, but was that not a viable concern? What was the point of making yourself needy and having to rely on God or the church or your friends when you could do just fine by yourself? Would it not be better for everyone if people just took care of themselves? Lived their own lives, made their own way, steered their own ship? Why did God, if that was indeed who was getting at Jack, want him to make himself dependent on others? How could that possibly make Jack's life better? After all, people let you down. Always. No matter how much they may care, or how close you might be to them, eventually, people always let you down. So, why make them that important? Why intentionally make them a vital part of your existence? Why knowingly put yourself into a relationship where you had to rely on each other?

Wasn't religion for the weak-minded people? Those who couldn't make anything of themselves, so, in desperation, they jumped on the 'Jesus' bandwagon to give themselves a feeling of importance and an identity that they otherwise could never have achieved? Why would someone like Jack, or Kirt or Phil for that matter, who appeared to really have it all together, need to get into religion? Kirt had said that it was the relationship that was so important. Well, what did that mean? Praying for your food before you ate, and saying goodnight before you hit your pit? How do you have a relationship with a thing that isn't really there? I mean, Jack had never *seen* God, had he? It wasn't like he popped in for tea twice a month or anything. He was nothing more than an illusive 'spirit' thing, some lofty ideal that people who could find no meaning in their lives had conjured up for the sake of having something to identify themselves with; some link to something that could give them a sense of belonging. Well, that was just plain freaky. Like those people who have lost a spouse, but keep on setting the spouse's place at the dinner table and talk to him or her all the time. Those people were not right in the head, man. When their significant other had died, something in their noggin' had bought it, too. Jack didn't want to become one of those people.

But, then, what about his new church friends? None of them seemed mentally unstable. They didn't seem like freaks who's brain waves would be unable to cause a disturbance in a mud puddle. They were just regular, normal people. Jack loved them—loved being with them—he just couldn't understand them. He had always thought of himself as a pretty intelligent person. Not the brightest bulb in the chandelier, perhaps, but certainly able to cast his fair share of light. So, what was he missing? Some piece of the puzzle just wasn't fitting into place. There had to be something obvious that he wasn't seeing.

"I smell smoke, Jack," Phil said, pointing to his head. "What in the world are you thinking about, buddy? That look on your face is not lovesick for Megan anymore. What else did you guys talk about?"

"I am just trying to make some sense of all this church stuff," Jack said, obviously frustrated. Megan, he could deal with. In fact, missing her was part of the magic; part of what he enjoyed about having a girlfriend. Missing her when they were apart, experiencing the joy when they were reunited. But the church/God thing—that was irritating, and it just wouldn't go away.

"Ah," Phil replied. He nodded his head, knowing Jack would continue when he was ready. Then he began to pray. Silently, but fervently, he began to pray. He asked God first to give him wisdom, so that he could give Jack the direction and guidance that he needed to find his way to a saving knowledge of Jesus Christ. He asked God to send the Holy Spirit to speak to Jack, to make Himself real to him, to convict him of his sinful state and to draw him into a position of surrender where God could dispense his loving forgiveness and create a new life in the old, dirty soul of Mr. Jonathan (Jack) Douglass. Whatever needed to happen for Jack to finally understand his need for God, Phil prayed that it would be done.

Jack took a deep, cleansing breath, still unable to speak. There was so much turmoil inside of him, he didn't know where to start. He should have been elated, especially after the wonderful conversation he had had with Megan the previous evening, but he wasn't. He felt frustrated and edgy. Nothing tangible had changed in his life, except for the entrance of Megan, and that could, in no way, be construed as a negative change by any stretch of the imagination. Sure, he had acquired a few new friends, but even that had been nothing if not a positive development in his life. He could think of no significant event or circumstance that was now a part of his life, and had not been before, that should be causing him to feel like he was feeling.

He was certain that Phil would understand, would more than likely even be able to offer some advice or other assistance to help him figure it out, but he simply didn't know where to begin. It was as if his entire belief system had been challenged to a duel, and Jack was out of ammunition. He couldn't answer his own questions based on what he knew, or thought he knew, to be true.

"Phil, I think God is trying to tell me something," Jack blurted out, surprising even himself.

A pause.

"Hmm," Phil grunted. "What is he trying to say, Jack?"

"I don't know. That is the frustrating part."

"Well, when you say he is trying to tell you something, what do you mean? Can you hear something?"

"No, it's nothing like that-"

"Okay, is it a feeling? A renegade thought rattling around in your head?"

"No, it's—I don't know, Phil. I have just never felt like this before. I have always been very much in control of myself. Always been in charge. Always kept my feelings in check. I have worked very hard not to be a petty person, not to let insignificant things bother me. I have always been able to figure out my own emotions—you know, to understand what I was feeling at any given moment—and eventually even why I was feeling it, what had sparked it, and what would be the best way to deal with it. But now, all of a sudden, I can't figure out what is going on inside me. I can't place my finger on any significant change, but something is different, and it doesn't feel right. Something has changed, and I don't know what or how or why."

"Well, what does it feel like, Jack?" Phil prodded. "I mean, the feelings you are having, what do they remind you of?"

"It's sort of like when you leave the house, and you know you have forgotten something. For the life of you, you can't remember it at the time, but you just know you have missed something. Plus there is a restlessness; like maybe I have forgotten to do something that I was supposed to do. I don't get it, Phil. How come all of a sudden, everything is different? I should be feeling great, looking at how my life has been going lately, but I don't. I feel awful. Uncomfortable. Like the time period between 'You just wait until your father gets home' and the point when he actually gets home. Or the time period after you have passed a cop at ten miles per hour over the speed limit, after you have slowed to the posted limit, while you are waiting for the inevitable flashing lights to appear in your rear-view mirror."

Phil processed what Jack had said. "You mean, sort of... guilty? Perhaps not guilty of something specific, but just plain old guilty?" Phil offered.

Jack tossed the idea around. Just guilty, huh? Not necessarily of anything specific, but guilty. Nothing he could place his finger on, or admit to, or make restitution for, and yet guilty. "Hmmm...yeah, kind of." Another pause. "Yeah, that's pretty much it, Phil. So, what's the deal with that? Don't you have to DO something before you can feel guilty about it?" he asked.

"Jack, old buddy, I hate to tell you this, but you have just described the convicting work of the Holy Spirit on the heart of a lost soul."

Jack huffed out a breath. "Right, Phil. Come on—"

"Why is that so difficult for you to believe, Jack? Is that not possible? Does the fact that you don't understand something make it inherently *im*possible? If someone is completely ignorant of the laws of electricity and the flow of electrons, does that mean that their light switches won't work? They fail to understand it, so it can't be so? That's pretty arrogant, Jack. I would have thought that someone with your intelligence would have been a little more open-minded and... I don't know... *logical* about it."

"Hey, ease up, Phil! Sheesh!"

"Why 'ease up'? Just because we are talking about God and religion? Neither of us would let the other get away with that kind of narrow-minded, obtuse thinking on any other subject, so why should I let you get away with it on this one?" Phil asked. "Just think about it for a minute, Jack. I'm not trying to be a jerk, but I think you are ignoring a potential answer on the grounds that you really don't want that to be the answer. At least give equal consideration to every possibility.

"And one more thing: let's not consider my opinion 'preaching'. On any other topic, you would let me have my say. You would listen carefully, then you would weigh it in your own mind, probably against things you already knew, and decide if my ideas were reasonable or unreasonable. Once you had come to a conclusion, we would then logically discuss whether you had deemed my ideas to be reasonable or not, and why you took that particular stance."

Jack thought it over for a moment then conceded. "Fair enough, Phil. So, explain it to me."

"Love to!" Phil quipped. "Although, you have already described the first half of it very well by stating the symptoms of your discomfort. You said yourself that you have unusual feelings inside you that you have never felt before, or at least never felt without being able to point to a specific event or action that either definitely or most likely resulted in those feelings manifesting themselves. Yes?"

A nod.

"And you further stated that you can find no such event or action in your current life or in the recent past that could possibly have resulted in those feelings manifesting themselves. Yes?"

Another nod.

"And, knowing you as I do, I am confident that you have thoroughly and completely searched your own heart and mind, and if such a reason did exist, I am quite certain you would have found it. Therefore, I must by default assume and agree that there has been no such catalyst at work in your life. That leaves only one possible conclusion: the feeling is coming from within your own soul—your own heart, mind, and emotional center. Not only are you responsible for it, but also you alone have the power to remedy it."

"You see, Jack, that is the way we were created. Now, we have to assume, for the sake of this argument, that my perception of God is correct. If I am wrong, then there is no help for you. But, if I am right, then the solution is very simple. You need God, Jack. Although it is true that God loves you and deeply desires a fellowship-relationship with you, he doesn't need you. He does not *need* any of us. It is we who need him. God did create us so that he could fellowship with us and have a relationship with us, but that's only something he *desires*; it isn't something he *requires*. We, on the other hand, do require it. To live as fully functional human beings, the way we were created and intended to live, we need God to be an active part of our lives. You may have heard the phrase 'There is a God-shaped void in all of us, and only God can fill that void.' That is a completely true statement, Jack.

"It's like an engine. Take my little GMC pickup for example. When the engineers in Detroit designed it, they designed it to run on six cylinders. Six pistons, six combustion chambers, six spark plugs. Now, what if the line workers decided to only put in five spark plugs? What if all the other vehicles they made got six spark plugs, but all the GMC pickups were shipped out with only five? Let's say that I went to the lot, bought one, brought it home assuming that all was in order, and began driving it around. Would it work? Would I be able to get to school or work or the store? Of course I would. It may be a little choppy, but it would get me there. It might have only a fraction of the power it was meant to have, but it would still get me from place to place. Over time, I might even get used to it. Might not even notice it anymore. But then, what if my neighbor had bought a new vehicle, too. What if he had bought the same kind, a GMC pickup, but his ran as smooth as a purring kitten? What if his could take off from a stoplight and be several blocks down the road before mine even got up to speed? Holy cow, all of a sudden, I see that there is something wrong with my pickup! They are the same kind, the same make, model and year, nearly the same manufacture date, but his runs so much better! What is the deal? Did I get into a wreck with mine and mess it up? No. Did I do something to the engine to make it function improperly? Of course not. So what is the deal? Well, let's just keep an eye on his pickup and see if we can see anything different between the two. They look the same—have the same tires, the same sunroof, the same steering wheel. Okay, let's ask him. So, I ask him what makes his run so much better than mine, and he tells me about the missing spark plug. We lift our hoods and, sure enough, his has six spark plugs and mine has only five!! How can this be?!? We get into a discussion about our trucks, and it turns out that, even though they are identical in every other way, without that sixth spark plug, mine has been deficient since the day I bought it. Somewhere along the way, someone else had shown my neighbor what his had been missing, and he had installed a sixth spark plug. The results had been astounding—practically creating an entirely new vehicle from a deficient crippled one.

"So, now I have figured out the problem: a missing spark plug. Now, what should I do about it? How can I fix it? Well, what if I tried to put a new head gasket into the spark plug hole? Would that help out my situation? No way. How about a new thermostat? A cam shaft? A fuel intake sensor module? No, none of that will help. Even a spark plug of the incorrect size or type wouldn't help. To make my engine complete, I will have to install the specific part it is lacking.

"And that is how it is with God. Every one of us, whether we want to admit it or not, was created to have a relationship with God. If we don't have that relationship, something is lacking, and we will never be what we were originally intended to be without it. Oh, we may function fairly well, may do okay by ourselves, but at some point, we will notice that other people are in better shape than we are. Other people have something that we don't. Other people seem to be getting through life with a lot more joy and peace than we are. And, just like with the engine, nothing else can fill the void like God can. Booze, drugs, or illicit sex can't do it. Even an innocent and 'good' replacement like a good job, money, or a family can't do it. Even becoming active in a local church can't do it. Doing 'godly' things is not the same as cultivating a *relationship* with God. And that is the only thing that can cure the symptoms that you just described to me, Mr. Jack Douglass."

Phil sat back against the bulkhead upon which Jack was perched. He tipped up his cup and took a swig of his cooling coffee. Lucky for him, he didn't mind cold coffee.

Jack sat up. "Okay, Phil, for argument's sake, let's say that you are right, that my problem is a lack of God. Well, why now? After all these years, why all of a sudden? Why have I not always felt this way? How come, out of nowhere, God has to tell me this now?"

"Simple, Jack," Phil started to explain.

"Somehow, I knew it would be…"

"Look at Adam and Eve. They were the first to have your problem. There they were in the Garden of Eden, going about their daily business, when Satan deceived them and they sinned. Do you remember what they actually did when they sinned?"

"Sure," Jack answered, "they disobeyed God."

"Yes, but how? What did they actually *do*?"

"They ate fruit from a forbidden tree, right?" Jack said.

"Exactly. Do you remember which tree?"

"Not really…"

"It was the Tree of the Knowledge of Good and Evil. And do you recall what one of the immediate results of eating the fruit was?" Phil asked.

"Yeah, they realized they were naked and they hid."

"Right," Phil agreed. "The Bible says that their eyes were opened, and they saw that they were naked. You see, Jack, before they ate the fruit, they didn't know the difference between good and evil. It was only after they had eaten the fruit that they could see the difference. After they had disobeyed God's commands and eaten the fruit, they realized that they were in a sinful state. It is the same way with you. Tell me, Jack, what have you been doing lately, say, the last month or so, that you haven't been doing for many years?"

"Well, keeping my answer in the same context as this conversation, I would have to say going to church," Jack volunteered.

"Exactly. And, have any of the messages gotten to you? Have you seen or heard anything at the church or with the church people that has spoken to your heart, in either a pleasant or an unpleasant way?"

"Well, some things that Kirt Radford said have been on my mind a lot recently. Why?"

"Jack, you are eating the fruit, man," Phil explained. "You have gained some knowledge of God and of his ways, and the Holy Spirit is therefore convicting you, or possibly *convincing* you, that you are in a sinful state and that you need to do something about it. You need to do some business with God and get it taken care of."

"Yeah, but Phil..." Jack began, but Phil cut him off.

"Yes, Jack?" he invited with raised eyebrow. "Yeah, but, what?"

"It's just a lot to digest all at once, man."

"Very true, Jack. Very true. But, it's really not all that complicated, either. You just have to look at the facts."

They sat in silence on the signal bridge of the USS *Mississippi* CGN-40, Jack Douglass deep in thought, Phil Prescott deep in prayer.

Above them, filling the sky immediately around the signal bridge of the great American warship, an unseen battle was taking place. The principalities and powers of darkness, evil demons and devils from the pit of Hell itself who had been deceiving Jack Douglass for years, were fighting to retain control of his immortal soul, while a legion of mighty angels sent down from Heaven were slowly subduing them, forcing them to release their sinister death-grip on Jack's mind... his heart... his will... his very soul...

In the small town of Sandusky, Michigan, Connie Douglass knelt beside her bed, as she did every night at about this time, to offer prayers to her Savior. Tonight, however, her prayers were different. She didn't follow her normal routine of praise and thanksgiving followed by worship, then intercession and petitions, then more praising. Tonight, her heart was heavy and she was scared. Something was wrong with her son. She had been sitting in the living room, reading her Bible and preparing for the Sunday school lesson she would have to teach the next Sunday, when a spirit of oppression had come over her like a thick quilt falling across a bed. She had felt stifled—afraid—and she began to pray. She nearly ran into the bedroom, dropping to her knees so quickly that it should have hurt a woman of her age, and began sobbing into her bedspread. She pleaded with God to come to her aid, not knowing what was wrong, but feeling that only God would be able to help her.

Suddenly, her small bedroom was filled with a blazing light. Her head jerked up involuntarily at the change of illumination she could sense even though her eyes had been closed and covered with her hands. There, in the corner of her room, hovering above the antique rocking chair, was the figure of a man. He was dressed in a white gown, his left hand gripping the handle of a glistening sword which was tucked into a bejeweled gold belt around his waist. He had no face that she could discern, but he had eyes that were glowing with the brightness that had illuminated her bedroom. His other hand was raised up to point at her, the index finger extended.

"Pray for Jack," the voice commanded, "for he is in great danger!" Then it disappeared in a brilliant flash of light, leaving Connie Douglass alone again in her bedroom.

Fear gripped her. Terrified, she cried out to the Lord. The sobbing became deeper, the fear greater. Connie prayed as she had never prayed before, that God would protect her beloved son, and give him the strength he needed to get through whatever was happening to him. As soon as she was physically able, she snatched the telephone from its cradle on the lamp stand and dialed the familiar number of her pastor. His wife answered, which was who she had wanted to talk to anyway. Between sobs, she quickly relayed the story of what had taken place and what the visitor had told her. She hung up the telephone, knowing that within minutes, most of the ladies in the church would join her in intercessory prayer for Jack. She returned to her praying, pleading to God with every ounce of her being.

In Norfolk, Virginia, Kirt Radford slammed on his brake

pedal, locking the wheels of his Ford F-150 pickup and causing it to skid off the road. There in front of him, not ten feet away, a man stood in the middle of the road. Even though it was after eight-thirty at night, the blinding light from his eyes made the roadway and the surrounding fields brighter than noon on the lightest day of the year. The man stood squarely in the road, one hand on top of the other and resting on the handle of a glistening double-edged sword. He looked straight at Kirt. He lifted the massive sword like it was a toothpick, pointing it at Kirt's chest.

"Pray for Jack!" he commanded, "for he is in great danger!" Then the man raised his sword toward the sky and disappeared in a flash of light to rival a space shuttle liftoff at Cape Canaveral, Florida.

Kirt slammed the gearshift into reverse, cranked the steering wheel all the way to the left, and punched the accelerator pedal. The truck lurched back onto the road, its front end swinging around to face back toward the farm. Dropping the gearshift back into drive, Kirt again stomped on the accelerator pedal, causing the old truck to spring into action. He headed back to his parents' farm, fish-tailing and slinging gravel in a rooster-tail behind him.

He spun into his parents' driveway, swerved around their car, then quickly stopped the truck, threw open the door and leapt from the vehicle. In six steps, he reached the back door, which he yanked open and ran into the house. His startled parents looked at him in alarm, wondering what could possibly be the matter.

"Mom! Dad!" he yelled, coming to a halt in the kitchen where they both looked at him inquisitively.

"My goodness, Kirt! What in the world—" Milly began, but Kirt cut her off.

"It's Jack!" he nearly yelled. "Pray for Jack!" he pleaded, as tears were beginning to form in his eyes.

They needed no more encouragement. All three of them dropped to their knees right there in the kitchen, leaning their elbows on the old chairs and covering their faces with their hands. They praised God for his wisdom, thanked him for speaking to Kirt, and pleaded with all their hearts that he would take care of Jack.

After the first ten minutes of fervent prayer, Kirt told his parents about the visitor he had seen in the road who had told him to pray for Jack, because he was in great danger. He also took a minute to call Laura Wright and quickly relay the story, to which she reacted by calling the rest of their small group of friends and getting all of them to pray as well. Then he resumed his place at the kitchen chair.

"I gotta take a leak," Jack announced as he jumped down from his perch. "Back in a bit."

"All right," Phil said. "You know, I could use a Coke. You want one?"

"Sure," Jack said. "If you're buying, I'm drinking!"

"Works for me," Phil said. "See ya in a few." He presumed that Jack just wanted some time to himself, which was fine with him—and probably even a good idea, given the subject matter they had been discussing. The pop run would give them both some time to reflect on their discussion thus far and to formulate additional questions or comments for the conversation that would almost certainly continue upon their collective return to the signal bridge.

Jack was in the signal shack talking to the bridge on the squawk box when Phil returned nearly half an hour later. He finished his conversation, made a couple of notations in the log book, then motioned for Phil to join him on the weather deck. They walked over to Jack's perch and popped open their beverages, each taking a couple of healthy swigs.

Phil looked at Jack, attempting to assess his mental state by his outward appearance. He looked defeated. He looked like a man who was accustomed to having it all together, being in control of any situation life threw at him, and always having the right answers; but who at the moment had no idea how he got where he was and no more of an idea of how to get himself back to normal.

Jack was just plain confused. Could Phil be right? Could Kirt and the others be right? Could a relationship with God really be that important? Jack wanted to just blow it all off and not worry about it, but he couldn't. His mind was racing, his heart was beating hard, and he couldn't shake the feeling of warmth that was overtaking him, making him sweat in the cool breeze of the evening. Not a good or a comfortable warmth, but a painful warmth, coming from the inside out. His chest felt tight; breathing was almost difficult. Well, if this was God, he was certainly making his point clearly enough. But still, Jack doubted. He just wasn't sure he could give control of his life over to an unseen thing; some celestial 'being' that was supposedly up there somewhere, watching from the sky as humans fumbled through life trying to live up to its standards.

Phil set his pop on the bulkhead. "Well, what do you think, Jack?" he asked. "You aren't the kind of person I feel the need to tread lightly around. I've shared the Gospel with other people before, and I've had to be very sensitive to them, so that I wouldn't come on too strong and freak them out. But I don't feel like I have to worry about that with you. For one thing, I like to think that we have a somewhat stronger relationship than your average friends do, given the length and depth of most of our discussions out here. Also, I think your logical approach to life gives you the ability to process information apart from your emotional reactions to it.

"So, tell me where you're at, buddy. What are you thinking?" Phil challenged.

Jack shifted in his seat. The heaviness he was feeling weighted him down like a lead suit. "I just don't know, Phil," he said at last. "What you said makes sense, but still, I just don't understand it. It doesn't make sense that it should work that way."

"Well, Jack, that part I can't explain to you. You will have to figure that one out for yourself. But, I will tell you this: I don't understand it either. I don't know why God does the things he does, and I don't know why he set things up the way he did. I don't understand all is methods or requirements, and I don't pretend to be an authority on the subject. However, this I do know: since I turned my life over to Jesus and let him have control of it, I have never been happier, never been more fulfilled, and never been more at peace. Jack, I don't particularly like not having all the answers either, because I like to be in control and I like to have a complete understanding of anything I am involved in. But God has not deemed it necessary to ask my opinion on how he set the world in place, and he has not seen fit to include me in his strategy for redeeming mankind. I can't explain to you the process, I can only testify to you about the results. It works, Jack. It's true. God is real, Jesus is alive, and that's the only way for you to get out of your current situation.

"Besides, Jack, what have you got to lose? What is it that is really and truly holding you back from accepting God's gift of forgiveness and a new life?"

Jack thought for a moment. "I honestly don't know, Phil. I am just so torn up inside."

"Then put a stop to it, Jack. Put the devil in his place and let God take control. Let God remove the sin from your heart and replace it with joy and peace."

With a screech and a howl of pain, the last demon relinquished its hold on Jack Douglass' mind and retreated into the darkness. The mighty angels of Heaven surrounded Jack, waving their swords in the air and singing praises to God. They worshipped with songs, dancing, and shouts of joy, watching the haze clear from Jack's mind like the smoke from a burning pile of leaves being whisked away by the wind. One of the angels broke away from the others, swooping in close and coming to rest on the perch next to Jack. His voice boomed like thunder when he leaned into Jack's ear and spoke.

"You no longer need to fear, Jack Douglass. The enemy has been defeated; you are now free to make your own decision. Choose God and live. He sent us to free you from the grasp of the enemy; now we can remain only if you request it of God. The enemy we can battle, but the sovereign will of man we cannot cross. The choice is now yours alone, Jack Douglass. Choose God and live."

With that, he returned to the circle of angels and joined in the chorus of praise still being offered up to God.

"Jack, are you okay?" Phil asked.

The distant, glassy look in Jack's eyes had startled him. Jack could see Phil talking to him, but he couldn't hear the words. In his mind, he saw himself. He also saw Jesus; the Jesus his mother had always told him about, but whom he had politely ignored as if it were so much religious babble. He saw Jesus being whipped and beaten, cringing and groaning with the pain, but never accusing his tormentors. He saw the ruthless soldier slam a ring of woven thorns on top of Jesus' head, piercing the skin and causing blood to trickle down into his face and eyes. He could hear the angry shouts of the crowd as they ridiculed him, cursed him, chanted with approval and satisfaction at his cruel, torturous death. He could hear the soldiers mocking him, teasing him as they slapped him and kicked him and spit in his face. The roar of the crowd was nearly deafening, their viciousness and anger frightening.

Then his mind flashed to the hill where the crosses had been prepared. He saw the soldiers push Jesus to the ground beside the largest of the crosses. They kicked him over onto his back, rolling him onto the cross. Stretching his arms out away from him, they took nails and, placing them over his wrists, drove them through his wrists and into the rough wood of the horizontal beam of the cross. This time, he screamed in agony from the intense pain, but still he never accused. The roar of the crowd became more intense with each swing of the hammers. They hurled insults at him, taunting him to save himself as he claimed to have saved others.

Suddenly, the scene became silent. In slow motion, Jack could still see the hammers rise above the soldiers' heads then come down with a crash, each one sending a spurt of blood into the air from Jesus' wrists. He could see the merciless faces of the crowd contort with rage as they shouted vile insults at him. But Jesus didn't seem to even notice them. He looked over at Jack, his eyes piercing Jack to the depths of his soul. Then his face changed. His eyes became eyes of love. He lifted his head and began to speak. "I am put to death so that you may have life, Jack Douglass. I am here in your place, to pay the penalty for your sins and to make a ransom for your soul. I have come that you may have life, and have it to the full."

"Jack!" Phil repeated. "What is going on, buddy? Are you okay?"

The scene before Jack's mind vanished; his heart filled with grief, tears flowed from his eyes. Finally, he understood. Jesus had died for *him*. He wasn't merely a fairy tale or a crutch for people to push their problems onto, He was real. He was alive. And He loved Jonathan (Jack) Douglass enough to endure agony beyond comprehension simply to save his soul and redeem him back into a relationship with God. Jack's heart was filled with awe, reverence, guilt, shame, and a host of other feelings he couldn't begin to list.

Jack grabbed Phil's shoulders and looked directly at his face. "I just saw Jesus!" he exclaimed through his tears. "Phil, I just saw Jesus! He told me that He came and died so I could have life. I saw Him on the cross, Phil. I saw Him getting beaten by the soldiers, just like those stories I heard when I was a kid, but a lot more gruesome. He looked right at me, Phil. He talked to me and called me by my name."

"Wow, Jack, that is amazing," Phil agreed, awed by his Savior's work.

"Ain't that the truth!" Jack agreed. "Phil, I need to pray. Will you pray with me?" Jack asked.

"Absolutely," Phil said, already praying and praising God in his heart.

With that, Jack closed his eyes and called upon God. Phil silently joined him in prayer, asking God to make Himself real to Jack and to cleanse his heart.

Jack wept to himself, wiping his eyes on his shirtsleeve. He didn't know what to say, so he simply asked God to help him. He admitted that he had been living life on his own terms, completely leaving God out of the picture. He had not been a bad person, but, like Kirt, he had been a useless one. He didn't want to continue leading a life with no direction, with no purpose. He wanted what Kirt and Phil had been talking about. He wanted the peace and the joy and the contentment. And, however it was possible, he wanted a relationship with God. He repented of his sins, vowing to change his life to meet God's standards. He asked God to cleanse his heart from sin and to fill it with His Spirit.

God happily granted his request. Immediately, Jack's guilt and shame disappeared. The tears that flowed from his eyes were a living metaphor, paralleling the blood of Jesus that purged the sin out of his soul. He felt an inner peace like he had never imagined possible. This time, the warmth that he felt was like hot chocolate in front of the fireplace and a plate of fresh cookies. The joy that he felt came all the way from his toes, filling his body until he thought he would burst from the intensity of it. He leaned back on the bulkhead, basking in God's presence like a crocodile sunning himself on a rock, enjoying the peacefulness of having his sins forgiven and his soul purified.

Meanwhile, in the sky above the *Mighty Mississippi*, the legion of angels that had been fighting for Jack's soul joined in a victorious chorus of praise to God. They flew back and forth across the sky like shooting stars or bolts of lightening, swinging their swords and shouting a victory cry. Sparks trailed behind them like the train of a bridal gown, lighting up the sky like a million gigantic sparklers on the Fourth of July. As if in answer to their shouts, the sky suddenly opened up and all of Heaven joined in the celebration. The glory of God filled the sky, as hundreds of thousands of angels and heavenly beings worshipped God, singing praises to Him and dancing before His throne. The musicians played their instruments with passion, glorifying God with their songs. The singers raised their voices, singing praise to God and worshipping Him. The thunderous roar of adulation was deafening, echoing throughout the Heavens with more force than the loudest heavy metal rock band could ever hope to create.

Jesus stood, and the celebration fell silent. A smile came across His lips, and His face shone like a hundred suns. He extended His hands out in front of Him, His palms facing up. He curled and uncurled His fingers twice, signaling for the singing and praising to continue. The volume increased until He held one of His hands palm out, in a 'halt' signal. The heavenly host quietly continued chanting a rhythmic exaltation to God. Jesus let His hands fall down by His side and looked down at His Father, who returned His smile and nodded.

Jesus looked back out in front of Him to the assembled masses, then off to His right, to an enormous golden table situated atop an enormous elevated platform, upon which rested an equally enormous golden book.

Eight winged cherubim, twelve feet tall and proportionately sized, surrounded the platform, standing equidistant from each other and facing away from the great platform. One stood at each of the four corners, and one stood in the center of each side. They maintained their posts at a position of relaxed attention, wings tucked neatly behind their backs, legs shoulder-width apart, feet planted firmly on the floor around the platform. Each had both hands wrapped around the handle of a blazing, fiery sword, which he held out in front of his face at arm's length, perpendicular to the floor and pointing straight upward. Across their chests, they wore a meshed sash made of pure silver and dotted with precious gemstones, except for the Captain of the Guard, whose sash was a mesh of pure gold inlaid with diamonds. He stood in the center of the front side of the platform facing the throne. Behind the cherubim, seven marble steps led up each side of the platform, giving it the appearance of the bottom half of one of the great pyramids of Gaza.

At the top of the structure, the seventh step became a marble platform measuring fifty feet square. It held a golden table measuring forty feet square, which in turn held a book whose cover and binding measured thirty feet square when laid open. The tabletop itself was a slab of pure gold, unmarked on its top but intricately designed around the sides and down the four legs which supported it. At each corner of the tabletop, a diamond the size of a basketball rested in prongs that looked like shortened canoe paddles.

Jesus began to descend the steps from His throne, head held high, pride in His eyes like an Olympic champion leaving the presentation ceremony after receiving a gold medal. He walked confidently across the floor to the foot of the guarded structure. The Captain of the Guard snapped to attention as He approached, then sheathed his sword and bowed down onto one knee, shouting an order for his small detail to do likewise. Jesus nodded and ascended the stairs. He walked over to the table, reaching out to open the book. "The Book of Life" was the imprinted title on the cover, which Jesus lifted, swung open, and set down carefully onto the other side of the table. He flipped through about a third of the ancient parchment pages until He came to the one on which the writing seemed to stop. He closed His eyes, then clenched one of His fists. Blood began to bubble out of the nail scar in His wrist and trickle down His hand to His index finger, which He had stretched out to a point to receive the small flow of blood. When the blood reached the tip of His finger, He bent down over the book, and used His finger like a fountain pen to write "Jonathan James Douglass" with His own blood on the first available space.

Immediately, the blood on His hand disappeared. Jesus lifted the book in His hands, holding it open for the host of Heaven to see. The blood which had formed the name of the most recent addition to the Book of Life was still bright red, and the cheers that erupted from the assembled crowd would have deafened every human being on the face of the Earth, had they been allowed to hear it. Jesus shut the book, replacing it on its table, and returned to His throne at the right hand of God. The cherubim guard drew their swords and returned to their posts around the platform holding the Book of Life.

The heavenly beings continued their celebration, singing and shouting for joy, for a sinner's soul had just been saved. There was a new member in the family of God, and, just as humans rejoice at the birth of a baby, so Heaven was rejoicing at the rebirth of a lost soul.

Milly Radford leaned back against the cupboard door in the kitchen of their old farmhouse. Kirt and Tom both looked up, finally feeling released from the burden to pray for Jack. They all felt a peace come over them, thanking them for being faithful and encouraging them that they had done well. They joined in prayer one more time, this time in thanksgiving for the deliverance that they knew Jack had experienced.

A few minutes later, the phone rang. Laura informed Kirt

that she felt a peace about Jack, that whatever had befallen him had been taken care of. Kirt thanked her, confirmed that he also had no idea what it was all about, and hung up the phone.

In Sandusky, Michigan, Connie Douglass crawled up onto her bed, exhausted. The pile of damp tissues beside her testified to the emotion with which she had interceded for her son over the last thirty minutes. Finally, however, she felt at peace. She didn't know what type of danger her son had been in, only that it had passed. She knew that he was okay and that he was in God's hands. As soon as she could regain enough strength to get up from the bed, she would write him a letter relaying her story and asking him what it had all been about.

* * *

Jack Douglass lay in his pit that night, finally feeling at peace. The intense emotional high of the early evening had faded slightly, allowing Jack to attach a logical explanation to what had happened between him and God. Not that he was trying to reason it away, but rather to base his conversion and subsequent change of focus on logic, which he knew to be sound and trustworthy, rather than on emotion, which he knew to be fickle and untrustworthy.

Phil had advised him that he may experience a myriad of emotions and feelings over the next few days, possibly questioning the validity of what he had experienced. The enemy had lost the battle for Jack's soul, and he would not be happy about it. He would also be quite reluctant to give up on it. He would alter his tactics from merely encouraging Jack to continue an existence of complacency and self-reliance to an offensive campaign of outright deceit and manipulation. He would attempt to cause Jack to doubt the validity of his recent conversion. He would tell him that he had imagined it all, or part of it, or that it was nothing more than an emotionally charged, hype-driven reaction to talking to Megan on the phone, having no basis in reality and having no net effect on the final destination of his eternal soul. It wasn't really necessary for him to change his life, for he wasn't a bad guy to begin with. He had just fallen victim to the loneliness and isolation of being underway, where people can get sucked in to schemes more easily in the nether-world of the Navy deployment than they ever would while on land. He would throw every trick he had at Jack, attempting to reclaim his soul for the kingdom of darkness. And, he would be patient. He would wait until Jack was vulnerable. He would bide his time until Jack let his guard down, in the middle of some trial or difficulty, and then he would whisper evil lies into his ears, trying to convince him that the Christian life was too difficult for him to live. Too demanding. Too humbling. Not worth the effort.

What the enemy didn't seem to realize, however, was exactly how stubborn Jack Douglass could be. Phil had listed several Scripture verses that would prove to Jack that his experience had been real, and others that detailed the plan of salvation, the necessity of it, and the resulting requirements and benefits of it. He had said that when circumstances turn less favorable, and Jack didn't *feel* like a Christian any more, to look up the verses, because the facts never changed. But Jack just kept remembering the face of Jesus and the love in His eyes when He had looked deep into Jack's own eyes and had called him by name. He didn't think that *that* was something he would soon forget, deceptive evil prince of darkness or not.

And the logic of the situation was this: Jesus had died so that Jack could live. Even if he hadn't known that from the Bible training of his youth, Jesus had said so Himself. Jesus had paid the price of redemption that Jack's sinful nature required, so that Jack could live a life free of that burden. His ticket to Heaven had been bought with the blood of Jesus, extracted from his body with whips and nails and a crown of thorns. And, not only was Jack's salvation sure, but that same power that raised Jesus from the dead was available to Jack to help him live his life for Jesus every day. He had felt the presence of God and the power of the Holy Spirit. He believed that the grace of God that had saved his soul was also powerful enough to get him through any situation the enemy might throw at him. So Jack slept, his mind and his body peacefully at rest.

~6~

The next evening, while again on watch on the signal bridge, Jack began to write a letter to Megan. He had been too excited to concentrate on writing the night before, but the story of his conversion was something he definitely wanted to share with her as soon as possible. In spite of his enthusiasm, however, he realized the need to be mindful of the way he presented it to her. He had grown up in a churchgoing family and had at least been exposed to much of what he had typically referred to as 'religious theories and ideals,' but Megan had had neither the good fortune of receiving solid religious training as a child nor the inclination to seek out such knowledge as an adult. Therefore, he would have to be very careful how he relayed to her the story of his conversion, detailing exactly what it meant to him and what it would mean to them. He would essentially be tasked with explaining to her the entire plan of salvation, beginning with the Fall of Man in the Garden of Eden and the resulting entrance of sin into the world, and proceeding to the sacrificial death of Jesus that paid the penalty for sin, hence redeeming mankind back into a right relationship with God.

Jack spent most of the 12-hour watch working on his letter to Megan. He began it apologetically, realizing that, though they had briefly passed over the subject of the existence and/or significance of God over the past few weeks, they had never had any in-depth discussions about it, so he didn't know the extent of her knowledge on the subject. He apologized for boring her with details that she may already be aware of, but explained that, just in case she was not already aware of them, she would need to have that knowledge as a prerequisite to understanding both the gravity of what had happened to him on Friday evening, and the reason for his subsequent change of perspective. He carefully but clearly wove his way through the plan of salvation, throwing in as many Bible verses as he could remember or could locate quickly. He concluded the letter by telling her about his experience of Friday evening, relaying as best he could the feelings he felt and the changes he underwent. He encouraged her to talk to Kirt Radford about any questions she may have, and promised to go over the whole letter in detail with her, if she wanted him to, as soon as he returned, whenever that might be.

After being relieved from his watch, Jack stuffed the letter into an envelope and dropped it into the ship's mailbox, knowing that it wouldn't go out until Monday at the earliest, because no mail helicopters were scheduled to arrive until Monday morning. He prayed that Megan would receive the letter with an open mind, then he slapped the metal door shut and walked down the passageway toward his berthing compartment.

The announcement had come over the 1MC announcing circuit right before the end of the second workday after the *Mississippi*'s departure from Cuba. The XO had informed the men that CINCLANTFLT (Commander-In-Chief, Atlantic Fleet), in recognition of their superior performance in the case of the boarding of the private yacht *Rosa de la Mañana*, had authorized the crew of the USS *Mississippi* to enjoy an extended stay at the port of call of their choosing within a reasonable distance of their operational theater in the Caribbean Sea. The men were asked to fill out ballots expressing their top three choices and turn them in to their divisional chiefs at Quarters the following morning.

The men were excited, to say the least. It was common for them to visit a liberty port after the first two or three weeks of a deployment, then about every three weeks after that. On this trip, however, they had already been out for three weeks without a port visit, and due to the unusual scheduling of their current deployment, there were no concrete plans to schedule a port visit as of yet. The brief stop in GITMO was the closest thing they had had to a port visit, even though it was unscheduled and only an overnight stop. As a result, the announcement was received with great enthusiasm by the crew, and they talked of little else for most of the day. Even the officers were all but campaigning, trying to sway the votes of their shipmates to the port they most wished to visit.

"San Juan, Baby!!" one sailor would say. "The streets are lined with bars and dance clubs. Cheap rum and lots of girls!"

"Nah, Barbados, man. That's where we need to go. You've never seen more beautiful women..."

"No way!! It's Jamaica, mon! That's where you'll be findin' the beauties, mon. The beautiful women swaying to the steel drum rhythms, mon. Make a young boy go half out of his mind, I tell you..."

"Come on, y'all! Ain't no place better'n St. Thomas! Lots of good 'ole American boys down there. They speak English, and you don't have to try and figgur out how much a blasted peso is worth!"

"Pipe down, you dumb hillbilly! Give you a jug of moonshine and a coon dog, and you'd be happy pulling in anywhere. Let those of us with a little taste make the decision."

"Oh, yeah, and where'd you wont to pull in, Mister fancy-pants? Some dumb opry house or a wine-tastin' place? Well, yee-haw, bring it on! Jes' pour me some home-made watermelon wine in a dixie cup and git outta my way."

"You are hopeless, you know."

"Yee-haw."

"Hey, guys, how about Cartegena? I've heard that's a really fun port."

"Right, Bonehead, we just assisted in busting and confiscating a yacht with a million bucks worth of Colombian cocaine on it. I don't imagine anyone in Colombia would have a problem with our ship pulling in for an extended liberty visit. I don't know about you, but I don't really want to go out dancing wearing a flack jacket and bringing along a police escort."

"Oh. Yeah. I didn't think about that."

And so it went, from one end of the ship to the other, each man convinced that he had the only reasonable opinion about which port would be the best one to visit.

The senior officers and chiefs kept their opinions to themselves, chuckling at their subordinates and pleased that they had something to occupy their minds other than ship's business. Most of them had been to all of the ports in question multiple times anyway, so it didn't make much of a difference to them where they went. The fact that they were finally getting a liberty port where they and their men could blow off some steam was good enough for them. They would let the junior men decide exactly where it was to be.

The XO's voice boomed out of the 1MC announcing circuit speakers, informing the crew that their request for an extended port visit to Sint Maarten, a small tropical island in the French West Indies, had been approved and would commence the following Thursday morning. The votes had been cast and counted Wednesday morning, the request made Thursday morning, and permission had been granted Friday morning. The crew was ecstatic, even those who had voted for a different port, simply because a taste of freedom was imminent. Whether they had voted for Sint Maarten or not, they still knew that within the week, they would be walking on dry land. Land that didn't move beneath their feet. Floors and walls that didn't pitch and sway with the changing moods of the sea. They would be able to go to a restaurant of their own choosing, order whatever food they desired, prepared especially for them in the specific manner they requested, and brought to them by a cheerful and hopefully attractive female waitress. That was something to get excited about. Even though there were still six days until they would arrive at Sint Maarten, the morale of the ship made a drastic jump up the positive end of the scale.

Being underway for any length of time can be a very difficult situation to deal with, and as the length of time away from home increases, so does the degree of unrest experienced by the crew. However, it is made markedly more frustrating when there is no definite mission completion date given to the crew. Even an estimated time of return, or a definitive liberty port schedule would make a significant difference in the morale of the men. They needed something to which they could look forward. Even though there would still be drills, still be training, and still be mundane tasks to perform on a daily basis, they would at least be able to find one positive speck on the distant horizon of their minds if they were given a specific point in time to which they could look forward with positive anticipation. Whatever a liberty port might mean to each of them, they now had a common motivation and a common goal to work toward. For some, it would be the abundance of alcoholic libations available in the local restaurants, bars, and dance clubs. For others, it would include the company of one of the local ladies, whether voluntarily or for a fee. For still others, it would be nothing more than getting away from the ship, seeing a foreign land, enjoying the local cuisine, and merely hanging out with friends someplace outside of the gray, steel walls of the *Mighty Mississippi*. And for most, it would mean a chance to find a telephone and get in touch with family and loved ones back home in the States. This time, Jack decided, he had news to share with friends and family that was important enough to merit a series of telephone calls, regardless of the telephone bills that would show up in his name a month later.

From one end of the *Mississippi* to the other, there was a flurry of activity over the next several days. The Store Keepers' Mates in Main Supply were busily arranging for a stores onload to take place shortly after the ship got into port in Sint Maarten. The Supply Petty Officers from the various divisions aboard the ship inventoried their own supplies and put in their divisional replenishment requests so that all of the necessary items could be ordered at the same time and delivered while they were in port.

As was common among the khakis, lists of items that needed to be attended to prior to entering port were generated and passed down the chain of command until the blue-shirts knew exactly what needed to be accomplished to alleviate a delay of liberty on the first day in Sint Maarten. It was a useful motivational tool for the khakis, since the mood aboard ship had become rather apathetic with respect to ship beautification and routine equipment maintenance.

On the personal side, blue-shirts and khakis alike were digging their civilian clothes out of their steaming lockers, those possessing a higher degree of vanity so that they could be properly ironed prior to use, and others so that they could be at the head of the line to get off the ship for Liberty Call. They retrieved their civilian shoes from the depths of their steaming lockers, located their stashes of cologne and after shave lotion, and checked the status of their wallets. Soon, the ATMs in the main H-passageway would have long lines of men waiting to reclaim whatever pre-determined sum had been automatically deducted from their paychecks and deposited in the Disbursing Office ATM records over the past few weeks.

The small ship's store would probably sell out of camera film and suntan lotion as men prepared to capture their memories on film for ease in relaying liberty port stories to friends back home, and to protect themselves from burning while they were in Sint Maarten making the sea stories.

Jack Douglass was still nearly floating around the ship, basking in God's love and drinking in His presence. Several of his shipmates had noticed the change and had asked him about it, to which he had eagerly responded with a characteristically short and concise reply about God's love and forgiveness. Some jeered, some cheered, and some accepted it with a 'to each his own' shrug. Most expected it to be short lived, assuming that Jack would be back to normal in a few days; but Jack and Phil knew better. They had been meeting each day to discuss and study the Bible over lunch. Although Phil knew that the never-never-land of 'underway' would soon give way to life back on land, where priorities change and ideals seldom seem to materialize, he also knew that what Jack had experienced was real and lasting. It did, however, need to be cultivated by continued study of the

Scriptures and regular times of prayer and meditation in the presence of God. Phil also knew that he had been given a perfect opportunity to assist Jack in his early development as a Christian, since they would be spending a significant amount of time together on the *Mississippi* before this deployment was over.

As well as Phil knew Jack, he was still surprised at the intensity with which Jack approached his newly developed habit of regular prayer and Bible reading.

"All these years," Jack would explain, "I had unlimited opportunities to learn about God and His Word, but I didn't pay any attention to it. Now, I feel like I should know so much more than I do. It's like I came into a class half-way through the semester, and now I have to catch up with the rest of the class."

Phil wanted to explain that there was really no specific level to which one was supposed to have developed in any given amount of time, but he suspected that Jack already knew that. He preferred to hold his tongue rather than say anything that would discourage Jack from his newly acquired passion for studying God's Word and spending time in prayer. Why mess with that degree of motivation? Better to encourage him and enjoy watching him grow.

The day finally arrived. How six days could take a month to pass, Jack would never understand. To him, the figurative Father Time was an impish, cranky old man who liked to spend his free time—of which, unfortunately, he had an abundance—tormenting people and toying with them. Why else would time drag by so slowly when one was waiting in anticipation of a future event, so that hours seemed like days, only to multiply its swiftness exponentially when that event finally did occur, so that the whole event seemed to breeze by in a matter of minutes instead of the hours that had actually passed? "Someone to whom control of time had been given should be a tad more gentlemanly with his use of it," Jack thought.

The cruel antics of Father Time notwithstanding, the day of the *Mississippi*'s arrival in Sint Maarten finally managed to come. The Special Sea and Anchor Detail was set topside, condition 'Maneuvering' was set in the engineering spaces, and the *Mighty Mississippi* was piloted to her point of anchor in Great Bay, on the southernmost tip of Dutch Sint Maarten, in the middle of the Leeward Islands of the Lesser Antilles island chain. The first water taxi was scheduled to arrive in about an hour, at 0930 local time, when it would begin shuttling the enthusiastic men of the *Mississippi* from their gray, steel home-away-from-home to the white sand beaches of Philipsburg, the capital of Dutch Sint Maarten.

After Jack made sure everything was in order on the signal bridge, he properly secured the watch and locked up the signal shack. He didn't have duty upon arrival like he had in Cuba, so he and Phil had agreed to go ashore and experience Sint Maarten together. The few extra minutes Jack had spent on the signal bridge had, however, netted them a forty-five minute wait in the water taxi line on the fantail. Jack stood on the port side of the fantail, gazing across the clear blue water at the beautiful tropical island across the bay. He noticed the changing colors of the water as the sandy bottom gradually rose close enough to the water's surface to finally meet it at the shoreline. The harbor was littered with small fishing boats, pleasure yachts, sailboats and wind surfers. The beach was painted with the tanning bodies of hundreds of tourists and seasonal residents, drinking in the sun's rays without a care in the world. From the main deck of the *Mississippi*, they looked like multi-colored specks on the beach, the shrill voices of those tossing Frisbees or slamming home a volleyball made inaudible by the distance between ship and shore. Jack could see the buildings lining Front Street; an uninterrupted line of hotels, restaurants, bars and stores, each eager to obtain its share of the abundance of US dollars the American sailors would soon be pouring into their purses like syrup on pancakes.

Jack and Phil were at last able to find space available on the third water taxi, on which they eagerly rode across the bay and into the heart of Philipsburg. Before the bulky rectangular tour boat had even thumped against the end of the town pier, the fore and aft mooring lines had been tossed onto the pier and were being made fast to two of the large cleats that lined the edge of the pier. Jack and Phil gathered their carry-along bags and once again engaged in the all-too-common Navy task of waiting in a line; this time to disembark the shuttle boat.

The crowd of sailors slowly made its way down the pier and onto Front Street, Jack and Phil bringing up the rear of the processional. Jack looked back across his shoulder and saw the '*Mighty Mississippi*' anchored in the distance, her commanding presence at the mouth of Great Bay reminiscent of the Swiss guards standing their post at the Tomb of the Unknown Soldier. Jack allowed a small wave of pride to run through him as he took in the sight. He would take a couple of pictures of her from the beach before he left the island.

"Land Ho, Jack, my boy!" Phil said contentedly. "Land Ho."

"Amen, Phil. Feels great to step on dirt. Well, asphalt, but it is close enough."

Phil slung his backpack over his shoulder and adjusted his shirt. Taking in the panorama of the beach and the busy street with a slow rotation of his head, he said, "Shall we proceed according to the plan?"

"You know it!" Jack answered. "Mom should be home now, and I don't want to wait another minute to tell her the news. I figure we can walk straight through the marketplace here, bypass all these shops where most of the boys have stopped to look around, and find us a bank of pay phones in the lobby of one of those fancy hotels over there at the end of the main drag." He paused for a moment, then added with a dismissive shrug of his shoulders, "We can shop later."

"Lead on, Obuahu," Phil chided, bowing low in mock submission with his free hand outstretched in front of him. Jack nodded curtly, lifted his nose slightly into the air, and proceeded to lead the pair through the bustling throng as a nobleman would precede his servant. They chuckled at themselves as they emerged from the crowd and briskly walked along Front Street toward the west end of the town.

Sint Maarten was indeed a magnificent sight. As they passed building after building, they would catch short glimpses of

Great Bay off to their left, and the many buildings that comprised the rest of the town off to their right. Front Street itself was positively teeming with people. The shopping opportunities along both sides of the street reminded Jack of a strip mall back in Virginia or Michigan, except that most of the shops here seemed to be selling the same merchandise at relatively the same prices. Those shops nearer the pier had slightly elevated prices, however, in hopes of generating increased revenue at the expense of eager shoppers who recognized a good deal when they saw one and didn't want to wait to see if, perhaps, they might get an even better deal somewhere else. Trinkets, post cards, leather goods, woven sweaters, beach gear, and many miscellaneous items were on display, although T-shirts and jewelry took up the largest percentage of the available marketing space. Jack and Phil made mental notes of those places to which they wished to return later in the day, while continuing on toward the hotels at the end of the street. They did stop in one store to acquire a couple of Cokes and a delectable local pastry, but aside from that, they were undeterred.

The sun was bright and the air was hot, causing more than a few beads of perspiration to line the foreheads of Mr. Jonathan (Jack) Douglass and Mr. E. Phillip Anthony Prescott by the time they finally reached the cool, breezy lobby of the Great Bay Beach Hotel and Casino on the west end of the city of Philipsburg. Jack strolled purposefully through the lobby, searching for the bank of pay phones he knew would be located somewhere in the vicinity. As if on cue, a wooden sign became visible through the foliage of a potted tree which stood in a brass planter at the end of the registration counter. Jack rounded the corner, delighted by the sight of a bank of five telephones complete with padded desk chairs and thin yellow telephone books. The phones were unoccupied except for the one at the far end, where a man was engaged in a rather animated discussion with a business associate on the other end of the line. Jack snatched up the receiver of the first empty telephone and sat down eagerly on the edge of the chair.

His first call would be to his mother. Megan could wait for a little while longer. This news had to go to his mother before anybody else. He jumped through the numerical hoops required by his telephone company's international calling card, and was eventually connected to an old telephone ringing loudly in the equally old kitchen of his mother's house in Sandusky, Michigan. It had taken just over an hour for Jack and Phil to make their way through the town and into the hotel, which put the call at just after eleven o'clock in the morning in both Sint Maarten and Sandusky, Michigan.

Connie Douglass was in her kitchen stirring a batch of chocolate chip cookies which she had agreed to bake for the teen bake sale at the church on Saturday morning. She dropped the spoon into the bowl of goo and walked briskly across the room to where the telephone hung on the south wall by the doorway. She picked it up on the fourth ring, cheerfully said "Hello?", and was completely surprised to hear the voice of her youngest son at the other end of the line.

"Jonathan! What's wrong?" she asked, knowing he was underway in the Caribbean somewhere, and that this was the first time he had ever called her while he was underway.

"Nothing, Mom. I'm fine," he assured her.

"Are you sure, Jonathan?" she persisted.

"Yes, Mom, everything is fine. How are you and Dad doing?"

"Well, we're okay, I guess. I was just making some cookies for the teen bake sale Saturday."

"Really? Boy, it sure would be nice to get a box of those in about a week or so. I don't suppose you might have a handful of extra ones, would you?" Jack asked.

"Oh, goodness, I might be able to come up with two or three extra ones before I'm done," she teased. "So long as I can keep them away from your father, that is." She chuckled at herself, then waited for Jack to say whatever was really on his mind.

"Mom," he began, "I have something to tell you. Something has happened out here."

"Go on, son," she encouraged, realizing that he couldn't see her nodding. "I am listening." She assumed it had something to do with the strange visitor she had had a couple of weeks before—the one who had told her to pray for Jack—but she was confident that Jack would share it with her when he was ready. She let him continue.

Jack didn't hesitate. Instead, he blurted out, "Mom, I met Jesus a couple of weeks ago! Right out here on the signal bridge of the *Mississippi*!"

He told her about his talks with Phil, about how he had been feeling uneasy and uncomfortable for quite some time, and how Phil had suggested that God had the cure for what was ailing him. He talked non-stop for nearly thirty minutes, practically stumbling over himself in his attempt to get the whole story out to his mother. He told her about Phil's analogy of the faulty engine, of Kirt Radford's comment that he had been a worthless person, and about Phil's challenge that he let God be a viable possibility instead of a fanatical crusader's cause. He told her how his chest had tightened, how his breath had come in short gasps, how he had felt like he was being crushed by some invisible force bearing down on him. Then he told her about the vision—how he had seen Jesus on the cross—and he quoted to her the words Jesus had said to him after He had called him by name.

All the while, Connie Douglass sat in a kitchen chair by the telephone, tears streaming down her cheeks, praising God from the bottom of her soul for the redemption of her son. With the back of her cookie-dough-covered hands, she wiped tears of joy from her eyes. She sat there listening to Jack, completely entranced by his recollection of that Friday evening's events. When he finally finished speaking, she told him about the visitor she had had, and what he had said to her. Now, it was Jack's turn to be amazed. He sat silent, as the realization of what had transpired gradually came to him. As he slowly began to see the depth of God's love for him, a wave of warmth came over him. Tears filled his eyes and he sobbed like a baby, standing shameless before his Creator. He could barely comprehend how God could go to such trouble just to save an insignificant guy like Jack Douglass.

Eventually, economics finally getting the better of him, Jack said good-bye to his mother and hung up the telephone. Since Megan wouldn't be home at that hour anyway, Jack didn't have to talk himself out of placing a call to her as well. He got out of the chair and stretched, then walked around the corner and back into the hotel lobby to look for Phil. He found him sitting in a chair in the waiting area, reading a brochure about bicycle rentals. Jack relayed the highlights of his conversation with his mother, specifically about his mother's visitor that same Friday evening. Phil smiled and nodded his head, once again standing in awe of God's mercy and His love.

The pair strolled out of the lobby and into the bright Sint Maarten midday sun, the warm Caribbean breeze providing little relief from the soaring temperatures on the island. They left the hotel grounds, turned east onto Front Street, and walked purposefully toward the main part of town. Jack would call Megan later in the evening; as for now, it was time to shop.

Meanwhile, back in Sandusky, Michigan, Connie Douglass sat weeping in her kitchen chair. She thanked God over and over for going to such lengths to reach her son. She continued her worship and adoration for several minutes, then she went into the bathroom, dried her eyes on a strip of toilet paper, and returned to the kitchen where her mixing bowl of cookie dough patiently waited. She could hardly wait for Sunday to come. Boy, would she have a testimony to share this week! While the cookies were baking, she would call a few of her closer friends, those who had shared her burden of prayer for Jack, and tell them the wonderful news.

Phil sipped his frozen fruit drink while he looked at the pile of wool sweaters next to a rack filled with leather purses. They had been through several jewelry stores, each claiming to have the lowest prices on the island, and countless T-shirt and souvenir shops along the busy streets of Sint Maarten. Phil had picked up a handful of post cards and some T-shirts, while Jack had only succumbed to the urging of one aggressive T-shirt salesman. He was still looking for just the right piece of jewelry to buy for Megan, but thus far hadn't been able to find what he wanted. Something simple, not too extravagant but not too chintzy, personal—possibly even sentimental—but not too suggestive. They were still at that awkward place in their relationship where everything meant something, something could mean anything, nothing could also mean anything, but might mean nothing at all, and knowing the difference meant everything. "To a woman, that makes perfect sense," Jack had remarked to Phil, shaking his head with his hands up in the air and wondering aloud if he would ever even understand it enough to know whether he actually understood it or not.

"Yes, they are strange and wonderful creatures, Jack," Phil had countered. "Oh, and uh—no, you never will."

They exited the shop and walked into the next one, a fancy jewelry store. The jewelry stores were always busy, since one could purchase gold for prices well below those advertised back in the United States. Chains, necklaces, earrings, bracelets, ankle bracelets, broaches and rings were displayed in abundance in large white jewelry display cases which lined the walls and formed a maze of islands in the middle of the room. Jack eased his way through the myriad of shoppers until he came to a case full of gold earrings. The necklaces, which normally would have been his first choice, didn't seem to catch his eye. In each store, he had passed quickly by the necklaces but had lingered at the displays of earrings.

"That's it, Phil," Jack stated with finality. "That pair right there."

"What's that, Jack? Did you find something you like?" Phil asked.

"Yep, right there," Jack pointed. "That pair of gold hearts with the little golden dolphins dangling inside of them. She will love them!" he exclaimed.

"Any significance to the dolphins, or is it the hearts we are looking at?" Phil prodded.

"She will just like them, that's all," Jack replied. "Let's get a sales clerk over here."

Having purchased all the souvenirs and gifts they wanted, Jack and Phil found an outdoor café and ordered frozen coffee drinks. They chose a table near the street and sat down to relax and watch the passersby until it was late enough to make their way back over to the Great Bay Beach Hotel and Casino to call Megan. Or, maybe they would have dinner first. Either way, they were just glad to be in port for a while where they could enjoy the sights, sounds and smells of life on land.

Megan sat on her old couch in her sparsely furnished living room and stared blankly at the television. She had gotten home from work only minutes before, slipped her shoes off her tired feet, and flopped down onto the couch. She couldn't find the remote, but she didn't want to get back up, so she just sat there, happy to be off her feet. She couldn't remember what was on anyway, since her television viewing habits were as inconsistent and unpredictable as her work schedule.

The unopened mail lay in a small stack on the kitchen table. It remained unopened because it did not contain a letter from Jack, and whatever else was there could and would wait until tomorrow to be opened. Her life had been pretty mundane ever since her relocation to Norfolk, at least until she had met Jack. Now that he was away, it seemed more mundane than ever. Her crazy work schedule as a waitress prevented her from being very active in the College/Career group at church, and there was nobody at work she would elect to spend any time with away from the restaurant. They got along okay at work, but that was quite enough time together for Megan's taste. Jack had been willing to work around her schedule in order to spend time with her, but she wouldn't expect the church group to do that. Besides, it was much easier for one person to adapt to her schedule than it would be for the whole College/Career group to do so.

It had been several days since she had received any mail from Jack. He tried to write often, but he never knew when the ship would be able to send off mail, and Megan never knew when to expect it. Sometimes she would go for many days without any letters, then she might get three or four of them in a single day. "Best advice would be not to expect it, then be happy when it gets there," Jack had said. That was easy to say, but not quite so easy to do. She was sure he was fine, so she didn't worry about him, but still, she missed him.

The ringing of the telephone startled her. She jumped, glad that she hadn't been holding a glass of water or anything, then got up and walked the few steps to the kitchen where the telephone hung on the side of the cupboard at the end of the bar. She lifted the receiver, hoping it was Jack but knowing it wouldn't be, and whispered a tired "Hello?" into the mouthpiece.

"Miss Megan Gallagher?" a high-pitched, nasal voice inquired.

"Yes…" Megan said cautiously, "This is Megan…"

"Great. Miss Gallagher, I am calling from the Foundation for Unfounded Foundations. We represent people who have been found to have founded unsound Foundations simply for the sake of having founded a Foundation, with little concern expressed as to whether or not the founding of their founded Foundation was found to be founded soundly."

"What? I'm sorry, I don't have time—"

"Megan, it's me, Jack!" Jack cut in, laughing.

"Jack Douglass! You brat!" Megan yelled.

"Gotcha!" Jack teased.

Megan walked back over to the couch, untwisting the telephone cord as she went.

"Jack, you aren't supposed to be calling, remember?" she reminded him.

"Well, I could hang up…" he left the sentence hanging.

"No!" Megan cut in a bit more quickly than she had intended to. "You might as well talk to me now, since you have already wasted that hefty charge for the first minute. How are you?"

"Wonderful, Megan. I'm just wonderful."

"Really? That's not exactly what I expected you to say. What is going on out there? Did you meet some beautiful island babe and dance the night away with her?"

"Hardly." Jack said. "There is only one 'babe' I'm interested in right now, and she isn't out here on any island."

Megan sighed.

"Megan, there is something I need to talk to you about," Jack said seriously.

"Okay," she said, a question in her voice, "What's up?"

"Well," Jack began, "A funny thing happened a few days ago..."

He eagerly told her all about his lengthy discussions with Phil, which had led up to his questions, which in turn had led to Phil's explanation of how people need God in their lives. He told her how his heart had felt so heavy, like it would burst, and how he had felt light as a feather after he had prayed to God for forgiveness and cleansing. He summed up by trying to explain the contrast between how horrible he had felt before he accepted Jesus into his heart, and how good he felt, how peaceful he felt, the sense of belonging he felt afterwards. He knew she wouldn't understand, even as he hadn't understood before his conversion, but he wanted to tell her anyway. He left out many of the details, mentioning that she would be getting a letter soon that would do a much better job of explaining the whole thing to her. She hesitantly acknowledged, still trying to process all that he had told her. She asked a few questions, then dropped the subject with relief when Jack asked her how her job was going and what she had been up to.

Their conversation ended after twenty-seven minutes, with Megan feeling somewhat anxious and apprehensive about Jack's new life, and with Jack feeling concerned, but at the same time content to leave it in God's hands. He would continue to write to her and pray for her, certain that God would work out the details. She occupied the top slot on his new prayer list, because he wanted her to experience the same peace and joy that he had experienced since his meeting with God.

The USS *Mississippi* remained at anchor in Sint Maarten for six days. By the evening of that sixth day, all the supplies had been taken on and stowed properly, most of the crewmen had spent all of their extra money, and many were ready to get back into a more routine existence. Liberty ports typically didn't last that long, and many of the men needed a vacation from their vacation. Therefore, it was without the normal groans and whining that the *Mighty Mississippi* pulled up her massive anchor and steamed out of Great Bay into the Caribbean Sea to once again perform her function of patrolling the high seas.

*   *   *

Miguel sat at his computer in his study. At three minutes after midnight, he typed in "machoman22" and entered the 'entrepreneurs' chat room. If one of them had to wait, he would prefer that it not be him. He searched through the silly screen names until he located stella24. Yes, she was already there. He began to type.

machoman22: hey, stella.
stella24: bout time, machoman.
machoman22: what's going on?
stella24: you just missed a big sale. One of our distributors was out of commission since thursday, just got back on line this afternoon. But I just found out. sometimes news doesn't travel as fast as I'd like.
machoman22: 6 days? and I'm just hearing about it now? I might have been able to help.
stella24: sorry- I can't get specials out to all our customers on a moment's notice. A weekly flier may not be the most efficient way to advertise, but that's how we have to do it.
machoman22: you're right. can't win them all. maybe as your business grows, you can expand to a more effective communications network.
stella24: sure, some day. Anyway, nothing else going on here. The distributor is back up and it'll be business as usual now.
machoman22: understand. keep me in the loop- I'd love to cash in on one of those unexpected wholesale opportunities sometime.
stella24: sure thing. talk to you later.

Miguel logged off and shut down his computer. He hated missing golden opportunities, but that was the way with business. Sometimes the other guy got the good deal.

* * *

The *Mississippi* spent three more weeks patrolling the Caribbean before her next visit to a port of call, this time on the island of Aruba, where the men were allowed the usual three days to enjoy the sights. When they pulled up the anchor and set sail from Aruba back out into the Caribbean, the men were given some wonderful news. They were going back home! The top brass in Norfolk and Washington had designated the USS *San Jacinto* CG-56 to replace the USS *Ticonderoga* on the Counter Drug Operation rotation. Since the *Mississippi* had just completed the remainder of the *Tico's* rotation plus all of her own, she was ordered to return to Norfolk immediately. The men were elated. They celebrated as much as the rules and regulations of a deployed US Navy warship allowed them to, and they dove in to their tasks of cleaning and preservation with a renewed sense of purpose. They would bring the ship into tip-top shape while they were underway so that there would be no reason for any liberty to be denied after their arrival back in Norfolk. The *Mighty Miss* was cleaned, swept, washed, scrubbed, chipped, painted, polished, buffed, waxed, labeled, stenciled and anything else the men could think of to do to her. They had been out for too long, and they were motivated.

Jack and Phil stood alone on the signal bridge, sipping fresh coffee and dreaming of home. Of course, the coffee was Jack's special gourmet blend, reserved for times such as this, when a celebration was in order. This would be the last evening they would stand here with the wind in their hair, drinking coffee and talking about whatever came to mind. Tomorrow afternoon they would be mooring to the pier in Norfolk, Virginia, home at last, and this time for their full six weeks of in-port rotation before deploying again.

"So," Jack asked, "Are we gonna do it?"

"I can't think of any reason why not," Phil stated. Over the past three weeks, since leaving Sint Maarten, they had thoroughly discussed the idea of getting an apartment together when they returned to Norfolk. They were both single, both could afford half the rent and utilities, and both were completely sick of living on board the ship. They had decided to look for a two bedroom apartment somewhere in Norfolk, hopefully not too far from Megan's.

"Boy, that will be nice," Jack mused. "Having my own place to relax, and not having to come back to the ship every night. I can hardly wait!"

"I hear you," Phil agreed. "Plenty of space, our own TV and stereo setup, full size beds!"

They sipped their coffee in comfortable silence, going through the events of the next few days in the theater of their minds. Phil broke the silence with a question.

"What do you think Megan is going to say?" he asked.

"About the apartment?" Jack asked.

"No, about your new life in Christ," Phil corrected.

"Oh, well, I guess I don't know. I will just have to find out tomorrow. She seemed kind of taken back when I told her about it on the phone, but, now that she has had time to think about it, hopefully she will be okay with it. I think it's safe to say that she is not a Christian, but I don't think that she's totally opposed to the idea. I mean, I did meet her at church, and she's never said anything negative about it that I can remember."

"Well, I'll be praying for both of you," Phil said.

"Yeah, so will I."

~7~

On Sunday morning, Megan walked into the second floor classroom just as the buzzer sounded to announce the beginning of Sunday school. She crossed the room, draped her jacket across the back of one of the empty seats beside Kim, and sat down.

"Wow, Megan, you look wonderful!" Kirt and Laura said at the same time. "What's up?"

Megan tried unsuccessfully to repress a big smile. "Jack is coming home this afternoon!" she said, her eyes dancing.

She had been calling the *Mississippi*'s Ombudsman line every few days to check for updates to the ship's schedule. The message was nearly always the same, and never encouraging. The *Mississippi* would be on station in the Caribbean for CD-Ops until further notice. The mission completion date was unknown and subject to the needs of the Navy, thus a return date for the ship could not be estimated. Speculation would put it sometime before Christmas, but even that was uncertain, not to mention a rather huge window of time. She had called Friday night after her late shift at work, hoping for good news but not really expecting any. Instead of the same noncommittal announcement she had heard every time for the last three weeks, she had been thrilled to hear the announcement of the ship's anticipated arrival on Sunday afternoon.

She had nearly worked herself into a frenzy of cleaning, getting her little apartment ready for Jack to come over when he got home. On Saturday afternoon, since she only had to work the lunch shift, she had gone to get her hair cut and styled, had gotten her nails done, and had spent hours trying on dresses in the mall before she found the perfect one that she knew Jack would absolutely love.

On Sunday morning, she had gotten up early, showered, dressed, and primped in front of the bathroom mirror for what any man would call an eternity, and what any woman would modestly call a few extra minutes.

"Really?" Laura said, "That's fantastic!"

"That's great!" Kim exclaimed.

"Awesome!" Brad added.

"When this afternoon?" Kirt asked.

"They say at two-thirty, but you know the Navy. Could be any time after that, but probably not any earlier," Megan explained. "I am leaving from here right after the service to go to the pier."

"That's wonderful!" Kirt said. "Wow—hey, do you think he would mind if we all showed up on the pier to meet him?"

"I think he would love it!" Megan said excitedly. "Would you do that?" she asked.

"Well, I would sure like to," Kirt said, looking around at the others.

"Count me in!" Laura nodded.

"Me, too!" added Kim.

"Hey, I'm in!" Brad said.

"I'll need a ride, but I'm in!" Steve said.

"Oh, that would mean so much to him," Megan sighed, looking over the small group and remembering what Jack had said about feeling comfortable with them, and about them being different. She thought that possibly she was beginning to understand what he had meant by those comments.

Megan fidgeted all through the service that morning. The message was good, and Pastor Mackey's delivery was as smooth and professional as ever, but her thoughts were a hundred miles away, and sitting still seemed impossible. In reality, her thoughts were only about thirty-five miles away and traveling in her direction at twenty nautical miles per hour.

A caravan of vehicles followed Megan onto the base and into the huge parking lot behind the McDonald's at Pier 10. They all got out of their cars and gathered around Megan, who had suggested they get something to drink at McDonald's while they waited for the ship to pull in. She checked to make sure they were all there, then started the walk across the lot to the restaurant. They waited in the line, got their beverages, and congregated in the far corner of the dining room which afforded them a view of the pier. Megan wanted to be able to see, just in case the ship came in early.

At 1:50, Megan excused herself from the table and went to the ladies room to check her hair and make-up. Kim and Laura followed her, teasing her about her excessive primping and ensuring her that she looked great and that Jack would be thoroughly impressed when he saw her.

The girls exited the ladies room and called to the men to join them for the walk to the middle of Pier 10, where the *Mighty Mississippi* would be moored within the hour.

Once again, the dull thud of the tug boats against the hull of the *Mississippi* announced to the crew that they were almost home. Jack was behind the 'big eyes', as usual, scanning the crowd for Megan. He hadn't been able to tell her when they were coming home, so he knew there was a good possibility that she wouldn't be there. Still, he scanned the crowd in hopes that she somehow had found out and would be there waiting for him. He was not to be disappointed. Right there, in the middle of the crowd toward the back, he could see her standing beside—hey—was that Kirt Radford? And Kim? And Laura and Steve? And there was Brad, too! What were they all doing here? Jack yelled to Phil to come over and take a look.

"Wow, Jack, looks like somebody besides Megan is glad you are home," Phil said.

"Huh!" Jack said. "That is really weird. I wonder why they are all here?"

"Because they are your friends, Dummy!" Phil explained, "And friends do things like that for each other."

"Well, I know, but...well, I just didn't expect them to all show up," Jack said, trying unsuccessfully to defend himself.

The ship was moored, the brow was placed, and Liberty for the Crew was announced. The men flowed from the main deck like so many cattle rushing through a broken length of fence in the branding corral. They merged with the crowd on the pier, searching for the loved ones they had seen from the deck, but who were now lost in the sea of tear-stained faces lovingly greeting one another. Jack found his way to where his friends stood, with Phil right behind him. This time he carried his bag with him, so he could leave the ship and not have to return until Tuesday morning. Normally, Monday would be a workday, but the XO had generously declared it to be holiday routine, which meant that only the duty section was required to report to work, since they had arrived on Sunday and had thus missed the weekend.

Jack walked straight to Megan, dropped his bag and started to open up his arms. "I wasn't sure whether you would…" The rest of what he said was muffled by her hair as she threw her arms around him and hugged him tightly.

"I missed you, Jack," she quietly said into his ear. "I am so glad you are home!"

"I missed you, too, Megan," Jack sighed, his heart melting inside him. They stood there holding each other while the rest of the world faded away. Once again, Jack's fears and apprehension about coming home and seeing Megan had amounted to nothing. Although he was justified this time in being uncertain that she would be on the pier, he should have known that she would keep track of the ship's movements and be there waiting for him, especially on a Sunday. Deciphering the secret code of a woman's signals had never been his strong point. Even with a special secret decoder ring from his favorite breakfast cereal, he still would be unable to figure out what women were trying to say unless they just broke down and said it to him. He doubted that he was alone in this condition of incompetence. Though other men might not be too quick to admit it, most of their women would not hesitate to slap a figurative label on their foreheads and place them in that category.

"Oh, I'm fine, Jack. Thanks for asking," Kirt said mockingly while Jack and Megan were still lost in their own little world.

"No, it was no trouble getting here to meet you, Jack. Don't mention it!" Steve said sarcastically, joining in the banter.

"You two, leave them alone!" Kim said. "Can't you see they need a minute together?"

"A minute?" Brad asked in mock incredulity. "A minute? It will take longer than that just to pull them apart!"

They all started to laugh, including Jack and Megan, who succumbed to their chiding and turned to face the group. The guys gave Jack a firm handshake, while the girls both gave him a big hug to welcome him back. Jack introduced Phil to the group, and handshakes were exchanged all the way around.

"Wow, guys," Jack said, "I didn't expect such a big welcome! I didn't even know if anybody would know we were coming home today."

"We wouldn't have, if Megan hadn't come into church this morning looking like a Miss America candidate," Brad said. "And she was so antsy, she couldn't even sit still all morning."

"Shut up, Bradley!" Megan said, only half kidding.

"Yeah, and her face was lit up like a Christmas tree, Jack. We could have stuck a star on her head and dumped a bunch of gifts at her feet, and nobody would have known the difference," Brad continued, eating up the attention.

Jack turned Megan to face him, looking at her with raised eyebrow, as if to confirm that he had indeed heard something that he knew she didn't want him to know. She blushed and socked Brad in the arm. "Let's go get some lunch, okay?" she pleaded, trying to change the subject. "Jack, have you eaten yet?"

"Nope. The thing they called 'lunch' frightened me today, so I decided to hold out for some real food somewhere in town. And, of course, I am starving!" he said. He looked around the group. "Well, where are we going?" he asked them.

"Your choice, sailor," Kirt said. The others nodded their consent.

"Hey, I won't argue. Best possible speed to Pizza Hut!" he ordered, pointing a finger out into the distance. They gladly agreed and headed toward their vehicles.

Phil joined Jack and Megan in her car, which Jack drove to where Phil had parked his pickup. After convincing Phil to follow them to Pizza Hut and join in the celebration, Jack and Megan pulled out of the parking lot, chattering like a couple of high school girls on the first day of a new school year. They merged into the stream of traffic going off the base and drove in the direction of the restaurant.

The afternoon passed quickly. They had once again succeeded in acquiring their usual table in the back corner of the dining area and also, as usual, Jack found himself doing most of the talking. Everyone wanted to hear all about what he had been up to while he was underway. He had introduced Phil to them all, and they had taken turns sharing events and experiences from their previous eight weeks out to sea. Jack brought up the subject of the boarding of the *Rosa de la Mañana* and quickly turned the floor over to Phil. They listened intently as Phil described the boarding and the search, then the ironic event which led to the discovery of the illegal drugs in the dummy fire extinguisher. They talked briefly about their visits to Cuba and Sint Maarten, and relayed a few stories of practical jokes that had been played on their shipmates.

Finally, when he could stand the suspense no longer, Kirt jumped in and changed the focus of the conversation. He told Jack and Phil about the mysterious Friday night call to prayer that he had experienced a few weeks ago after leaving his parents' house. He described the visitor, then the call to intercessory prayer, then the sudden lifting of the burden a short while later. Jack's jaw dropped as he again sat in awe of his Savior, amazed that He would go to so much trouble for just one soul, for just *his* soul. It wasn't like Jack was a significant person or anything, he was just another guy. He had no contacts in higher authority, he had no friends in high places, he had no inside track to influence the impressionable minds of the huddled masses. He was just Jack Douglass, average guy. It completely amazed him that God would go to such lengths simply to get him to surrender his soul to God.

"I don't know if you can even remember that specific night, Jack," Kirt was saying, "but, can you think of anything that may have happened that night to initiate such activity in the spiritual realm?"

"Well, you know, Kirt, I think I can help you with that one," Jack began with a smile shared only by Phil. "I was going to keep a lid on this one until I could share it with Megan first, but I guess you guys all had a part in it, so I may as well let the cat out of the bag right now, while we are all here." Knowing he had the total attention of all of them, he made a dramatic show of taking a long sip of his Coke and re-positioning himself in his chair.

"Yes, Jack?" Kirt prodded.

Jack smiled and began his oration. "You see, my mom had an experience very similar to yours on that same night." He meticulously relayed the story his mother had told him about her visitor on that night, the command to pray for Jack, followed by the sudden lifting of the burden about half an hour later. He gave as many details as he could remember, thoroughly enjoying clobbering Kirt over the head with anticipation for the climax of the story. Then, without even telling him what it was all about, he steered the story back to the signal bridge of the *Mighty Mississippi* on the same evening. He began by describing the feeling of the wind, the appearance of the night sky over the Caribbean, the sound of the waves hitting the hull…

Suddenly, Kirt slammed his mug of Coke onto the table with a thud, making Kim and Brad jump and cutting Jack off mid-sentence. Laura didn't quite stifle a small yelp.

"Jack Douglass," Kirt growled through clenched teeth, displaying his best fake menacing look, "if you don't get to the point, and fast, I am coming across this table…"

Jack lifted his hands in a defensive posture in front of him. "Okay, okay, keep your shirt on, I'm getting there!" he teased.

Jack became a little more serious. He told them of the many talks he and Phil had shared up on the signal bridge; how sometimes when he would toss out a question, Phil would dodge it and guide the conversation in such a way that Jack would end up answering his own question, and how other times he would seem to spit out a blunt answer without a second thought and take Jack completely by surprise. Finally, he told them about that night. It had been the most intense chat they had ever had, with Jack not really saying much but feeling very troubled inside, and with Phil in rare form, spouting off Scriptures and analogies like an agitated can of Coke spewing forth its contents at the popping of the lid.

Jack gave them the very shortened version of the truck engine analogy, then quoted what Kirt had said about being a useless person. Then, he told them about the vision. He tried in vain to describe the intensity of it, the emotions it generated, the terrible feelings of guilt and shame that weighted down his heart.

"I would say that it was as real as you guys are, sitting right here in front of me, but it was a hundred times more than that. The rest of this table might as well be fifty yards away, so weak is the picture generated compared to the vivid, intense reality of the vision." Jack did his best to describe the vision to them, which he did with perfect accuracy. Each person felt as though he had been there by the time Jack finished his recollection. Kim and Laura were weeping quietly, while all the guys were glassy-eyed and sat in reverent silence. Jack was crying too; it was all so clear in his mind, as though it had happened only moments ago instead of several weeks ago.

Even after Jack had finished his story and taken a long sip of his Coke, no one at the table spoke. Each person seemed to be having his or her own little private time of worship with the Lord. It was overwhelming to them to think that the Creator of the universe would take such a personal interest in His creation.

Kirt broke the silence. "Wow, Jack, that is incredible. So…then what happened?"

Jack began again. "I told Phil I needed to pray."

"After something like that, I can imagine!" Kim said absently.

"So," Jack continued, "we prayed. For a long time. I asked Jesus to forgive my sins and make me the new creature Phil and Kirt had talked about. And then, this peace fell over me. I felt as light as a feather, like I could lift up off the signal bridge of the boat and float through the air across the Caribbean all by myself. I felt good. Not just 'fine', or 'okay', but *good.* I mean, like *I* was good. Like I had suddenly become a positive force in the universe, instead of merely one more glob of atoms floating randomly around the cosmos with no direction and no purpose, and with no contribution. Better than I have ever felt in my life. I just felt like everything was okay, and not just at that moment; I felt like everything was okay, and would be okay, for the rest of my life. You know, like I would never have to feel alone or useless or guilty again. They say that when God forgives a person, He never remembers the sin again. I think that is true. I felt like He separated my past from my future in such a way that I can still remember and finally understand my past, but that I no longer need to be influenced or controlled by it. I don't feel like I have to make anything up to God, but like I can just start today, wherever I am and go from there. It is such a freeing feeling! I can't believe I was stupid enough to live without it for all these years. Satan is so good at deceiving us."

"Well, his job is pretty easy in that respect," Steve put in. "All he has to do is convince us to do exactly what we want to do anyway. Nothing! To *not* make a decision to follow Christ is to make a default decision to follow Satan. There is no middle ground."

"Well said, Steve," Kirt agreed. Turning to Jack, he said, "Jack, that is as amazing and wonderful as any Bible story I have ever read. To have been a part of such a miraculous work of God even gives me a feeling of belonging. You know, like somehow we are all closer now, because God chose to unite us in the task of saving one of our own. Welcome to the Family of God, Jack."

"Thanks, you guys. All of you. Thank you for being faithful and praying when God told you to. I guess I can quote the old cliché and say that I would not be here tonight if not for your faithfulness!"

Since everyone had been sniffling and crying, no one thought anything about the tears slowly creeping down Megan's face.

Suddenly, she leapt out of her seat as if it were on fire. Everyone turned to look at her, startled by the sudden movement. She grabbed her napkin, pressed it to her nose, then said through flowing tears, "Please excuse me—I have to go!" With that, she turned and bolted from the table, weaving through the other patrons and rushing out the door.

For a moment, they all sat motionless, stunned with disbelief. Jack turned to look at the others, as if to ask for confirmation that what he believed he had just witnessed had actually happened. He turned back toward the door, then back to the others. He tried to speak, "Did...but...she...wha..."

Kim was looking at him. "Go!" she yelled, and pointed at the door.

Jerked back into reality, Jack grabbed Megan's jacket off the back of her chair and hurried toward the door. Kim followed at a distance, while Kirt led those remaining around the table in prayer for Megan.

Jack's hesitation gave Megan just enough time to reach her car before he emerged from the door of the restaurant. He heard a car door slam shut, then an engine being turned over. He raced between the rows of parked cars in time to see Megan drop her gearshift into Drive and step on the gas pedal. He yelled and waved for her to stop, but she held her palm up to the window and shook her head as she sped out of the parking lot and onto the highway. Kim ran up to Jack's side.

"What was that all about?" she wondered aloud.

"Got me," Jack said. He turned and headed back toward the building.

Back at the table, everyone looked up at Jack and Kim for a report. "No idea," Jack said, shaking his head. "She was backing her car out of the parking space as I got to it, but she wouldn't stop. Just raised her hand, shook her head, then squealed out onto the highway." He pulled out his chair and sat down. "You know, guys, I'm pretty new to this whole Christian thing, and I'm not too good with women anyway, but if you ask me, that seems like a bad sign."

"Jack," Kirt asked, "did she say anything earlier that might indicate what could have caused her to do such a thing? I mean, has something been bothering her?"

"Not that I know of," Jack replied. "She was fine before our conversation, then, well, I didn't really pay that much attention to her while I was talking, but I didn't notice anything that was obviously wrong. Was anybody else watching her while we were talking?"

"She seemed moved by your story," Laura said. "She was wiping tears away just like the rest of us, but nothing too out of the ordinary from what I could see."

"I thought she was very into your story, Jack," Kim said. "But she seemed more sad or confused than touched. Maybe she was under conviction?" she suggested.

"Could be," Kirt agreed, "but I still wouldn't expect such a reaction from the Holy Spirit's convicting. It may have been partially that, in addition to something else."

"That sounds reasonable," Jack concluded. "Did anything weird happen while I was gone?" he asked. "I mean, has she been okay all along, up until today?"

"Sure, she's been fine," Steve said. "I chatted with her after church most Sundays, and I never noticed anything unusual. Not until ten minutes ago, anyway."

"Well, she obviously wants to be alone, and that apparently includes you, Jack, so I suggest we pay for this pizza and go find someplace where we can pray. We will have to ask God to prompt her to call whichever one of us she feels she can talk to, and then wait it out."

Nobody liked the conclusion, but nobody could come up with a better one, so they decided to relocate their party to Kirt's house where they could pray for Megan. They each dug out some bills and tossed them onto the table until the food and tip were covered, then they piled into their cars and headed for the Radfor farm. Kirt's parents were always up for a good prayer session, and they would be thrilled to hear all about Jack's conversion drama after they prayed for Megan.

Jack didn't know how to feel. He had been looking forward to being with Megan for many weeks. When he learned that they would be arriving on a Sunday, he was even more excited because he knew that they would be able to spend the whole day together—talking, laughing, catching up on life and making up for the time that had been stolen from them. Instead, Jack was riding in Phil's pickup truck, headed for the Radford farm to spend the rest of the day with everyone except Megan. And it had started out so well, with everybody showing up to meet him at the pier, then the pizza place, then, Boom! All of a sudden, it was over. Someone had yanked the rug out from under his 'Welcome Home' party, and he didn't have the first clue who, or why, or what was going on.

He wanted to be mad at Megan for leaving, but she was obviously in great distress about something. She probably had not wanted to leave either, but perhaps she knew of no other alternative. He wanted to be scared for her, but he didn't even know what he should be afraid of for her. He wanted to be supportive of her, but he could not reach her. He wanted to help her through whatever it was she was going through, but he did not even know what it was or what she needed, or what he could do, and for some reason she would not tell him. Then he came right back around to wanting to be mad at her again. He wanted to be mad at somebody! Or something! He was angry that something had wrecked his homecoming and had stolen even more of his precious time with Megan, but even more, he was angry that something was hurting Megan and he couldn't fix it. That was a man's job—to make everything okay for his lady. Whatever might go wrong, it was the man's job to fix it. Especially where Jack was concerned. His was the problem-solving personality. Type A? Type B? He couldn't remember, but either way, that was what he did. Like Phil and Kirt, he usually could figure out the answers to problems and pass on the key to fixing them to whomever needed it. This time, it was Megan. Jack's heart hurt. There must be something he could do!

They arrived at the Radford farm a short while later and congregated in the living room. Kirt gave Tom and Milly the extremely abbreviated version of the afternoon's events, and they all began praying. After about twenty minutes, the alternating prayers reached what seemed like a natural end. They took a break, some getting liquid refreshment, some relieving themselves of previously acquired liquid refreshment, others making use of the nearby boxes of facial tissues. They chatted for a few minutes about Megan's situation, deciding that they had fulfilled their immediate responsibility of praying for her. They would all continue to remember her in their daily prayers, but for now, the Holy Spirit needed time to deal with her Himself. Jack would call her later in the evening and see if there was anything he could do for her. At the moment, though he really didn't feel like it, he was coerced into again recounting the story of his conversion on the signal bridge of the USS *Mississippi*, somewhere in the Caribbean Sea.

Megan Gallagher burst into her apartment, flinging the door shut behind her. She opened her hands, letting her keys and purse fall onto the floor as she ran into her bedroom. She dove onto her bed, buried her face under the pillows, and wept. She lay there crying until she fell asleep, to be awakened several hours later by the ringing of the telephone. She knew it would be Jack, and her heart leapt inside her at the chance to talk to him, while at the same time her mind cried in anguish at the thought of talking to him. While she sat on the edge of the bed battling her inner feelings, the ringing from the kitchen stopped. Her heart sank. It had to have been him. Nobody else ever called her. She had only received one 'wrong number' call and a small handful of telephone marketers the whole time Jack had been away—and none of them ever happened on a Sunday evening. She prayed that it would start to ring again, knowing that she wouldn't pick it up even if it did. She walked out to the kitchen and unplugged the line from the wall where it entered the base of the telephone. Now she wouldn't have to worry about it. She walked over to the door and locked it, then retrieved her purse and keys, which she laid on the small table by the door. She went back into her bedroom and slipped out of her clothes, leaving them in a trail on the floor like bread crumbs through the woods in a fairy tale. Aside from the clothes, the apartment was spotless—a result of Saturday's cleaning frenzy—but she no longer cared. She moved like a zombie in one of those cheesy black and white horror movies, as though her mindless body was animated by electrodes and moving of its own accord through a pre-determined course. She felt numb; trapped; like she was suspended indefinitely in that small fraction of time *after* you pound your thumb with a hammer and think 'Oh, boy, that is really going to hurt', and *before* the pain actually hits. There is nothing that can be done to avoid it, because the pounding has already occurred. The damage has already been done, but the reality of it has not yet taken hold, and so you cringe, hold your breath, hunker down and brace for impact. And all Megan could do was cry.

Jack was worried. Megan had never ignored him before, especially on the day he returned from a deployment. He was certain that she was at home, even though she wasn't answering her telephone. He had tried to call her several times, only to hear the ringing continue past the point at which her answering machine should have picked up. Jack assumed correctly that she had unplugged it. Finally, frustrated and feeling helpless, he called Kim. She was very sensitive and always enjoyed helping others. Jack thought she would be the best candidate to visit Megan tomorrow and try to talk with her. Whatever was bothering Megan was too big for her to handle by herself. Kim had a good head on her shoulders and a good spirit in her heart. Surely she would be able to get through to Megan.

Every so often throughout the day, Kim would offer quick, silent prayers for Megan. At some moments, the day seemed to drag by, since Kim was eager to get to Megan's place and find out what she could do to help. At other moments, she felt ill-equipped for the task, and the day seemed to rush by too quickly. Eventually, like it or not, quitting time came and went. The crisp fall afternoon found Kim behind the wheel of her Mustang, heading toward Megan's apartment.

She rounded the last curve on the directions Jack had given her, weaving back and forth to avoid the mountains of leaves piled up along the curbs at the end of concrete driveways. The apartment complex was at the end of the subdivision. What once had been a giant cul-de-sac was now a circular all-way-stop, where the two lanes providing access to the apartment buildings met the old road coming in from the subdivision and the new road going out to the four-lane highway. Kim drove around the circle twice, noticing the road she wanted after passing it the first time. She turned right onto the access road, then right again at the intersection where parking lots from the outer sides of both buildings spilled out into the access road. She followed the curve and entered the parking lot next to the building, continuing on to the end of the pair of buildings. She recognized Megan's car parked in the last space in front of the apartment entrance bearing the number Jack had given her. "Well, here goes!" she said to herself. She got out of her car and walked confidently up to Megan's door, assaulting it with three hard raps. She waited just a little bit longer than she should have had to, then repeated her knocking. There was movement inside. "Please invite me in, Megan!" she whispered to the air. The sound of approaching footsteps permeated the door, then silence reigned for a moment. Kim surmised Megan was watching her through the peephole and deciding whether or not to invite her in. She must have decided in the affirmative, because the door was slowly pulled open and Megan stood on the other side. Her eyes were red and puffy, she wore no make-up, and evidence of a hairdo was completely absent, aside from a failed attempt at a pony tail. She was dressed sloppily in paint-stained gray sweat pants and a ragged black sweatshirt, pink fuzzy slippers on her feet. She stepped back from the door, then turned and shuffled back into the living room, leaving the door hanging open. Kim took that to mean, "Oh, hi, Kim! Thanks for dropping by. Please, come in and make yourself at home," which she cautiously did. She followed Megan into the living room, where she seated herself on the cushion of a big arm chair, directly across from Megan, who had seated herself on the far end of the couch.

"Hi, Megan," Kim said. "I was worried about you and I wanted to stop by and see if you could use a friendly ear or anything."

"Jack sent you, didn't he?" Megan asked, hardly letting Kim finish what she was saying. She pulled her legs up underneath her and looked hard at her visitor.

"He is very concerned about you," Kim answered.

"He wouldn't be if he knew me," Megan said, absently but with finality. She turned away from Kim and seemed to focus on something totally out of sight, yet still visible in the distance.

"What do you mean, 'if he knew you'?" Kim asked. Megan

was still acting very strange and Kim's concern about her was not being lessened at all by her behavior.

They sat in silence. Usually, such a silence would be completely uncomfortable, but this was different. Kim didn't feel unwelcome, nor did she feel the need to speak. She silently prayed for Megan to open up to her, while she simply sat in the big chair and waited for God to work.

Megan whimpered. It was obvious to Kim that tears didn't come easily or often to Megan Gallagher. She could tell that it bothered Megan to be crying at all, especially in front of Kim, whom she really didn't know all that well to begin with. It was equally apparent that Megan had given up hope. Whatever burden she was carrying was defeating her, and she could no longer deal with it by herself. What would normally have been an award-winning portrayal of toughness and control had been reduced to the real-life drama of a fallen star nursing a broken heart. She reached for a tissue and quietly wiped her eyes and her nose.

Kim waited a few more seconds. She leaned forward in her chair. "Megan," she said quietly, "you don't have to do this by yourself. You have friends here who love you and want to help. You just need to let us in."

"You don't understand, Kim!" Megan said. "It's not that easy." A new flood of emotion overtook her, evidenced by an equal flood of tears.

"I didn't say it would be easy, I just said we want to help. *I* want to help." Kim stood up and walked over to the couch. She sat down sideways in the middle, facing Megan. "It is obvious that this involves Jack, but I know it is more than some silly lover's thing. I know you love Jack, and he loves you, but you two didn't have enough time together to get into any arguments or anything like that, so this has to be about something else. And, judging by the way it is affecting you, it has to be huge."

"You have no idea!" Megan huffed.

"Then give me an idea!" Kim challenged. "Look, I don't want to be nosy and butt into your business, but I do care and I do want to help. Nothing we say has to leave this room, Megan. Anything we talk about will be completely confidential."

"Megan Gallagher is the person I want to be, Kim, but

that is not the person I am. You are right, I do love Jack, but it will never work. He doesn't know the real me, and if he did, he wouldn't want anything to do with me. He would drop me like a bad habit. I am not the good person he thinks I am."

"Hey, we all want to be better people, Megan. That's what going to church is all about. God can forgive us for the way we have lived in the past, for our failed attempts at measuring up, and He can teach us to be better people in the future. We don't have to hold on to the bad and the ugly that is inside us—we can turn it over to God and let Him change us…"

"Kim-"

"…anything we may have done in the past will be forgiven and forgotten, never to be mentioned again…"

"Kim!"

"…God will give you a new heart, new priorities, a new will…"

"Kim!! I am not Megan Gallagher! My name is Belinda Gallagos!"

Kim sat, stunned, uncertain whether she had heard Megan correctly. "You… you're…what?…who?…Who is…" she stammered.

"I am not Megan Gallagher. I am Belinda Maria Gallagos, a poor farm girl from Venezuela. I am living here temporarily under the assumed identity of Megan Gallagher, college dropout and now waitress by profession, working under the evil thumb of a rotten creep back in Venezuela."

Kim was speechless. "Uh…" was all she could get out.

Now that Megan had cracked open the dam which held back the dark secrets of her tortured soul, her emotions tore through it and the truth poured out like a mighty river of lies, deceit and oppression. She held nothing back, revealing to Kim the sinister plot that held her captive from across the globe.

Megan continued, "I am here under a forced agreement with a very bad man in Venezuela. I do certain things for him, and he takes care of my family back at home. My family is very poor, mostly because this same man stole our small farm and our land from us several years ago. He now pays my father a small pittance to work the farm for him as long as I keep my end of the bargain here. It isn't much, just barely enough for them to survive. But, if I fail to keep my end of the deal, he will kill them. All of them. My mother, my father, and my little sister.

"So you see, Kim, as much as I may want your God to forgive me, and as much as I may want to be the person Megan Gallagher is becoming, and as much as I may adore Jack Douglass, my hands are tied. I am a prisoner, and there is no way out!" She burst into a new torrent of tears, her body shaking as she released the terrible secret she had been holding inside of her. Kim reached out and pulled Megan's head to her shoulder. She held her while she cried, feverishly praying and begging God for wisdom.

The wave of weeping passed, and Megan excused herself to go and clean herself up a little bit in her bathroom. She encouraged Kim to help herself to a drink or whatever she needed from the small kitchen.

After a few minutes, they regrouped on the couch. Kim asked questions and listened intently as Megan described every detail of her arrangement with the man called Miguel Ramirez from Venezuela. She told Kim about the Internet meetings, the money she would receive every month, and the not-so-subtle reminders of what would happen to her family should a glitch ever develop in their evil little scheme.

"Kim," Megan said, "I don't want it to be like this anymore. I want out. Ramirez is an evil man, and I don't want anything to do with him, but I can't sacrifice my family. How could I ever forgive myself if I betrayed my family into the hands of Miguel Ramirez so that I could have a happy life here in America without them? But how can God ever forgive me if I continue the arrangement with Ramirez? It is wrong, and Pastor Mackey says that God will not tolerate sin, right? "

"Right—"

"So, what am I supposed to do? There is no right answer. There is no way out!" Megan's tears started to return, but she forced them away.

"Do you want God to forgive you, Megan, or Belinda, or..."

"Please, keep calling me Megan. That is the person I want

to be. And yes, I do want God to forgive me. I have listened to Pastor Mackey speak every Sunday, and I have seen how different you and your friends are. I have been torn up inside about this for a long time. I am deceiving everybody. I only started going to church so that I could get close to Jack. I wasn't supposed to be listening to the sermons. I've been using Jack to get information about the ships' operating schedules. He'll never believe that I really care about him! My whole life up here in America is a big lie. I wouldn't expect you all to forgive me and still be my friends, but either way, I want God's forgiveness. I want to eventually experience the happiness that Jack was talking about last night at dinner. I can't imagine how God could do that, but I believe that somehow He can.

"It was bad enough just being in the church services and hanging out with you guys, but then, when I heard Jack telling about how he had—what did he call it—gotten saved? Yes, gotten saved, and how wonderful it felt, I just couldn't handle it any more. I had to leave. That is why I left in such a hurry last night. Oh, poor Jack!" she cried. "He will be so hurt. He will never want to see me again after he learns what I have been doing. How I have been using him!" The tears continued, but she remained in control.

"Megan, listen to me. Listen carefully. If you want to change your life around, it is up to you. God can and will do it if you just ask Him to. Where is your Bible?" Kim asked. Regaining her composure, she decided to take one issue at a time. The web of deceit and espionage was way over her head, but the repentance/becoming a Christian part she could handle. That was more important anyway.

Megan quickly walked into the bedroom, plucked her Bible off her night stand, and returned to the couch, handing the book to Kim.

Kim opened it up to the book of Revelation. "Look right here, Megan, in Revelation 3:19-21:"

> Those whom I love I rebuke and discipline. So be earnest, and repent. Here I am! I stand at the door and knock. If anyone hears my voice and opens the

door, I will come in and eat with him, and he with me. To him who overcomes, I will give the right to sit with me on my throne, just as I overcame and sat down with my Father on his throne.

"And then over here in John 3:16-17…"

For God so loved the world that he gave his one and only Son, that whoever believes in him shall not perish but have eternal life. For God did not send his Son into the world to condemn the world, but to save the world through him. Whoever believes in him is not condemned, but whoever does not believe stands condemned already, because he has not believed in the name of God's one and only Son.

"And just one more, over here in First John 1:8-10:"

If we claim to be without sin, we deceive ourselves and the truth is not in us. If we confess our sins, he is faithful and just and will forgive us our sins and purify us from all unrighteousness. If we claim we have not sinned, we make him out to be a liar and his word has no place in our lives."

Kim handed the Bible to Megan and leaned back against the back of the couch. Megan read through the last passage again to herself, clearly contemplating the message.

"You see, Megan, we all have sinned. In God's eyes, every one of us is a sinner. It isn't a matter of how many sins you have committed or of what kind of sins they were. It doesn't matter how bad you were or even how good you might have been. It's a matter of wanting to change your heart. It's a matter of wanting to be obedient to Him and wanting to have a relationship with Him. He wants to have a relationship with you, bad enough to send His Son to earth to die for you. All you have to do is accept His free gift of forgiveness."

Megan finished reading and sat up straight. Latching on to

the first rays of sunlight to pierce the storm clouds of her life for quite some time, she looked over at Kim. "So, what do I have to do?"

"Pray," Kim said.

"That's it? Pray?" Megan asked incredulously.

"That's the first step. You have to pray. First, you have to admit to God that you are a sinner. Admit to Him that you have not been following His ways or living like He wants you to. Then, you have to tell Him that you believe that His Son, Jesus, was sent to earth to die, thereby paying the penalty for your sins and providing the way out for you. And last, you have to repent of those sins and ask Him to forgive you. 'Repentance' means a total changing of direction. Second Corinthians 5:17 says, 'Therefore, if any one is in Christ, he is a new creation; the old has gone, the new has come!' To repent of your sins is to confess that you have committed sins, then vow to change your life in such a way that you will not commit them any more. You have to ask God to cleanse your heart from all sin, just like those verses said."

Megan looked somewhat uncomfortable. She shifted in her seat and looked back down at the Bible. "But, what about Miguel?" she asked. "What about the arrangement?"

"God will take care of it, Megan," Kim assured her. She lifted the Bible off Megan's lap, turning to the book of Romans. "Look at this, Romans 8:28 says, 'And we know that in all things God works for the good of those who love him, who have been called according to his purpose.'" She placed the open Bible back on the coffee table. "Sin carries consequences, Megan. I wouldn't try to tell you otherwise. Just because God forgives you for the sin you have been involved in and will no longer hold you accountable for it does not mean that the consequences of the sin will be reversed or canceled. The relationship between the sinner and God will be restored, on the spiritual plane, but on the earthly plane, the consequences of sin will still have to be dealt with. You can repair a busted water pipe to stop a house from flooding, but that won't do anything to alleviate the water damage caused by the flooding prior to the repair. It's the same with sin. You can trust God to work this situation out for you, but it may still come at great personal cost to you. He won't simply make it go away, although He does promise to help you through it, and eventually to use it for His own glory and for your benefit."

Silence returned. Megan sat motionless on the couch, deep in thought about the words Kim had shared. Kim was silently praying for the Holy Spirit to get through to Megan. Kim got up and walked to the kitchen, where she retrieved two ice cubes from the freezer and dropped them into her empty glass. She refilled it with water from the tap, made sure that Megan didn't want anything, then reclaimed her seat in the middle of the couch.

"Megan, would you like me to pray with you?"

"Yes, I would," Megan answered without hesitation. "I don't really know what to say… "

"All right, I will pray first, and then you can just repeat my words from your heart. Okay?"

Megan nodded and they bowed their heads. Soon, all of Heaven was rejoicing just as it had when Jack had turned his life over to Christ.

The tears that rolled down Megan's face now were welcome tears. They were tears of joy, of freedom, of peace. Her situation was still grim, her oppression by Miguel Ramirez still a reality, but somehow it wasn't all that significant. Now, the peace of God that washed over her and filled her soul assured her that everything would be all right. There may still be pain, there would probably still be suffering, but now it would be different. The Holy Spirit would be there to share the burden with her. At last, she felt free from the personal bondage that had held her soul captive to sin. At last, her head was clear, so she could think and reason and pray to God to find a way out of her predicament with Ramirez. At last, she was confident that there actually would be a way out of her predicament.

Kim smiled and gave Megan's hand a reassuring squeeze. Megan leaned over and hugged her. "Well, the cat's out of the bag now," Megan said. "Now, what do I do?"

Kim leaned back onto the back of the couch. "I think you have to tell Jack," she said.

"I can't, Kim!" Megan was immediately defensive.

"Megan, you have to. He has a right to know, and he needs to hear it from you." She paused. "Okay, we will get around to Jack later. Now, what about your situation with this Ramirez guy? What can be done about that?"

"I don't know, Kim. He is a very dangerous, very powerful man. People who cross him once don't get a chance to do it again, if you know what I mean."

"I think we need some help. This is way too big for either of us to deal with. I think we need to go to the professionals."

"The professionals? Who would that be?" Megan asked.

"Well, the FBI, maybe? CIA? The information you are giving to Ramirez is spy-type stuff, isn't it? There has to be something illegal about it."

"Yes, but CIA? FBI? Won't that get me into trouble, too?"

"Don't you watch movies, Megan? They can give you immunity in return for your testimony against Ramirez. Or something like that. Either way, we need to talk to somebody who knows more about this kind of situation than we do."

"What about Pastor Mackey? I know he's not a cop, but don't you think he could point us in the right direction? And they may even be a bit more receptive if a respected preacher approached them first."

"Not a bad idea," Kim agreed. "But first, you need to talk to Jack. I won't be involved in something that hits him this close to home and not tell him about it. It wouldn't be right."

"Well, what about Phil?"

"Huh?"

"Phil—couldn't we talk to Phil, and maybe have him break it to Jack first, then I can talk to him later? I just don't think I could handle the hurt look of betrayal on his face. I wouldn't even be able to talk—" she choked back a sob and looked at Kim with pleading eyes.

"I guess we could talk to him. It couldn't hurt. But I am calling him right now."

Megan nodded her assent as Kim stood up and walked over to the table where her purse was sitting. Jack had passed out his and Phil's beeper numbers to them last night, since they planned to spend all day today apartment hunting, and he wanted any news about Megan to reach him immediately. She dialed the number, listened for the series of beeps, then entered Megan's number followed by the pound sign. She hoped that Phil would return the call without remembering who's number it was, since he would probably let Jack return the call if he knew it was from Megan.

A few miles away, on the other side of town, Phil grabbed his beeper off his belt and looked at the number. "Been away too long," he thought to himself. "I probably know who this is, but I can't place the number off the top of my head."

Luckily for Kim and Megan, the boys had just gotten a bite to eat at McDonald's. Phil was waiting for Jack to finish using the bathroom before they went to their last red-circled apartment ad from the Sunday paper. He walked out the front door, turned left, and fished a couple of coins out of his pocket. Dropping them into the appropriate slot on the front of the public telephone, he dialed the number on the screen of his beeper.

Kim answered after one ring. "Phil?" she asked.

"Uh, yeah, who is this?" the vaguely familiar voice said.

"Phil, this is Kim, from last night. One of Jack's friends."

"Oh, yeah," Phil said, mentally calling a picture of her to the front of his mind. "Black hair, right?"

"Yep, that's me," Kim said. "Phil, we have a problem. Can you talk right now? I mean, is Jack within earshot?"

Phil's mind triggered an immediate alarm. "He is in the rest room here at McDonald's. I'm outside. What's going on?"

"Phil, I can't get into it over the phone, but it is urgent that we meet at Megan's place. Right now, if you can get away. For the moment, Jack can know nothing about it. I promise you will understand as soon as you get here. Can you do it? Please, Phil, it's extremely important."

"Does it have anything to do with the episode last night?" Phil asked, not yet convinced.

"Absolutely. I will tell you this much: I have been here at Megan's place for over an hour. We have read Scriptures, we have prayed together, and we have cried together. She has even accepted Jesus as her personal Savior. But there is a situation—a huge situation—that I don't know how to deal with. It definitely involves Jack, but she won't talk to him about it until she bounces it off your head first. So, Phil, can you come? And can you get away without arousing Jack's suspicions?"

"I think so. I mean, yes, I can get away, and I should be able to split without making Jack too suspicious. I can blame it on the Coast Guard or something. I will have to take him back to his car though, so it will probably take me about an hour to get there. Where does she live, anyway?"

Kim gave him directions to an apartment complex that was actually quite close by, so Phil cut his anticipated arrival time down to about thirty minutes and hung up the phone.

Jack ran his fingers through his hair and placed his Miami Dolphins ball cap squarely on his head. He tossed the crumpled hand towel into the trash bin and pulled open the heavy door. Rounding the corner of the small hallway and entering the small dining area, he found Phil sitting at their table with the paper spread out in front of him.

"You know, Jack," he said, "I am about hunted-out for today. It's getting pretty close to time for the offices to be closing up anyway, so how about we call it a day? I have some other things I need to do before work tomorrow, too. We don't all get a holiday vacation when we pull into port like you Signalmen do."

Jack smiled at the ribbing. "Sure, Phil. No problem. I need to get in touch with Kim and see how she made out with Megan anyway, so that will work. Maybe we can bug out a little early tomorrow and hit the rest of them then."

"Sounds good, buddy. Let's hit the road."

Phil pulled up alongside Jack's Honda. He came to a stop but didn't put the gearshift into Park so that he could take his foot off the brake. Jack took the hint and climbed out of the truck. He leaned down and poked his head back in before closing the door.

"Hey, come on up to the signal bridge after quarters in the morning. I'll have some of that gourmet coffee I just bought all brewed up and ready," Jack said.

"You got a deal. See you in the morning."

"Yep, see ya."

Phil hated sneaking around his friend like that, but Jack was Kim's friend too, and if she thought it was necessary, then he wouldn't argue until he knew the facts. He took his foot off the brake and punched the gas pedal, zipping out into a small break in traffic barely large enough for him to take advantage of. Ten minutes should put him at Megan's front door.

In reality, twelve minutes put him at Megan's front door. Traffic lights were such a pain. Hardly had he knocked twice when the door was whisked open. Kim and Megan both stood there, obviously very anxious for his arrival.

Greetings were quickly exchanged, Phil was offered a beverage which he declined, and the trio settled into the old and worn, but comfortable, seats in the living room.

"Okay, so what is this all about? And why all the secrecy?"

"First, Phil, let me introduce you to the newest member of the Family of God, someone you already know, Miss Megan Gallagher." She stretched out her hand in Megan's direction, just in case there was any confusion concerning which one of them was Megan.

"That is wonderful, Megan. I am so happy for you!" Phil said as he quickly got up and walked over to her to give her a welcome-to-the-family hug. As he returned to his seat, he continued, "Jack was really worried about how you would take his own conversion out there on the ocean. He will be very relieved."

"Maybe not," Kim countered. "And now, Phil, let me introduce you to someone you *don't* already know, Miss Belinda Maria Gallagos of Venezuela." She again stretched out her hand in Megan's direction.

"Kim, what are you talking about?"

Megan took over. "Phil, it is true, I am not Megan Gallagher. Well, technically I am. I mean, if there were a Megan Gallagher, I would be her, but I am not. My real name is—or was—Belinda Maria Gallagos, like Kim said. I am from a small village in Venezuela, where my family used to own a small farm from which we made our living..."

Phil sat open-mouthed, but silent, while Megan told her story.

"Uh—Wow?" Phil said. "That is quite a story. Uh...man, let me think for a minute. So, what about Jack? When will you tell him?" he asked.

"Honestly, that is why we wanted you," Megan admitted.

"You probably know him better than anybody else down here. How do you think he will take it?" Kim asked.

"Well, holy cow, Kim, how do you think he will take it? I mean, it's not every day you find out your girlfriend is an international spy who is using your relationship to gain access to classified information which she then passes along to a known mobster/drug lord somewhere in Venezuela! Call me kooky, but I would imagine that he may find the whole thing just the slightest bit unsettling!"

"Okay, okay, I guess I deserved that," Kim admitted, raising her arms in surrender. "You see, I have already had a chance to digest this whole thing and to get over my initial reaction, but I realize that this is the first time you have heard the story. Sorry."

"No, I'm sorry," Phil said, shaking his head. "I shouldn't have reacted that way. You just completely took me by surprise. Uh—man, this is going to kill Jack."

"I was hoping you could break it to him for me," Megan stated boldly. "It was hard enough telling you about it, even worse telling Kim. But telling Jack—that would be terrible. I don't think I could do it without bawling my head off and stumbling over my words. I *want* to talk to him about it, I *need* to talk to him about it, but only after he already knows the truth. I would do anything in the world to patch things up between him and me, but I just don't think I can be the first one to tell him about it. Do you understand?" she asked.

"I suppose I do," Phil said reluctantly. "But I'm not so sure I want to be the one to break it to him, either. Why did you pick me?"

"Because you are his closest friend down here. He talks

about you all the time, about all the evenings you two spend on his signal bridge 'chatting and saving the world', as he puts it. He really respects you, and I think he would take it better coming from you than from anybody else." Megan explained.

Nuts, that made sense, too. How was he going to get out of this? For Jack's sake, he supposed he couldn't. The girls were right—Jack would need Phil to help him get through this. It was probably a very good thing that they would be moving in together.

Phil hammered Megan with questions, much the same as Kim had done, in order to gain a thorough understanding of the situation he would be presenting to his friend, probably within the hour. He advised Megan to keep her afternoon free tomorrow, because Jack got off at three-fifteen and he would almost certainly want to stop over and see her before she went to work at five.

"What should we do now, Phil?" Kim asked. "I mean, about her Venezuela thing. Who should we talk to? The cops?"

"Well, it is actually a federal offense, sharing classified information about a government operation with a foreign national, so I don't know if the local Norfolk cops would have jurisdiction. The schedules of naval vessels is classified information, and Ramirez is definitely a foreigner, but I'm not sure which agency handles that kind of stuff. I would probably start with the NCIS, the Naval Criminal Investigative Service, since it is a naval vessel we are dealing with. I can probably get in touch with the appropriate offices tomorrow, and let you know what they say, or at least where we should start. In the meantime, I guess you should keep doing whatever Ramirez would expect you to be doing, so that he doesn't suspect anything. That's what they say in the movies, anyway," Phil said with a wry grin. He gave Megan a supportive hug, then Kim walked him to the door. With a quick hug from her, Phil left the apartment and walked to his pickup. This was going to be a very difficult evening.

Jack Douglass had had a very bad day which, although he couldn't realize it at the moment, was about to get substantially worse. For starters, he hadn't been able to spend the day with Megan. It was his extended weekend, compliments of the XO, and he had spent the day with Phil, looking for apartments. That in and of itself didn't make it a bad day, but it had not exactly been the day he had been looking forward to. To make matters worse, it was also the only day before Friday that Megan didn't have to go to work, so the whole day would have been, *should have* been, theirs to enjoy. And, as if that weren't bad enough, Jack didn't even know *why* they weren't spending the day together! Megan had not said a word to him since she had bolted from the restaurant the previous afternoon. She wouldn't answer her telephone, and wouldn't answer the messages he had left on her answering machine. He didn't know how to feel. He was angry, disappointed, hurt, confused, worried, afraid, and probably a whole list of other feelings that he couldn't think of at the moment. Why was she doing this? What could have happened in two hours between his arrival and the conversation in the restaurant that would make her go off the deep end like this, and not even offer any sort of an explanation that a guy could hold on to? Even bad news had to be better than no news! After all, man's greatest fear is the fear of the unknown. Why else would the first question to be thrown out in a time of crisis be the question of 'why'? Knowing something bad was easier to deal with than not knowing anything at all. Better antagonistic treason than absence without reason.

It was shortly after seven in the evening on board the *Mighty Mississippi.* Jack was feeling pretty low, and being in the complex where he would have to listen to all of his shipmates talk about their awesome day back in port was not the way he wanted to spend his evening. He would hide out up here on the signal bridge until almost bedtime, then he would go back down just in time to crawl into his pit and go to sleep. What a sad way to end a perfectly pathetic day.

~8~

BM2 E. Phillip Prescott flashed his military ID and walked across the brow from Pier 10 onto the main deck of the *Mississippi.* He had noticed during his walk down the pier that the lights in the signal bridge were still on, which could only mean that Jack was up there sulking about Megan. Phil went to Jack's living complex first, hoping to find Jack there and save himself a trip to the signal bridge. Those present in the complex assured Phil that they hadn't seen Jack since right after dinner, and a quick peek into his pit revealed a neatly folded blanket and a CD player, but no Jack Douglass. Satisfied that his initial impression had been correct, he stopped at the vending machine, dropped sufficient coinage into the slot to procure an ice cold Coke, and punched the appropriately labeled button. Inside the machine, the next honorable warrior in the battle against thirst stood on end, saluted his fellow soldiers, then slid down the chute onto the battlefield, where he would provide his proponent with a cold dose of caffeinated refreshment, valiantly serving until his life was extinguished. Phil repeated the process for Jack, then picked up the two Cokes and set out for the signal bridge and the awful task that awaited him.

It was chilly enough outside to require a jacket, which neither Jack nor Phil had worn, so the watertight doors to the signal shack had been shut on both sides and the heating unit thermostat had been adjusted to make it comfortably warm inside the shack. Jack sat at the big desk staring off into space, holding the handle of his coffee cup which was still half full of water that had long since warmed up to room temperature. Phil peered at him through the window, then pulled up on the dogging handle which retracted the dogs along the inside of the watertight door and allowed it to be opened. Jack was startled by the sudden moving of the dogging mechanism, the result of which was a small stream of water running down the inclined desk to the floor, as well as a significant amount of it soaking into his right sleeve.

"Sorry, Jack, didn't mean to startle you," Phil said, handing over one of the Cokes, which now seemed more like a peace offering than a gift.

"Hey, no problem," Jack said, regaining his composure. "I was way out there in my own little world, you know. Didn't expect anybody to be coming up here tonight."

"Yeah, I saw the light on when I was coming down the pier. I figured it was you, so I thought I would come on up."

"Well, I'm afraid I'm not going to be very good company tonight, Phil. Feeling kind of low, you know? I haven't been able to get hold of Kim, and I really want to talk to her before I go over to see Megan tomorrow. I was hoping to get over there tonight, but since I can't get hold of Kim, well, you know."

"Speaking of Kim and Megan, Jack, I have something to tell you." He popped open his Coke, stalling by taking several long slugs.

"Come on, Phil, out with it. What's going on? Have you talked to either of them?"

"First, the good news," Phil began. "Yes, I have talked to both of them. Megan is a Christian now. Kim did meet with her today, and they talked and prayed, and Megan asked Jesus into her heart."

"Well, Phil, that is wonderful! She—what? What else? That news should have you all fired up, but you are far from fired up. What else do you know, Phil?"

"Never could fool you, Jack. I wouldn't try anyway. You are right, there is more. Much more. And it is ugly. You know that I am one to just shoot from the hip and let the truth reign, so I need for you to be receptive..."

"Come on, Phil! Out with it! WHAT IS GOING ON?"

"All right, all right, I am getting there. I will tell you everything I know, but you have to sit there and listen. Let me finish, then we can discuss it. Deal?"

"Yes, Phil, whatever, just talk!"

"Megan Gallagher has only been Megan Gallagher for about a year. She was born Belinda Maria Gallagos in the state of

Sucre in Venezuela. She is working here under the assumed identity of 'Megan Gallagher,' a fictitious college student who moved from Iowa to go to school here in Norfolk. She has a counterfeit birth certificate, social security card, and passport to identify her as Megan Gallagher.

"Well, that's not so bad," Jack interrupted tentatively. "I mean, it would have been nice to know that, but—"

"Jack, there's more," Phil said abruptly, cutting him off. "The reason she's here at all is that she is a spy."

A shocked look covered Jack's face. He stood up, starting to object, but Phil raised a hand to cut him off so that he could finish.

"She is connected to a very dangerous and powerful Mafia kingpin/drug lord in Venezuela. She has been using you to get information about the classified schedules of naval vessels, which she in turn delivers to him via Internet chat rooms. The reason she does this is because this guy, this Ramirez, has taken over her family's small farm. He pays her father a sorry wage to work the farm, which he will continue to do as long as Megan keeps him happy with information from here. From you. He has threatened to kill them all if Megan fails to deliver. She hates the whole situation and she wants out, but her family's safety is in jeopardy if she tries to do anything about it.

"Jack, I know this is a lot to deal with, but she truly does love you..."

"What?! She 'truly loves me'? What in the heck is that supposed to mean? She really cares for the pawn she is using to help her drug-lord-boyfriend in another country? How am I supposed to believe that? Why would I even CARE if she loves me or not? I don't even know this woman, Phil! If Megan is not Megan, but Belinda or whatever, then I don't know her. I don't care what she does or doesn't want or anything else. She lied to me, used me, and betrayed me, and I don't want anything to do with her!" Jack grabbed his nearly full Coke and fired it at the wall of the signal shack, sending sprays of Coke in all directions. He jerked the dogging handle across the watertight door and kicked it open. It slammed against the exterior wall with a crash, somehow managing to hook into the latching arm that held it open, thus preventing it from swinging back and smacking him square in the face. He paced the weatherdeck, mumbling to himself and throwing his arms up and down as he spoke. He looked like a TV evangelist bringing home the final point of his message.

As Jack stormed back and forth across the weatherdeck, Phil silently prayed for his friend. He shut and dogged the door, took some paper towels out of the cupboard and cleaned up the spilled Coke, then settled into a chair to wait for Jack's tantrum to wear itself out so they could continue their discussion like mature adults. He supposed he would probably have reacted in much the same way as Jack, so he didn't feel the need to say anything about it.

After a few minutes, Jack had calmed himself down somewhat. Phil saw the dogging handle slowly slide across the door, which Jack swung open so he could enter.

"Sorry about that," he said to Phil as he regained his seat.

"About what?" Phil asked in mock ignorance.

"Oh, I seem to have spilled my beverage. Sorry."

"Hey, no problem. Stuff happens."

"Really, Phil, I am sorry I reacted that way." He paused. "I am assuming that what you told me was merely the highlights, and that there is a lot more detail you have yet to share with me. Would that be correct?"

"You have assumed correctly, Colombo. I am almost afraid to ask, but shall I elaborate?"

"Uh, tell you what, why don't I go and replace my desecrated beverage, and perhaps blow off a little more steam and excess adrenaline, then you can fill me in on all the details. Okay?"

"Good call," Phil confirmed. Whatever it took for Jack to deal with this terrible mess was fine with him. "I will wait right here," he added, pointing to his chair.

Jack left the signal bridge to get another drink, and Phil started to pray. He asked God to give Jack the grace to deal with this horrible situation. He asked for the right words to say to Jack that would bring him comfort, yet at the same time give him the courage to do the right thing in this difficult situation. His was a multi-faceted situation with implications reaching much farther than his wounded pride and his broken heart. Many lives would be affected by the outcome of the conversation he and Phil would have tonight, not to mention that the newly saved souls of two baby Christians hung in the balance. Since Megan was now a child of God, Jack was required to forgive her. He wasn't required to maintain the relationship they had begun, but he was required to honor her request for forgiveness. Anyone would have a hard time with that, particularly considering the personal nature of her offenses. Since they were both new Christians, they would both need wise counsel to arrive at Biblically sound decisions with respect to making reparations to their damaged relationship, at least enough so that they didn't harbor destructively negative feelings toward each other. Resentment and ill will would eat a person up from the inside out, making him bitter and ugly. Phil didn't want that to happen to either one of them.

"Okay," Jack said, stepping back into the signal shack and shutting the door. He plopped down on his seat and popped open his new Coke, looking at Phil expectantly. "Let's hear it. Everything you know, down to the last detail."

Phil did exactly that. He told Jack every single detail he knew about Megan and Belinda and the entire situation. When he was finished, he sat back in his chair and sipped at his own Coke, allowing Jack to ask questions like he and Kim had both done with Megan. Satisfied that he knew all he was going to learn from Phil, Jack sat back in silent contemplation, the pain obvious on his face.

The next day, promptly at three-fifteen, Jack bolted from the ship and made a beeline for his Honda. He cranked it up and raced out of the parking lot, heading for Megan's apartment. He arrived eighteen minutes later, parked the Honda and walked up the sidewalk to her door. She opened the door after the first knock and invited him to have a seat in the living room. He did so, after which Megan vainly attempted to break the uncomfortable silence with pleasant, relatively meaningless conversation.

"How are you, Jack?" she asked. "I have been worried

about you."

"You don't have the right to be worried about me, Megan, or Belinda, or whoever you are! Don't you dare sit there and be nice to me! The only reason I came over here is that I want to hear it all straight from you. All of it, from the beginning. It was very clever of you to make Phil break it to me, so that my initial reaction would be wasted on him and not be taken out on you in full force, but you aren't getting out of it that easy. I want you to tell me all about it. If you are going to betray me, you can do it to my face. Phil isn't here to do your dirty work for you this time. You get to do it. So, let's hear it."

He sat back on the couch, folded his arms and crossed his legs with his feet up on the coffee table. Megan was already in tears as a result of his outburst. This was already worse than the worst scenario she had conjured up in her mind over the past two days. It was absolutely not going as she had hoped that it would. Didn't he know that she was sorry? Couldn't he see how much she really loved him? She reached for another tissue from the box by Jack's feet.

"Come on, enough with the sniffling!" he said angrily. "You were tough enough to use me like a cheap toy for the past few months, so let's see some of that toughness now. Quit pumping out those 'poor little old me' sympathy tears and start talking."

Okay, so that was it. He was punishing her. He was going to get back at her by tormenting her. He would take his revenge by tearing her apart with vicious words. This was really not what she had been hoping for, but if it had to be this way, then it had to be this way. Kim had shown her what the Bible said about this type of situation. Megan had sinned against God, and she had sinned against Jack, and now she was required to go to both of them to confess her sins and ask for forgiveness. The only thing God required of her was an admission of guilt and total repentance. His forgiveness was free and complete, contingent upon those two things. There was no propitiation required, no atonement that she must make, no percentage of the penalty that she was expected to endure. Apparently, it was not so with Jack. He seemed to need to lash out in retaliation for the pain she had inflicted on him. Her spirit sank. Her heart was breaking all over again. She had so wished that they would be able to salvage the wonderful relationship they had begun, but her dreams were crashing and burning at her feet. All she could do was stand there and watch it burn, attempting to douse the flames with the tears from her eyes.

With a quick, silent prayer for courage and composure, she began relaying her story to Jack. She didn't gloss it over to make it seem better or worse than it was, she simply told him the facts as she understood them. She began with her life on the farm as a poor peasant girl and the family's dealings with Miguel Ramirez during her early teen years. She ended with the 'bargain' he had forced her into, to come to the United States and be his eyes on the American Navy, in return for 'the protection of and provision for' the rest of her family. She described the tearful departure she had made from the family she loved with all her heart, led away by two thugs with guns tucked under their coats. She had vowed to do whatever Ramirez wanted as long as he agreed not to hurt her family any more.

Only after she finished telling the story did she attempt to pour out her heart to Jack. She told him how she had broken down and told the whole story to Kim, and how Kim had led her to a saving knowledge of Jesus Christ. Now they were trying to figure out a way to get her out of the deal with Ramirez without sacrificing her family in the process. She explained how much it had hurt her to have to lie to him and to all of their friends, but that she had been trapped, with no way out that she could see. She confessed her love for him, adding that she was willing to do anything he needed her to if they could only salvage their relationship.

Jack had pretty much turned her off as soon as she finished the details of the story and switched over to the personal babbling, but he still let her go on. There was a certain amount of perverse satisfaction to be gained by listening to her grovel and beg for his forgiveness. Not that she would get it, of course, but the groveling was a pleasant perk nonetheless.

Jack leaned up to the edge of the couch, sitting with his elbows on his knees and his hands clasped in front of him. Megan looked up at him expectantly.

"Well, that was quite a little story, Megan. It is only missing two things."

"What do you mean? What two things?" she asked, swallowing the bait.

"A white knight and 'happily ever after.'" Jack shot back at her, his voice dripping with bitterness and sarcasm. "Hey, too bad for your kinfolk down there in the Venezuelan jungle, but just because some drug lord cracks down on your dad, that doesn't give you the right to come up here into my country and mess up my life! I don't like being lied to, I don't like being used, and I certainly don't like you coming crying to me about how awful your pathetic little life is and thinking I will just forget everything you did to me and pat you on the head and tell you everything will be all right just because you started feeling a little guilty and said a prayer or two for Kim's benefit! I'm not buying it, Megan. Everything is NOT all right! And it is not GOING TO BE all right! You can't just slap down your 'I am a Christian now' trump card and expect me to hand over the jackpot to you and just sit back and wait for the next deal. I'm out, Megan. I don't like the way you deal. New deck, new cut, and new dealer. Good luck in prison if the Feds don't buy your little fairy tale and cut you a good deal of their own. Either way, I am out of here." And with that, Jack Douglass walked out the door, slamming it with just enough energy to knock a picture off the wall, which he supposed was fake anyway, and drive the point home that he was finished with her.

Megan fell over onto her face on the couch and cried. Aside from the safety of her family, the one thing she wanted most in the world was for Jack to forgive her and still want to be with her. Unfortunately, she had to admit, the prospects did not look terribly good. She had hurt him. She had deceived him, hurt his pride and broken his trust, not to mention his heart. He had pursued her and opened himself up to her, and she had returned the favor by using him for her own personal gain. Everything he had said about her was true, all except his doubting the sincerity of her conversion. In that assumption, he was absolutely wrong. Even so, she didn't blame him for his reaction. She probably would have said the same sort of things to him, had their roles been reversed. Knowing that she had gotten exactly what she deserved did not, however, ease the pain that came with getting what she deserved.

She eventually got up off the couch. She had to get a shower and pull herself together so she could be at work by five o'clock. The telephone rang while she was putting the finishing touches on her mascara. She ran to the kitchen and snatched it up, knowing that it wasn't Jack, but hoping with all her heart that it would be. Instead, Kim's soft voice came through the line.

"It did not go well," Megan reported. She gave Kim the ninety-second version of the confrontation, summarizing the gist of what had transpired.

"Oh, Megan," she said softly. "I was really hoping that he would take it better than that. Well, it has only been one day. Maybe he will cool down in a few days and you two can talk about it again."

"Yeah, that would be nice, but I won't clear my schedule just yet, if you know what I mean," Megan said.

"Just don't give up hope completely. God can still work this thing out for the two of you. Hey, have you heard anything from Phil yet?" Kim asked.

"Nope. He said he would try to set something up with someone on Friday, and that I should keep the afternoon open just in case."

"Okay. Well, let me know if I can do anything for you, okay?"

"Sure," Megan said, hanging up the phone. She huffed out her breath. What could anyone possibly do for her?

Four minutes before midnight that same night, Megan rushed into her apartment, tossed her keys onto the counter and her jacket onto the couch, then punched the button on her computer that would bring it to life. After listening to a chorus of beeps and whirrs, she clicked the 'connect to the Internet' button on her computer screen and logged on to the Internet. She entered the 'entrepreneurs' chat room under the name 'stella24' and typed a greeting to 'machoman22', to Miguel Ramirez in Venezuela. Tears rolled down her cheeks as she answered his questions about her 'source', confirming that there was nothing new to report and that all was going well with the source. She agreed to keep him posted, then turned off her computer and walked out of the room. Entering her bedroom, she dove into the bed with her face in her hands and cried. She humbly asked God to forgive her one more time for her part in Miguel's scheme, and for keeping it going until the authorities could get her out of it. Eventually, she allowed God's peace to once again envelop her, silently encouraging her to remain faithful because He would see her through her situation. She went into the bathroom, took a hot, cleansing shower, then returned to her bed. She fell asleep reading how God had always been faithful to deliver the psalmists from their troubles so many years ago.

Late Wednesday morning, Jack and Phil met at the *Mississippi Café* for lunch. They hadn't had a chance to talk since before Jack had gone to see Megan, and Phil was eager to hear how their meeting had gone. They waited in line, got their trays of food, and strode over to an empty table under the television which, unfortunately, was on and tuned to CNN. Phil spooned the brown gravy out of his peas and back onto his mashed potatoes where it belonged.

"Well, Jack, how did it go last night? Did you and Megan get anything resolved?" he asked.

"Oh, we sure did," Jack answered with a cocky, self-satisfied grin. He recounted their meeting for Phil with surprising accuracy, only slightly embellishing about his remarks right before he had stormed out of her apartment and slammed the door. He expected Phil to congratulate him on putting her in her place, maybe give him a high-five hand slap or a 'bug juice' toast or something. Instead, Phil was silent. He looked at Jack with sad eyes, then looked back at his food, sighing and shaking his head.

"What gives, Phil?" Jack asked. "I thought you would be proud of me, telling her off, letting her have it with both barrels. One more point for the men in the big game, eh?"

Phil remained still, unimpressed by Jack's 'victory for all

that is maleness'.

"Come on, Phil!" Jack prodded. "What do you think?"

"I think you are a hypocrite, Jack. That is what I think."

Jack froze, stunned by the remark. His jaw hung open, but he didn't know what to say. Phil shoveled the last bite of roast beef and mashed potatoes into his mouth and dropped his fork onto his tray. Standing up, he looked down at Jack.

"You really screwed up, Jack," he said. "I thought you had it together more than that. What a disappointment." With that, he picked up his tray and headed for the scullery.

He was half way across the mess deck before Jack collected himself enough to speak. "Hey, wait just a dog-gone minute!" he yelled to Phil's back. He speed-walked across the mess deck to catch up with Phil at the scullery. "Did I miss something, here? I am the one who got boned over, Phil! She lied to me and used me, but just because she has an attack of guilty conscience and spills her guts about it, I am supposed to roll over and pretend nothing happened and be her best friend? That's ridiculous!" Jack almost shouted.

Phil whirled around to face Jack. He looked straight into his eyes, straight into his soul. "No, Jack, I don't expect you to be her best friend, but I don't expect you to be a big jerk, either! I saw her, Jack, remember? I saw the pain in her eyes. I saw the fear in her heart for her family. I saw her repentant spirit, and the Grace of God surrounding her like a blanket. And I saw the pain she was in over you, Jack. I saw the love in her eyes for you, full of fear that you would do exactly what you did when she confessed to you. I have her tear stains all over my shirt, Jack. The tears she cried because of what she had done to you; the tears of grief because of the way she had hurt you; the tears of fear that you wouldn't be able to forgive her. I saw the wide open, hurting, vulnerable soul of one recently won to Christ; someone trying with her whole heart to do the right thing, out of love and duty to her new Lord and Savior, at the risk of losing the one she truly loves, and possibly even causing the deaths of her entire family at the bloody hands of a madman; someone willing to lay her whole being at the feet of Jesus and let Him have complete control. I saw the new creature that she has become since the blood of Jesus washed her sins away. But you, Jack Douglass, were so worried about Jack Douglass, that you wouldn't even allow her to try to make things right! You wanted to punish her for the sins she had committed, when God, whose only Son was beaten and killed to pay for those very sins, instantly forgave her and let her go free. All He required from her was a repentant heart, but that wasn't enough for you.

"Don't you think she is in enough pain, Jack? Don't you think she has suffered enough for the life she has been living? And, even if you don't think so, don't you at least think that her punishment should be left up to God, and not up to poor little Jack Douglass, who got his little feelings hurt by a manipulated, innocent young girl who was forced into doing a despicable thing simply to keep her parents and her little sister from being butchered by a maniac?

"I don't expect you to be her best friend, Jack, but I certainly don't expect you to be a selfish, petty, self-absorbed, vindictive, cold-hearted hypocrite, either!" Phil stormed away, clearly showing that the conversation was over, and that the debate had most certainly not been won by Mr. Jack Douglass.

Jack stood outside the scullery, still too stunned to speak. He had never heard Phil go off like that before, and he had never expected that it would be him that he would go off on. Jack walked back to his living complex, because he couldn't remember what it was that he had planned on doing for the rest of the lunch hour anyway. He wanted to be alone to think, so he disrobed and crawled up into his pit.

It was hard to see through the fog. It all seemed to settle on the ground—or maybe it was even coming up out of the ground—nearly two feet deep and thick enough to make Jack all but invisible as he crouched down among the dead tree stumps and twisted, misshapen bushes. He could hear the shouts of the men coming up in front of him, could almost smell the sweat running down their backs. His own heart was thumping in his chest like the bass drum in a marching band, making his body shudder with each pulsating throb. The sweat running down into his eyes carried with it a cargo of dirt and mud as it slowly flowed through his matted hair and across his mud-smeared forehead. He didn't know how long he had been running, or even how far he had come. This place was just like the place he had fled from earlier, when he had first heard the mob approaching. Too familiar. How could it be the same, after all the running? Had he been running around in circles? How would he ever get away? How could he ever escape from where he was when he didn't even know where he was?

The sense of a presence directly behind him sent a chill through his body. He leapt to his feet and bolted from behind the bushes at a full run. Low hanging tree branches and tall weeds slapped at his face and tore the skin along his forearms. He dove behind a tree and curled up into a ball deep beneath the layer of fog. He willed his breathing to slow itself, his heart to calm its furious beating. He carefully lifted his head, peering through the fog to gaze across the weeds. There was no one in sight. He was finally alone. He could no longer hear the angry shouts or the clanging of metal on metal. Still captivated by fear, he crawled across the muddy ground, twigs and small rocks poking into his knees through his pant-legs. At last, he stopped. He must have lost them. He was finally safe.

Suddenly, a huge hand reached down and grabbed him by the hair, lifting him up to a standing position. He yelped in pain and surprise, then choked back the scream as his eyes focused on his assailant. The head was easily twice the size of his own, covered with scraggly black hair, curly and matted down onto the rugged, leathery skin. The eyes were yellow and glowing, the mouth snarling and venomous. In a split second, the huge hand released his hair and grabbed the back of his shirt, lifting him a foot above the ground. Jack hung there, suspended in the air by this powerful creature's massive arm. The arm rotated, spinning Jack half-way around so that he could see the ruins of a small building several yards away. There was no fog in front of the building, so Jack could plainly see Megan kneeling in front of it, surrounded by three lifeless lumps in the dirt. She was crying loudly; the heart-wrenching cry of someone who has cheated death, but whose life has been forever scarred and altered by the fate of loved ones who didn't emerge as victors from the same battle. Sensing his presence, she looked up and searched her field of vision until her eyes came to rest on Jack. As recognition registered in her mind, her face twisted in anger. Her eyes bore into him, piercing his soul with a sharp pain as though the blade of a red-hot sword were slowly being driven through his heart.

"You killed them, Jack!" she growled through gritted teeth. "You killed them!"

Another of the massive, evil creatures backhanded Megan, sending her head-over-heels through the air. She landed with a thud against the blackened wall of the destroyed building, several yards away from where she had been kneeling. Blood was running from a long cut on her cheek where the creature's huge hand had made contact; bruises were already forming on her back and shoulders where she had struck the broken bricks in the wall. The creatures laughed their sinister laugh, feeding on the pain they were inflicting. Jack bristled, then twisted his body so that his shirt ripped. He fell free of the creature, leaving the torn fabric of the back of his shirt still in the creature's grasp. Megan slowly began to rise. Jack yelled for Megan to run, but the creature who had hit her reached out again and batted her to the ground as if she were a stuffed toy. Her body thumped as it hit the ground, the air rushing out of her lungs. She gasped for breath, her chest heaving as she tried to inhale, unable to lift herself out of the mud. Jack started to run to her, but the creature threw the remnant of his shirt to the ground and grabbed his hair again, stopping him in his tracks.

"Leave her alone!" Jack yelled at them, writhing to get free of the monster. "Let her go!"

But they just laughed at him. "You don't care about her anymore, remember?" they taunted. "'New deck, new cut, new dealer', remember?" they laughed. "Now she is all alone! What an easy target!"

"No!" Jack yelled. "Noooo!"

The creature beside Megan reached out his monstrous hand. He snatched a handful of her hair and lifted her to her feet, slipping his other hand around her neck. He looked over at Jack, a terrible, evil grin coming across his hideous face. With the slightest twitch of his wrist, Megan's neck snapped. Her body, now limp and lifeless, hung from the creature's hand like a cooked spaghetti noodle dangling from a fork.

"Megan!" Jack screamed in terror. He would have sat bolt upright in his pit, had the unforgiving metal bottom of the pit above him not stopped his movement halfway up into a sitting position. His forehead made contact with the cold steel, then his body fell as quickly as it had risen, flopping back down onto the mattress and appearing as lifeless as Megan's body had appeared in his dream. He slowly lifted his hand up to his forehead and moaned.

Startled by the loud bang and the subsequent moaning, two of his roommates rushed to his pit to investigate. They found a very dazed Jack Douglass attempting to emerge from his pit, his shaky hand covering the reddened lump on his forehead. Jack slowly made it to an upright position, steadying himself by holding the edge of his pit with his other hand. He refused any assistance, assuring them that he was okay, and staggered to the head to splash some cold water onto his face. After drying his face off and fixing his hair, Jack returned to his pit, retrieved his hat from behind his pillow, and carefully made his way to the signal bridge.

As soon as they were cut loose that afternoon, Phil headed straight for Megan's apartment. She must be feeling horrible about the confrontation with Jack. Phil wanted to make sure she understood that Jack was being stubborn and cold, and not at all Christ-like. If he had found out about Megan before she had confessed, that would be a whole different animal. He would have had the right to read the riot act to her, because she would have been clearly in the wrong. His mistake, however, was in not recognizing the fact that she had already confessed her sins to Kim and to God, and that she was merely following God's requirement of making things right with those against whom she had sinned when she met with Jack.

He knocked on Megan's door at ten minutes before four. She opened it up and invited him in.

"Hi, Phil! What brings you out here?" she asked.

"I talked with Jack over lunch today," he explained. "More accurately, I should say, he told me about the meeting the two of you had yesterday, and about the appalling way he behaved. I gave him one Class A, US Choice, Grade A, Number One butt-chewing."

"Oh, you did…"

"Yes, I most certainly did. You see, Megan, Jack's behavior was inexcusable. Confession of sin is supposed to be met with grace and forgiveness, not with condemnation and bitterness. That isn't how God works. Yes, you wronged Jack, and you needed to ask his forgiveness; but he had no right to lecture you about how evil you are and to refuse to forgive you. I chewed him out because I know he can handle it. He will think about it, realize he was wrong, and then it will be up to him to make things right with you.

"I also wanted to make sure you understand that I am here for you, Megan. I want to help you learn how to live your new life properly, and the episode with Jack was a classic lesson in how *not* to act. Jack will come around, you just have to give him some time. I know him well enough to know that my words hurt him today. He was acting all cocky about what he had said to you, and I put him right back in his place very harshly. I didn't enjoy it, but that is what it takes to get through to some people.

"You rely on God, Megan. Give Jack some time and some space, and he will get back on track. You have enough to worry about right now without concerning yourself with Jack."

"Well, thank you, Phil. I must admit, it did take me by surprise when he said those things. I have never seen that side of him before. Oh, did you make any progress as far as the legal aspect of my situation is concerned?" she asked.

"Not yet, but I am putting all the effort I can into it. Don't plan anything for Friday yet. I'm still trying to get something lined up for that afternoon."

"Thanks, Phil," Megan said, pulling him tightly into the frightened embrace of a woman feeling very alone in a troubled sea of confusion and uncertainty.

Jack felt horrible. Aside from the knot on his forehead and the accompanying headache, he was an emotional wreck. In only two short days, he had gone through a wide variety of emotional highs and lows—but mostly lows. He had experienced the excitement and anticipation of coming home to his girlfriend after an eight-week separation. He had been greeted on the pier by all of his friends from the church. Megan had fled the 'welcome home' dinner at Pizza Hut and refused to speak to him, he had endured a frustrating day of apartment hunting with Phil while wondering what in the world could be wrong with Megan. He had been informed that what was wrong with his girlfriend was that she was actually somebody else living under a new name and working undercover as a spy for a drug lord in a foreign country. He had confronted her about it and had brutally let her have it for using him as a spy source while pretending to care for him. Phil had let *him* have it just as brutally for letting *her* have it because he was supposed to have forgiven her. And, to top it all off, he had had this freaky nightmare during his lunch-time 'nooner' where Megan had blamed him for killing her family and then she had gotten herself killed by those huge demon things. Then he had almost cracked his head open on the pit above him when he woke up from the terrible nightmare. He had definitely had better days.

Now here he was, walking by himself across the Navy base along the bank of the Chesapeake Bay. This was a less traveled part of the base, the undeveloped area between the main working portion of the base and a seldom-used back entrance to the base. Up ahead on the left was a small parking lot. Like a low-budget roadside park, it had several picnic tables, a pet walking area, a platoon of trash cans and no restroom facilities. Across the road from the lot was a small health facility, complete with a collection of free weights and nautilus weight machines, a fleet of exercise machines and a big television mounted at the ceiling in the corner of the room. Jack entered the park area and walked across the asphalt to the grass along the water's edge. The bank was covered with a layer of white rocks, beginning several inches above the water line and extending down into the water as far as Jack could see, like the lining of a swimming pool. There was a line of dried green and brown algae a few inches above the edge of the water, marking the normal water level so that the bay knew how high to rise when the next rain came. Dusk had arrived in full force, bringing with it a very chilly fall breeze which raced the diminishing rays of sunlight across the water to the place where Jack was walking. He buried his hands deep into the pockets of his jacket and stopped walking, defiantly facing the incoming wind.

Squatting down to reach the ground, he picked up a handful of the white rocks and threw one out into the bay as far as he could. "Why did she have to pick me?" he wondered aloud. He threw another rock, this one even further into the bay. Strike one. "Of all the guys in Norfolk—of all the *churches* in Norfolk—why did she have to pick me?!" he yelled at the falling darkness. He pitched another fast ball into the water. Strike two. "After all this time, I finally meet what appears to be a nice girl, and meet her at church no less, and we hit it off wonderfully, and she turns out to be nothing more than a liar and a spy!! I finally meet a 'nice girl' *at church*, and she is a SPY! I could have done better in a singles bar somewhere! At least there, I would know what I was getting. If I dated her for a while and looked around one day to find myself with a drunk, or a sleaze-ball, or even a sweet girl with loose morals, at least I wouldn't be terribly surprised. But to meet a sweet girl in the church, someone who may not claim to be 'Little Miss Religious Fanatic' or even claim to buy into the whole religious ball of wax, but who still gives the impression of being a good girl, someone of high moral character and strong values, only to find out later that she is a liar and a deceiver and a user who can't be trusted, who has ties with some drug guy down in Venezuela which she claims is based on threats to her family, but who knows what her real relationship with him is! And then she thinks that if she apologizes for it that it will all just go away and I am supposed to just say 'Oh, that's all right, Megan, I forgive you. I know you didn't mean to finagle your way into my life, slowly get into my head and heart, then in one fell swoop rip my heart out of my chest, jump up and down on it, then pull your mask off and say 'Sorry, Jack, I didn't mean it, I really do care, the Venezuelan drug guy made me do it; forgive me?' –Hey, don't give it a second thought. We all have those days when we obliterate the heart of someone we love under the guise of blackmail by the international drug cartel.'

"What a crock! It's not my fault she got mixed up in this mess, so why should I have to play the role of supportive friend and help her through it? I am the one who got the shaft in this whole situation. It's easy for Phil to tell me to forgive her and be her friend, she wasn't curled up with *him* on the couch in front of the TV set watching movies until the wee hours of the morning. She wasn't writing *him* letters about how much she enjoyed her time with him and how she couldn't wait until he came home. She didn't give *him* the googely-eyes all through dinner, then rest her head on his shoulder as they walked arm-in-arm along the beach talking about what they hoped their life would be like in the years to come. And she didn't just tell *him* that all of it had been merely a farce; a cover created for her by her Venezuelan drug guy.

"Why would I want anything to do with her ever again? How could I ever trust her, even if I wanted to? There would always be the doubt. There would always be the fear that it would happen again. When would it end? When would the next sadistic surprise happen? What if she just made up all this guilty confession stuff to throw me off the track? What if it is all part of her plan, to make me think that it is all over, only to dig her claws in deeper and get even more sensitive information out of me? What if she meets me one day with a gun to my head because I can no longer provide her with information good enough to satisfy her boss across the sea? What a messed up woman! Who would be stupid enough to walk back in to that mess on purpose? Not Jack Douglass, that's for sure! No way, I am cutting my losses. I don't need that kind of aggravation. I'd be better off with the bar wench—at least I would know what I was in for before I got involved." He heaved another rock out into the bay. "Strike three. She's outta here," Jack spat out bitterly as he dug his hands back into his pockets and started walking toward the ship.

The chilly breeze became colder as Jack trudged along the road on his way back to the ship. The cold air circled around his neck and shot down inside his jacket. It would come in cold bursts, slapping him in the face and taking his breath away. Inside his heart, Phil's words were having the same effect. Like cold fingers of ice, they poked him and twisted away at his conscience. "What if Phil is right?" they suggested. "What if Megan really is sorry for what she did to you, and what if she really is trying to get out of her deal with Ramirez? What if she really does love you and wants to repair the damage she has done to you and to your relationship? What if Phil is right, that she has truly repented to God for her sins, and He has forgiven her? Then what? What will you do, Jack?" The doubts in his mind tormented him almost as much as thinking about what Megan had done to him.

Jack reached the *Mississippi*, stormed into his complex and flopped down into an empty chair in front of the TV. He watched three shows, two dumb comedies and a boring drama, before he gave up and walked back to his pit. He had hoped that the mindless entertainment would prevent him from thinking about Megan, but he was sadly disappointed. Unable to stand it any longer, he took off his clothes and crawled into his pit, hoping that sleep would quiet the war that was raging in his mind.

The next morning, half an hour after Quarters, Jack stood behind the desk in the signal shack waiting for the coffee pot to provide him with a good, hot cup of coffee. Something had to go right this morning, even if it was something as insignificant as a refreshing cup of Morning Blend coffee. He had awakened with a headache, probably an after-effect of slamming his forehead into the pit bottom the previous afternoon. He had cut himself shaving, like he was still sixteen or something, and the breakfast he had been served in the galley was one of the worst he could remember. It could probably have been his favorite food, expertly prepared by a professional chef, and it still would have been awful, simply because of his foul mood. When the coffee had finally finished dripping from the grounds, Jack picked up the carafe and poured himself a cupful. He was about to place the carafe back onto the heating element when Phil stepped through the doorway, extending his empty cup toward Jack.

"Can you spare a cup?" he asked.

"Sure, Phil. Come on in," Jack invited, not at all entertained by the idea of listening to another lecture from Phil about Megan. He positioned the carafe over Phil's cup and let the hot, black liquid flow into it.

"How's it going, Jack?" Phil asked, trying to break the awkward tension and ease into conversation.

"Been better," Jack said, replacing the carafe and hopping up onto one of the stools. A little bit of coffee splashed out of Jack's cup and landed on his knee. "Sure," he said through gritted teeth while the hot coffee on his leg cooled off and the burning subsided, "you just had to do that, didn't you?"

"Rough morning?" Phil asked.

"You could say that," Jack retorted.

Phil leaned up against the desk, quietly sipping at his coffee. He could see that Jack was in turmoil over Megan, but he didn't volunteer to start a conversation about it. Jack, on the other hand, was irritated that Phil wasn't saying anything. He was casually sitting there drinking his coffee, acting like nothing had happened between them yesterday. A few moments of silence passed.

"Hey," Phil said, breaking the silence, "do you want to go out and look at some more apartments this afternoon?"

"Okay, Phil, I have been thinking about what you said, all right?!" Jack almost yelled.

"Yes..." Phil said, content with the total change of subject and prodding him to continue.

"Yes, and I think you are wrong," he said sternly. "She betrayed me, Phil. She lied to me, she used me, and she betrayed me. I don't care if she does feel guilty about what she has done. Good! She should feel guilty because she IS guilty! And you think I should just forgive and forget and carry on like nothing ever happened? No way, man. It doesn't work like that. I let her in, Phil. I cared for her, and she used me like a piece of scrap paper. And I am not going back for any more. You know the old saying, Phil, 'Fool me once, shame on you; fool me twice, shame on me.'

Well, shame on her, and I am out of there. She can clean up her own mess."

"Really," Phil said.

"Yes, really," Jack agreed viscously.

"So, you are done with her, then?" Phil asked. "No second chances? No mercy?"

"Second chances? For what? To work me over again? Why would I want to do that? I have seen her true colors now, and I don't like the shade. Yes, I am done with her. She is free as far as I am concerned. Why, are you interested?" Jack said with bitter sarcasm.

"Not romantically, but yes, very interested."

"What is that supposed to mean?" Jack asked.

Phil paused and looked knowingly at Jack, as though the answer had suddenly come to him. "You love her, don't you Jack?" Phil asked.

"What?? Are you out of your mind? After what she did to me? Why can't you understand this, Phil? You are so smart in some ways, but you sure seem to be an idiot where women are concerned."

"You do, don't you?" Phil persisted.

"If you are up here just to bug me, then you might as well leave. I have work to do," Jack said, plopping his cup on the desk and hopping down off of his stool.

"Jack, I know it hurts when someone you love betrays you, but you have to get past that and—"

"Get *past* that?? GET PAST IT ?" Jack yelled. You don't just 'get past' something like this, Phil!"

"Why not, Jack? What is so different now? Where is that logic you are so proud of using all the time? Does that only apply to other people during their crises, and not to you during yours?"

"What are you talking about, Phil?" Jack asked, still seething with anger.

"What am I talking about? Now who is being an idiot? You see, Jack, there are two aspects to the situation here that you have to deal with. The first is the betrayal. Yes, she betrayed you, and yes, she was dead wrong. There is no question about that."

"Finally!" Jack shouted, throwing his hands into the air.

"Let me finish," Phil said sternly. "The first is the betrayal. The second is the forgiveness. The first is singular and personal, a one-fold affair between you and Megan. The second is also personal, but it is a two-fold predicament; on one hand, between you and Megan, and on the other hand, between you and God."

Jack looked blankly at Phil, understanding him so far but having no idea where he was going with his explanation.

Phil continued, "In the first case, that of the betrayal, your options are clear. She wronged you, there is no doubt. The only issue to be dealt with there is whether or not to continue the relationship. You and Megan have begun to develop a strong and wonderful relationship; but if you elect not to attempt to repair the damage done to that relationship, that is your prerogative. You are under no obligation to continue to cultivate that relationship, any more than you would be obligated to continue it if there had been no betrayal at all. It is completely up to you. In my opinion, however, considering what I believe the state of Megan's heart to be, you would be a fool to walk away."

Jack began to argue, but Phil silenced him with a pointed finger from an upraised hand. Jack conceded and leaned back against the desk.

"The second case is much more complicated. There are two dynamics at work in the second case, as opposed to only the one in the first. The first dynamic is the issue of your forgiveness of Megan with respect to your relationship with Megan. It is my firm belief that Megan has truly and freely repented of her sins and has become a new creature in Jesus Christ, in accordance with the same Biblical principles and requirements that I have adhered to for many years, and that you have only recently made the decision to adhere to. It is in this capacity that she has prevailed upon you to forgive her for her sins against you. Now, removing *you* from the equation and looking exclusively at Megan, she has followed those Biblical requirements where you are concerned. Whether you elect to forgive her or not, she has already been forgiven by God and is no longer being held accountable to Him for her sins. Should you refuse to forgive her, the effect on her is purely personal and emotional, not spiritual. Although she desires your forgiveness with all her heart, she doesn't need it to be in a right relationship with God. That brings us to the next point.

"The second dynamic is the issue of your forgiveness of Megan with respect to your relationship with God. You see, Megan doesn't need your forgiveness to maintain her relationship with God, but you *do* need to forgive *her* to maintain *your* relationship with God."

Phil reached around Jack and pulled open the steel drawer marked 'LPO'. He removed Jack's Bible from it and placed it on the desktop, flipping it open to the New Testament. "Look, Jack," he continued. "Look at what Jesus said in Matthew 7:2, 'For in the same way you judge others, you will be judged, and with the measure you use, it will be measured to you.' And back here in chapter six, after Jesus taught His disciples how to pray, He said in verses fourteen and fifteen, 'For if you forgive men when they sin against you, your heavenly Father will also forgive you. But if you do not forgive men their sins, your Father will not forgive your sins.'

"You see, Jack, it's not like you caught Megan doing you wrong and, instead of owning up to her actions, she is trying to weasel her way out of it. On the contrary! She came to you about it of her own free will, confessed her sins to you, and humbly asked for your forgiveness. I firmly believe that the Holy Spirit got hold of her heart and caused her to see her sinful state, which she honestly repented of in Kim's presence. Now she is trying to do right by God and 'clean up the mess', as you so eloquently put it. She knows what she did, Jack. She knows how much it hurt you. And she also knows how much she loves you and wants to make it right.

"I am your friend, Jack, and I love you like a brother, but I must tell you, if you don't forgive her and work through this, number one, it will eat you up inside and destroy your soul; and number two, you will be throwing away a chance to make something wonderful with an incredible lady who loves you with all her heart. Why do you think she came clean, Jack? Why do you think she couldn't tell you about it sooner, or even later, without me breaking it to you first? She was afraid she wouldn't be able to get the words out because her own heart would be breaking and she wouldn't be able to speak. She wanted you to understand, or at least to get the whole story, so she asked me to tell you the details first.

"Please don't take this lightly, Jack. This is a very big deal, with great potential for far-reaching repercussions. The decisions you make in the next few hours or days could quite possibly affect the lives of many people. Take it to God, Jack. That is what Jesus meant when He said in Mark 8 that we must deny ourselves and take up our cross and follow Him. He made that statement after Peter had argued that Jesus would never be killed by the chief priests and teachers of the law. He said that Peter had in mind the things of men, not the things of God. He said we must deny that selfish thought process and allow God's thoughts to prevail, and we would live. The cross we are to take up is the cross of letting God be number one and not always looking out for ourselves."

Phil drained his cup and walked out of the signal shack, leaving Jack alone to process what he had said. He walked toward the forward bulkhead and looked out over the bay at the merchant ships slowly steaming their way out into the open sea. "Oh, God," he prayed, "give Jack wisdom. Let him see beyond his own pain and hurt feelings to the bigger picture. He is hurting right now, but he can still do the right thing. Give him grace and peace."

Back inside the signal shack, tears streamed down Jack's face as he looked back over the verses Phil had read and unknowingly joined him in his prayer to God for wisdom and strength.

Later that morning, Phil hurried through his lunch and walked to the pay phone on the aft quarterdeck. He dropped the required coins into the slot and dialed Megan's number from memory.

Megan shut off the vacuum sweeper, thinking she may have heard the telephone ringing. It rang again, so she quickly locked the machine in its upright position and ran out of her bedroom to where the telephone hung on the wall at the end of the kitchen cupboard. She picked it up and breathlessly said, "Hello?"

into the mouthpiece.

"Hi, Megan. Phil Prescott, here," Phil said. "Are you all right? You sound out of breath."

"Oh, hi, Phil! Yeah, I am fine. I was just vacuuming, and I'm a little winded from running across the apartment to get to the telephone. What's going on?"

"Just checking on you. How are you doing?"

"About as well as can be expected, I guess," she answered. "I am trying to keep myself busy. You know, keep my mind from wandering to painful things that I can't control and don't need to be thinking about."

"Smart girl," Phil said. "Hey, speaking of painful things that you can't control, I talked to Jack this morning. He was much more calm than he was yesterday, and he was even somewhat receptive to discussing the subject of you. I think he will be coming around before long."

"Oh, I hope so, Phil. I wouldn't be surprised if he decides to end our relationship, but I hope we can still be friends."

"Just give him time, Megan. This has been quite a blow to him. Pray and wait."

"Yeah, I know. I'm trying."

"Well, keep it up."

"Right. Hey, any luck getting in touch with—uh—whomever you were going to get in touch with about me and this mess?"

"I am making progress. I talked to Lieutenant Hensley, my unit commander, and he is making some calls for me. He agreed that we should probably talk to the NCIS about it first, but he is checking around just to be sure. I will probably hear something from him later today or first thing tomorrow. You will know as soon as I do, Megan. Just hang in there."

"I'm hanging, Phil. I'm hanging."

"All right, then, I'll talk to you later."

"Hey, Phil?"

"Yes?"

"I was thinking about getting together with everybody who was at the Pizza Hut on Sunday and filling them in on what is going on. They are probably wondering what in the world is wrong with me, and I really owe it to them to tell them the truth. What do you think? I mean, legally, or whatever, should I be telling people about it?"

"I don't think it will hurt to tell your closest friends, but I wouldn't be spreading it around or anything. Who knows, this Ramirez guy might have other eyes and ears up here."

A cold chill swept through Megan in an instant, causing her to shiver and get goose bumps all over her arms. "True. I hadn't thought of that. Well, I think I'll call Kirt Radford and see if he can arrange for everyone to meet me somewhere tonight. The sooner, the better, I guess."

"I think that is a good idea," Phil agreed. "You could really use the added support right now, not to mention in the near future."

"I don't even want to think about that part," she chuckled. "One crisis at a time. Uh, Phil, if you don't have plans tonight, I would like to have you there if I can set up a meeting tonight. You know, just to have someone in my corner?"

"Sure, Megan, give me a beep. I may have to cancel tea and Cricket with the Queen, but I suppose I could do that for you."

She chuckled again. "Thanks, Phil. Talk to you later."

"Yep, bye," he said.

Megan hung up the phone and flipped through the wrinkled papers clipped to the memo clip magnet on her refrigerator door until she came to the one with Kirt Radford's name and phone number scribbled on it. She dialed the number and waited through four rings, a short yet professional message solicitation, and one very long beep. "Kirt, this is Megan," she began, only to be interrupted by Kirt's voice.

"Hi, Megan! How are you?" he inquired anxiously.

"I am fine, Kirt. Thanks for asking."

"Sure. I talked to Kim last night at church, and she told me the good news about your decision to become a Christian. That is wonderful, Megan. I am very happy for you."

"Thanks, Kirt. Hey, the reason I am calling is that I want to get together with you and everybody who was at the Hut on Sunday. I feel like I need to explain myself to all of you, and I would rather get everybody together and catch you all at the same time."

"Sure, Megan, we can do that. How about tomorrow night? We can meet at my parent's place, if you don't mind. They have been busy in prayer for you, and they would appreciate hearing about it from you, too."

"Okay, I guess that would be all right," she said.

"Great, I'll make the calls. What time? About seven? I'll have Mom bake some cookies or something."

"Oh, she doesn't need to go to that kind of trouble…"

"Are you kidding?" Kirt interrupted. "She lives for that kind of stuff. She wouldn't feel like she was doing her part if she couldn't bake *and* pray about something. 'Grace for the soul, cookies for the peace of mind', she always says."

"Okay, Kirt, thanks. See you tomorrow night."

"Sure, see you then. Bye."

The work day seemed like it would never end. Every time Jack got a few minutes to himself to think about Megan, someone would interrupt him for something. Three-fifteen could not come soon enough. The situation was eating him up inside, and something needed to be done about it. He needed time alone to figure out exactly how he felt about the whole deal. He needed time to consider what Phil had said, both times, and to pray for God's guidance. He had to admit, he was feeling a little bit guilty about the episode with Megan, even though part of him still believed she had deserved it. Either way, it hadn't been a very nice thing for him to do.

At 3:00, Jack locked up the signal bridge and went down to his living complex. He washed his face and fixed his hair, then selected a matching set of civilian clothes out of his pit locker. He swapped his black low-top boots for a comfortable pair of sneakers, and his black socks for a clean pair of white ones. As he was tying his sneakers, Phil entered the complex. They had agreed to continue their search for an apartment as soon as they were cut loose on liberty. They exchanged greetings as Phil waited for Jack to finish getting ready.

The sudden burst of static coming across the 1MC

announcing circuit was all the announcement they needed. Before the Petty Officer of the Watch had even begun to deliver his 'Liberty Call, Liberty Call' speech, watertight doors from one end of the ship to the other were being flung open as eager sailors bolted from their complexes to the quarterdeck for a day's worth of freedom. Jack and Phil were near the beginning of the line of sailors spilling out onto the pier in search of food, shopping, movies, and whatever other sort of business or entertainment they could find.

Again, Phil and Jack opted to take Phil's pickup because it was the first of their vehicles they came to in the parking lot. They drove over to the Oceanview area, one of the few areas they hadn't searched yet, and turned north on Oceanview Drive.

"We may as well have a view of the ocean," Jack said. "They cost a little more, but between the two of us, we can afford it."

They checked out several apartment buildings with advertised vacancies, but most were too small or too dirty or both. The third apartment they actually stopped to look at, however, was the one they had spent the last week trying to find. It was way up at the north end of Oceanview, where highway 60 goes on up to the small peninsula of Willoughby Beach and runs the length of it. The small piece of land looks like a witch's crooked index finger, pointing to the west then curling south at the first knuckle to form Willoughby Bay, the small body of water between Willoughby Beach on the north and the Norfolk Naval Base on the south and east. The apartment was at the end of Eleventh View Street, a stone's throw beyond the place where Toler Place intersects it perpendicularly and links it to Twelfth View Street. As soon as they opened the front door, they knew this was the place for them. Two bedrooms, big living room, small but suitable kitchen, and a sliding glass door opening up from the small dining area onto a balcony overlooking the Chesapeake Bay. Sold. They filled out the necessary paperwork, performed their move-in inspection, and arranged to take possession Monday. Phil would call Friday and get all the utilities turned on, and they could pick up their keys Monday morning at the rental office.

"Let's grab some dinner," Phil said as he slid behind the wheel of his pickup. "What are you in the mood for, Jack?"

"Something that does not require conscious thought," Jack replied.

"That bad, eh?" Phil asked.

"I am just trying to figure out this Megan thing, Phil," Jack said. "Of course, you were right with the stuff you said yesterday, but it's not that easy. I can't just pinpoint how I am supposed to feel, wave my magic wand and, POOF! That is the way I feel."

Jack's mood had calmed significantly, but he was still irritated and upset. The anger and hostility he had initially felt had given way to a combination of the hurt from the betrayal and the sense of loss and emptiness he felt without her. The shock of the realization of what had happened was diminishing, giving way to the survival instinct to assess and repair the damage.

"It is more than the forgiveness that you talked about," Jack continued. "For Kim and you and the rest of them, all you have to be concerned about is the fact of her being an impostor. But for me, it is much more than that. The relationship Megan and I have—had—whatever—didn't stop at mere friendship. Sure, we were becoming close friends, but we were also working the girlfriend/boyfriend angle of it. As you well know, I was getting in very deep with her, and I thought she was doing the same with me. But now, all the trust we had is gone. Whenever I think of Megan, I still get all stupid inside, because I am absolutely crazy about the wonderful girl I was falling in love with. But now, I find out that that girl may not even exist! How much of what I loved about Megan is going to be present in Belinda? And, even more frightening to consider, how much of what I don't know about Belinda is actually going to be present in Megan? Phil, I have fallen in love with a woman who doesn't exist! Now, let's put aside the whole betrayal aspect of it. Let's look at it from a purely psychological point of view. How can I attempt to date and develop a relationship with Belinda, who looks, acts, sounds, smells, laughs, walks, and talks exactly like Megan, without allowing my pre-conceived notions of who and what she is to enter the picture and cloud my judgment? Can I really be fair and honest in my impressions of her? Is it possible for me to put out of my mind every bias I have about Megan and get to know her as Belinda? Wouldn't that be like trying to switch from one identical twin sister to the other, halfway through a courtship ritual, without letting any impressions of the first come into play in the form of a bias for or against the second?"

"Jack, I think you are thinking too hard about this," Phil interrupted. "Believe me, I understand where you are coming from, but I think that possibly you are going *too* deep this time. You see, I don't believe that Megan and Belinda are two distinctly different people. Rather, I think that Megan and Belinda are one in the same person; same thoughts, same dreams, same ideals, same desires. However, I do believe that what separates them and makes them different is their theater of operation and what it is that they are required to do in that environment to ensure their survival."

"Phil, I think you have lost it, man. You are really reaching on this one—"

"I'll get there, Jack, just give me a minute. A little latitude, Your Honor," Phil requested in mock formality and with a pathetic English accent.

"*Very* little latitude, Counselor," Jack smiled. "You may proceed..."

"I believe that the person you got to know and fell in love with, Megan, is the same person that Belinda is. Like you said yourself, same looks, smile, smell, talk, walk, laugh, etc. In my opinion, I believe that Belinda is the girl you got to know and fell in love with. *Megan* is the impostor. In Venezuela, Belinda Gallagos was a poor farm girl who probably had a very small and happy life, until Ramirez came along and tore it all to shreds. But still, she loved her family enough to do whatever she could to keep them safe. When she came to the United States, she became Megan Gallagher, traitor and spy. She was supposed to get close to you and use you as Megan Gallagher, to finesse information out of you and pass it along to Ramirez, in return for the safety of her family. However, the Belinda Gallagos side of her was too dominant. Instead of keeping herself aloof and concentrating her contact with you on getting information, she fell in love with you. Ramirez tried to force Belinda to become Megan, but he couldn't. She caved and blew her cover because she loved you too much to carry it on any longer. I think that she loves you enough to risk losing you in order to keep you. She knew that it would eventually come out anyway, and she also knew that the longer it took to come out, the smaller the chance that you could forgive her and still want to work it out with her. The result? The events of this week."

"I hate it when you are right, but that does make sense. So, you are saying that all the good that I saw in Megan was actually the true person of Belinda, and that the good in Belinda overcame the bad in Megan? Almost like a schizophrenic whose dominant good personality suppresses the bad ones and becomes the dominant character of the person?"

"Right. Now, I am not at all suggesting that she has any type of personality disorder. I am only saying that she is one person trying to fulfill the roles of two very different people, one here and one in Venezuela."

"Hmm..." Jack took a moment to ponder Phil's opinion.

Phil took the opportunity to start the pickup and head out toward Luciano's. He knew Jack wouldn't mind. Three stop lights later, Jack cleared his throat and looked over at Phil.

"Okay, so let me ask you this, Phil. Bear in mind, however, that this does not constitute agreement with your explanation. This is simply a hypothetical question using your explanation as the assumption, and my current dilemma as the example."

"Understood. Please, continue," Phil said.

"Okay, let's suppose that what you have said is correct, that Belinda really did fall in love with me. Several questions come to mind. One: do you think she really is in love with me?"

"Easy one—absolutely. I have watched her with you, Jack. Nobody can act that good. And, even if she could, she would have no reason. She could get the information she needed from you by merely being a friend, like she is with Kim and Laura, or even Steve or Kirt. To carry it as far as she did would be way above and beyond the call of duty for a spy, not to mention detrimental to the mission itself, as we have clearly seen."

"Two: what if she is faking all of this, and just trying to endear herself to all of us so she can get even closer?"

"Again, no need," Phil stated bluntly. "She could get all the information she needed as a friend to any of us, or even a specific few of us. All of the scheming that would be required would serve no purpose. And, even if the story of her family was a fabrication, she is still in very grave danger as a result of her confessing her activities to all of us. Treason is a capital crime."

"Three: can I ever trust her again? I mean, after she betrayed me like she did?"

"Do you love her, Jack?"

Silence.

"Come on, Jack, I already know the answer. Do you love her?"

"All right, all right! Yes, I do. I love her. If I didn't, this stuff wouldn't bother me so much, now would it?"

"Then I don't even have to answer that one."

Jack nodded and looked out the window as Phil turned the pickup into the parking lot of Luciano's and steered into an empty space behind the building.

"Jack, just talk to her. And, more importantly, listen to her. Be skeptical going in if you need to, but *go in.* Try to see it from her point of view. You are an innocent victim, but so is she. Talk to her, Jack. See for yourself if her conversion is real. See for yourself if her love for you is true. Take it one step at a time. Start the relationship over, pace yourself, whatever you have to do, just don't give up after one little snag. Okay, or after one incredibly humungous monster snag." Phil smiled at his friend as he slammed the shifting lever into Park and opened up his door. "Come on, let's go get some food."

"Right behind you, Bro. Lead on."

~9~

Ltjg Malcolm Hensley shouted, "ENTER!" and looked up from behind the small desk he had been given during his TAD assignment to the USS *Mississippi* as Commander of the Coast Guard Drug Interdiction Team. What had previously been a storeroom in the aft, port corner of the Combat Systems computer support control room had been emptied, painted, and sparsely furnished to become the temporary new office of Ltjg Hensley. BM2 E. Phillip Anthony Prescott opened the small door and stepped through it. He had gotten the word during lunch that Ltjg Hensley wanted to see him ASAP in his office, to which he had responded anxiously and with great haste. He pushed the door shut behind him and, at the Lieutenant's behest, took the single paint-speckled folding chair opposite the small desk and sat in it.

"Mr. Prescott," Ltjg Hensley began, "you have managed to get the attention of many people with your unusual request. The inquiries I made for you this week have stirred up a flurry of activity in a variety of offices all over the city. At the moment, however, jurisdiction for a suspected espionage case at this level falls within the confines of the Naval Criminal Investigative Service. I have been instructed to ask you no questions, but only to give you this telephone number and a direct order to make a call to Resident Special Agent In Charge William H. McDowell immediately. You may use the telephone at my desk. I will be back later this afternoon. You have my permission and my order to provide Special Agent McDowell with any and all assistance he requests. If your compliance with his requests requires any time off to meet with him, fill out a special request chit to that effect and place it on my desk before you leave. And you had better be prepared to fill me in on every detail of this situation as soon as security allows it, Prescott. It sounds pretty exciting!" Ltjg Hensley slapped Phil on the back as he exited the tiny office.

Phil walked around the desk and plopped down into the

chair. It was only slightly more comfortable than the folding chair he had been using, he thought. He dialed the number and waited while it rang. It was picked up after the second ring.

"Naval Criminal Investigative Service, Norfolk Operations, how may I help you?" a friendly voice asked.

"Special Agent William McDowell, please," Phil replied.

"One moment," the voice said.

Another voice came on the line before Phil could even identify the classic rock song that was being brutally butchered by a symphony orchestra on the hold line.

"Special Agent Bill McDowell" said a deep, scratchy voice, the tone of which suggesting that he was happy it was Friday and was quite eager to leave for the weekend.

"Good afternoon, Special Agent McDowell, my name is BM2 Phil Prescott. Ltjg Hensley instructed me to call you immediately."

"Ah, right, Prescott." Phil heard the shuffling of papers through the telephone. "Prescott, Phillip, BM2, possible espionage contact, right?"

"Yes, Sir, that is correct," Phil answered.

"What ship are you on, Petty Officer Prescott?" McDowell asked.

"The *Mississippi*, Sir. CGN-40."

"Okay, Petty Officer Prescott. Now, the remainder of this discussion needs to take place in our office, for security reasons. Do you know where our office is located?"

Phil responded that he did not, and Special Agent McDowell gave him directions.

"I would like to meet with you today, if that is at all possible. I hate leaving a new case in limbo over the weekend."

"Sir, I am not the actual subject of the espionage," Phil said. "There is a civilian spy who is currently dating a military person. The civilian was the one to expose her involvement in the espionage, of which the military member was completely unaware until four days ago."

"So, you are saying that you are not technically involved, but are aware of the situation because you are acquainted with both of the subjects who are involved?"

"That is correct."

"And do they both know you are making this call?"

"The civilian does, the military member does not. He and the civilian have had something of a falling out since the truth came out. She asked me what she should do, so I told her I would ask my Lieutenant how to handle it, and he directed me to you."

"Understood," Special Agent McDowell said. "All right, then, do you believe that the military member would meet with me freely?"

"Absolutely. He just found out about the whole situation, and he is not at all happy about it. Of course, his displeasure is not due to reasons of national security, if you get my meaning. I don't imagine he has even considered the legal ramifications of the situation."

"Okay, Petty Officer Prescott, would you give me the names of the subjects involved, please?"

"Certainly, Sir. The civilian is a Miss Megan Gallagher, the sailor is Signalman Second Class Jonathan Douglass."

"Thank you, Petty Officer Prescott. Now, would you and Miss Gallagher be able to meet with me today? Say, around one-thirty? I would like to talk to the two of you first, then bring Mr. Douglass into it on Monday morning."

"Better make it two, if that is okay. I will have to call Megan, then go and pick her up on my way to your office."

"Two is fine. See you then."

"Yes, Sir. Bye," Phil said, then hung up the telephone. He lifted the receiver again and called Megan to tell her to be ready in thirty minutes, to which she nervously agreed. Then he filled out a special request chit requesting the rest of the day off to meet with the NCIS agent and placed it neatly in the middle of Ltjg Hensley's desk. His adrenaline started building. This was getting complicated.

It had taken Phil exactly eighteen minutes to get to his complex, change into appropriate civilian attire, and walk from the ship to his pickup. He fired it up and zipped out of the parking lot to the main road heading off the base. He wove through traffic as best he could, not really saving himself any driving time, but giving himself the false impression that he was.

Megan answered the door and invited Phil into her apartment.

"Be just a minute," she said.

"All right. Hey, I have a question for you," Phil said loud enough for the sound to carry into the bedroom.

Megan poked her head through the doorway, "Yeah?" she asked.

"You said you were living here temporarily under the identity of Megan Gallagher. Do you have any legal documentation to that effect?"

"All I have is whatever is in here," she said, reaching into her dresser drawer and extracting a plastic pouch. "Ramirez said this was all I would need, and that no one would ask me any questions that these documents wouldn't answer." She handed the plastic pouch to Phil, who removed a pen from his shirt pocket and used it to flip through the papers contained in the pouch.

"A birth certificate, a passport, and a social security card," he said. "Pretty thorough, this Ramirez guy."

"I had another passport, too, but he told me to burn it after I got here from Venezuela. It was in some other name I had never heard of, but I guess I looked a lot like the picture in it, because nobody ever confronted me about it."

"We should take these to the NCIS guy. I am sure he will want to see them."

"Okay," she agreed nervously. "Phil, those are false documents. Am I going to get into trouble for having counterfeit official documents in my possession?"

"I don't know, Megan. Hopefully you will be able to work something out with the authorities, since you are voluntarily going to them and turning yourself in."

"I hope so, Phil. I am getting really scared. What if they lock me up? What if they charge me with treason and throw me into some prison where women who look like men run around beating up the new inmates and stealing their toothbrushes? What if—"

"Megan!" Phil said. "Get a grip. They only want to talk

with you to find out what you know. They aren't going to throw you into prison today. You will just have do what is right and trust God to take care of you. He will do it."

"I know, I know. Okay, let's go."

They climbed into Phil's pickup and started out for the Norfolk office of the Naval Criminal Investigative Service, both a little tense and both praying furiously in their hearts.

Phil had no trouble following Special Agent McDowell's directions. He pulled into an empty parking space in front of the Federal Building at seven minutes before two o'clock. The building was one of those all-glass structures, seven floors tall, with a huge revolving door at the front entrance sheltered from the elements by a big gray awning suspended above it. Phil and Megan exited the vehicle and slowly made their way toward the entrance of the building. Special Agent McDowell had told Phil that his office was located on the third floor at the south end of the hall, the last office on the left. They entered the same wedge-shaped section of the revolving door and baby-stepped around in a half-circle until they were deposited into a cavernous foyer with a large information desk along the wall directly opposite the door. On either side of the desk were heavy brass stands holding thick polished wooden poles that had to be forty feet tall from base to tip. Each bore a flag of proportionate size; the State of Virginia on one side, the United States of America on the other. High up on the wall behind the desk attendant was a round metal molding of the logo and seal of the United States Navy, and beneath it, the smaller bronze molding of the Naval Criminal Investigative Service.

There was a bank of elevators directly behind the information desk, opening up into the corridors that began at the end of the information desk and ran to the back wall of the building. The corridor to each bank of elevators was separated from the foyer proper by a walk-through metal detector and an x-ray machine. A uniformed marine stood guard at each of the two security checkpoints, directing those entering to place their belongings onto the x-ray machine belt, and to remove any metal adornment prior to passing through the metal detectors.

Phil and Megan followed the marine's orders and passed through the security point without incident. They walked over to the bank of elevators and pressed the appropriate button to call an upward bound car. Presently, the 'ding' of an arriving car invited them to step inside, after which Phil pressed the stainless steel button with the number '3' engraved on it. The car quickly and silently ascended to their destination, announced their arrival with another 'ding', then whisked the door open. They stepped out onto the dark blue carpeting and looked straight ahead at a light blue papered wall with a framed black felt board whose white letters formed the names of the offices that could be found at this end of the third floor.

"South end, last office on the left," Phil recited. They walked over to the main corridor, turned left and began walking. The hallway they found themselves in was nearly five feet wide, the right wall made up of the mirrored external glass that could be seen from outside the building. The left wall was made up of a three foot high brick wall supporting the remaining glass wall, which extended up to the ceiling. Through the glass, they could see a great square room, the middle of which was crowded with desks. Some of the desks were partitioned off with portable cubicle walls, while others were separated only by the strategic arrangement of the myriad of messy desks themselves. At the far end of the great room was a series of offices and conference rooms, each separated from the main room by glass walls, thick vinyl blinds, and heavy glass doors. The back wall of the row of offices was bricked, separating that office mass from the identical one behind it, where Phil and Megan would shortly find the office of Resident Special Agent In Charge, William H. McDowell, Naval Criminal Investigative Service.

Phil tentatively pulled open the door to the second office mass. No one seemed to notice his intrusion, so he and Megan entered the room and proceeded to the last office on the left, the larger one in the corner, and knocked on the door.

A brawny man in his early forties looked up from a stack of paper he was leafing through. He stood up and walked around the desk while he motioned for them to enter. He was taller than he had appeared while sitting down, but was light on his feet and agile. His pale gray-blue suit was rumpled from having been worn behind a desk all day. His tie had been loosened and his top shirt button had been unbuttoned. His suit coat hung on a hook by the door, and his shoulder holster hung across the back of his chair. Phil assumed his government issue 9mm handgun had been safely unloaded and placed into one of his desk drawers. He was lean and muscular, with coal black hair that showed the first signs of graying but gave no indication of receding or thinning. His iron grip handshake was of the kind used to intimidate criminals and project power and control at the beginning of an interview, which it had done very well in the case of Phil Prescott and Megan Gallagher.

"Bill McDowell," he said as he clasped Phil's hand and pumped it a single time.

"Phil Prescott," Phil said. "Pleased to meet you. And this is my friend, Megan Gallagher." He nodded to Megan, whom McDowell greeted with a somewhat lighter version of the handshake Phil had gotten.

"Have a seat, folks," McDowell said, motioning to the pair of padded chairs across from his desk.

McDowell returned to his seat, then slid the pile of papers aside and produced an empty manila folder and a clean legal pad from somewhere out of Phil's view behind the desk. He pulled a cheap black ball-point pen out of his shirt pocket and clicked out the ink barrel. Then he looked up at his guests.

"With your permission, I would like to tape record this interview," he asked. "Simply to ensure that I don't make any mistakes when I copy my notes over to any official paperwork I might have to do for this case. Any objections?" Both guests shook their heads, and McDowell retrieved a mini cassette recorder from his top desk drawer. He popped out the tape to make sure it was a new one, then, satisfied that it was the correct one, returned it to the machine and placed the unit in the middle of the desk. He pressed the record button and watched to make sure the reels had begun to spin.

He cleared his throat, then stated the time, day, date and year, followed by his official title, rank, position, and the organization for which he worked.

"I have been contacted by a member of the U S Coast Guard regarding an alleged incident of espionage involving a civilian and a member of the U S Navy. The civilian and the Coast Guard member are present at this interview, the naval member is not." He looked up at Phil and Megan. "Please state your name, birth date and occupation for the record."

"Boatswain's Mate Second Class E. Phillip Anthony Prescott, born April 17, 1970. Occupation, United States Coast Guard, Temporary Active Duty assignment to the USS *Mississippi* CGN-40 for Drug Interdiction Operations in the Caribbean Sea."

"Megan—er—Belinda Maria Gallagos, born May 13, 1973. Occupation, waitress at the Admiral's Steakhouse, Norfolk, Virginia."

"I thought your name was Megan Gallagher—who is Belinda Gallagos?" McDowell asked with obvious confusion.

"I was born Belinda Maria Gallagos, in Venezuela," Megan answered. "But since I have been living in the United States, I have been going by Megan Gallagher."

"I see. And, how long have you been in the States?"

"Sir, if I may, I think it will make more sense if I just tell you my story from the beginning. Would that be all right?"

McDowell nodded. "Of course, please, proceed."

Megan relayed her story to the best of her recollection, beginning from her early childhood and her father's earliest dealings with Miguel Ramirez. She even told details that she hadn't told Phil and her other friends, about how Ramirez would send men to destroy her father's crops so that he would be forced to pay a protection fee to keep them away. Every so often, her father would try to stand up to Ramirez, and each time he would be put down worse than the time before. When Ramirez had finally had enough, he sent his men to completely destroy everything her father had; the fields, the equipment, the barns. Ramirez even bribed or threatened the bank owner into selling him the mortgage on her family's land, so that they would be completely at his mercy.

"That is when he came to me," she continued. "I was a good student in school, and I was particularly good at English, which we were taught as a second language. I even tutored some of the other children in our area. One day, when I was on my way home from one of my tutoring sessions, two men in one of Ramirez's fancy black cars stopped me in the road. They forced me into the car with them and took me to Ramirez's house. I was escorted to his study, where he offered me a sickening proposition. He said that if I would agree to go to America, to Norfolk, and pose as a waitress where I could meet Navy and Coast Guard men, he would do two things for me. One, he would give me a new false identity, set me up in an apartment, and send me a small sum of money once a month. Two, he would let my family live. He promised me that if I refused him, or if I failed in my mission once I got here, that he would kill my family, one at a time, and send me parts of them through the mail." Megan began sobbing. McDowell offered her a small box of tissue from his desk.

"I have seen him kill before, and I know that he isn't bluffing. He will kill my family if he ever hears that I am here talking to you, or if he is not satisfied with the information I send to him."

"And exactly what kind of information is he looking for?"

"Mostly schedules of ships. He has to smuggle his cocaine and marijuana to the United States across the Caribbean. He wants me to tell him whenever the ships are switching duty, going to a liberty port, or anything else that would allow him a couple of days to push a shipment through when they might not be watching so closely."

"Go on," McDowell encouraged. "Tell me everything that has happened since you arrived here."

Megan quickly told him about how she had taken a plane to Washington DC, then another to Norfolk. She found an apartment close to the base, which she rented with the money Ramirez had sent with her. She bought a computer and signed up for Internet access, which she uses to deliver the information to him. She got a job at the Admiral's Steakhouse, and began searching for a target.

"I figured that a church would be a good place to look for a target, because you never know what you might find in a bar, but a guy would automatically be more trusting of a girl he met in church."

"Clever," McDowell interjected.

"Yeah, well anyway, it worked. That is where I met Jack Douglass."

"Jack?" McDowell asked, searching his notes from his conversation with Phil over the telephone.

"Signalman Second Class Jonathan Douglass, but he goes by 'Jack'," Phil said. "He is assigned to the USS *Mississippi* also."

"Got it," McDowell said, adding some markings to his notes.

"Well, Jack and I really hit it off, and to keep the story professional, I got too close to my target. I mean, what do I know about being a spy? I am a farm girl from Venezuela who tutors neighborhood kids in English! Anyway, Jack and I were getting very close, and it was getting very uncomfortable lying to him all the time. Then, the worst part happened. I mean, it is really wonderful, it is absolutely the best thing, but it completely screwed up my plan. I'm sorry, I am rambling." She paused while she picked a tissue out of the box and wiped her nose.

"Well, some of the church sermons were starting to get to me. I was feeling terrible about what I was doing, partly because of Jack and partly just because it was wrong. Then the bomb dropped. Jack came back from his last deployment and told me that he had become a Christian. He was telling all of us at Pizza Hut how awesome and free he felt, and I couldn't stand it. I ran out of the restaurant and drove home. Our friend Kim came over the next day, and I couldn't hold it in any longer. I spilled the whole terrible story to her, and she did a strange thing. She supported me and asked me how she could help. She didn't judge me, she didn't condemn me, and she didn't tell me how rotten I was. What she did do was ask me if I wanted God to forgive me for that and for all my sins, and help me to start a new life. So, I became a Christian, too. That is when I talked to Phil here, and asked him what I should do. And, here we are.

"I hate what I have done, but I can't undo it. I'm putting my family in terrible danger, not because of America, or the Navy, or the Coast Guard, or even my friends or Jack. I am doing this because as a Christian, I can no longer participate in something that is clearly wrong. I would give anything to be able to help my family, and I pray to God that you can help me to do that, but one thing I will not give to save them is my soul. I have to be obedient to God first, and look after my family second."

"Well, I'm not so sure about the Christianity thing, but I will say this for you, you have guts. Guts and passion," McDowell said. "Okay, just a couple more questions. How exactly are you getting the information to Ramirez?"

Megan outlined the Internet meeting schedule and their code names for each part of the month. Finally satisfied that he had all the information she could give him, he turned to Phil. "Now, how about you? What else can you tell me?" he asked.

"Nothing," Phil said. "Megan actually just told you more than I knew before I came in here. But, she is my friend, and I wanted to be here to support her and offer any assistance I could."

"Right. Okay, then, let me make a few calls. I will meet with Petty Officer Douglass on Monday, then I will get back with you probably the following Monday. I need to caution both of you not to leave town until I give you the okay to do so, all right?"

They both nodded and stood up to leave.

"Miss Gallagher," McDowell said, "you need to understand that you are in serious trouble, here. I am assuming, since you have voluntarily come to me with this situation, that you are seeking some sort of immunity from prosecution in return for providing information about Ramirez. While that is definitely a possibility, I can make no guarantees of any leniency at all. You have confessed to participation in the crime of treason against the United States of America, a crime which we do not take lightly. Because of the nature of your confession, I am going to let you leave my office on your own recognizance. But I must warn you, if you make any attempt to leave the area, or if your actions become in any way suspicious, I will have you arrested and thrown in a cell faster than you can say 'John Pollard'. Is that understood?"

"Yes, Sir. Completely," she replied.

McDowell took down their addresses and telephone numbers, then escorted them to the door. He handed them both

NCIS business cards with his cell phone number handwritten on the back. "If you think of anything else that I should know, please call me. Otherwise, I'll be in touch," he said, then he returned to his desk.

At 6:45 Friday evening, Megan pulled into the Radford's driveway and parked her car on the grass in front of the barn behind Kim's Mustang. She was at the same time nervous about sharing her secret life with everyone, and relieved that she wouldn't have to hide it from them any longer. She knocked one time on the screen door and yelled 'hello!' as she entered the kitchen.

"Come on in, Missie," Tom Radford called to her, using his own informal version of "Miss" which he found to be a little more personal. "We are all in the living room!"

"Grab a drink on your way in," Kirt added. "There are cookies in here on the coffee table."

Megan followed their instructions, pouring herself a cup of hot coffee before she walked into the living room. Tom and Millie were on the couch, Kirt sat in the very ugly and very worn arm chair, and Kim sat on the hearth in front of the fireplace. Still feeling a chill, and that only partially from the crisp autumn air outside, Megan joined Kim in front of the fireplace. She had selected two small cookies and a brownie before taking her seat, because she knew that Tom would razz her about it if she didn't, and Millie would be pleased about it if she did. As always, the goodies were wonderful.

They chatted about this and that until everyone who was expected to show up was there. Brad and Steve came in together about ten minutes after Megan, Phil arrived just after seven, and Laura hurried in at seven-ten, apologizing about losing track of the time while studying at the library. Kirt got their attention and addressed the group.

"Thanks for coming, everyone. Megan called me yesterday and asked if we could all get together to discuss the unusual events of this past week, of which I am told there have been many." Mumbles of agreement were dominated by sarcastic expressions, like "Really?" and "Ya think?" As Kirt attempted to calm them down and continue speaking, he heard the screen door shut. Jack walked through the kitchen and stopped at the entrance to the living room. Megan rose quickly to her feet, unsure what to do, nearly dizzy by the instantaneous flood of emotions that had started a churning in her stomach and a tightness in her chest. The only sound that could be heard was the soft electric whine of the cuckoo clock that hung on the wall above the couch. Every eye in the house was riveted on one of them, either Jack or Megan, wondering what would happen next and who would be the one to make it happen.

Jack walked into the living room and stood in front of Megan. Kirt quietly sat back down. No one else moved. Jack looked deep into Megan's eyes, searching for the person who Phil said was still in there, had been there all the time. Tears welled up in Megan's eyes until they overflowed and streamed down her face. She made no effort to wipe them away, nor did anyone offer her a tissue. Seconds ticked by as the couple stood facing each other in a moment that belonged only to them; a moment that no one else dared to interrupt, neither with voice nor with movement. Finally, Megan tried to speak.

"Jack—" she began. Jack silently shook his head back and forth. Megan stopped talking and waited. Still, he looked into her eyes, almost through her eyes, as if he were dialoguing with an unseen entity somewhere deep inside her. Suddenly, Jack's countenance changed. A spirit of oppression seemed to physically lift off of him, allowing his face to exhibit the slightest hint of a smile at the corners of his mouth. Without warning, he threw his arms around Megan and drew her to him, holding her tightly with one hand while lovingly stroking the back of her head with the other. Megan's tears flowed even faster, but this time they were tears of joy, of release, of happiness. Her body shuddered with relief as the strong arms of the one she loved held her in a protective and possessive embrace.

Every eye in the room was moist to some extent, some more than others, as each of them praised God and thanked Him for the successful negotiating of one more step in the resolution of the terrible situation their friends had found themselves in. One at a time, they all got out of their chairs and surrounded the couple, laying their hands on them and praying for them. Most of them didn't know anything about Megan's secret life or why she and Jack had had a falling out; they only knew that something significant had come between them, and that now it was apparently being resolved. In the absence of complete understanding, they rejoiced that something positive was happening between their friends and that the problem was being worked out. Whatever it was, it was obviously a big deal, and it was also obviously being worked out right in front of them.

Megan's tears subsided and her intense emotion ebbed. She and Jack separated, still holding hands. "I didn't really want to do this in front of an audience," Jack said, "but I need to do it either way. Megan, I am sorry about how I reacted. You came to me willingly confessing and asking for my support, and all I did was react like a jerk and put you down. You hurt me, Megan. You lied to me, you betrayed me, and you used me, and that hurt me very badly. But it only hurt me so much because I love you so much. I realize now how hard it must have been for you, and how much pain you must have been in even before you came clean about it.

"I'm not suggesting that this will be easy to get through, and I'm not even sure what will happen next or how it will all play out, but I want you to know that I'm sorry for the way I behaved, and I need to ask your forgiveness."

"Of course, Jack, I forgive you!" Megan said. "But how about me? Can you ever forgive me, Jack?" she asked.

"I already have, Megan. Once I realized why you did what you did, and realized the great risk you have taken by putting it all out in the open, I knew that you were sincere. But I had to look into your eyes to be sure of how you felt about me. I forgive you, Megan, and I love you, and I promise to stay by your side and help you get through this, no matter what I have to do."

She hugged him again, basking in his love.

"Uh, excuse me, I don't mean to mess up your moment here, but I just have one little question," Brad said. Everyone looked at him. "Exactly what in the world are you people talking about?!"

Those who already knew laughed, while those who didn't continued to look at them as though they had lost their minds.

"Okay," Megan said. "I'll give you the whole story. Are you ready?"

"YES!!" they all shouted.

Megan stifled a giggle as she began her story. She started with her childhood in Venezuela, then continued right up to the episode with Jack a few minutes earlier, assisted at some points by Kim and Phil and Jack. Tom, Millie, Kirt, Brad, Steve and Laura sat big-eyed and open-mouthed by the time Megan finished her story. Even Brad could think of no smart comment to make.

Megan also filled them in on her meeting with Special Agent McDowell of the NCIS, and his predictions of what may transpire in the not-too-distant future. After answering a few questions from various friends, they wrapped up the evening by having a special prayer session for Megan. They asked God to bless her new life in Him, and to bring a quick and acceptable end to the situation in which she was very deeply involved.

When the cool autumn breeze dances past, carrying with it the slightest hint of smoke from burning leaves and causing the tiny hairs on the back of your neck to stand on end; and when the endless black sky is painted with countless dots of fiery white stars spread out as far as the human eye can see; and when the trees have shed most of their multi-colored leaves onto a blanket of green grass that has not yet given in to the dormancy of winter, well, that is when you know there is a God. And when you can experience that magnificent scene while strolling across that grass and through those fallen leaves, looking up at that beautiful sky, arm in arm with the one you love the most, huddled in close to each other against the comfortable chill of that delightful, teasing breeze, well, that is when you know that God loves you.

Jack and Megan were taking just such a stroll together through the landscaped grounds of her apartment complex after leaving the meeting at the Radford's. Because of Megan's hasty exit from the pizza place the previous Sunday afternoon, and as a result of the communication difficulties they had experienced during the rest of the week, she and Jack had not yet had the opportunity to discuss anything since his return from the extended eight-week deployment. Tonight, they would make up for lost time. They walked and talked for hours, kicking through the neat piles of leaves along the edge of the streets that the maintenance men had worked so hard to rake from the lawns. They sat on the concrete wall of an elaborate foot bridge over the little creek that ran through the apartment complex and into the adjacent woods. They chatted and chatted, enjoying the friendly banter and the new discoveries as a young couple in love sharing with each other their hearts and minds, fears and dreams. This was the first time they had really talked with each other about themselves, their childhood, their teenage years, and even their young adult years thus far. Eventually, Megan got a little too chilly, and they returned to the warmth of her apartment. They curled up on the couch under a blanket and watched TV, pausing to order a pizza when the munchies got the better of them.

"So," Jack said between bites, "what did the NCIS guy say the next step is going to be?"

"He didn't. Except that he wants to meet with you Monday afternoon. Phil said he probably called your ship earlier today to set it up."

"Well, I suppose I am a significant player, since I am the source of the information you have been passing along."

"Yeah, I suppose so," Megan agreed reluctantly and with a lingering twinge of guilt.

"So, are you going to go by 'Megan' still, or should I start calling you 'Belinda?'" Jack asked.

"I don't know," Megan answered. "I really like the name Megan, but it doesn't really sound like me, you know? I am Belinda. But, everybody here knows me as Megan. I don't know if it would be worth trying to change it back now."

"What do you mean, 'now'?" Jack asked. "Are you saying 'now', with the implication that there will at some point in the future be a 'later' which significantly differs from what you are at this juncture referring to as 'now'?"

"Jack, why do you have to do that?" she asked. "What are you trying to say? Or, what are you trying to ask me?"

"You said you didn't know if it was worth trying to change your name back 'now'. I was simply wondering if you were thinking of trying to change it back at some point in the future, like after all this mess has been cleaned up," he explained.

"Oh," she said, then she paused, taking a big bite of pizza to conceal her pondering.

"Well," Jack admitted, "I suppose it is up to you. It is your name, after all. Or, should I say *they* are your *names*, after all."

They munched on their late supper while they watched the rest of the Tonight Show. Jack broke the silence with a very disturbing question.

"Megan," he asked, "what will you do when this is all over? I mean, you are an illegal alien, living here under false pretenses and a false identity, with counterfeit government documents. Assuming you can avoid jail time by cutting a deal with the authorities, what will you do then?" His voice was becoming tense.

"I don't know," she said. "I would assume that deportation would be a condition of my 'testimony in lieu of incarceration' deal. I can hardly expect the government to grant me an automatic citizenship, complete with green card and voting rights, now can I?"

"I wouldn't think so," Jack agreed. He picked up the last piece of pizza and took a bite. "Megan, I can't let them take you away from me," he said with a sorrowful fear in his eyes.

"No, Jack. Not tonight," she said. "Don't even do that tonight. This has been one of the worst weeks of my life, but it is ending up to be the best, so let's not ruin it with stupid thoughts of what may or may not go wrong in the future. We have tonight, Jack, and nobody is going to do anything to take that away from us. Now, shut up and give me that last bread stick."

Jack smiled. No, nobody would take tonight from them. And nobody would take her from him, either. He simply couldn't let that happen.

Eventually, fatigue overtook the happy couple, and they pried themselves from the couch to say goodnight. Jack held her in his arms for a long time, knowing that any moment they had together could be their last, or at least their last for a long time. He didn't know what the future would hold for them, or how God would work out their situation, so he grasped every moment he could get his hands on and held on for dear life. He kissed her gently on her lips and ran the back of his hand along her face.

"I love you, Belinda Maria Gallagos," he said. "Goodnight."

A tear slipped from her eye and dripped onto Jack's fingers. "I love you, too, Jack," she said.

He walked out her door and across the parking lot to his Honda. He slowly drove back to the base for what would be one of his last nights of sleeping on board the *Mighty Mississippi* until they were underway again in five weeks.

The entire class erupted into a resounding applause at the announcement that both Megan and Jack had accepted Christ as their personal savior since the last time they had been to class. They were each asked to give a brief recounting of the conditions under which they made their life-changing commitments, which they did, again to a resounding applause. The fact of their recent conversion was also announced during the morning worship service, but without the requested sharing of details.

Pastor Mackey asked Jack and Megan to join him at the Country Kitchen after church to celebrate their 'birthdays' as Christians. They gladly accepted, as did the rest of their little group of friends.

As usual, the long table in the conference room of the Country Kitchen had been reserved for Pastor Mackey and friends from the Hampton First Church of the Nazarene. They filed in, removing their jackets and placing them over the backs of the chairs they had chosen. Pastor Mackey had directed Jack and Megan to the pair of chairs to his immediate left, while his wife took the one to his right. The remaining chairs were quickly filled, after which a prayer of thanksgiving was offered and the food they would soon gather from the lunch buffet was corporately blessed. As if they had been poised in front of a runner's block and had just heard the starting gun, the assembled group disappeared at the sounding of the 'Amen', filing out of the banquet room for the yellow tape finish line of the lunch buffet. Pastor Mackey lingered behind, as did Jack and Megan.

"I would like to meet with the two of you, individually, of course, sometime this week," Pastor Mackey said. "I like to have follow-up meetings with new Christians as soon as I can after their conversion experience. I think it is good for the individual and for me to touch base and find out how you are doing, answer any questions you may have, and entertain any pertinent requests for prayer that you may have." He pulled a pocket calendar booklet out of the inside pocket of his suit coat. "Megan, I know you have a weekly schedule, which is mostly afternoons and evenings, but would you happen to know when you might be free this week for an hour or so? If mornings work better for you, I can easily accommodate that."

Megan pulled her photocopied schedule for the next week out of her purse and set up a meeting with Pastor Mackey for Tuesday morning. Jack scheduled his meeting for early evening on the same day, after Megan would already have gone to work. Business having been taken care of, the threesome made their way to the buffet line, which had nearly diminished enough so that they could begin filling their plates upon arrival.

During the meal, Pastor Mackey asked Jack and Megan to briefly tell how and why they had made the decision to follow Christ, both of whose stories were met with praises to God and nods of approval. After lunch, several of the church members came by to hug Jack and Megan, wishing them well and encouraging them to read their Bibles and pray and to remain faithful. They responded with appropriate pleasantries, promising to do their best and to let God take care of them.

"Little do they know how rough it is really going to get for us!" Jack said quietly to Megan. She smiled in agreement, pulling on her coat and picking up her purse.

"How do you think they will react when they hear the news about me?" Megan asked as they walked across the parking lot to their cars. "Do you think it will change the way they treat you?" she asked.

"What do you mean, the way they treat ME?" Jack said.

"Well, I know they will treat me differently, but I don't want them to treat you any differently just because we are together. I mean, you didn't do anything wrong, but you will still be considered guilty by association because of your relationship with me."

"Now who is thinking too much!" Jack teased. "I am sure they will be just fine, once they get over the shock of learning the truth. It may take a while for them to accept it, but I'm sure they will be fine."

"Well, I hope so, but I doubt it. You know how people are."

"Yeah, I sure do," Jack agreed. "What are you going to tell Pastor Mackey Tuesday? Are you going to spill the beans to him, tell him all about what is going on?"

"I don't know. I haven't had time to think about it yet. What do you think I should do?"

"I don't know either," Jack said, shrugging his shoulders. "I don't suppose the added prayer support would hurt, although I don't imagine that he would be able to help you out in any other way. I mean, the legal aspect of this is way above his head."

"True," Megan agreed. "I guess I will just do whatever seems right at the time."

"Sounds good, but be sure to let me know what you did and did not tell him, so that I don't say too much when I meet with him that evening."

They each climbed into their respective vehicles and drove to Megan's apartment, where they spent the day much like they had the previous Friday night; trying desperately to squeeze every second of quality time out of every minute they had left before the impending legal action of the coming week separated them for another indefinite period of time, even as the 'needs of the Navy' had done for the previous couple of months.

Monday morning, Jack awoke at reveille and headed for

the shower. He shaved, waited for his turn in the shower, then put on a clean uniform and went up to Phil's complex to see if he wanted to join him in the galley for breakfast. Jack waited for Phil to finish dressing, after which they made their way to the food line.

As they sat at the galley table eating their food, they shared what had transpired for each of them over the weekend, then they speculated about what might happen during the current week. Jack said that no, he hadn't been told of any meeting with the NCIS yet, but that he expected to receive such an order at Quarters. They discussed the possible fate of Megan, what the government might do to her, and what might happen to Jack, since he knew of an active spy and didn't report his contact with her.

"Under the circumstances, I don't think the fact that you didn't report it right away will be a big deal for you. Or, against you, I should say. And it will certainly work in Megan's favor, since she had the opportunity to freely confess of her own volition, and not as a result of the authorities breaking her down during an interrogation after she had been turned in by someone else."

"Yeah, I suppose that is true. Hey, do you have time for a fresh cup of hot joe up on the sig bridge before Quarters?" Jack asked.

"Always," Phil said, picking up his tray and heading for the scullery.

"I am really afraid, Phil," Jack said quietly. "They could do all kinds of things to Megan if they get the notion. They could lock her up, they could deport her, they could execute her—"

"Hey, hold on, Jack. Let's not get carried away, here. Sure, she was involved in espionage, but it wasn't terribly sensitive information that she was passing along. I mean, schedules for surface ships are not all that hard to figure out anyway, since they can not hide under the water like submarines can. All you really have to do is watch for them."

"Well, I guess that's true."

"Jack, I don't want you to think that I am taking this lightly, because I'm not. But there is absolutely nothing you can do for her except pray. Her fate is in the hands of the legal system, and they will not consult you about her punishment. You just have to pray and trust God to do what is best for everyone."

"But what if taking her away from me is best for everyone? Then what?" Jack asked, starting to get choked up.

"Stop it, Jack. You need to be strong for her. Pray and trust God to work it out. I know that can sound pretty lame when you are the one going through the turmoil and I'm not, but you know it's true. You are going to have to deal with this mess one piece at a time. Cope with each step before going on to the next one. Don't try to do it all at once, because it all hasn't happened yet, and you have no clue what is going to happen anyway. It will be difficult enough without you making it worse by unfounded conjecture. Let it come, and deal with it then."

Phil filled the cups and replaced the carafe. "I'll come back up here after Quarters to see when you go to meet with McDowell. He seems like a nice enough guy, but he has a job to do like everyone else. Do you want me to ride over there with you? Hensley will let me go if you think you could use the company."

"Yeah, that would be great, Phil. I just might need the company, depending on how he answers my questions about what will happen to Megan."

"No problem, I'll take care of it," Phil said.

The meeting with Special Agent McDowell was at eleven o'clock, after which each man had been granted early liberty until the next morning. At ten, each could be found in his complex packing his sea bag in preparation to spend his first night in the new apartment. They exited the ship together at ten-thirty, walked to Phil's pickup, then drove to Jack's Honda. Jack said he wanted to drive, so they locked their sea bags in his trunk and left Phil's pickup there, to be picked up on their way back from the NCIS office.

Phil led the way around the information desk to the bank of elevators, entering the first one to respond to his pressing of the call button. They exited the elevator on the third floor, and Phil led Jack down the hall to McDowell's office. McDowell met them at the door. He shook Phil's hand and motioned for him to take a seat outside his office, while he shook Jack's hand and directed him to one of the chairs in front of his desk.

McDowell walked over to the chair behind his neatly arranged desk, pulled it out, and lowered himself into it. He seemed to have all the time in the world, while Jack, in contrast, was extremely anxious to get the meeting going. He had questions about Megan that he needed answers to, but he thought it best to let McDowell run the meeting as he saw fit.

The NCIS Agent pulled out the long bottom drawer on the right side of his desk and extracted a manila file folder, placing it gingerly in the center of the marked-up calendar on his desk. Jack couldn't read what was scribbled on the title tab, but he hoped that whatever it was, it would be just the thing McDowell needed to get this meeting going. Jack looked around the office, noting the Criminal Justice Degree from Purdue University hanging in a cheap frame on the wall to his right, a dusty plastic tree standing in a tarnished brass pot in the corner, and a large collection of reference books on a bookshelf along the left wall. The desk was a common metal desk with a Formica top and drawers on each side. McDowell opened one of the drawers and removed his mini-cassette recorder, which he placed along the edge of the desk in front of Jack. He informed Jack that he would be taping their conversation, then he went through the same ritual of introduction that he had with Phil and Megan.

"Signalman Second Class Jonathan James Douglass, born January 14, 1970; occupation, United States Navy, serving aboard the USS *Mississippi* CGN-40."

McDowell nodded. "Thank you, Petty Officer Douglass. Now, I am sure you know why I asked for this meeting, but just for the record, let's start at the beginning."

Jack nodded.

"Last Friday afternoon, I met with a Boatswain's Mate Second Class E. Phillip Anthony Prescott, and a Miss Belinda Maria Gallagos, a.k.a. Megan Gallagher. Please state the nature of your relationship with each of the people I just mentioned."

"I met Phil Prescott about four or five months ago on the *Mississippi*. We were assigned to a rotating six-week tour schedule of Counter Drug Operations in the Caribbean working with the Coast Guard. Phil is the leader of one of the search teams for when they do boardings of suspect vessels. He has a lot of free time while we are underway, so he comes up to the signal bridge to shoot the breeze. We got to be pretty good friends over the last two underway times."

"I see. So, the nature of your relationship is a combination of professional and social, correct?"

"Sure, I guess so. We are friends, but we work together, too," Jack added.

"Okay, and how about the girl, Miss Gallagos?"

"I met her at the Hampton Church of the Nazarene, oh, about five and a half months ago, a few weeks before that first deployment that Phil went on with us. Anyway, we started dating, and have also gotten pretty close. I guess you could say she is my girlfriend," Jack volunteered.

"I see. And, are you two sleeping together?"

"Excuse me?" Jack said, surprised and annoyed. "What kind of a question is that?"

"Routine, Petty Officer Douglass. I need to ascertain the exact dimensions of your relationship with Miss Gallagos."

"No, we are not sleeping together. She is my girlfriend. We spend time together, go out on dates, hang out with our church friends. But we do not sleep together."

"I understand. Thank you. I didn't mean to imply anything." He paused while he scribbled something down on the legal pad. Without looking up, he asked, "And when did you first find out she was a spy?"

"A week ago today," Jack said. "Our ship had just pulled in after eight weeks out, so we all went out to Pizza Hut for dinner to celebrate and catch up."

"And 'we all' would refer to..."

"Me, Phil, Megan, and a bunch of our church friends. Do you need their names, too?" Jack asked.

"Yes, please. It may not be relevant, but at this point I am merely gathering information, so I must consider everything to be relevant. Please, continue."

"Okay, there was Kirt Radford, Kim Perkins , Laura

Wright, Brad Coulder, and Steve Denison. So, there we all were eating some pizza and talking, when all of a sudden, Megan jumps up out of her chair and bolts. Just runs out, without a word to anyone. I ran after her, but she took off in her car before I could get to her. I tried to call her later that night and the next day, but she wouldn't talk to me. I had no idea what was going on.

"The next day, Monday, Phil and I were out apartment hunting, and after we quit, I went back to the ship, but he went over to Megan's. I had called Kim Perkins and asked her to go and check on Megan and see if there was anything I could do, and Megan had spilled the beans to her, then called Phil to tell him before they would tell me. Anyway, that night, Phil came back onto the ship and told me the whole story, or at least as much as he knew. I went over to Megan's the next day and chewed her out good for lying to me and using me, then I went back to the ship. She was all crying and sobbing and stuff, but I just left. I figured she deserved it for what she did to me. I told her off good, then I left.

"Well, the next day, Phil came and chewed me out for being a jerk to Megan; said he believed she was really sorry about what she had done, and that she had become a Christian, so I should forgive her and move on. I didn't buy it."

"You didn't buy the conversion?"

"No, I didn't buy that I should forgive her and move on. She had betrayed me! What did I want with a girl like that?"

"So, you did buy her conversion story, then?"

"Well, not at first. Actually, I just didn't care at first. I didn't care if she was a Christian now or not, that didn't change what she had done to me, you know? So I just blew her off. But I felt awful, and Phil talked to me again about forgiveness, which made me feel even worse, so then I went and talked to Megan."

"Right, and when was that?"

"Uh, that would have been on Friday. She had Kirt gather everybody—same ones who were at the Pizza Hut party—at Kirt's house so she could tell them all what was going on. You see, I had become a Christian a few weeks before, when we were still underway, and that is why I was feeling so awful about what I had said to her. So I prayed about it a lot, and I felt like I did need to forgive her and move on. I crashed her little 'coming out' party at Kirt's, and we patched things up."

"So now you are okay with her, with everything she did to you?" McDowell asked.

"Of course not! I will never be 'okay' with what she did to me, but it is done and over with now. She is not the same person she was before. Whatever she did in the past is just that—in the past. Just like Phil, I believe her conversion is real, and I support her 100 percent."

"Okay, now let's move on to you, Petty Officer Douglass. Why didn't you contact the NCIS when you first learned that Miss Gallagher was a spy? Did you at least talk to your leading chief about it? Or you division officer?"

"No, I didn't talk to anyone about it except for Phil."

"Why not?"

"Hey, forgive me for being a bad sailor, but national security was not really on my mind at the time, okay? My girlfriend had just told me that she was not the person she had said she was, and that she was really a spy from Venezuela who had been using me to get information. My first thoughts were completely and totally selfish. I was heartbroken, and that is all I could think about. Turning her in for the safety of the country never occurred to me. Telling her off and getting her out of my head was all I wanted."

"Fair enough. While you were dating, did she ever ask you any pointed questions about the Navy or the Coast Guard or anything of a technical nature?"

"No. Not any more than you would expect a new friend/girlfriend to ask about her new friend/boyfriend's job."

"No questions about ship capabilities, armaments, weaponry?"

"No. She didn't seem to have any more interest in that type of stuff than the average person would who has never seen a warship before. She says that all she was after was the scheduling information, which she could easily get without raising the slightest bit of suspicion simply by dating me, or anyone else on a naval vessel."

"Two final questions, Petty Officer Douglass. What is

your current relationship with Miss Gallagos, and what are your intentions where she is concerned?"

"I am currently very much in love with Miss Gallagos, and my intention is to stand faithfully by her side through this whole mess, hoping against all odds that the situation can be resolved in such a way as to permit us a long and happy life together."

"I see. Okay, thank you Petty Officer Douglass, for your time and your honesty. Please don't leave town for the next few weeks, in case I need to get in touch with you." He handed Jack a NCIS business card with his name and number on it. "If you think of anything else, please feel free to call me any time. Good afternoon." He stood and shook Jack's hand firmly, indicating that he could get the door for himself and find his own way out. This he did with urgency.

Jack hurried out of the office and motioned for Phil to follow him as he continued on toward the hallway.

"Boy, he is a very intense guy," Jack observed. "I wanted to ask him about Megan, about what could happen to her, or what probably would happen to her, but he didn't seem the type to want to chit chat about stuff like that. I just wanted to get out of there."

Phil nodded. "Yeah, he does seem driven."

"Plus, I think he thought I was a fruitcake for wanting to stay with Megan after what she had been doing. He probably thinks I am in on it with her."

"It is his job to be suspicious, Jack. He doesn't know the first thing about any of us, so he is probably being very careful to consider every possibility and cover all possible angles. I don't think we should read anything into it. Hey, what do you say we get out of here, eh? We have a new apartment to move into."

Tuesday night Jack was sitting with Megan in front of her computer at ten minutes before midnight. He wanted to be there when she chatted with Ramirez, her tormentor from across the seas. She logged on to the Internet at two minutes before midnight and entered the 'entrepreneurs' chat room. She typed in 'stella24' and waited. Suddenly, the name 'machoman22' appeared on her screen.

machoman22: hey, stella, how are things?
stella24: pretty good here. same old, same old, you know.
machoman22: how's the new meat loaf recipe? bringing in the customers?
stella24: it's great. no new customers, but the regulars like it.
machoman22: right. any specials that are too good to miss this week?
stella24: nothing new this week. we'll keep working the meat loaf as long as sales keep up
machoman22: well, you might want to run two specials side by side. might bring in even more customers. sometimes more is better.
stella24: don't push it, machoman. it is hard enough to keep one main dish going. I don't have the energy to try two. this is still just an amateur operation, you know.
machoman22: fine, don't get uptight. I'm only looking out for your future, stella. what if there is a beef shortage? why put all your eggs in one basket?
stella24: you've never seen my basket, machoman. I won't run out of beef and my eggs are fine.
machoman22: suit yourself. I only hope your business doesn't suffer.
stella24: thanks for your concern. gotta run. kitchen opens early tomorrow.
machoman22: right. bye.

"What a jerk!" Jack yelled. "Is he suggesting what I think he is suggesting? That you get another guy and work both of us?"

"Yes, that is what he is suggesting," Megan confirmed.

Jack calmed himself, remembering that Megan was no longer actively involved with Ramirez. "Well, I truly hope you're not thinking of taking him up on his suggestion," Jack said with an impish grin.

"No," Megan said. "I am pretty content with just the meat loaf for now."

"For now??" Jack yelled, grabbing her and wrestling her to the floor. "For now?" he repeated, tickling her until she was laughing hysterically.

He stopped tickling her and looked into her eyes. He brushed her hair out of her eyes with his fingers and kissed her. "Time to go home," he said, standing up and walking across the living room to get his jacket. I'll see you tomorrow."

She waved to him from the floor. "Goodnight, Jack. I'll dream of you."

"Goodnight, Megan," Jack said as he closed her door. "I am already dreaming of you."

~10~

"Something is wrong," Miguel said under his breath to the empty room. "Something is wrong with her."

It was nothing he could put his finger on. There was no one specific thing she had said or had neglected to say that he could point to, and yet something was out of sorts. It was an ability Miguel had developed over the years which had allowed him to know when someone was not being completely truthful with him. Call it instinct, call it a sixth sense, call it what you must, but it had worked to his benefit many times in the past. And, if he had mistakenly eliminated an occasional subject or source unnecessarily, well, that was really of little consequence to him.

Sources were easily bought and sold. There would always be someone waiting in the wings to sell their knowledge to Miguel Ramirez as soon as one of his current sources took early retirement, voluntarily or otherwise. In his position, it paid to be paranoid.

This situation, however, would be somewhat different. This wrinkle in the fabric of his information network couldn't simply be cut out and replaced. Belinda was his special project. She was an investment in his future, not to mention something of an object of his desire. She had blossomed into a very beautiful girl over the years, and Miguel held aspirations that she would one day come back to Venezuela to rule with him the kingdom he was building for himself. She would be a worthy queen, would give him a son to carry on the business and rule the kingdom after his death, and would be a source of pride to him as he paraded her about the cities of his conquest. But something about her had changed. It couldn't even be blamed on a voice inflection, because they had only chatted on the Internet, and yet he could sense the change. He pondered the exchange they had had in the chat room. "This one must be dealt with carefully," he thought; "carefully and personally."

Miguel Ramirez woke up the next morning angry and annoyed. Although he wasn't a terribly pleasant man to work for when he was in a good mood, when he was grouchy, he was unbearable. From the first growl that passed through the thick wooden door of his master bedroom suite to reach the ears of the upstairs maid as she diligently dusted the ornate spindles in the banister outside his door, word was quickly spread throughout the staff for everyone to be on his best behavior, and to avoid contact with the boss whenever possible.

After a hot shower and a shave, Miguel slipped on his thick terrycloth robe and walked out of his carpeted bedroom and onto the cold hardwood floor of the hallway. He yelled from the shock of the cold floor, sputtered out a few expletives, then returned to his room for his slippers. He stormed down the curved oak staircase that led to the main floor, then turned to his left to pass by the kitchen on his way to the terrace outside the dining room. "I will take my breakfast out on the terrace!" he yelled into the kitchen as he passed. A nervous young servant girl picked up a silver tray containing a matching pair of silver pitchers. One was filled with his favorite coffee, the other with his favorite tea. A warmed cup and a cool saucer were added to the tray, as were a variety of condiments and a spoon. She hurried out the door, through the dining room, and onto the terrace where Miguel had seated himself at the glass topped table, facing the distant woods with his back to the house. She gingerly placed the tray beside him on the table.

"Good morning, Don Miguel," she timidly said. "Coffee or tea, Sir?"

Miguel continued to stare out into the distance for a moment longer, then growled, "Coffee. Cream and two sugars."

The girl quickly obliged him. She poured the steaming brew into the warmed cup, added a shot of cream and two lumps of sugar, then stirred it. She gently tapped the spoon on the inside of the cup, placed it on the saucer, and carefully placed in front of him on the table. "And what would you like for breakfast this morning, Sir?" she asked.

"The same thing I always have for breakfast!" Miguel snapped.

"Of course, Sir," the girl said, nodding and backing away. "Right away, Sir." She turned and quickly walked back into the kitchen. "The usual," she said to the chef, "and I would put a rush on it if I were you."

Moments later, the girl returned to the terrace with a larger silver tray containing Miguel's breakfast of two poached eggs, one piece of rye toast with a small dish of marmalade, three slices of melon and a glass of fruit juice. She refilled his coffee cup, asked if there were anything else he required, then executed a hasty departure at the dismissing wave of his hand.

At ten minutes before nine, Victor knocked twice then entered Miguel's office. The boss was standing beside his desk, looking out across the lawn.

"You wanted to see me, Don Miguel?" Victor asked with professional respect.

"Yes, Victor. Take a seat," Miguel said curtly.

Victor walked around the leather high-backed chair in front of Miguel's desk and plopped himself into it. Though he still considered Miguel to be his superior and himself a loyal subordinate, he wasn't as easily intimidated as the rest of the staff. Victor looked up at Miguel, inquisitive but patient.

"I believe we may have a problem with one of our information sources in America," he began. Victor nodded, waiting for him to continue.

"We have a source in Norfolk, Virginia, working an American Navy sailor for scheduling information concerning what they call the CD Ops ships."

Victor nodded again to indicate his comprehension thus far so that Miguel would continue.

"I was in contact with this source last night, and I sensed that there is something wrong. Nothing specific that was said, it is more a gut feeling of mine."

"Another elimination, Miguel? My men can have the trash taken out by dinner. How would you like it done? Anything specific? Make it look like an accident? A robbery gone bad? Gang related shooting?"

Miguel raised his hands, palms out to his guest. "Easy, Victor," he said. "This one must be handled a little more delicately. I am speaking of the daughter of Diego Gallagos, one of our tenant farmers. She is living in the United States posing as a waitress near the naval base in Norfolk, Virginia." Victor smiled inwardly as a picture of the lovely Belinda Gallagos entered his mind. The smile was the result of a combination of the pleasant picture in his mind and the inside knowledge he possessed concerning his boss' affections for Miss Gallagos. Miguel lifted two manila file folders from the top of his desk and handed them to Victor. "The top one is her file, the other is her family's. Familiarize yourself with them both, then return them to me. I want you to go to Norfolk and watch her. I want to know everything she does, everyone she sees, every place she goes. I want you to search her apartment, her car, her locker at work. I want to know everything there is to know about 'Miss Megan Gallagher', but she is not to have the slightest idea that she is being watched. Be invisible. Make no contact with her of any kind. You will leave immediately. Take one man with you to support twenty-four-hour surveillance. She will be contacting me next Tuesday night at midnight, after which I want you on the first flight back here. You will call me from the airport and wake me when you arrive, immediately after which you will come directly to this office and make your report to me. Is that understood?"

"Yes, Miguel, it is understood." Victor stood up and walked out of the office while reading the contents of the first file.

* * *

"Ladies and gentlemen, thank you for coming today. Let's get right down to business." Special Agent William McDowell closed the thick glass door to the conference room and walked over to his seat at the head of the table. His assistant, Special Agent Harvey Mesko, followed him in with a stack of documents that had been prepared for the guests sitting around the table. McDowell introduced himself and his assistant, then he went around the table and introduced each person present as Mesko handed him or her a copy of the documents he was carrying.

"Special Agent Rob Paxton, FBI, Counter-Espionage. Special Agent Debbie Jacobs, FBI, Narcotics. Special Agent Angelo Ferrelli, DEA. Special Agent Lucas Brock, Immigration. And, last but not least, Agent Don Stiles, CIA." McDowell walked back to his chair and sat down. "The documents you have been given were collected by my office over the past three days. First, you have a transcript of three interviews conducted by me in my office, times and dates as indicated in the opening statements of the interviews. The first interview, with a Boatswain's Mate Second Class E. Phillip Anthony Prescott of the US Coast Guard, was the initial contact in this case. With him during the interview was a Miss Belinda Maria Gallagos, a.k.a. Megan Gallagher, who is the foreign operative involved in the case. Third, we have a Signalman Second Class Jonathan James Douglass of the US Navy who was the target of the alleged espionage. Under normal circumstances, a case of this magnitude would have been handled quietly by my office, with no external assistance needed. However, as the next document will indicate, my research took me into an arena which I consider to be much larger and much more significant than the espionage case itself, and for which I feel the assistance of other branches of law enforcement will be required to achieve a satisfactory result.

"Miss Gallagos is an information plant in the employ of one 'Don' Miguel Ramirez of Venezuela, the head of one of the largest and most ruthless drug cartels in all of South America. I am sure that this name is familiar to most of us, but if not, a quick skimming of the information you were given will be sufficient for you to understand my position.

"As much as I would love for the NCIS to bust this guy and to be able to take all the credit for it, it is more important for me to involve some or all of you in the bust, so we will be able to charge him with a much wider variety of crimes. That way, even if he gets a slick lawyer to get him off some of the charges, he won't be able to escape them all, and we will still be able to lock him up for the rest of his natural life. Of course, the NCIS will retain primary jurisdiction and operational command, but I am authorized to formally request the assistance of any of you whose parent organizations have a vested interest in and/or would like to offer operational or technical assistance for the arrest and conviction of Mr. Miguel Ramirez."

The guests were given sufficient time to read through the prepared documents, after which the meeting resumed. A flurry of questions came from all around the table, to which McDowell provided the best answers his information permitted.

After several hours, many cell phone calls and a handful of faxes, the meeting broke up. It had been decided that every organization represented wanted a piece of the action, except for Special Agent Lucas Brock of Immigration. Though he had no immediate official interest in the case, he agreed to stand by on a consulting basis to provide additional technical support, and to press additional criminal charges if the need and/or opportunity presented itself.

The NCIS would maintain primary jurisdiction over the

case, operational command of the sting, and would provide initial surveillance of the subjects. The other agencies involved would inform and consult with their superiors to organize the bust into a well planned-out operation that would take into consideration every conceivable contingency and/or irregularity such that, in spite of any erratic and unpredictable behavior on the part of the subjects, the government would be able to successfully execute the arrest and prosecution of those subjects involved—particularly Mr. Miguel Ramirez.

*   *   *

The A320 Airbus from Caracas, Venezuela to Dulles International Airport in Washington DC landed eight minutes late and taxied to the terminal. Victor and his companion, Luis, joined the line of travelers as they exited the plane and gathered around the baggage claim conveyor. Victor and Luis each retrieved a small suitcase and proceeded to the US Customs checkpoint separating the International Arrivals area from the rest of the airport. They dutifully placed their suitcases and carry-on bags on the x-ray conveyor and produced passports to give to the customs agents. After determining that "Julio Gonzales" and "Mario Castillo" were low level executives from the Maracaibo Oil Company in town for a business conference, a bored customs agent stamped their passports, returned them, and expressed his insincere desire that they enjoy their visit to the United States of America.

Victor and Luis passed through the turnstiles and entered the main airport, where they consulted an airport map to locate the rental car booth. On their way to the booth, they stopped in the men's room where they washed their faces, checked their hair, straightened their suits, and deposited the claim tickets from their suitcases into the trash can.

Luis took the pair of phony passports and placed them into a small leather shaving kit bag from his suitcase, which he then shoved into the back of an airport locker. He deposited the required coins into the slot and removed the key, which he dropped into the pocket of his sport coat.

While Luis was taking care of the passports, Victor was at the rental car booth renting a mid-size two-door sedan, which he paid for with a credit card bearing the name of Raul Chavez.

Victor drove the three and a half hours from Washington DC to Norfolk, where they checked into a chain hotel which catered to business travelers. Victor explained to the desk clerk that he, Constantino Argurro and his associate, Pedro Servantes, would be in town for a week doing some consulting and repair work for their office machine company in Detroit. The tired desk clerk assigned them a room on the second floor and pointed out its location on a laminated map which hung beside her on the wall. Victor thanked her, picked up the two key cards she had laid on the counter in front of him, and walked out of the lobby.

Thursday morning Victor and Luis rose early, showered, shaved and dressed themselves, then took their rented car to the diner across the street for breakfast. On the way they stopped and bought two maps of Norfolk and the surrounding areas from the gas station on the corner. A cheerful waitress brought them silverware, menus and coffee cups, then asked them what she could get them to drink. Both men asked for coffee, after which they placed their orders for the breakfast special. Victor also asked to see the local yellow pages, which he used to locate two rental car facilities, one nearby and one on the other side of town. He found the two locations on his map, as well as the directions to Megan's work and her apartment, then he folded up the map and put it away as the waitress placed his breakfast on the table in front of him.

Victor and Luis chatted quietly while they ate their food. When they were finished, they paid for their food, left a generous but not extravagant tip for the waitress, and exited the restaurant. They rode together to the nearest rental car agency, where they rented two of the most common cars in the city; each style different from the other, but each a type that would be seen all over town at any given moment in time and would therefore not be easily recognizable or memorable. After Argurro and Servantes had each rented a vehicle, they drove the "Raul Chavez" car across town, turned it in to the proper rental agency and settled the bill with Chavez's credit card. When they had traveled about half of the distance back to the place by the diner where they had rented the other pair of vehicles, Victor pulled into a gas station and stopped the car by the pay phone. He pulled some coins out of his pocket , dropped them into the slot, and dialed a telephone number written on a small piece of paper he had pulled out of his pocket with the change.

"State your business!" a stern voice at the other end of the line commanded.

"This is Louie the Leprechaun. I am searching for the pot of gold at the end of the rainbow."

"Third stall, downtown library men's room. Downtown Greyhound." The line clicked and there was silence.

"Talkative fellow," Victor said to himself. He hung up the telephone and resumed the drive back to their other car.

Once they reached Luis' car, Victor instructed him to locate Belinda's apartment and her workplace, familiarize himself with each of them, then begin surveillance at the apartment. Victor would join him in two hours. Luis acknowledged his orders, jumped into his car and headed for the Admiral's Steakhouse. Victor turned his own car toward the Norfolk Public Library, main downtown branch, and joined the flow of traffic.

Victor parked his car across the street from the old Norfolk Public Library building. He crossed the street, opened the door and walked into the main entrance area. He noticed a sign pointing to the men's restroom up on the second floor, so he crossed over to the other side of the room and climbed the worn wooden steps to the second floor. The floor creaked as he followed another sign to the opposite corner of the room and pulled open the door to the men's room. He went into the third stall and locked the door. He searched behind the stool, then up inside the paper dispenser, but found nothing. Then he removed the lid from the old tank and peered inside, where he found a silver colored key similar to the one he had in his pocket from the airport locker. It was hanging from the front edge of the tank on the end of a paper clip which had been bent at the other end to hook onto the edge of the toilet tank. He retrieved the key and dropped it into his pocket, then replaced the lid, threw the mutilated paper clip into the trash can and walked out of the men's room. He stopped by the big desk at the main entrance to ask the librarian how to get to the downtown Greyhound bus station, which she was happy to tell him, then he continued out to where he had parked his car across the street.

"One thirty?!" Victor asked in disbelief. "Are you sure?"

"Yes, Sir, the bus from Richmond is scheduled to arrive at one-thirty this afternoon."

"I can't believe it!" Victor said, exasperated. "That dope of a little brother of mine said *ten*-thirty! Boy, is he going to get it when he gets off that bus!"

Victor walked over to an empty plastic bench and sat down heavily, his frustration obvious. He sat there fuming for twenty minutes, after which he got up, purchased a copy of the local paper, and returned to his seat. There had been four other people in the bus terminal when he arrived: the older lady sitting across from him against the wall, the tall bearded man in the long overcoat standing by the window reading a magazine, and two younger girls in a corner talking continuously about their clothes, hair and make-up. Shortly after Victor sat down, the older lady boarded a bus for Pittsburgh, and the pair of wanna-be fashion consultants were joined by a third of their kind, who added her part to their jabbering with the same intensity but with even more volume from the second they saw each other until they were outside the building and the door shut behind them.

The tall man continued reading his magazine over by the window. Victor eventually got up and made a lazy visit to the men's room, after which he purchased a Coke from the machine by the lockers and returned to his seat. He glanced at the man as he opened up his paper, but he couldn't tell if the man was watching him, the lockers, or neither. He could simply be waiting for a bus to arrive or depart; or he could be an undercover cop who knew something about locker number 307, to which Victor held the key in the right inside pocket of his sports coat.

The terminal wasn't as busy as Victor had anticipated. Several lone travelers and a few couples had come in, waited for a little while, then left with friends or by themselves to wait elsewhere. Victor was just about to abort the pickup, to return at a later time when the tall man would be gone, when he saw movement out of the corner of his eye. The tall man closed his magazine, dropped it onto the chair beside him, and walked over to the counter. He mumbled something that Victor couldn't hear to the girl behind the counter.

"I don't know when she will be back, Ted!" the girl snapped. "Her lunch was over ten minutes ago, but I can't leave until she gets back, so you will either have to keep waiting, or go on without me!"

The man huffed, walked over to a chair, and sat down. Victor didn't try to hide his smile. Paranoia was necessary in this line of work, he thought, but it certainly did waste a lot of time. He stood up, fished the locker key out of his pocket, and inserted it into the keyhole for locker 307.

He opened the locker, extracted two small gray suitcases and a black nylon duffel bag, then quickly exited the bus terminal. He unlocked the trunk of his rental car, carefully placed the luggage on the floor, then hopped into the driver's seat and pulled out into traffic. When he had made enough erratic turns to be certain that neither he nor the luggage was being followed, he drove back to the hotel. Entering through the side entrance, he took the elevator to the second floor, gained access to his room with the plastic key card, then locked and bolted the door behind him. He placed the suitcases and the duffel bag onto the bed, then he removed his sport coat and hung it over the back of the hotel's desk chair, which he pulled over to face the corner of the bed.

Victor decided to begin with the duffel bag. He pulled it over in front of himself and unzipped it. Inside he found an unmarked white envelope containing five thousand dollars in cash, two walkie-talkie radios, a pair of lock-picking kits, a pair of black halogen flashlights, two shoulder holsters, two back-up holsters, and a pair of utility belts upon which to carry each of those items plus four extra semi-automatic handgun ammunition clips. This gave Victor a pretty good idea of what to expect when he opened the suitcases. The duffel bag also produced a pair of binoculars and two small pocket notebooks, each with a pen and a pencil for keeping notes on Belinda's activities. He took out two thousand dollars, one for him and one for Luis, then stuffed the envelope into the outside pouch of his suitcase. He stuck the two thousand into his wallet, then reached for the first suitcase and opened the lid.

Nestled safely in custom-cut pockets in the gray foam padding were four Colt .45 handguns, two in what was now the lid of the suitcase, and two in the bottom. Each handgun was accompanied by two extra clips full of rounds, and there were four more boxes of extra rounds secured along the bottom of the suitcase. Miguel did believe in being prepared.

The second suitcase contained camera equipment packed the same way in gray foam padding. It was a 35mm camera with a couple of extra telephoto lenses, one of them large and powerful enough to allow him to sit on the bed in his hotel room and read the prices on the menus in the diner across the street.

Victor checked over all the equipment, disassembling and reassembling all the guns, unloading and reloading all the clips, checking the action of the guns and the working features of the camera. Once satisfied that all would perform properly if called upon, he put on his shoulder and back-up holsters, tucked a loaded .45 and two full clips into the pockets of each one, then slipped into his sport coat. He slid the lock-pick kit into one breast pocket, the notebook and pen into the other. Then he returned all the remaining miscellaneous paraphernalia to the duffel bag, along with the other two Colts, the rest of the extra clips, and a box of ammunition for Luis. With the duffel bag's carry strap slung over his shoulder, he picked up the suitcase containing the camera equipment and walked back out the side door to his car. Now, they were in business. He quickly checked his map, then drove over to Belinda's apartment complex where he would properly equip Luis and assist him in the surveillance.

*　　　　*　　　　*

Captain Emilio Escobar sat back in his chair. "Very interesting," he sighed. "Very interesting, indeed."

He had been deep in thought, studying the document laid out on the top of his desk. It was a copy of the latest proficiency reports collected from the commanders of both his regular Puerto Cristobol Police Force and the six-man Special Operations team. The numbers had improved markedly since the previous report, thus Captain Escobar was quite pleased with what he saw. He didn't want his own forces to be regarded as inferior to those of the DISIP, if and when the course of this operation took them into a live-fire combat situation. Perhaps slightly inferior, he admitted, due to the significant difference in funding and training, but certainly competent, motivated, and willing to learn.

His concentration had been broken by the beep of his intercom and the pleasant voice of his office manager, Miss Veronica Santos.

"Line one for you, Chief. It is Inspector San Tielo with the DISIP."

"Thank you, Veronica," he had said, quickly punching the appropriate button to connect the telephone on his desk to that of Inspector Eduardo San Tielo of the DISIP. "Inspector, this is Captain Escobar. What can I do for you?" he said into the mouthpiece.

"I believe it is I who can do for you, Captain. I have just received a most interesting telephone call. Can we meet for lunch today? It would be best to discuss this matter in person."

"Of course, Inspector. Did you have a time and place in mind?"

"How about Lupe's at noon?" the Inspector suggested.

"That would be fine," Escobar agreed. "Lupe's at noon. I will see you then."

"Splendid. Good-bye, Captain."

Captain Escobar was certain that his lunch appointment would have something to do with the Ramirez case, although he had no idea what the subject of the Inspector's telephone call had been or how it would relate to the case that had become his own top priority. Anticipation, at times considered to be an aphrodisiac, under different circumstances could be more accurately described as a nuisance.

Lupe's was a small delicatessen two blocks south and two blocks west of the police station, scrunched in between a dry cleaning service and a shoe store. It was a common lunch spot for the beat cops, upon whose plates Lupe herself would always add a little extra food at no extra cost. Captain Escobar didn't find himself frequenting Lupe's as often as he had during his own beat cop days, so he decided to take an early lunch and wait for Inspector San Tielo at the deli.

The moment he walked through the door, he was assaulted by the strong aroma of Lupe's infamous soup counter. Three large pots of soup sat in steamers along the back wall, their mouth-watering smells drifting up through the hole in the lids where the spoon handles protruded from inside. The place was small and always full of customers. Lupe and her daughter were working feverishly behind the counter, taking orders, cooking dishes, and serving customers. When she recognized Captain Escobar, Lupe smiled and waved, absently tucking into her bonnet the same stray lock of graying black hair she had been fighting with all morning.

"Emilio!" she shouted. "It has been much too long since you come to see me. I should make you go to Antonio's and suffer through his lunch buffet, but I will forgive you and serve you here. You eat alone?"

"Oh, no," Escobar said. "I am meeting someone here at noon. How are you doing, Lupe?"

"I am very good. Lupe's is as busy as ever. I always give enough food to stretch their stomachs, so they have to come back here to get enough next time," she whispered conspiratorially.

"Oh, so that is your secret! I should have guessed!" Escobar chuckled. He missed this part of his beat cop days. Spending time with the people on their own turf had made him feel connected to them. It made the job seem more personal and important. It was no longer merely wearing a badge and busting criminals. It was protecting the rights and safety of the common people; the good people who lived their small lives happily from day to day, oblivious to the hard realities of the world outside their small existence and having no desire to learn about them. These people and their happy lives were what had motivated him to become a police officer in the first place. Corruption in the ranks was what had motivated him to advance. Experiences like he was having at this very moment would motivate him to do his job with honor and integrity, to the best of his ability as long as he remained in office.

"It is very good to see you, Lupe," he said.

She smiled a knowing smile and slid a small bowl of soup in front of him. "Before your friend arrives," she said. "It is a new recipe you have never had. Try it."

Escobar picked up a spoon and took a taste of the soup. It was unbelievable. Lupe saw the compliment written on his face. Beaming, she turned back to the grill and continued her cooking.

A few minutes later, Escobar saw San Tielo walk through the door. He got up from the bar and nodded to an empty booth in the back corner, toward which both men walked. They met at the table, shook hands, and took their seats.

"Thank you for seeing me on such short notice, Captain," San Tielo said.

"My pleasure, Inspector," Escobar replied. "Even if your information turns out to be less than I anticipate, visiting here again will have made the meeting worth while."

"I don't think you will be forced to base the success of our meeting on your dining experience, Captain. What I have to tell you should give you great pleasure, indeed."

Just then, Lupe stopped at their table. "What can I get for you two handsome gentlemen today?" she asked.

They placed their orders, which she carefully wrote down on her order pad and waddled back into the kitchen.

"This morning, I received a telephone call from the United States Drug Enforcement Agency. Special Agent Angelo Ferrelli, the agent in charge of the office in Norfolk, Virginia."

"Interesting. Do go on, Inspector," Escobar encouraged.

"Special Agent Ferrelli was rather vague in his details, but I gathered from him that the name of Miguel Ramirez had come up as the subject of a very large joint operation involving several different agencies of law enforcement in the United States. As a matter of professional courtesy, he was calling to inform us that the Americans were gearing up to take steps against Mr. Ramirez, and to ask if we had any particular interest in this man from a legal standpoint. He wanted to ensure that their operation would not interfere with any ongoing investigations or other legal action we may be actively involved in.

"I told him that Miguel Ramirez is a name many of us know well here, and that we were always eager to hear anything another organization may have to say about him. Also that we were nearly always involved in legal action against him in some way or another. I ended the call by informing him that I needed to bring other individuals in on this topic, and that I would be getting in touch with him later today or tomorrow."

Escobar smiled a devilish smile. "Indeed," he said. "So, the Americans have some design for our old friend as well. Inspector, this could be just the break we have been looking for. No—I will not speculate until we speak with this person further. He is your contact, Inspector. How do you recommend we handle it?" Escobar asked.

"First, I believe we should verify his position as a Special Agent in the DEA. Then, once satisfied that he is who he claims to be, I propose we arrange to meet with him in person immediately to exchange notes and determine exactly what we are dealing with. If they are interested in launching some sort of an attack on Ramirez as well, it could take some of the load off of us. I mean, I would love to be the one to bust him and put him away, but most importantly, I simply want to see him put away. If the Americans can do it for us, using their finances and resources, so much the better. Free trash disposal."

"Exactly what I was thinking, Inspector. Let's make some calls."

*　　　*　　　*

"NCIS, Special Agent McDowell speaking."

"Hey, McDowell, Ferrelli here, DEA"

"Oh, hi, Ferrelli. I was just on my way out. What's up?"

"Cancel your dinner plans, buddy. I've got some news for you."

"Shoot."

"Out of professional courtesy, I telephoned the Directorate of Intelligence and Prevention Services down in Venezuela, that is their equivalent of our DEA, and talked to an Inspector San Tielo, the head of the local office in Cumana, the closest one to Puerto Cristobol, which Ramirez uses as a home base for his business. I didn't want to tell him too much, you know how corrupt they can be down there, but I said that multiple law enforcement agencies up here had an interest in one of their citizens, Mr. Miguel Ramirez, and were considering taking legal action against him. I wondered if he could share with me if they knew of this man, and whether they had any ongoing investigations or anything of that nature that our potential activities might interfere with."

McDowell nodded, then grunted into the telephone for Ferrelli to continue.

"Well, he seemed very intrigued by the idea of our action against Ramirez. He said he needed to talk with some people and that he would get back to me later in the day. He called me an hour ago, and said that he and a colleague of his would like to meet with me somewhere safe and private to discuss some 'very important matters,' as he put it."

"And did he suggest where such a meeting might take place?" McDowell asked. "You know he could be working for Ramirez, and this could all be an elaborate trap to lure us down there and bury us in the jungle. Ramirez does not appreciate opposition, from what I have gathered."

"Actually, he suggested St. Thomas. He said we could make it look like a vacation, then nobody would suspect that anything was going on. I don't know about you, but I could certainly use a Caribbean vacation, even if it is only for a day or two!

"I checked with our embassy down there in Caracas, and they couldn't find anything bad on our friend, Inspector San Tielo. They said as far as they knew, he was straight and above board. Our undercover DEA people down there say he is a straight arrow, too. I believe we are looking at a joint venture between our two countries to pull out all the stops and put this scumbag away forever. I say we go to St. Thomas."

"Excellent work, Ferrelli. The DEA does not disappoint. I completely agree. Set it up ASAP and I'll start filling out the paperwork. Just to be safe, take Stiles with you. He is CIA, and on the off chance that something goes down while you are there, he will have more resources in that area to assist than either of us. Agreed?"

"Agreed. May I also recommend that you set up another meeting of the operational heads for the day we get back? If this is as big as I think it is, we will want to move on it immediately."

"Done. Good luck, Ferrelli. Don't forget your suntan lotion."

"Thanks, McDowell, I'll remember that. See you in a few days."

McDowell hung up the telephone and pulled out his file cabinet drawer to select the mountain of paperwork this little trip would require him to generate. Ferrelli and Stiles would be out having fun in the sun, and he had to sit in here and fill out the extra paperwork that would make it possible. Man, he missed being a field agent.

*　　　　*　　　　*

"Megan, let's go!" Jack yelled from the living room. "Kickoff is in twenty minutes, and you know what traffic is like on a Friday night!"

"Uh! You men and your football!" Megan said, exasperated. "It's not like it's the Super Bowl or something. It's only a high school game."

"That's not the point. You want to see the whole game, including the kickoff. That's just the way it is with football. You wouldn't want to go into an opera halfway through the opening scene, would you?"

She stopped trying to get her barrette in place and looked at him. She started to say that his comparison was among the silliest things she had ever heard, when she noticed how handsome he was. Instead, she smiled and finished doing her hair, a little more quickly than she had been.

"Besides, the others will all be waiting at the gate for us in ten minutes," Jack added.

As Jack had predicted, Kirt, Steve, Kim and Laura were standing by the gate when Jack and Megan finally arrived at the school, two minutes before kickoff.

"Boy, you are lucky I caught most of the lights green, young lady, or you might have found yourself walking home!" Jack teased.

"Oh, keep talking, smart boy!" Megan countered. "I'll just sit down here with the girls, and you can snuggle up to Kirt and Steve to keep warm!"

"Ouch! You are ruthless, Megan. That isn't even funny!"

"Oh, come here, you dope!" Megan said, pulling Jack closer to her and kissing him on the cheek. "You know I am only kidding."

Jack smiled and nodded.

"Besides, if anyone snuggles up to Kirt and Steve to keep warm, it will be me!" Megan let out a shriek of laughter and darted between the girls as Jack lunged for her.

"Brat." Jack said, walking ahead to join the guys.

The small group of friends walked along the track to where they could enter the bleachers. They chose seats halfway up the bleachers, in the middle of the crowd right next to the aisle. They scanned the playing field, looked at the scoreboard, and took in their surroundings, talking and teasing, laughing and shivering. They all needed to blow off some steam, and a high school football game seemed like as good a place as any.

The players and cheerleaders for the opposing team were pacing back and forth across the field from them, and the home team was getting ready to enter the field. All the cheerleaders were holding a huge ring covered with paper, which the players would break through in a magnificent display of the formidable force which they would be bringing with them to unleash onto the playing field. The opposition didn't stand any more of a chance than that paper did.

The coin toss went to the visiting team, who opted to receive, and the players took their places on the playing field. The home team kicker slammed the ball deep into visitor territory, and the game was on. The cheerleaders jumped and yelled, some watching the game, others completely oblivious to what was going on behind them.

Aside from being a good way for the friends to have some fun, their attendance at the football game also served the needs of someone else. Had they but known what to look for, they would have seen the short man in the bulky blue ski coat sitting ten rows above them and talking into a radio.

"Yes, we are at the football game. They appear to be staying here for all of it, so now would be a good time to search the apartment," Luis said into the radio. "I will let you know when they get ready to leave, but you should have a couple of hours. I am told that the game won't be over until about 9 p.m., and it will take a while after that to get out of here with all the traffic."

"Understood. Keep me posted," Victor said.

Luis clipped the radio back onto his belt and looked out at the field. What a curious game, this American football.

Across town, Victor stepped out of his rental car and casually made his way over to Belinda's door. He made a show of knocking on the door, just in case there was an unseen observer somewhere in the vicinity who had escaped his notice, and also to allow himself the opportunity to visually inspect the lock in the doorknob. Once satisfied that there were no people about, he pulled his lock-pick kit out of his coat pocket and made a quick selection of the necessary items. Kneeling in front of the doorknob, Victor inserted his tools into the keyhole and popped the door open as quickly and easily as he could have using Belinda's key. With a final surveying glance at the parking lot and sidewalk next to it, he slipped into the apartment and quietly shut the door.

He went directly to the windows, where he noted the positioning of each of the blinds before he closed them. He pulled the flashlight from the nylon case on his belt and clicked it on, careful to keep from shining it directly onto the window coverings. He looked around the apartment, room by room, observing the general condition, the placement of furniture, and the presence of any unusual items. This was the easiest kind of search—he wasn't looking *for* anything, he was simply looking *at* everything. His mission was to take in every aspect of Belinda's life, to find out what magazines she read, what foods she kept in her refrigerator and her cupboards, what brands of perfume and clothing she favored. Miguel would want to know the content of any computer disks she had, as well as anything she had loaded onto her hard drive. He would expect Victor to give an account of every significant move she had made since she had been living in the United States.

Victor's general survey of the apartment ended in the bathroom, where the detailed search would then begin. The small mirrored medicine cabinet hanging above the sink revealed nothing of interest; a bottle of non-aspirin pain reliever, a selection of common toiletries, some female products and a small first aid kit. There were no prescription drugs, and all bottles and boxes were found to contain exactly what their labels indicated. Under the sink was a four-pack of bathroom tissue with three rolls remaining, two bars of soap, small piles of bath towels, hand towels and washcloths, and an assortment of cleaning supplies.

In the bedroom, Victor started in the closet, where he found nothing but clothes, an ironing board, and an iron. No boxes of keepsakes up on the shelves, no secret panels along the walls; only hanging clothes on a solid wooden bar and a rack of shoes on the floor. The dresser was littered with cheap jewelry in glass and ceramic jars and bowls of different sorts, none matching and none noteworthy. He removed and searched the drawers, careful not to disturb the neatly folded clothing in each one, then checked the bottoms of the drawers and the inside of the dresser. The beat-up old vanity along the wall contained a variety of hair, nail, and make-up items, from application tools to unopened packages of cosmetics and hairpieces. Two curling irons and a blow dryer were lying on the surface, all still plugged in but none turned on. Victor checked under the bed where he found one sock, a old copy of a women's magazine, and a plastic pencil sharpener.

The kitchen was much easier than the bedroom or the bathroom. A very small assortment of cooking pans and storage bowls was in the cupboards on either side of the stove, their accompanying utensils in the drawers above them. In the cupboard above the counter were glasses, cups, and dining service for four. The cupboard above the bar held paper plates and cups, a thick telephone directory, and the miscellaneous selection of items that people keep for absolutely no reason, fearing that the only time they could ever possibly need such a thing would be immediately after they got rid of it. The third drawer contained a set of silverware, a bottle opener and a cheap manual can opener.

Along the wall, between what served as an entryway and where the living room began, was a small computer desk holding Belinda's meager computer system. The desk had two drawers along the right side, with the computer tower on the floor beside it and the monitor up on the desktop with the mouse and keyboard. Victor leafed through her files, making little notes of the commonly called numbers on her telephone bills and the receipts she had kept from department store and bookstore purchases. He switched on her computer, searching her hard drive for anything out of the ordinary. He made notes of any programs she had loaded onto her hard drive and made copies of all floppy disks that showed evidence of use. Satisfied that this area held nothing that would be of interest to Miguel, he turned his attention toward the living room.

Though the living room was the easiest and quickest of all to search, it ended up being the only room which gave Victor anything of interest to report to Miguel. The TV and VCR occupied two of the three shelves on an old wooden cart along the far wall, and a portable AM/FM stereo/CD player provided mood music from a limited selection of CD's on the floor beside it. A beat up coffee table sported a universal remote control for the severely lacking entertainment center, a current copy of the same women's magazine that had found its way under the bed, and a plain black leather-backed book with "Holy Bible" printed along the spine. Victor chuckled, picked it up, and began to leaf through it. He was about to drop it back onto the coffee table and consider his search 'completed but unrevealing' when he noticed a bookmark sticking up from somewhere toward the back of the book. He flipped it open to that page, disregarding the text as his eyes focused on the business card that was being used as a bookmark. It was the official government business card of the Naval Criminal Investigative Service, this one belonging to William H. McDowell, Resident Special Agent in Charge, East Coast Operations, Norfolk Branch Office. The office telephone and fax numbers were listed on the front of the card, along with an email address. On the back was a handwritten number, probably written by Special Agent McDowell himself, and most likely ringing in to his personal cell phone. A sadistic smile formed on the face of Victor Mesones.

"Miss Gallagos," he whispered to himself, "you have made a very big mistake." He returned the Bible to its original position on the coffee table and did a quick visual inspection to make sure he hadn't left anything in a condition other than it had been in prior to his arrival. Satisfied with his night's work, he returned the blinds to their original positions and watched out the windows until the parking lot was deserted. He quickly and silently exited the apartment, locking the door behind him, and resumed a casual strolling pace to his rental car on the other side of the lot. When he reached the car, he let himself in the driver's side and stuck the key into the ignition. The smile returned. "Well," he said to himself, "this mission just might be upgraded to a hit after all." He began to whistle as he drove out of the parking lot and made his way back to the hotel for a nap, from which Luis would call to wake him when Belinda returned to her apartment. Luis would follow the boyfriend back to his place in preparation for reconnaissance the next day, after which he would go back to the hotel and sleep. Victor would take over watching Belinda for the first half of the night shift, Luis would relieve him for the second.

Saturday morning at 8:13, the radio beside Victor's pillow cackled to life. He fumbled for it, finally pushing the button to answer Luis after he had called him the third time.

"What is it?" Victor growled into the microphone.

"Subject number one is up and about."

"Understood. Any action last night?"

"Nothing. Not even a potty break during the night."

"Right. See you in an hour."

Victor crawled out of bed, plopped the radio onto the back of the toilet, and revived himself with a hot shower and a shave. He dressed himself and pulled out his notebook, flipping to the page where he had written down Belinda's home phone number. Keying the button on his radio, he announced to Luis that he would be calling Belinda, so any communication between them should be with single words and then only in an emergency. Luis replied that he understood, and Victor picked up and dialed the hotel telephone. Luis watched Belinda hurry through the apartment and pick up her own telephone.

"Hello?" she said.

"Hi, Miss Gallagher, this is Mike Ramsey from Special Agent Bill McDowell's office at the NCIS. I am very sorry to bother you on a Saturday, but I have been working on typing up the transcript of your meeting with him, and there is a section of the interview here where the tape is garbled and I just can't figure out what was said. I was wondering if you might be able to help me fill in a few of the details?"

"Well, I can try," Megan/Belinda answered. "What information did you need?"

"Ah, well, you are talking about a Navy man, about your involvement with him..."

"You mean with Jack?"

"Yeah, with Jack." Victor jotted "Jack" down on the notepad beside the bed. "And, uh, it is something about why you came to the NCIS to begin with... is any of this sounding familiar, Miss Gallagher?"

"Yeah, sort of, I guess. It's hard to remember what exactly was said. But coming to the NCIS about it was Phil's idea."

"Phil's idea? And Phil would be... let me flip back a page, here..."

"Phil is Jack's friend, the Coast Guard guy."

"Yes, of course, it's right here on the last page," Victor lied. "Okay, thanks, this is really helping. All right, and one more section, here near the end, talking about the deal, how you wanted the deal or something?"

"The deal? Oh, you mean *out of* the deal. How I wanted out of the deal with Ramirez."

"Right," Victor said. "Yes, that fits. Well, thank you, Miss Gallagher. That is all I needed. You have been a great help. Good day."

"Bye," Megan said, hanging up the telephone.

Victor laughed and keyed his radio.

"Yeah," Luis answered.

"Burn up some film, Luis. Our little mole is turning out to be a rat. The boss is not going to like this one bit, and we will need to be able to prove it to him."

"Got it. I will get a few now, then a bunch more when the boyfriend comes over."

"Right," Victor answered. "Out."

*　　　*　　　*

Two American tourists walked out of St. Thomas' Cyril E. King Airport arrivals terminal and waved for a taxi. One was dressed in tennis shorts and a polo shirt, the other in khaki shorts with a tank top and a loose fitting cotton button-down, unbuttoned and flapping in the breeze. Both were without luggage, except for the carry-on bags slung over their shoulders, and each had a cell phone clipped to the waistband of his shorts.

"Blackbeard's Castle, please," one of them said to the taxi driver, who quickly pulled away from the curb and shot out into traffic.

"So, what is our agenda, Angelo?" Stiles asked. "Shopping first, or hit the beach?"

"I was thinking maybe a nice lunch first," Ferrelli said. "That bag of stale peanuts didn't seem to hit the spot."

"Sure, lunch works," Stiles agreed.

They arrived at Blackbeard's Castle in what must have been record time, considering the aggressive driving of the cabby. They paid the cab fare and walked into the lobby. The cheerful desk clerk looked up their reservations in her computer, punched in a couple of entries, then handed them each a room key, wishing them a pleasant stay and encouraging them to call her at the desk if they needed anything at all. They politely thanked her, then picked up their bags and made their way to their rooms, up the stairs and to the right, side by side on the second floor.

They took a few minutes to freshen up from the flight before they met in the bar beside the hotel restaurant. Each enjoyed a local cocktail before asking the hostess to seat them at a table for four out on the balcony, where they could take in the spectacular view of the city directly below them and the glistening blue water of the St. Thomas Harbor in the distance.

Blackbeard's Castle, located on Government Hill north of the capital city of Charlotte Amalie, was built by Danish governor Jorgen Iverson in 1678, and was originally called Fort Shytsborg. It is said to have been the hideout of the legendary pirate Blackbeard, whose real name was Edward Teach, while he terrorized the Caribbean during the early 1700s. It was now a quaint twenty-four room inn, a historical landmark, and one of the oldest buildings on the island.

Stiles was right in the middle of sharing an extremely amusing, but very classified, CIA story when two men approached their table. The taller of the two looked at the short, stocky Italian seated at the table and smiled.

"Angelo Ferrelli?" the tall man asked.

"In the flesh," Ferrelli said. "And you must be Eduardo San Tielo, yes?"

"Correct," the Venezuelan said, then continued in very passable English, "I am Inspector Eduardo San Tielo, Senior Operations Officer of the Cumana, Sucre office of the Directorate of Intelligence and Prevention Services, and this is Captain Emilio Escobar, Chief of Police of the city of Puerto Cristobol, Sucre, Venezuela."

Ferrelli and Stiles stood to shake hands with their guests.

"Pleased to meet you both," Ferrelli said. "I am Special Agent Angelo Ferrelli of the Drug Enforcement Agency, and this is Agent Don Stiles of the Central Intelligence Agency. Thank you, Inspector, for your willingness to cooperate with our government on this venture." He looked out across the harbor and smiled. "And for choosing such a pleasant setting for our business meeting!" he added with a friendly smile.

A waitress came by, quickly jotted down their drink and lunch orders, then disappeared back inside the restaurant.

"Gentlemen," San Tielo said, "I propose we get right down to business. I received some new information only yesterday that I believe could be quite pertinent to our discussion, not to mention rather time-sensitive."

"By all means, proceed," Ferrelli invited. Stiles nodded.

San Tielo outlined the case from the Venezuelan perspective, sharing what information they knew about Ramirez and about the present case in particular, along with their strong desire to put Ramirez away for good. Ferrelli reciprocated, outlining their own plan for nabbing Ramirez. He also questioned them concerning the story told to them by Megan/Belinda about her family's hardships at the hands of Ramirez, which the Venezuelans confirmed with no small degree of sadness. By the end of the meeting, it had been concluded that it would be far more effective for the United States to apprehend Ramirez and prosecute him on American soil for crimes against the State. Those crimes carried much heavier sentences and a conviction was much more likely than mere drug trafficking and smuggling allegations in Venezuela. San Tielo and Escobar agreed to provide any assistance requested of them, including protection of the family of Belinda Gallagos to begin immediately and to last until the trial was over. The Americans were granted unrestricted access to Venezuelan law enforcement agencies and resources pertaining to and in support of the arrest and conviction of Miguel Ramirez.

"And one more thing," San Tielo added. "The new information I received yesterday confirms that Victor Mesones, Ramirez's number two man, has disappeared. He was seen in Caracas last week, but hasn't been seen or heard from since. I fear Mr. Ramirez may be getting a bit suspicious of his transplanted flower up in Norfolk, Virginia."

Ferrelli and Stiles shared a concerned look. "Thank you, Inspector. We will address that concern immediately. Again, thank you very much for your assistance. We will be in touch with you soon."

"Anything we can do, Special Agent Ferrelli. Do not hesitate to call," San Tielo offered.

The men shook hands and the meeting was ended. Ferrelli and Stiles walked out to the beach. "We have to get this word to McDowell," he said. "If we lose the girl, it's all over."

"Agreed," Stiles said. "I will get my people to provide a couple of guys for the surveillance. This Victor Mesones guy is a brute. Things could go south in a heartbeat." Stiles pulled his cell phone off his waistband and began to dial.

"Right, I will too," Ferrelli said, pulling up the antenna on his own cell phone. "I hope we can get hold of enough people on a Saturday. Waiting until Monday could mean curtains for our little Venezuelan canary."

McDowell paced around his office, yelling into the telephone. "I don't care if you had plans to dine at the White House! You will be in my office in one hour, is that clear?" He slammed the receiver back into the cradle and ran his fingers through his hair. It wasn't supposed to go down this soon! He was supposed to have had time to think, and to plan; to make a quiet, forceful attack against an unprepared enemy who didn't even know there would be an attack. Now, there was evidence that the enemy not only knew about his involvement, but also that they already had operatives in place, possibly with orders to remove Miss Gallagher from the equation. This would bring his whole plan crashing to the floor around him.

McDowell shook his head in a futile attempt to clear his mind, as though the physical act of shaking his head would cause the jumbled mass of thoughts within it to fall quietly into place, neatly arranged in logical order. Sometimes even the most valiant of efforts results in little more than instant dizziness and the need to find a chair. Well, at least he had gotten in touch with enough agents to cover surveillance for the remainder of the weekend. The DEA had provided two men for the Sunday day shift. The NCIS would be taking the Saturday night and the Sunday night shifts. CIA would begin immediately by covering the remainder of the Saturday day shift. They would take over again Monday morning while McDowell and the rest of the team met in the NCIS office to finalize their plans, somewhat sooner than they had originally anticipated. He had briefed the men about Victor's possible presence, ordering them to shadow the girl unnoticed, watching for Victor to show up, and to intervene only as necessary to prevent loss of life, particularly that of the girl.

Victor Mesones made a decision. His orders were to observe and gather intelligence until Tuesday night, then fly back to Venezuela and brief Miguel on the details. However, the fact of NCIS involvement raised the stakes of the game high enough that Miguel would want to know about it immediately. He keyed his radio and waited for Luis to answer.

"Go ahead, Victor" Luis said into his radio.

"What's going on? Any visitors?" Victor asked.

"Nothing, man. Oh, wait, the boyfriend just drove up in his little car. He is walking up to her door right now."

"Right. I need to go back in. I'll be over in thirty minutes. We will wait until they leave, then you can follow them while I go back into her apartment and get a message to Miguel on her computer."

Jack finished off his glass of water and sat the empty glass back down on the coffee table. Megan walked out of the kitchen and snuggled up beside him.

"How are you holding up?" he asked.

"About as well as can be expected, I guess," she replied. "It is the waiting around and wondering what is going to happen that is driving me nuts."

"Yeah. Me, too," Jack said. "I wish that NCIS guy would call back and give us some news."

"Well, he probably won't even do anything about it until Monday, Jack," Megan said.

"Oh, that's right, it is Saturday. Great."

"So let's enjoy my last weekend of freedom before they lock me up in a federal penitentiary and throw away the key," Megan teased.

"That isn't funny, Megan!" Jack said, completely not amused.

"Hey, lighten up, Jack. There is nothing we can do about it now anyway. God will take care of it, and I will have to tough it out and face whatever happens as a result of my actions."

"But, you were coerced by a lunatic! That should exonerate you from some of it!"

"And it probably will, so just take it easy. Let's not waste the time we have now worrying about something that may or may not happen in the future, okay?"

"You're right. Maybe McDowell will call on Monday. Let's go take a walk outside."

"You're on," Megan agreed, standing up off the couch and walking to the closet for her jacket.

The happy, but uptight couple strolled through the grass around the parking lot, then walked over to the concrete bridge, where they sat and threw stones into the shallow water. They were so afraid of losing each other as a result of the mess they were in that they could hardly enjoy just being together like they had before.

"Megan," Jack said.

"Yeah?" she answered.

"I think we should pray about this whole predicament."

"I have been, Jack! All the time!"

"No, I mean together. I think that our relationship is what each of us is most concerned about, so why don't we spend some time in prayer about us, and ask God to work this out so that we can still be together?"

"Good idea, Jack. I think we should."

They spent the next 45 minutes sitting on the concrete railing of the old foot bridge talking with God. They asked Him to take control of the situation and work it out however He saw fit. They asked for grace to be able to accept whatever ending He had in store for the whole matter, and for peace and strength to be able to stand up through it. Jack and Megan declared their love for each other, and for God, and their willingness to let God work out the details of the case and of their lives. Through tears and emotional anguish, they pleaded with God to work out the circumstances so that they could stay together, so that her family would be protected, and so that somehow it would all work out for good in the long run.

After thanking and praising God for a little while, they both felt much better. It amazed them how the peace of God could instantly calm them even in the midst of such intense personal unrest. They got up and returned to the apartment so Megan could get ready for work. She had to work the lunch shift and the dinner shift, because she had agreed to cover for a girl who needed the weekend off. Of course, she now wished she had not agreed, but it was probably best that she keep busy anyway, and the extra money never hurt.

Megan changed into her work clothes then followed Jack out of the apartment. Jack was heading home to spend the rest of the day hanging out with Phil. He would see Megan in the morning at church. They shared an intensely passionate hug, after which they climbed into their cars and drove out of the parking lot in different directions.

As soon as Jack was out of sight, Luis dropped his camera onto the seat beside him, fired up his rental car, and carefully tried to catch up to Belinda. Victor keyed his radio. "Luis, I am going into the apartment. Notify me at once if anything unforeseen happens."

"Right, Victor."

Victor got out of his rental car and walked up to Belinda's door, which he again opened with ease, and slipped inside.

As if occurring in a parallel universe but reading the same script, one of another pair of surveillance automobiles pulled out of the parking lot behind Megan Gallagher, while a man in the second vehicle of the pair picked up a portable radio and pushed the button.

"Command, Diggs here. Subjects are mobile. Bonnie has a tail, call him Bert, Laughlin is shadowing both. Clyde is without tail; none of ours, none of theirs. I am remaining at post one to investigate penetration of domicile by second shadow, call him Ernie. Copy, Command?"

"Diggs, Command copies. Proceed with caution. Command out." McDowell threw the microphone onto the desk and cursed. Bert and Ernie could only be Victor Mesones and accomplice.

Victor switched on Belinda's computer and logged onto the Internet. He entered her email program, clicked the mouse on "Create Mail" and typed in a coded message to a contact in Miami who would then forward it on to Miguel. The message was addressed to the parent of a school child, supposedly written by that child's teacher.

Dear Mr. Bellevue:

I am sorry to inform you that your child is a problem child. Although you will find no outward evidence of her intolerable behavior, it is confirmed that she has been to see the principal at least one time, and much was discussed during this interview. Of course, she pointed to you by name as the cause for her bad behavior. I am afraid this may change our prior disciplinary agreement. I will be in my office for the next two hours. Please advise.

Mrs. Brubaker

Victor clicked the mouse arrow on the "Send" button, then got up and walked over to the couch, where he reclined to await Miguel's response. One hour and forty minutes later, the computer beeped and announced to the user that a piece of electronic mail had just been received. Victor jumped off the couch and walked back over to the computer. He opened the email from Mr. Bellevue and read a short response:

Dear Mrs. Brubaker:

The news about my child is very disturbing. We must meet to discuss a revised disciplinary plan immediately. I will be at the downtown library at 4 Monday afternoon.

Mr. Bellevue

"Wow, he must be mad," Victor whispered to himself. "He is coming up here to deal with Belinda personally. Enjoy your last weekend alive, little rat," he smiled to himself. He quickly removed all evidence that the computer had been tampered with then left the apartment to catch up with Luis and make plans for his boss' arrival.

~11~

"Command, this is Diggs."

"Go ahead, Diggs," McDowell said.

"Ernie sent and received email, then exited Bonnie's domicile, destination unknown. I am shadowing him, but you may want to send a computer whiz over here to find out what went back and forth."

"Copy, Diggs. Command out." McDowell grabbed the telephone receiver out of its cradle and punched in some numbers. He arranged for a field agent to escort a computer whiz over to Megan's apartment to recover from her hard drive the data that had just passed between Victor and his contact, most likely Miguel Ramirez, himself.

Two hours later, Special Agent Mesko handed McDowell a printout of the correspondence between Victor Mesones and an unconfirmed party, suspected of being Miguel Ramirez.

McDowell cursed. "They know we are on to her! And, according to this, Ramirez himself is coming here to deal with it personally. This is great! Terrible, but great. Now we can catch him red-handed, right here in the good old U S of A, with no jurisdiction issues or transportation problems to worry about. Mesko!" McDowell shouted.

"Right here, Boss!" Mesko said.

"Get hold of Paxton and Jacobs with the FBI. Tell them we will meet here at noon tomorrow. Advise them of our latest intelligence and ask them to come prepared. When are Ferrelli and Stiles getting back?"

"Not until Monday morning, Sir."

McDowell cursed again. "Get them on the phone, advise them of our situation, and tell them to take the first available flight out of there. This whole situation is a ticking time bomb that will probably blow sky-high by Monday night! I need them here NOW!"

"Yes, Sir!" Mesko yelled, already scurrying back to his desk.

The rest of Saturday and Sunday passed without incident.

Megan's shadows were themselves shadowed by government agents under McDowell's command, while some of Stiles' men accessed Victor and Luis' hotel room and searched it. They found two sets of counterfeit identification papers, a wad of cash, the empty suitcase with the gun-shaped hollow spots cut into it, and a couple of envelopes containing pictures of Megan at work, at home, with her friends and by herself. They determined that "Constantino Argurro" and "Pedro Servantes" had been in town since very late the previous Wednesday evening, and that they intended to vacate the following Wednesday morning.

McDowell himself went home for some sleep late Saturday evening. He returned to his office Sunday morning to meet with FBI Agents Paxton and Jacobs to formulate and fine-tune a series of game plans for apprehending Ramirez. Which one was actually put into action would depend almost entirely upon what type of action Ramirez decided to take against Megan.

DEA Agent Ferrelli and CIA Agent Stiles returned early from their Caribbean vacation to join the command meeting late Sunday afternoon, adding their knowledge and expertise to the most likely of the operational plans.

Jack and Megan had gone to church on Sunday morning, just like always, and out for pizza in the evening with Kirt, Phil and the rest of the group. The small group of friends continued to be very supportive of Jack and Megan, praying often to God on their behalf. The evening was a bit uncomfortable, however, due to the expectation of a call from Special Agent McDowell Monday morning, which could be bringing terrible news for Megan just as easily as it could be bringing good news for her. The painful, stark reality of it was that the government had every right to arrest and try Megan for treason, of which she would doubtlessly be found guilty. Adding to their discomfort was the fact that, even though McDowell seemed to be a level-headed, if not caring man, he also had to answer to his superiors, who most likely would not share his lenient and trusting attitude toward Megan. McDowell only wanted to bring down the big boy, not Megan. She was a victim in this; insignificant in the big picture.

He wanted the man responsible, but, even if they were unable to reach the man responsible, someone above him would still demand some type of justification for all the man-hours invested. If Megan were the only party left with any guilt, she would be sacrificed to appease the gods of the criminal justice system and the bean-counters who vocally demand responsible disbursing of federal funds.

While Megan was across town enjoying some time with her friends at the Pizza Hut, Agent Stiles of the CIA had a crew inside her apartment, planting listening devices in every room and tapping her telephone. They even bugged her computer, so they would be able to monitor her Internet movements from a remote laptop computer set up in McDowell's office. They placed tracking devices underneath her car and listening devices on the inside. McDowell had decided that contacting her in any way could prove to be very dangerous to her well being, and that alerting her to the true gravity of the situation would be even worse. If she knew that Victor and Luis were following her, she would act differently, she would look for them unintentionally, and she would draw undue attention to herself. He didn't even want to consider how she might react if she knew Ramirez was on his way to Norfolk to deal with her personally. He decided to plant listening devices everywhere she might be, so that they could keep on top of any new developments without alerting her to their actions. And, if somehow Ramirez or his goons were to abduct her, or lie in wait for her at her apartment, they would be able to monitor the situation and take appropriate action when the timing was right. They would plant similar devices in Jack's car tonight while he slept, provided neither Victor nor Luis was watching him; thus far, they had only watched him when he was with Megan, not when he was alone.

Special Agent Ferrelli slapped his cell phone shut and walked into McDowell's office with a smile on his face. A call to Inspector San Tielo prior to his departure from St. Thomas had just netted him the flight plans of a private Learjet 31A belonging to Miguel Ramirez. The Learjet was scheduled to depart from Puerto Cristobol, Venezuela on Monday morning bound for Miami, Florida. It would almost certainly refuel and take off again immediately, as the tone of "Mr. Bellevue's" email to "Mrs. Brubaker" suggested a strong sense of urgency to arrive in Norfolk as soon as possible. Ferrelli could have his colleagues in Miami confirm a flight plan for the Learjet to depart Miami for Norfolk within an hour of the plans being filed, which would still give them just over two hours before Ramirez arrived at the Norfolk International Airport. He made his report to McDowell, who thanked him and jotted some notes down on a piece of paper beside his telephone.

Special Agent McDowell called for the attention of the group of Special Agents in Charge assembled in and around his office.

"Ladies and gentlemen, I think that is enough for today. We have two or three very workable assault/takedown plans, with several contingencies should Mr. Ramirez turn out to be more crafty than we give him credit for. His plane will leave Puerto Cristobol, Venezuela tomorrow morning at seven. Agent Stiles will have some of his CIA colleagues working in conjunction with the local Venezuelan authorities to verify the departure of the plane from Puerto Cristobol as well as the presence of Mr. Ramirez on that plane. Agent Ferrelli's DEA colleagues in Miami will monitor the plane's arrival in and subsequent departure from that city later in the morning, keeping a close eye on any movements of Ramirez while he is on the ground. When he lands in Norfolk Monday at about noon, FBI Agent Paxton will lead the shadow team for Mr. Ramirez, monitoring his every movement from the second his plane touches the tarmac until he is safely in our custody. Agent Stiles and his CIA team will take over the shadowing of Miss Gallagher/Gallagos and the Learjet pilot. My NCIS teams will continue doing the same for our Signalman target, Mr. Douglass, as well as Bert and Ernie, Ramirez's henchmen. FBI Agent Jacobs and DEA Agent Ferrelli, I will need your teams to stand by to assist in the takedown. It is unlikely that this will be a drug-related matter, even though Ramirez does have a slot near the top of your personal and organizational most-wanted lists; therefore the intelligence and counter-espionage units will be running the operation with your support.

"Command members, we will meet here at seven tomorrow morning for a final briefing, after which we will brief all of the teams in the conference room at eight. Have your men and women here promptly at eight, assembled in the conference room in full assault dress, armed only with side arms. After the full briefing, all teams will remain on alert until the bust goes down. If Ramirez is really upset, it could very well be tomorrow night. If he wants to watch her for a while or toy with her, then it could drag on for a while. Either way, we will be ready. Are there any questions?"

No one had any questions or comments, so McDowell adjourned the meeting.

"My thanks to all of you for your support in this matter. See you in the morning."

The office emptied quickly. McDowell also locked up his office and left, eager to get home to the last good night's sleep he was likely to see for several days.

Everyone at the table tossed bills at Laura until there was enough accumulated to cover the bill for the food plus a moderately generous tip for the waitress. She neatly stacked the money in the middle of the table, placed the bill on top of the stack, and secured it in place with a half empty glass of Coke. Sensing the increasing amount of tension in the group, Kirt had recommended that they all meet at his parent's house and have a good old-fashioned intercessory prayer session for Megan. Some had verbalized agreement, while others had simply nodded their heads in agreement and dug into their pockets for their money.

As they exited the restaurant, a cloud of gloom seemed to follow them, dampening their mood and chafing at their souls. The peace of God could easily overwhelm the spirit of despondency they all felt, but not until they agreed to let go of their fear and let God take control. Fear is normal and often healthy, especially in a situation such as the one Megan was facing, but fear should not be permitted to be the dominant emotion, affecting what we do and how we act. It is only a feeling; merely a warning bell telling us that something may be wrong, and that we should proceed with caution. It is not the final authority on how we should act. Fear would always stay in the castle and hide under the bed; how then would the dragons ever be vanquished? The hard and fast truth was that God was in control. Megan had surrendered her soul to Him and had agreed to let Him rule her life. She had boldly taken steps to remove herself from the trap Ramirez had placed her in, following God's leading even at the possible expense of her family's safety. She had given up all hope of getting out of her predicament under her own power, and had completely given it over to God. She no longer needed to rely on her own strength, and she no longer needed to be held captive by her own irrational fears. God was in control and, though He was under no obligation to prove anything to her, He had already offered her the undeniable proof of the softening of Jack's heart. Not only was Jack able to see the sincerity in her own heart and forgive her for her betrayal, even though he himself had been severely wounded by it, but he had also decided to remain faithfully by her side throughout the whole ordeal, supporting her and loving her. Only God could have caused such a transformation in Jack's heart, allowing him to see beyond his own pain and anger to rationally view the situation as it really was, and not as his selfish anger had wanted to see it. Like Jesus said in Matthew 19:26, "With man this is impossible, but with God all things are possible."

However, even though she knew God would take care of her, and that she would again experience His peace when this whole mess was over, she still couldn't rid herself of the apprehension she felt about the potential outcome of the approaching week. Even though a basketball player with a dislocated finger may know that getting it popped back into place will ease the pain and will allow him to finish the game, turning his hand over to the person who will do the popping is still met with some degree of apprehension. The certainty of the pain inherent in a cure can sometimes be intimidating enough to prevent someone from accepting that cure, and to cause them to resign themselves to the reality of living life with a debilitating ailment. So it is with God's cleansing, freeing spirit. Sometimes the pain of giving up control, admitting one's faults, and righting one's wrongs can cause a person to decide against God's love and to continue living life with the ailment of sin, which will eventually lead to death. Even though the pain of the cure is but a moment of pain in contrast to a lifetime, not to mention an eternity, of joy, peace, and freedom, many will choose the ailment out of sheer irrational dread of the cure.

The caravan of cars pulled into the Radford driveway and parked along the grass. Tom and Milly were sitting in the living room, watching all the cars enter their driveway. Milly got up and went to the kitchen to get drinks and cookies for everybody. Nobody was allowed to leave Milly Radford's house on an empty stomach. The kids entered the house, greeted the Radfords and selected their cookies and drinks from the counter. With the formalities out of the way, Milly invited them to all go into the living room and find a seat. Kirt began to share with his mother the heaviness of spirit they had all been feeling and his suggestion that they come on over to the Radfords to pray about it. Milly happily agreed, suggesting that they sing a couple of soft worshipful songs before they began praying.

As they were reverently singing the third song, the presence of God filled the house. Each reacted in his or her own way, most of them softly weeping tears of joy. The singing got louder, the crying harder. Steve's body shook with the power of God; he felt like an electric pulse had hit the top of his head and run down through his body to his hands and feet. Tears streamed down the cheeks of the girls and most of the men as they stood in the presence of a holy God. They sang and praised God for nearly half an hour, basking in His love and drinking in His presence. Eventually, the intensity of the exchange between the God of love and His loyal servants slowly diminished, leaving them all feeling tired but peaceful. They hadn’t even prayed for Megan and Jack yet, but somehow they knew that God was in control and that everything would be okay.

As they began to fall back into their seats, Tom Radford reached over to the lamp stand and picked up his Bible, opening it to Ephesians. He announced that he would be reading from chapter six, verses 10-12. The group quieted down as Tom began to read:

> Finally, be strong in the Lord and in his mighty power. Put on the full armor of God so that you can take your stand against the devil's schemes. For our struggle is not against flesh and blood, but against the rulers, against the authorities, against the powers of this dark world and against the spiritual forces of evil in the heavenly realms.

"Megan and Jack," Tom continued, "what you must realize is that this terrible situation you find yourselves in is not even about you; not really. Before you became children of God, when you still lived in sin, the 'evil' aspect of your predicament was not a factor. Now that you have seen the truth, however, it has become very significant. You asked God to save your souls and to cleanse you from all your sins, which He instantly did. But now He requires of you that you remain faithful so that He can continue the work. For, you see, the aspect of this situation that you can see with your eyes is only a very small part of the whole thing. The two of you are now nothing more than a battlefield. A battle will indeed rage on this battlefield, but it is a battle that is no longer yours to fight. It is between God and the devil. The forces of darkness are waging war against the God of light for the occupied territory of your souls. You have chosen to give the right of occupancy to God, not to Satan, and therefore the battle can only be lost if you give up. If you remain faithful and stand by your decision to follow Jesus, Satan will be defeated. You don't need to actively fight Satan; God will do it for you. You need only to actively stand firm in your faith and allow God the opportunity to be victorious.

"Before you became Christians, the devil had already won. By not choosing God's way, you had by default chosen the devil's way. All he had to do was keep you there. However, when you deserted him and crossed over to God's side, the devil got very angry. He will now do everything in his power to get you back. He will attempt to make the Christian life too difficult for you to live faithfully. He will make the sacrifices God requires of you seem too great. He will try to burden you with guilt, stifle you with fear, shame you with failures, crush you with opposition.

"Make no mistake, the devil is a formidable adversary, one who you absolutely can not defeat in your own strength. But God is on your side now and, as Paul says in his letter to the Ephesians, the struggle does not even belong to you. All you need to do is call upon the name of the Lord and remain faithful. Here is another example: back in the Old Testament when the armies of Moab and Ammon were about to attack Israel, King Jehoshaphat prayed to God. In Second Chronicles 20:12 he prays, 'For we have no power to face this vast army that is attacking us. We do not know what to do, but our eyes are upon you.' Then the Spirit of the Lord came upon a man named Jahaziel, who stood up to speak to the whole assembly. This is what he had to say, beginning with verse 15:

> He said: "Listen, King Jehoshaphat and all who live in Judah and Jerusalem! This is what the Lord says to you: 'Do not be afraid or discouraged because of this vast army. For the battle is not yours, but God's. Tomorrow march down against them. They will be climbing up by the pass of Ziz, and you will find them at the end of the gorge in the Desert of Jeruel. You will not have to fight this battle. Take up your positions; stand firm and see the deliverance the Lord will give you, O Judah and Jerusalem. Do not be afraid; do not be discouraged. Go out to face them tomorrow, and the Lord will be with you.'"

"Megan, Jack, you are just like those Israelites now. The battle is not yours. You have to trust God to fight it for you, and be willing to accept whatever solution to the problem He offers you. It may mean some very hard times for a while, but God will make it all worth it in the long run."

Megan smiled and nodded, thanking Tom for his support

and his wisdom. They all gathered around Jack and Megan, laying their hands on them and praying for God to take care of them and to work out their lives according to His will for them.

The meeting broke up shortly after the last prayer, and the cars departed the Radford driveway on their way to several destinations around the area. Jack and Megan turned left onto the highway and headed back to Norfolk, unaware of the two unmarked shadow vehicles that were following them; one belonging to Victor Mesones, the other to two of McDowell's NCIS agents.

*   *   *

The small speaker above Miguel Ramirez's head crackled with a clearance announcement from his pilot. The control tower at the Puerto Cristobol Airport had finally given them permission to taxi to runway two for take-off—not at 7 a.m. as he had requested, but at thirteen minutes before eight. Funny how the smallest things got under a person's skin when he was already irritated about something else.

Miguel was still trying to decide how best to handle Belinda and her most unfortunate change of loyalties. He had wisely opted to wait until Monday to go to the US, allowing his anger to recede enough so that he could decide intelligently how to act on his new information, and not simply react in his anger. He would probably still kill all or at least part of her family, and possibly Belinda herself, but before he carried out her punishment he wanted to survey the situation for himself to make an accurate assessment of her actions. He could not tolerate disloyalty, not even in its smallest form, and not even from one of his closest associates. The smallest chink in his armor would be a sign of weakness to his enemies, and they would swarm in and pounce on him like hungry lions devouring a wounded antelope. No, he had to maintain his iron-fisted rule in every facet of his existence, demanding respect from friend and foe alike, ensuring both his own safety and his dynasty's longevity. But *Belinda*, of all people!

Why did it have to be her? Had it been any of his other associates, he would have ordered the hit immediately, spectacular and obvious, warning everyone who heard of it to never entertain the idea of crossing 'Don' Miguel Ramirez. But, this was different. Belinda was a project, an investment. He didn't want to simply dispose of her like he had several of his other subjects. This one, he wanted to reform. He wanted to break her, like a wild mare who refuses to be domesticated. Once she was finally broken, what a magnificent prize she would be! And yet, this treachery could not go unpunished. He would have to wait and see for himself exactly how far gone she was. Perhaps she could still be saved from herself.

The plane touched down at Miami International Airport just before 9:30 a.m. The pilot's voice again interrupted Miguel's thoughts with the announcement that it would take anywhere from thirty minutes to an hour and thirty minutes to refuel. He also asked if Miguel desired to exit the plane during the refueling.

"No, just get us back into the air!" Miguel barked into the intercom.

"As you wish, Sir!" the pilot said.

One hour and twenty-seven minutes later, the Learjet was taxiing to its designated runway to take off for the Norfolk International Airport in Virginia.

"Got it. All right, great. Thanks a lot, Joe. Sure will. Well, if it all works out, it will be in all the big papers and you can read about it there. See ya, Joe," Agent Ferrelli said, flipping shut his cell phone. He walked into the NCIS conference room and cleared his throat. "It's a go, gentlemen. Ramirez's Learjet departed Miami International about forty minutes ago, bound for Norfolk. ETA at Norfolk International is 1:00 this afternoon, which puts him on the ground in our back yard just over one hour from now. Since he does have an established cover as a legitimate businessman, customs won't be a problem for him, so we will have to be on alert immediately."

"I agree. Thanks, Ferrelli," McDowell said. "Ladies and gentlemen, there you have it. The game is underway. You all know what is required of you. Let's do it!" Everyone left the conference room with cell phones and radios crackling, alerting their crews and giving out the details of Ramirez's arrival.

All the mobile teams were alerted and apprised of the latest developments. Jack Douglass' team was hanging out at the end of Pier 10 on the naval base, and Megan/Belinda's team was in the parking lot of the steakhouse, as were Victor and Luis. The teams assigned to shadow Victor and Luis were parked in the lot of an adjacent shopping center, waiting for the word that their targets were mobile so that they could follow them.

At the Norfolk International Airport, three shadow teams in six different vehicles waited for Miguel Ramirez to walk out of the airport. The airport itself was positively crawling with government agents. FBI Agent Paxton, who was responsible for the shadowing of Ramirez, had himself and four other agents inside the airport in addition to the three teams in vehicles outside. His counterpart in Narcotics was also present with two other agents inside the terminal. CIA Agent Stiles was in the airport's security office with the Head of Security and the Airport Manager. The three had worked together from time to time in the past, whenever the CIA had a special interest in a certain plane or a certain passenger that they needed to keep an eye on.

DEA Agent Ferrelli had three agents on their way to the downtown library, where one would be stationed on each floor to await the arrival of Victor and Luis, plus a mobile team waiting in a car outside the library to watch for Ramirez's arrival. He wouldn't be able to so much as scratch his head without the full knowledge of the United States government. His every step would be monitored. The second he crossed a line big enough to bury him under, the government would attack, and Miguel Ramirez would become a trophy of the American justice system instead of a threat to American ideals.

"Roger, Norfolk International, copy permission to land on runway six," the pilot of the Learjet said into his headset. He reduced speed and altered his course to one that would bring him to the end of runway six, the older and shorter runway in the back of the airport used predominantly for small private business jets and other smaller planes providing 'hop' service between relatively close neighboring cities. The pilot flipped a switch on his console and spoke into his headset again.

"Mr. Ramirez, we are approaching Norfolk International Airport. We will be landing on runway six in twelve minutes."

"Thank you," was all Ramirez said in reply. He carried the remains of his lunch over to the small galley and disposed of it in the trash can. He piled the dirty dishes in the sink then closed the door to the galley, securing it in place with the devices provided. In the small restroom in the front of the cabin, he checked his appearance, straightened his suit coat and tie, then shut off the light as he walked back to his seat. He buckled his seat belt in preparation for the landing and closed his eyes. He usually enjoyed this part of his business, but this time it was different. He had had such a different future in mind for Belinda Gallagos.

"Stiles!" Doug Marshall, the Head of Airport Security yelled from across the security room. "Your pal's Learjet is coming in for a landing on runway six."

Stiles crossed the room to where Marshall was standing. "Runway six? Great. Are you going to have him park it out there by the old hangar, too?" Stiles asked.

"We can if you want us to," Marshall volunteered.

"Yes, if you could, that would be great. Right there, in full view of this camera. And, Doug, I am also going to have to ask you to keep an eye on it for me. I may be able to send a guy here to monitor it with your boys, but either way I need to know if there is any activity anywhere near that plane. If bird droppings fall on it, I need to know what kind of bird it was and how far the poop fell before it hit. Okay?"

"Well, sure, Don, if that's all you need! Why didn't you just say so? Heck, maybe we can just have them park it right there outside our window, then we will be sure not to miss anything!" Marshall chided.

"Just watch the plane, smart aleck!" Stiles said. "And I will need to be contacted immediately whenever they file their next flight plan." Stiles handed him a CIA business card with his cell phone number written on the back. "Any activity of any kind, you let me know. Who knows, do a good job, there may be a six-pack in it for you."

"Now you have really sweetened the pot, Don!" Marshall teased. "No problem. I will call you if we see anything."

"Thanks, Doug," Stiles said, turning back to the security monitors to watch the plane come in.

Since it was an international flight, airport personnel were required to meet the plane near the terminal to escort its passengers and flight crew through a United States Customs checkpoint. After they had passed through customs and had their passports stamped, the flight crew would be allowed to return to the plane to take care of the necessary shut-down procedures and any maintenance they had to do. The passengers would be free to enjoy their visit to the United States at their leisure.

There were only two of them, Miguel Ramirez and his pilot. Ramirez passed through customs and carried his single suitcase through the airport and out to the line of taxis waiting for fares. He climbed into the first one, said something to the driver, and sat back against the back of the seat. The driver deftly pulled the cab away from the curb and into the traffic leaving the airport. Six unmarked government vehicles joined the flow of traffic in previously determined intervals, and from previously designated places, to tail Miguel Ramirez. They would switch shadows often, because Ramirez may become suspicious if he saw the same vehicle behind him for a long period of time.

The pilot returned to his plane, performed his routine shut-down maintenance checks and radioed to the ground crew that he was finished and that they could move the plane. They pushed it backwards into a fenced area away from the main traffic area, beside an old maintenance hangar. The gate in the fence was promptly shut and locked, providing some security for the plane but mostly providing airport security with the opportunity to keep an eye on it.

Stiles thanked the Airport Manager and the Head of Security for their assistance, then left the airport to return to the Command Center in the Federal Building.

Promptly at 3:15 p.m., Jack Douglass walked across the brow of the *Mississippi* and onto the pier. He was supposed to go to the steakhouse and wait for Megan to get off work, which would be whenever it got really slow after the lunch rush. She hadn't beeped him yet to say that she had gotten off early, so he went to his car and took off for the steakhouse. He would have a big glass of tea and maybe some French fries while he waited for her. It wasn't all bad watching her work. He would sit back in a booth and allow his head to be filled with all kinds of things; like visions of sitting in his mom's living room and watching her while she helped his mother prepare Thanksgiving Dinner…

He walked into the restaurant, got her attention and waved to her, then climbed up onto a stool at one of the tall tables in the bar area. He declined a beverage until Megan stopped by to let him know how long his wait was likely to be.

When she came up behind him 3 minutes later, it was with her jacket in her hand.

"Hey, you! Good timing, eh?" Jack said.

"Well, I didn't ask to leave until I saw you come in. It has been kind of slow, but I figured I could use the extra money. Did you have a good day on the Miss'?"

"Not bad," Jack replied. "But it is wonderful now. What about you? Have you heard from Agent McDowell yet?"

"I don't know, I haven't been home since 9:30. Let's go there now and find out."

"Works for me. Let's go."

They walked out of the steakhouse together, enjoyed a long hug, then separated to go to their own cars. Megan took the lead, and Jack followed her to her apartment. In the air all around them, radio signals shot through the sky from all the various surveillance teams reporting the couple's movements to their superiors.

Once relatively certain that Jack and Megan were headed to her apartment, Victor radioed Luis to tell him that he would be heading off to the library to meet Miguel, and Luis would be on his own with the happy couple. Luis acknowledged, and Victor turned at the next corner to head back toward the downtown library. The shadow team behind him announced his change of direction, opined that he was headed for the library, and turned around at the same corner to continue their surveillance.

"Ferrelli One, be advised, the train is on the track. Repeat, Ferrelli One, be advised, the train is on the track," McDowell said into his radio.

Outside the library in a blue Ford Taurus, a DEA Agent picked up his radio and keyed the button on the side. "Command, Ferrelli One. Copy train is inbound. Ready at the station." The Agent forwarded the message to the men inside, alerting them that Victor would soon be arriving.

Victor arrived at the library parking lot at eighteen minutes before four, parked the car and walked toward the side door. He strolled through the main level, casually walking around as if looking for something. He searched the top floor, then the basement, then returned to the main level. Finding no sign of Miguel, he went to the "Periodicals" section and sat down in an old cushioned chair to flip through a magazine while he waited for Miguel to show up.

Megan unlocked her apartment and walked inside with Jack at her heels. They both walked straight over to the answering machine and willed it to be flashing with at least one message. The zero seemed to laugh at them from the LED display. McDowell hadn't called.

"Megan, did he say he would contact you Monday? Or did

he just say something about trying to figure out what to do by Monday?"

"I don't remember, exactly. I thought he said he would at least figure out a plan of action by today, and I just assumed he would be sharing that information with me. I don't recall if he actually said that he would call me about it. I did get a call from somebody named Ramsey on Saturday. He said he was typing up a transcript of the meeting we had with McDowell and he asked me to clarify a bunch of stuff about the interview. Do you think I should call him and see if he has gotten anywhere?" she asked.

"It seems to me that he said he would try to get back with you by today. But, if he is just getting around to making a transcript of our meetings on Saturday, maybe it is taking him longer than he expected."

"Well, is that good? What if longer is bad?"

"Relax, Megan. He will contact you when he contacts you. Believe me, he is not going to forget about this one. If Ramirez is as big as you say he is, this could mean a huge star on McDowell's resume'. Let's just try to be patient and let things run their course. I know it's hard, but there isn't really anything else we can do anyway."

"You're right. He will call when he is ready."

"You want to go out for some dinner?"

"I could be persuaded. Where did you have in mind, Sailor?" she asked.

"Well, I was thinking Venice, but I am a little short on change, so how about we compromise and go out to La Cantina? Could you go for some Mexican?" Jack asked.

"I think I could handle that. Let me change out of these work clothes. Be right back." She ran into the bedroom and quickly changed her clothes. As she ran back out of the bedroom, Jack stepped in front of her and caught her in his arms as she ran into him. She looked up into his eyes.

"I love you, Megan" Jack said, smiling at her with his hands around her waist.

"And I love you, Jack Douglass. Now, feed me!" she giggled as she wrenched herself free from his grip and ran out the door toward his car.

"Brat," Jack said to himself, locking the door and running after her.

Miguel Ramirez stepped out of the taxi and walked into the downtown library at 4:06 p.m. Victor was in the process of switching magazines when he saw Miguel out of the corner of his eye. He dropped his magazine back into the rack, walked past Miguel without looking at him, and exited through the same side door he had used to enter the library half an hour earlier. Without a word, Miguel followed him at a great enough distance so that no library patrons would suspect them of being together. He exited through the side door, crossed the street and stepped into Victor's waiting car in the parking lot. Victor exited the parking lot and sped off to merge into the flow of traffic.

"Command, Ferrelli One. Train has taken on stores and left the station. Repeat, train has taken on stores and left the station. Shadow in place."

"Copy, Ferrelli One. Proceed with extreme caution. It gets sticky from here," McDowell said. "That's it!" he said to the small command group assembled in the conference room/Command Center. Ramirez was just picked up by Victor and they are mobile. Ferrelli One is on them."

The rest of the agents inside the library returned to the NCIS office to await further instructions while Ferrelli One and Victor's NCIS shadow maintained the tail on Ramirez.

Victor took Miguel back to the hotel where he showed him all the information they had collected on Belinda since their arrival. He showed him pictures of Belinda and Jack, and of the business card she had in her Bible. He relayed the details of his conversation with her when he had portrayed himself as someone from the NCIS office to confirm her suspected involvement with the authorities. He recounted her usual daily activities, her dates with Jack, and her attendance at the church.

Miguel was irate again. Seeing and hearing the evidence first hand lit anew the fire of rage and jealousy that burned inside of him. When a man betrayed him, he simply had him tortured, killed, or both. But when a woman betrayed him, it was personal.

"Take me to her," Miguel growled. "I want to see her for myself."

Victor keyed his radio. "Luis!" he said.

"Yes, Victor."

"The Boss is here. Status report."

"We are eastbound on Military Highway, passing Military Circle Mall. Subject plus one in his car. Probably going out to dinner."

"Understood. Thank you. We will join you soon."

They left the hotel and climbed into Victor's rented car. He quickly exited the parking lot and headed toward Military Circle Mall.

Jack and Megan were seated at a table in front of one of the big windows looking out across the parking lot. Their waitress, Debbie, was getting their drinks and their chips and salsa while they pored over their menus. She returned with an overflowing basket of chips, two bowls of hot salsa and a pair of beverages. She jotted their order down on her pad and dashed off to deliver it to the kitchen before she rushed across the room to take care of her other customers.

Jack and Megan sat with their arms across the table, fingers interlocked between the salsa bowls, and eyes locked onto each other's. Although it is very common for couples in love to crave time with each other, the uncertainty of their future together caused Jack and Megan to do so even more. It was a painfully real possibility that any moment they were sharing could very well be their last moment together. They could be separated by incarceration, by deportation, or if things took a terrible turn for the worse, by death at the hands of Miguel's henchmen. Nothing was said by either of them, because there was nothing to say. Their love for each other was so strong they didn't need to confess it. They could feel it. They could see it in each other's eyes. And that meant more than any combination of words could ever say anyway.

. . .

Out in the parking lot, in the passenger side of a rented sedan, Miguel Ramirez was putting together a combination of words that really meant very little, but served to adequately vent his anger and accurately describe the severe lack of approval of what he was seeing.

"That is her Navy boy?" Miguel spat out.

"Yes, that is Jack Douglass. He is a Signalman on the USS *Mississippi.*"

"Well, I think she has gone above and beyond the call of duty in maintaining her relationship with this fellow," Miguel fumed. "No wonder she didn't want to acquire any other contacts! She has fallen in love with this American!"

"Yes, it would appear so, Miguel," Victor agreed. "Will we take care of both of them at one time?" he asked.

Miguel started to speak, then paused. His angry face underwent a change, becoming placidly evil. His mouth twisted into a sadistic grin. "No," he said with satisfaction. "No, Victor, we will not dispose of him. Instead, we will let him suffer the loss of his lover. We will let him live, but only after he has had the pleasure of seeing his lover violated, defiled, and eventually killed before his eyes."

Victor smiled and chuckled. He would definitely enjoy this assignment. She was a prize to behold, after all.

"Victor, when she contacts me on Tuesday nights, is he there with her?"

"I don't know, Miguel, we didn't arrive here until Wednesday. But they do seem to spend nearly every moment together."

"This is what we will do. Tomorrow, I will have the Learjet fueled and readied for a 1 am departure. If she works tomorrow night, we will be in her apartment waiting for her when she gets home. If she doesn't work tomorrow night, we will wait until midnight, then break in and surprise her while she is trying to contact me on the Internet. If the boyfriend is there, we will take them both to the Learjet. If we have to, we will have her call him and invite him over, then we will have them both. We will fly to Puerto Cristobol, during which time you and Luis may do as you please with the very lovely Miss Gallagos, while her lover is tied securely to a front row seat to watch. Then, once we get to Puerto Cristobol, we will gather her family together, slaughter them all in front of her, then kill her and burn them all in their pathetic little house.

"We can then send lover-boy home to mourn, threatening him with a similar fate for his own family if he ever breathes a word about what happened to the soon-to-be late Miss Gallagos and her family."

Jack and Megan finished their dinner and decided to take in a movie together. Jack paid the bill and they went on their merry way, completely unaware of how close at hand death was lurking. They didn't pay any attention to the two men in the car that pulled out and exited the parking lot while they were walking to Jack's car. But they would be paying attention to them soon.

They chose an action-drama, figuring that they were emotional enough without watching some sappy love story or an intense dramatic presentation. Action would be just fine. After the movie, Jack walked Megan to her door, which she unlocked and entered. She turned on the lights, kissed him good-night, and closed the door. Jack drove back to his apartment floating on a cloud.

"Hey, I don't want to sound like a low-budget horror movie, boss, but it's too quiet," Special Agent Mesko said to McDowell as they sat in his office monitoring the radio. "He must be planning something big, sitting back and watching her like this. Maybe he is waiting for the right time."

"Whatever it is, it won't be going down until tomorrow, probably at night. Ramirez and Mesones are at their hotel, and Luis is watching Megan sleep. The Signalman is going home to sleep, too. I think I will follow their lead and go next door for some 'rack time'. Continue all surveillance and call me if anything out of the ordinary happens."

"You got it, Boss," Mesko agreed.

McDowell walked over to his office and flopped down on the old couch that sat along the side wall. He still wanted to be available in case something did happen tonight, but he needed to get some sleep in case it did not.

Off the eastern coast of Virginia, a huge ball of gas and fire penetrated the sky along the line where it met the ocean in the distant horizon. It appeared to rise directly out of the chilly waters of the Atlantic Ocean as it slowly worked its way into the early morning sky, dispersing the nighttime shadows and announcing the beginning of a brand new day. Some of its brilliant rays passed through the windows in Special Agent William McDowell's office in the NCIS wing of the Federal Building downtown and drilled into his eyes through his closed eyelids. He grudgingly pulled himself into a sitting position and rubbed his tired eyes to convince them to open up and focus. He stood up and walked out of the office and over to the bathroom, where he splashed cold water on his face and wiped it off with a paper towel. The sight he saw in the mirror did not have a positive effect on his demeanor, so he threw his paper towel into the trash can and walked over to the conference room where he was sure to be able to come up with a hot cup of coffee. Maybe he would even be able to find some food left over from the night crew.

It was nearly 7:30 on Tuesday morning. Mesko sat in a chair by the coffee mess reading the morning paper. A handful of agents from various agencies were sprawled out over chairs or on the floor, trying to get as much rest as the conditions allowed.

"Good morning, Mesko," McDowell offered. "What is the status of the game?"

"All quiet, Boss," Mesko answered. The girl is sleeping at her apartment. The Signalman is doing the same at his. Ramirez and his two thugs are up but they haven't left their hotel yet."

"Good. Did you get any sleep?"

"Couple of hours, couple different times. I'm good."

"Tell you what," McDowell said, "I'm going to go home and get a shower and some fresh clothes. I'll be back in an hour, then you can go home and get a couple hours of sleep and put yourself back together. Deal?"

"You got it, Boss. See you in an hour."

"I'll keep my radio with me all the time. Anything of any significance happens, you call me," McDowell ordered.

"Sure thing, Boss," Mesko agreed, eager to get his boss on his way so that he could go and get his own hot shower and fresh clothes.

"Victor! Luis!" Miguel yelled, pounding on their hotel room door. He had taken a room two doors down and across the hall. "Get up! We have much work to do!"

"We are up, Miguel!" Victor yelled back, slightly irritated. This was the first night they had both been able to get a decent amount of sleep since their arrival in the States. Miguel could at least give them a few moments of peace this early in the morning. He walked over to the door, cracking it open to look at Miguel, shaven, dressed and ready to go.

"Check out of your room and meet me in the diner across the street in thirty minutes. We can throw your things in the trunk of one of the cars for today, until we can get it out to the plane later this evening."

"Miguel, we have been eating in that diner all week. Perhaps it would be better if we met at the McDonald's. It is down the street a few blocks on the same side. No one will know us there, and no one is likely to take notice of us in a place like that, as a waitress might if she had to wait on us all together."

"Very good, Victor," Miguel agreed. "Yes, that would be much better. Thirty minutes, then." He turned and walked down to his own room.

Miguel tucked his clothes and his toiletries into his suitcase and placed it on the floor beside the door. He checked around the room to make sure that he hadn't forgotten anything, then he sat down in the chair at the desk and picked up the telephone. He dialed the Airport Holiday Inn and punched in the extension for room 223. A groggy voice answered on the fifth ring.

"Hello?"

"Armando, good morning!" Miguel said cheerfully.

"Good morning, Mr. Ramirez," Armando said. "Are we leaving already, Sir?"

"Not quite yet. We will be leaving late tonight, between midnight and one o'clock. Have the plane fueled and ready to go by eleven. Do your pre-flight and be ready for anything by eleven o'clock. Understood?"

"Yes, Sir. Flight-ready by eleven. Got it, Mr. Ramirez."

"Good. See you there," Miguel said, then hung up the phone. He picked up his suitcase and walked down to the elevator. On the first floor, he turned in his key, paid his bill with cash and walked out to one of the rental cars. He dropped his suitcase into the trunk and hopped into the driver's seat. He would wait in the parking lot of McDonald's for his associates to arrive.

"Command, Paxton One. Big Bird is mobile. Repeat, Big Bird is mobile. Shadow is in place. No sign of Bert and Ernie."

"Paxton One, Command. Copy Big Bird is mobile. Transmit destination when known. Command out."

Forty minutes later, Victor and Luis pulled into the parking lot of McDonald's and parked two spaces over from Miguel. The three entered the restaurant together, while an assortment of government agents watched them from inside and outside the building.

"Command, Paxton One. Sesame Street cast party at McDonald's up the street from the hotel. All cast members present."

"Copy, Paxton One. Laughlin, do you read?"

"Laughlin here, listening in on the basement extension."

"Laughlin, go back to the hotel and see if our friends have

checked out yet."

"10-4, Command. Laughlin out."

Special Agent Laughlin of the NCIS walked into the lobby of the hotel. He smiled at the pretty young girl on duty at the front desk and flashed her his NCIS badge.

"Miss, I need to ask you a couple of questions," he said.

"Sure, Special Agent Laughlin. Fire away."

"A man in a business suit left this hotel approximately 45 minutes ago, then another pair in more casual clothing left approximately ten minutes ago. I need you to tell me if they have checked out of their rooms." He smiled his best flirty, put-them-at-ease smile and leaned on the counter.

"Sure did, Special Agent Laughlin. Guy named Ed Winters and one name of—here's a real winner for you—Constantino Argurro. Winters just came in last night, but the Argurro guy's been here almost a week."

"Really. Tell me, this Argurro guy, he had a friend with him. Would you happen to know his name, too?"

"I think so. Hang on a minute. Yep, here it is. Pedro Servantes. Are they in some kind of trouble?"

"Nothing to worry yourself about, Miss. Thanks, you've been a big help." Laughlin smiled again, backed away from the desk and walked back out to his car.

"Command, Laughlin," he said into his radio.

"Go ahead, Laughlin."

"Big Bird, Bert and Ernie have left the building. Paid their bill and flew the coop. But get this, the girl at the desk told me their names. Big Bird is Ed Winters, Bert and Ernie are Pedro Servantes and Constantino Argurro."

"Nice names. Thanks, Laughlin. Command out."

The three businessmen ordered their breakfasts and found a table in a deserted corner of the dining area. While they ate their food, Miguel laid out the plan for the day's festivities. When they finished their meeting, Luis went directly to Belinda's apartment to resume his watch while Miguel and Victor took the other car and drove in the direction of the airport. The night before, Victor had studied the map and found that the fenced area beside the old hangar bordered a small sliver of wooded land that stretched the entire length of the field beside it, which in turn ran parallel to Runway Six. Behind the old hangar was another field with a cemetery running along the road at its edge. The access to the field was on the other side of the fence at the end of the cemetery. Since the field had recently been harvested, they would be able to drive their car into the field, along the back fence of the cemetery, and park it in the corner where the cemetery shared the border with the wooded strip of land.

Victor was already wearing his black clothing. He popped open the trunk, retrieved his binoculars, a black ski cap, and a small packet of tools, then jogged into the woods while Miguel stayed at the car and waited. Victor ran through the woods until he came to the old rusty fence at the edge of the tarmac next to the maintenance hangar. The fence was about eight feet tall with barbed wire in a "v" along the top. It was covered nearly half the way up with vines and briars that had grown through the fence, intertwining themselves with it, and fastening themselves to it. They would provide him with an easy way to cover his entrance for the rest of the day until they had to use it after sunset.

First, he pulled out his binoculars to survey the area. No people in sight, no pop machines outside the building to attract them. The big hangar doors were shut and the windows were all on the upper level. Victor walked along the fence, stopping every fifty feet or so to survey the area through his binoculars from his new vantage point. The only obstacle he could find was the security camera mounted on the corner of the building. It was pointed directly at the Learjet. No, wait—it was rotating, but it paused at three points during its rotation; once at either end and once in the middle, each time for about twenty seconds. He would either have to go up there first and reposition it, or be very careful to keep his movements concealed by the underbrush and then timed perfectly so as not to be caught by the camera while he entered the plane. Repositioning the camera might draw attention to the area, which he definitely didn't want, so he decided that he would have to plan out the operation so as to be invisible while he did his reconnaissance now, and while he loaded their cargo into the plane later tonight.

He walked back to the entry point he had chosen, directly behind the Learjet and out of view of the camera, and pulled the wire cutters out of his tool packet. He went to work on the fence, snipping an eighteen inch long horizontal line along the fence about six inches from the ground, then a vertical line extending up from the right end of the first line for about four feet. Next, he duplicated the first line at the top end of the vertical line, giving himself a four by one-and-a-half foot doorway into the airport grounds. He pushed the fence back and slipped through the opening. Judging the distance to be about five hundred feet, he sprinted to the plane, crouching behind the wheels when he arrived. He pulled the key Miguel had given him out of his pocket and poked his head out from behind the wheel just far enough to see the camera. It was rotating from the nose area of the plane to the center. He stuck his head back behind the wheel and counted. Twenty seconds for the camera to complete its rotation to the center position, twenty more in that position, then another twenty before it was focused on the tail end of the plane. He poked his head out again, then dashed around the wheels and over to the door on the plane's left side. He inserted the key, turned it, and yanked the door open. He rushed up the steps and into the plane, tugging at the cord which would shut the door behind him. When the door slammed home, he grabbed the handle and twisted it to latch the door in the shut position. Looking out the window at the camera, he counted to eight before the camera began to move again. Eight extra seconds. If the pilot left the door unlocked, that would shave off three or four seconds, allowing him and Luis and their two guests plenty of time to enter the plane and get the door shut before the camera would come back around to focus on the plane's door. Wonderful.

He turned to look at the seating cabin. Yes, this would work. He could easily get the little rat and her boyfriend in here without anyone seeing them. He would take them to the back of the plane, handcuff them, gag them, and lock them in their seats until after takeoff. Then the real fun would begin. He began to get excited just thinking about it. Miguel would rant and rave about loyalty and trust for a while, then he would go into his own private part of the cabin and let Victor and Luis have their fun with Belinda.

Victor shook his head. Enough of that. One thing at a time, he thought to himself. He watched the camera until it rotated to the nose of the plane, then quickly unlatched and opened the door. He poked his head out to make sure that no one was around, then he trotted down the stairs, pushed the door shut, latched it and raced back around the plane to again hide behind the wheel. He looked from side to side again, watching for observers, then sprinted back to the fence, jumped through the opening, and positioned it back the way it was before he had ever opened it. Now it was time to get some supplies.

"The airport?" McDowell asked. "What were they doing at the airport?"

"Don't know, Boss," Mesko said. "Paxton One and Laughlin tailed them to the cemetery along the road east of the airport. Said they drove in behind it, parked for over an hour, then came back out. Ramirez waited by the car while Mesones went off into the woods. When he came back out, they left. Right now, they are heading into the mall. Luis is still tailing Megan, who so far has not left her apartment."

"All right, Mesko, go home and get some sleep. I'll see you back here at four."

"Right, Boss. See you then," Mesko said as he walked out the door and down the hallway.

McDowell pulled FBI Agent Jacobs aside. He relayed to her what Mesko had just told him and asked her to send a couple of agents out there to see if they could find out what Ramirez and Mesones had been up to.

"They may be back later, so caution your agents to leave no evidence of their investigation. Have them contact you with the details, then you can relay the important parts to me."

Special Agent Jacobs called two of her agents in from the hallway, gave them a quick briefing and sent them off with McDowell's instructions.

An hour and a half later, FBI Agent Jacobs clipped her

radio back onto her belt and walked into McDowell's office.

"Yes, Agent Jacobs, what did you find out?"

"My men found a doorway cut into the fence along the back perimeter of the maintenance hangar area where the Learjet is being stored. That is the only fact we were able to gather. I believe we would be justified in suspecting that Ramirez intends to load some type of cargo onto the plane that he doesn't want to have to take through customs or explain to anybody. In my area of expertise, and also considering who the subject is, I would immediately suspect a major drug shipment. However, using his own plane and transporting the drugs personally would be very stupid. He hasn't made it to his position in the drug world by being stupid. Therefore, I can only suspect that he may be intending to load your spy girl on board and take her back to Venezuela with him without any interference from the United States government, and particularly from your office. He knows you are on to him, so he may be here to tie up loose ends before something gets out that he doesn't want to get out. Or maybe he just wants to dump her out over the Caribbean as a lesson to whoever he blackmails into taking her place as his spy."

"I would lean toward possibility number two. He could have had his boys kill her a week ago. I have to think that he has come up here personally to take care of her betrayal punishment himself. Or maybe he is taking her back so that he can carry out his promise of killing her family with her watching. Either way, he's not leaving this city with that girl, I can promise you that!" McDowell said forcefully. He walked out into the hallway between his office and the conference room. "Ferrelli!" he yelled. "Ferrelli! Are you out here?"

"Yeah, I'm here," a voice called from the other end of the conference room. DEA Agent Ferrelli got up, stretched, and walked into McDowell's office. "What's up, McDowell?" he asked.

"What kind of protection is in place for the Gallagos family right now in Venezuela?" McDowell asked.

"I don't know, exactly," Ferrelli said. "The DISIP man said they would handle it, that was all."

"Could you call him and check it out, please?" McDowell

asked. "I have a gut feeling that our friend Mr. Ramirez is planning a very unpleasant family reunion for them in the next couple of days. They need to be protected. Tell them we can send agents in if they want us to."

"I'm on it," Ferrelli said. He walked out into the hallway, unclipped his cell phone from his belt, and began punching in the number to Inspector San Tielo's personal cell phone.

The sharp ringing tone of the cell phone startled Inspector Eduardo San Tielo, causing him to jump and spill his tea down his pant leg. He yelped, jerked the hot, wet fabric away from his skin, and picked up his cell phone.

"Inspector San Tielo" he said tersely.

"Hey, Eduardo! Angelo Ferrelli, DEA. How are you?"

"Not bad, Angelo. Except that your call startled me and I dumped some very expensive tea all down my pant leg. How are you doing?"

"Good. Hey, I have a question for you. The man running the operation up here wants to know what kind of protection you are providing for the canary's family. He believes a storm is brewing, which will find its way to them, fast and furious, if you don't stop it. We strongly recommend that they be taken to a government safe house until this blows over."

"Not to worry, Angelo. My men picked them up this morning and took them to a safe place nearby. Thank you for your concern, and rest assured they are fine."

"Great!" Ferrelli said. "That will put his mind at ease. It will all be over soon, Eduardo. Probably tonight. I will talk to you soon and let you know how it all turned out."

Agent Ferrelli punched the button on his cell phone to end the call and returned to McDowell's office.

"It has been taken care of, McDowell," he reported. "The DISIP picked up the entire Gallagos family this morning and relocated them to a safe house pending confirmation from us that the threat has been neutralized."

"Excellent," McDowell said. "One less thing to worry about. Now, let's concentrate on taking this guy down." He walked over to his door and poked his head out into the hall. "Agents Paxton, Jacobs, and Stiles!" he yelled. "Please join me in my office."

The trio quickly answered his request after stopping along the way to refill their coffee cups at the coffee mess in the conference room. Once they were all seated in the office, McDowell brought them all up to speed on what they knew so far. Ramirez and his goons had checked out of their hotel. Bert was still tailing the girl, while Ramirez and Ernie were making preparations around town. He told them of their visit to the airport, and was explaining what the FBI agents had found when Stiles' cell phone began to ring. He answered it without leaving the room, expecting it to be pertinent to the case anyway.

"Did he, now? Interesting. Refueling ASAP and an anticipated departure time of midnight, plus or minus one hour? Beautiful, Doug. Thanks. Sure, I owe you a six-pack, Mooch." He flipped his phone shut and looked up at his colleagues. "The rooster is getting ready to fly the coop!" he said. That was Doug Marshall, Head of Security for Norfolk International. He says that Ramirez's pilot just put in a request to top off the fuel tanks on the Learjet ASAP and filed a flight plan to take off for Havana International Airport in Cuba at midnight, give or take an hour, definite time still to be determined."

McDowell jabbed his right fist into the palm of his left hand. "We've got him!" he said excitedly. "That is exactly the piece of intelligence we needed to green light the second phase of the operation. Let's take him down." McDowell walked across his office to look out the window. The adrenaline began to flow through him as he thought through the take-down in his head. Everything had to be right. After all, this was why he had joined the NCIS in the first place. Today, all his training would be made worthwhile. Not only would he finally get the opportunity to be involved in the removal of a major player in the drug/espionage trade, he would be the man running the operation!

He turned back to his colleagues and began barking out orders, delivered in the form of respectful requests.

"Pull in all your people. Get them all dressed out in full night assault gear, fully armed with silenced weapons. Have them get into their positions as soon as darkness falls. This is no longer a surveillance detail; it has now become an active take-down operation. Suspects are to be considered armed and very dangerous. Weapons status is 'free', but your people should only fire if engaged by the enemy.

"Agent Stiles, I want that plane disabled. If something unforeseen happens, I don't want Ramirez or any of his thugs to be able to take off. Instead of topping off the fuel tanks, drain them. Apprehend the pilot and replace him with one of your men who knows planes and speaks Spanish. Also, get in touch with your friends in airport management and fill them in on our plan. Tell them to keep all personnel away from the maintenance area, and have one of your teams in position in the maintenance hangar to back us up.

"Agent Jacobs, your men will cover the woods and take up positions along the fence surrounding the maintenance area.

"Agent Ferrelli, have your men cover any part of the maintenance area left uncovered by Jacobs' people. Spread them out so that they will be able to stop a runner if one of our friends gets loose.

"Agent Paxton, choose two men to accompany you. I will bring one of my teams, and we will disperse throughout the inside of the plane itself. From the intelligence that we have collected, I think we can safely assume that Victor Mesones and his companion will attempt to bring the girl to the plane through the hole they made in the fence. Ramirez will most likely join them on the plane from the airport itself, having gone through the proper channels as though he were returning home after completing a two-day business conference.

"We will let Mesones and company enter the plane, at which point we will apprehend Mesones and his friend and get the girl to safety in the cockpit of the plane. When Ramirez attempts to board the plane through the passenger door, he will also be apprehended. Afterward, we will transport them all to the Federal Detention Center and come back here to spend the next year doing all the associated paperwork. I think that will do it. Any questions? Comments? Suggestions?" he asked.

FBI Agent Paxton spoke up. "I am assuming you want my

men to maintain the shadow on Ramirez, right?"

"Correct. Let's keep one team on Ramirez, and one team on the girl. I think we pretty much know what is going to happen tonight, but let's not take anything as a guarantee. Bring the rest of your teams in to assist in the actual take down. Also, maintain active monitoring of the listening devices in the girl's apartment and car. If anything changes, I want to know about it immediately. We can afford no surprises tonight."

They all shook their heads, giving their consent to the plan as presented.

"Then let's do it. Good luck." McDowell said, dismissing them.

The afternoon passed without incident. Megan went to work at 4:00, Jack left the ship at 3:15 and went directly to his apartment, which he did not leave all evening. Ramirez and Mesones picked up a few odds and ends while shopping, but appeared only to be killing time until the party at midnight. McDowell and all the agents involved paced impatiently around the NCIS offices, waiting for the night to come.

As afternoon gave way to evening, then evening to night, Jack and Phil finished off the last of the pizza and tossed the box into the trash can in the kitchen. After taking a quick potty-break and grabbing two fresh Cokes from the refrigerator, Phil pushed the 'play' button on the remote control and the movie they were watching resumed.

Jack had decided that he wouldn't go to the steakhouse to see Megan tonight. He had just spent the evening with her the night before, and he was tired. Sometime he had to start getting enough sleep. She would be fine tonight, and he would see her after her shift on Wednesday.

This line of thinking got him to about ten-thirty. By eleven, he thought it would be really good of him to go over to her place and kiss her good-night, just as a gesture of good will. Or something. Maybe she is having a bad night, and she'll need to talk.

"Or maybe," Phil interjected, "you are going over there because you are a big love-sick dope who can't survive even one day without seeing her."

"Yeah, that could be it," Jack smiled. "Where are my keys?" And with that he grabbed his jacket and ran from the apartment.

"Wimp," Phil said to himself as he killed the TV set and walked into his bedroom.

Jack drove quickly over to the steakhouse, arriving at 11:02. He rushed inside, greeting the hostess and asking if Megan was still there. She yelled to one of the waitresses, who replied that she had just left. Jack had probably just missed her in the parking lot. He thanked her and rushed back out to his car. If he was that close behind her, he could probably catch her before she got to her apartment. Either way, it would be fun to try, so he stepped on the gas pedal and squealed out of the parking lot after her.

He did catch her, but only as she was stopping at the circle-stop right outside her apartment complex parking lot. She pulled into an empty spot in the middle of the lot, and Jack zipped in right beside her, honking his horn. She jumped back against the car beside her and let out a high-pitched yelp. Jack cracked up laughing at her as he flung his door open and jumped out of his car.

"Jack! You brat!" she yelled, swinging her purse at him. "You nearly scared me to death!"

Jack hurried around the car and picked her up in a big bear hug. She laughed and wrapped her arms around him.

"What are you doing here?" she asked.

"Well, duh, I came to see you, silly! I knew you had to talk with that creep on the Internet tonight, so I thought I would pop in and cheer you up when you are done. Is that okay with you, or do you want to be alone with him?" Jack teased.

"Yeah, Jack, I don't want you to hear our x-rated conversation. Maybe you had better wait out here."

They walked arm in arm up to her door, which she unlocked and pushed open. Jack politely allowed her to walk in first, following closely behind and giving the door a shove. Megan would always flip on the light as she shut the door, but Jack was between her and the switch, so she hung her purse on a hook by the kitchen and began taking off her jacket.

"Jack, do you smell cigarettes?" she asked.

Jack had been reaching for the light switch on the other side of the door when she asked about the smell. He stopped reaching and turned back to face her. As he did, he noticed that the tiny dot of orange glowing on the other side of the room suddenly got brighter. He had absently taken it for the stereo light when he first saw it, forgetting that she didn't have a stereo on that side of the room. In the same instant that the voice spoke, a huge hand was clasped over Megan's mouth while a thick muscular arm wrapped itself around her waist, and the cold barrel of a pistol was jammed into Jack's temple, slamming his head up against the wall.

"I know, it is a nasty habit. I have been trying to quit, but I can't seem to kick it. Hello, Belinda. I am a little early for our chat, but I didn't want to miss it, even though I am not at my office."

"Megan, who—" Jack began, only to receive a sharp knee jab in the stomach by the man with the pistol at his head. He coughed and gasped for the air that had been pushed out of his lungs.

"It's Miguel!" Megan blurted out.

~12~

Jack's heart stopped. Fear gripped him as the realization of what that meant became clear to him. Of all the things they had worried and prayed about over the past couple of weeks, the idea that the creep from Venezuela would ever come here had never occurred to him. How had he known? There were a million thoughts racing through Jack's mind. The next one he latched on to was that McDowell would help them. After all, he knew the whole story, didn't he? Yes, he would—no, wait a minute. He had never even called Megan to let her know what he could do for her. He may not have even believed her story. Of course not! How could he even know that Ramirez was here, in Norfolk, taking care of Megan himself? Jack was on his own. Three thugs that he could see, all armed, against him and Megan, scared and unarmed. Not good odds. Jack began to pray.

The burly moose that had taken hold of Megan dragged her over to the couch and plopped her onto it. The man who had taken charge of Jack eased him over to the arm chair and shoved him down into it, keeping the pressure of the gun applied to his temple. Ramirez nodded to him, and the man placed his empty hand on Jack's shoulder, removing the gun hand. Seconds later the hand returned, and this time Jack felt the cold steel of a large knife blade against his neck.

"This will be much quieter if we are forced to take any action to encourage your cooperation, Belinda," Ramirez said. He nodded to the other man, who turned on the kitchen light, providing an eerie, gloomy illumination to the living room. The blinds had all been shut, and all the interior doors closed.

"So, Belinda, let's chat. Tell me how you have been doing," Ramirez said.

"Miguel, what are you doing?" Megan asked pleadingly. Why are you here? And why are you holding us at gun-point like prisoners?"

"Belinda, I was disturbed the last time we talked. I had the distinct feeling that something was not right, so I came up here to check on you and to make sure that everything is as it should be."

"Miguel, everything is fine!" Megan yelled. She became emboldened by anger. "You didn't come here just to check on me, either. Because now you have blown my cover, since Jack here is my source, so there is another reason you are here. What is going on?"

"Why don't you tell me, Belinda? What is going on with you?"

"What do you mean, Miguel? What do you want me to say?"

"I want you to stop lying to me. I want you to tell me that you have fallen in love with your 'source', and that you have gone to the authorities about our arrangement. I want you to admit that you have betrayed me!" Ramirez shouted at her through clenched teeth.

Suddenly it became clear to Megan. She didn't know how, but somehow Miguel knew all about everything she had been doing. The other two guys must have been spying on her. Her boldness diminished and left her, fear remaining as the only replacement.

"McDowell, it's Mesko" McDowell's radio crackled.

"McDowell here. Go ahead, Mesko."

"Ramirez and his two thugs are at the girl's apartment. Douglass is there, too. He is holding them at gun-point, trying to get her to confess to betraying him."

"Copy, Mesko. Thanks. Keep me apprised."

"10-4, Boss. Mesko out."

"Where is your cockiness now, Belinda? Not so bold now, are we? Now, before Luis starts carving up your boyfriend like a holiday goose, tell me what I want to know. Why have you betrayed me? Was it his idea?" he asked, throwing a CD case at Jack. It hit him in the forehead, slicing the skin and sending a small trickle of blood into his eyes.

Megan, gasped, lunging for Jack.

"Back!" Luis growled, pushing the knife into Jack's throat.

"Okay, okay!" Megan said, raising her hands up in front of her in surrender. "I'm sitting back down."

"I am not a patient man, Belinda. Start talking," Ramirez commanded.

"All right, Miguel. I'll tell you. As I am sure you can imagine, I have always hated you. You are a selfish, evil, horrible man. You took my family's land away from us. You abused my father and ruined his life. Then you forced me to come here and be your spy. I have always despised you and the things you have made me and my family do for you.

"But still, I came here and did as you asked. I met Jack, a sailor on the USS *Mississippi*, and developed a relationship with him. But then the unexpected happened. Not that we fell in love; that is not so unexpected. What happened is that I also met Jesus."

"You *what*?" Ramirez screamed. "You met *Jesus*?? And that is why you betrayed me to the authorities?"

"Are you going to let me finish, Miguel?" Megan asked with raised eyebrows, looking directly into his eyes. Jack was continuously praying for her, and she could feel the Spirit of God giving her confidence and boldness.

"Okay," she said, like a teacher who had just reprimanded a naughty child for his outburst. "As I was saying, I met Jesus. I had always felt guilty about the things I did for you, but I knew of no way out. But with Jesus, I learned that I could be free. I didn't have to bow to your oppression any more. You see, Miguel, I asked Jesus to come into my heart and forgive my sins. I asked Him to forgive me for all the rotten things I have done for you over the years, and I asked Him to help me to get free from you.

"Of course, I also asked Him to save my family, but that's not a guarantee. You see, threatening to hurt or kill my family is no longer something that you can use against me. I am working for Jesus now, and the only commands I follow are His. *He* doesn't want me to deceive Jack and squeeze him for information any more. *He* doesn't want me to give you information that will help you build your evil empire of lies and murder and deceit and who knows what other kinds of evils. *He* doesn't want me to have any part in the workings of the kingdom of darkness. Jesus has saved my soul from hell and has given me a new life in Him. In God's Word, He says,

> Cast all your anxiety on him because he cares for you. Be self-controlled and alert. Your enemy the devil prowls around like a roaring lion looking for someone to devour. Resist him, standing firm in the faith, because you know that your brothers throughout the world are undergoing the same kind of sufferings. And the God of all grace, who called you to his eternal glory in Christ, after you have suffered a little while, will himself restore you and make you strong, firm and steadfast. To him be the power forever and ever. Amen!

"And His Word also says that if I love even my family more than I love Him, I am not worthy to be His disciple. Well, Miguel, I have left the care of my family up to Jesus, because I do have something to lose if I betray *Him*! Praise God!" Megan yelled, and sat back into the cushions of the couch.

Miguel slowly stood up from the chair he was sitting in, growling like a mad dog. Spittle was dripping out of his mouth as he cursed Megan and blasphemed God under his breath. He walked over to Jack and turned to face Megan.

"Your God will take care of you, heh? Well, let's see if He can keep your boyfriend here from bleeding to death." He grabbed the knife out of Luis' hand and plunged it into Jack's thigh until the tip came out the other side. Jack screamed. Miguel smiled the evil smile of Satan himself as he jerked up on the knife's handle, ripping it out of Jack's leg, flinging blood up onto the ceiling and splattering the wall. Jack screamed again, clutching his leg and writhing in pain.

"Victor!" Miguel said. "Bring up one of the cars. We will all ride to the airport together, so that we can all watch God prevent the boyfriend here from slowly bleeding to death."

Victor laughed as he walked out of the apartment.

"Stiles! Stiles, it's Agent Mesko! Do you copy?" Mesko nearly shouted into his radio.

"Stiles here. What's up, Mesko?"

"Ramirez just stabbed Douglass in the leg. He wants to

make the girl watch him bleed to death. They are getting into a car now to go to the airport."

"Copy, Mesko. I'll alert the airport medics and get them over here to provide EMT support until help arrives. Call 911 and have them dispatch two ambulance units to the airport. Tell them to park in front of the terminal, lights out. We will bring the injured man to them ASAP."

"10-4, Stiles. Mesko, out."

FBI Agent Jacobs' two-way radio headset came to life. "Lights at the cemetery. Repeat, we have incoming lights, going behind the cemetery."

All the teams wore headsets tuned to a common frequency so that they could all hear as the drama unfolded. From the cemetery to the woods to the people inside the plane, an intensity overtook them, shooting another dose of adrenaline into their bloodstreams.

"Past checkpoint one," the radio crackled. The subjects had entered the woods.

Seven or eight minutes later, "Passing checkpoint two." The subjects were passing through the hole Victor had cut in the fence.

"Now listen up," Victor growled. "When I say go, we are all going to run straight toward the landing gear of that Learjet, got it?" He glared at Jack, who was trying his best to stand up, but failing miserably. Tears and sweat ran down his face and soaked his shirt, while the blood from his leg ran down his pants and into his socks. "Navy boy, one peep about that leg, and I'll make the other one look just like it, understand?" Jack nodded. "GO!" Victor said, leading the way. Megan followed him, then Jack, then Luis was in the rear pushing Jack along and dragging him when he stumbled.

Inside the plane, McDowell, Paxton and the rest of their

miniature assault team crouched behind seats, behind curtains, behind the restroom door and up in the cockpit.

The foursome huddled behind the wheels of the Learjet. Victor, realizing that they would really be cutting it close on time because of Jack's wounded leg, barked out instructions in a hushed growl.

"Luis, we will have one shot to do this." He directed Luis' attention to the camera mounted on the roof of the hangar. "That camera up there moves in twenty second segments; twenty to get to a position, twenty at rest, then twenty to get to the next one. As soon as it begins to leave the middle position on its way to the nose of the plane, we will make a run for it. The girl and I will go first. I will open the door, we will go into the plane, then I will help you drag the boyfriend in. We will have at most 45 seconds to get the door shut and be out of sight. Get ready, it is rotating to the center. As soon as it starts to move again, we go."

"GO!" Victor shouted, and the foursome leapt to their feet and raced around the plane. Victor yanked the door open and bounded up the stairs, nearly pulling Megan in behind him. He turned back toward the door and grabbed Jack's arm, lifting him off his feet and tossing him across the cabin against the far wall. Luis leapt into the plane and crossed the cabin, grabbing Jack from behind and leaning up against the seat while Victor reached for Megan to take her to the back of the cabin.

Suddenly, a loud voice from farther inside the cabin shouted, "Freeze, FBI!"

In one split-second motion, Victor whirled around, pulled his .45 out of his shoulder holster, grabbed Megan by the neck and jammed the end of the barrel into her temple. Luis had his hand on his gun also, but he was afraid to let go of Jack to pull it out of his jacket. He needed Jack's body as cover.

In the same split-second, the plane was filled with government agents dressed in black with weapons trained on Victor and Luis.

Special Agent Roy Matthews, commander of the FBI counter-espionage assault team, positioned the red dot from the laser sights on his assault rifle in the center of Victor's forehead. He cleared his throat and said forcefully, "Nobody has to die here, Victor. Drop the gun and let the girl go."

Victor cursed and spit at him. "Back off, or I'll kill her!" he yelled.

"Last chance, Victor. Nobody has to die here. Drop your gun and let the girl go."

"I said back off! I swear I'll kill her!"

The next thing that crossed Victor's mind was a trio of 9mm bullets rapid-fired from Special Agent Matthews' Heckler & Koch MP-5 SD assault rifle. In fact, they physically removed his mind from his instantly lifeless body, which reeled backwards from the impact of the bullets, releasing its hold on Megan and crumpling to the floor of the plane. McDowell lunged forward and grabbed Megan, pulling her back to a safer place behind one of his team members. Matthews repositioned the red dot onto the middle of Luis' forehead.

"Okay, now let's try this again," Matthews said loudly but politely, this time glaring at Luis. "Nobody *else* has to die here, Luis. Let go of the gun, slowly pull your hand out of your jacket and place both hands on your head."

Luis did as he was told. Three agents cuffed him, frisked him, disarmed him and dragged him to the back of the plane, where they placed duct tape across his mouth so that he couldn't alert Ramirez to the trap that was awaiting him. Two more agents tended to Jack, who had slumped to the floor when Luis had released his hold on him. They carried him to the back of the plane, out of sight of the door, and performed first aid as best they could until they could get him off the plane and into an ambulance. Megan ran back to Jack and held onto him, softly crying and fervently praying.

McDowell keyed his radio. "Victor has been retired. His accomplice has been disarmed and restrained. We are back into position and awaiting the arrival of Ramirez."

Thirteen minutes later, the wait was over. Stiles announced that Miguel Ramirez had just cleared customs and was on his way out of the building. He would never know how many pairs of eyes were watching him as the FBI Agent in an airport worker's uniform drove him from the main airport building to the maintenance area in an old golf cart. The Agent stopped at the locked gate and stepped off of the cart. He unlocked the gate and pushed both halves back on their rollers until there was an opening large enough for the Learjet to navigate through. The Agent returned to the cart and drove it over to the Learjet, parking it next to the door of the plane. He politely wished his customer a pleasant flight before he returned to his golf cart to make the short journey back to the main section of the airport.

Ramirez reached up and unlatched the door to the Learjet. He pulled it down and climbed up the steps. Pausing in the doorway, he turned and looked out at the scene before him as if to snub his nose at the United States one last time before returning to his own country. He turned and stepped into the plane.

"Armando!" he shouted. "Get us out of here!" He could hear Belinda crying in the back of the plane. He pulled the door shut and latched it, then turned in the direction of the crying sound when he sensed that something was wrong. He stopped, instinctively reaching inside his suit coat for the gun that was not there. He cursed and went over to the storage area above the first passenger seat where he always kept a loaded gun hidden behind a Velcro flap in the wall. As he lifted up the door, reached inside and yanked back the flap, he froze at the sound of an unfamiliar voice.

"That's far enough, Ramirez. I am Special Agent in Charge Bill McDowell, Naval Criminal Investigative Service. You are under arrest by the United States government for the kidnapping of Megan Gallagher and Jack Douglass, the criminal assault and attempted murder of Jack Douglass, espionage against the United States, and whatever else I can come up with between now and the time I file the list of charges back at my office. Now turn around, very slowly, and put your hands on your head."

McDowell had his 9mm pistol pointed at the back of Miguel's head. The handful of agents, who had appeared as if from nowhere, also had their weapons trained on Ramirez. Miguel knew he had lost. These government jerks had all the evidence that they would need to lock him up forever right here in this plane. Well, Miguel Ramirez would not be spending the rest of his life in a prison cell. He would make one last valiant effort to run for the door and blast his way out. His left fingers tightened around the hand grip of a nickel plated semi-automatic Colt .45 pistol. He took a breath, then sprang into action. Whirling around to his left, he swung his left arm out in the direction of the government agents and opened fire with his Colt while lunging for the Learjet's passenger door. He got off three rounds before every agent in the cabin of the airplane opened fire on him, slamming his body up against the cabin's front wall and tearing it to shreds in less than a second.

*   *   *

The brisk October breeze pitched brown leaves against the window of Jack's room in the Portsmouth Naval Hospital, carrying with it the faint smell of smoke from piles of leaves being burned nearby. Megan looked up from Jack's bedside as Special Agent McDowell walked into the room.

"Hi, Petty Officer Douglass, Miss Gallagher," he said, nodding at each of them. "How's the leg?"

"They are going to let me keep it," Jack said. "as long as I promise not to stick any more bowie knives through it, that is."

"Well, that's good. You getting out of here soon?"

"This afternoon, if the Doc is happy with how it's healing up from the last surgery. Four days in this place is long enough, believe me. Of course, I really don't remember the first one, or much of the second, either. Megan says I was pretty messed up."

"Yeah, you were almost a goner. Lost an awful lot of blood. We weren't sure if you were going to make it there for a while," McDowell said. He turned to Megan. "Miss Gallagher, I just got off the phone with Special Agent Brock of Immigration. He says that there is nothing he can do legally to allow you to stay here in America. Due to the extenuating circumstances of this case, and as a result of your cooperation with the Ramirez business, plus the fact that you came forward and turned yourself in of your own free will, I was able to get you a thirty day extension on your deportation date. Sorry, but that's the best I could do. You will have to be out of the United States thirty days from today. For the time being, you will be free on your own recognizance. I am sorry that I couldn't do more for you. Perhaps after you get back to Venezuela, you can apply for citizenship and immigrate here legally. I can't speak for the rest of the country, but I think there are two men in this room who would be proud to call you an American."

"Thank you, Agent McDowell," Megan said. "For everything."

He smiled and shook her hand. "As for you, Douglass, I don't know what the Navy has in store for you. They typically consider someone who has been involved in a case of espionage to be a security risk. Even if you weren't actively involved in the spying, merely being associated with it makes them very nervous. And being the target really puts them on edge."

"Would that mean that I might be able to get an administrative separation from the Navy, effective as soon as my medical care is completed?" Jack asked.

"Very possible, Douglass. Very possible." He grinned. "I could put in a bad word for you if you like."

Later that afternoon, Jack did get discharged from the hospital. Megan helped him into her car and drove him to his apartment to begin his twenty days of free convalescent leave. The twenty days off couldn't have come at a better time. It would allow him to spend every minute of the next three weeks with Megan, leaving only ten days after that before she was deported. He suggested that she quit her job and join him at his parent's home in Sandusky, Michigan. That would give Jack some time with his mother, it would allow Megan and his mother to meet and, most importantly, it would allow him to spend every minute of the next twenty days *uninterrupted* with Megan. She agreed completely. She would work her shift tomorrow and inform her boss that it would be her last.

The following Monday morning, Phil helped Jack climb aboard the *Mississippi.* He had become fairly adept at using the crutches, but steps were still difficult for him. He was in his complex, collecting a few personal items from his pit when his leading chief walked up beside him shaking his head.

"What gives, Douglass? Who do you think you are, the lead character in a Tom Clancy novel? Hooking up with a gorgeous female spy...getting into a brawl with a Venezuelan drug lord...can't you just go to a movie and play Nintendo on your off time like normal people do?"

"Sorry, Chief. It wasn't really the way I had my week planned out, either," Jack said.

"Only you, Douglass. Only you." SMC Johnson chuckled. "Well, I just came down to deliver a message. XO wants to see you in his stateroom ASAP. I wish I could give you a heads up as to what it is all about, but I am completely uninformed. Nobody's talking. Good luck, Douglass," the chief said. He turned and walked out of the complex. Jack tossed a few more things into his duffel bag, locked up his pit, and hobbled up the steps.

The pain in his leg made climbing the stairs difficult, but he eventually made it to the XO's stateroom. He was breathing hard and cringing when the XO looked up from his desk through the open door.

"Douglass!" he shouted. "You shouldn't be climbing steps by yourself! Get in here and sit down."

"Sorry, XO," Jack huffed, gingerly lowering himself into a chair. "I'm not exactly back at 100 percent yet."

"I guess not, Douglass! Not after what you have been through this last week." He shuffled through some papers on his desk, then pulled a manila envelope out of his 'in' box. He handed it to Jack and leaned back in his chair. Jack took the cue and opened the envelope, removing the small sheaf of papers held together by a large paper clip. The XO let a couple of minutes pass by while Jack skimmed through the top two or three pages.

"There really is no policy on this, Douglass. We have no precedent to follow. After a major espionage case goes down, there usually aren't any pieces left to pick up. Usually, the service member is actively involved in the criminal transfer of information, and is thus prosecuted at a military court marshal. In this situation, however, that's not the case. It has been determined by the investigating authorities that, although you were not knowingly involved in the sharing of information, or in the subsequent distribution thereof, you were still deeply involved in a circumstance which involved not only a noted criminal element, but that resulted in an international incident during which the lives of two foreigners were taken in the name of United States justice.

"Now, this whole thing looks really good for the FBI, NCIS, CIA, DEA, and all those cop organizations, but it doesn't look very good for the Navy. One of our members was involved with this drug lord fellow, whether voluntarily or involuntarily. Any espionage case reflects very poorly upon the particular branch of service involved. It is with this in mind that the Department of the Navy would like you to consider the offer outlined in that packet. Since you don't have sufficient time in service to take advantage of an early retirement, the Navy would like to offer you an Administrative Separation from the US Navy, due to circumstances which will remain classified for a period not to exceed thirty years from the date of separation. The Severance Package will include complete medical care for your current injuries and any subsequent medical problems that arise as a direct result of your current medical condition, as well as a separation check in an amount equal to six months worth of your regular base pay at your current rank and time in service."

"The Navy does not wish to trivialize the service you have given to your country, nor do we wish to imply guilt in any way. We do, however, feel that it is in the best interests of the Navy at this time to end our professional relationship with you and to encourage you to seek alternate employment. If this Separation/Severance Package meets with your approval, I have been authorized to execute it immediately, thanking you for your service to your country and wishing you the best of luck in whichever civilian path you may choose."

Inside, Jack was jumping up and down, bouncing off the walls, and screaming praises to God at the top of his lungs.

Outside, he solemnly told the XO that he understood the Navy's position and that the Separation/Severance Package was acceptable. Two hours later, Jonathan (Jack) Douglass, civilian, walked off the brow of the USS *Mississippi* CGN-40 for the very last time.

The following Friday evening, all of Jack's friends from the church threw him a farewell party. He was unsure what he would do in his unexpected and recently acquired civilian life, but whatever it was, he did not intend to do it in Norfolk. He would stick with his plan to recover at his parents' home in Michigan, during which time he would figure out what his next move would be.

The adventure that Jack and Megan had experienced over the past few weeks had served to strengthened their relationship and bring them to a point which may have been months down the road in a typical dating relationship. They were walking hand in hand along the beach in Port Sanilac, Michigan, about thirty minutes east of Sandusky and just south of the thumb on the western shore of Lake Huron. The October breeze was very cool coming off the lake. Jack and Megan huddled together, looking out across the beautiful water. They had been in Sandusky for just over a week, which left Megan two more weeks until she had to go back to Venezuela.

She had gotten in touch with her parents to tell them that she was coming home soon. They were thrilled that she was coming home, and they shared with her the wonderful news that the Venezuelan government, in appreciation for Belinda's part in the destruction of Ramirez's empire, had returned ownership of the Gallagos family land to her father. He would now be able to get the family back on its feet, working the land the way his father had taught him years before.

Jack was silently praying as they walked along, thanking God for working out the details of his life so far and pleading with God to give him guidance in his present dilemma. The struggling in his own mind about what he should do with his life was a constant source of frustration for him. It was more than just a career change. People did that all the time. His case, however, was a tad more complicated. His entire life had been turned upside-down. Over the course of the previous three months, he had started going to church, had met a wonderful girl, had fallen in love with the wonderful girl, had become a Christian, had made a close friend of Phil Prescott, had moved into an apartment with Phil, had the very foundation of his new faith challenged by finding out that his girlfriend was a spy, had gotten into a confrontation with a Venezuelan drug lord who had stabbed him in the leg and nearly killed him, had spent four days in the hospital as a result of that confrontation and the resulting injury, had found out that his girlfriend was going to be deported in a month, had been 'let go' from the Navy, and had moved away from all his new friends in Virginia to live with his parents again in his hometown in Michigan. And now he was trying to make some kind of sense out of what was left so that he could somehow figure out what he was supposed to do with it. On one hand, he had lost his job. Not a big deal. His generous severance compensation would give him ample time to make a new career choice. Of course, that still didn't make the choosing any easier. On the other hand, there was Megan. This couldn't be the end. It just couldn't be. It couldn't end like this; not after all they had been through together. There had to be something else left for them.

He squeezed Megan close to him and looked out across the lake. Cold as it was, there were several sailboats cruising around in circles out on the water. Suddenly, it hit Jack. It may as well have been a huge neon sign hanging on the sail of one of those sailboats. He had been so pre-occupied during church on Sunday that he had only partially paid attention to the sermon; but now, somehow, the passage of Scripture that they had read popped into his mind. Just like it did with Megan when she had spouted off that Scripture to Ramirez in her apartment, the Word of the Lord came to Jack as if the Bible were lying open in front of him. The preacher had read from the Old Testament book of Ruth. The message was on faithfulness and loyalty, using Ruth as an example of family sticking by each other; but that's not how it was meant for Jack. For Jack Douglass, back at his childhood church in Sandusky, Michigan, it was marching orders. Even though he hadn't read it, and had hardly paid attention to it when the pastor had read it Sunday morning, the words were emblazoned on his mind. He began to quote the verses quietly to himself as he walked in the sand:

> Don't urge me to leave you or to turn back from you.
> Where you go I will go, and where you stay I will stay.
> Your people will be my people and your God my God.
> Where you die I will die, and there will I be buried.
> May the Lord deal with me, be it ever so severely, if
> anything but death separates you and me.

Megan stopped and looked at him. "Jack, what are you mumbling about?"

He grabbed her by the shoulders and looked deep into her eyes. "Megan," he said matter-of-factly, "I am coming with you to Venezuela."

"What?" she asked incredulously. "What are you talking about?"

"Don't you see?" Jack explained. "The Bible verses from Sunday morning! That's what I am supposed to do!" He said the verses again for her benefit. "You see, I have been feeling terrible about you leaving and about not knowing what to do with my life now. I thought I was only feeling bad because I love you and I don't want you to go out of my life, but it is more than that. Those verses just popped into my head like a billboard on the highway, telling me which way I am supposed to go. Megan, I am going to Venezuela with you. We can be together there. I can work on your father's farm—help him get it back on its feet. What do you think?"

Megan smiled, a single tear running out of her eye. "Oh, Jack! That would be wonderful!" she said. "Would you really do that for me? Leave the United States? Your parents? Your home?"

Jack thought for a moment. "Probably not," he said. "But *you* didn't ask me to, did you? And the One who did ask me didn't really put it in the form of a question. I am coming to Venezuela with you, Megan." Jack stated with finality.

"Then I guess you had better start calling me Belinda," she giggled.

Jack pulled her into his arms and held her, running his fingers through the hair that fell across her shoulders.

"I love you, Belinda," he said softly.

"And I love you, Jack," she replied.

Jack released her and turned back toward where they had left the car. "Let's go back and tell Mom," he suggested, excitement in his eyes. "After the ride we have just been on, I can hardly wait to see what God has in store for us next!"

Author's Note

I hope you enjoyed my first work of Inspirational Fiction. Even more, I hope you allowed the Holy Spirit to touch your heart as you read the book. I hope you were encouraged to walk closer with God, and to give Him more control over your attitude and your actions. God didn't call us to Himself to be mediocre or passive Christians. He called us to have a dynamic, exciting, active relationship with Him, and to mature in our faith as we nurture that relationship and share it with the people within our sphere of influence.

Thank you for purchasing your copy of ***Interdiction***. I would love to hear your comments! Please feel free to contact me at dinglemaypublish@cs.com or by regular mail, sent to me in care of the publisher.

In His Service,

Kevin L. Kingsbury

Dinglemay Publishing

Quick Order Form

Make your check or money order
payable to
Dinglemay Publishing
and send to:

Dinglemay Publishing
PO Box 2956
Elkhart, IN 46515-2956

(Please allow 4-6 weeks for delivery)

Please rush ____ copy(ies) of ***Interdiction*** to the address listed below. I have included payment in the amount of $16.95 plus $1.95 shipping and handling for each copy ordered. (Indiana residents, please add 5% state sales tax)

Ship to (please print):

Name____

Address______________________________________

____

Telephone____________________________________

Email address_________________________________

Dinglemay Publishing

Quick Order Form

Make your check or money order
payable to
Dinglemay Publishing
and send to:

Dinglemay Publishing
PO Box 2956
Elkhart, IN 46515-2956

(Please allow 4-6 weeks for delivery)

Please rush ____ copy(ies) of ***Interdiction*** to the address listed below. I have included payment in the amount of $16.95 plus $1.95 shipping and handling for each copy ordered. (Indiana residents, please add 5% state sales tax)

Ship to (please print):

Name____

Address______________________________________

____

Telephone____________________________________

Email address_________________________________